THE HOLY BIBLE

HISTORY

WORLD ENGLISH BIBLE TRANSLATION

Cover illustration: *Ruth & Boaz* - Gustave Dore, 1885

Book and Jacket design by KR15 Creative Services [KR15.com]
Set in Adobe Garamond & Avenir

ISBN (paperback) 978-0-9910041-4-0

First Edition: November 2017
Printed in the USA

CONTENTS

PREFACE

About this edition

When I told a friend that I was publishing a Bible she said "Why? Don't we have enough Bibles already?" I replied "You can never have too many Bibles!" But the 'why' is a fair question, and I have two answers.

First, I wanted a cheap paperback reader's Bible and I couldn't find one. A "Reader's Bible" is a Bible that has been formatted with none of the usual verse and chapter markers and a minimum of footnotes. This allows the reader to experience the text closer to its original form. A reader's Bible is not meant to be studied line-by-line or to be read by jumping back and forth between verses. A study Bible is great for that. These stripped-down texts are meant to be read straight through. Anything that might be a hindrance has been removed. You experience the text in a different way when you can drink it in one gulp, so to speak.

There are already a lot of wonderful reader's Bibles out there. The problem is that most of them are fancy, precious objects. They cost a lot and they look great on the shelf, but you might not want to throw your $200 hardcover in your bag to read on the bus or by the pool. Some reader's Bibles have stripped out the verse markers but they are still printed on ultra-thin transparent paper in a tiny space-saving typeface.

I wanted a reader's Bible that is small and light enough to take with you, but is set in 11pt. Adobe Garamond on real paper. I also wanted it to be as cheap as possible. The result is that you get a good reading experience but you can take it anywhere and not feel bad about the creases and dog-ears. Just being able to read the Bible in Garamond is reason enough for a new edition. I have also included an estimated time to complete a read through of each book. I have found in my own reading that I am more likely to start if I know what I have signed up for.

The second reason I made this is because I thought it would be fun. I am a graphic artist by trade, and I have spent my career designing all manner of marketing materials, corporate identities, websites, apps, and advertisements. Along the way I have done a little bit of book design and publishing. I have a deep love for the Holy Scriptures and I thought, "Man, wouldn't it be great to design a Bible." Half of the reason I made these volumes was so that I could design the covers and the icons. I initially intended to design one icon for each of the 63 books of the canon (counting Samuel, Kings, and Chronicles as one book each). After I completed the icons for the Torah I realized I would NEVER finish if I tried to design 58 more. I re-aligned my ambitions with reality and designed one more icon for each volume, and ended up with 10 icons.

On a more serious note, one of the ways we respond to the work of the Holy Spirit in our lives is with the desire to use our gifts to honor God or to advance his kingdom in some way. One of the ways that I responded to that desire was to create the book you are holding in your hands. I hope that its accessibility will encourage people who are apprehensive about reading a long and confusing leather-bound tome to dive in and see what the Bible says for themselves.

I also need to give a shout out to Dave Braford. Without his technical expertise, I would not have been able to complete this project. Thanks Dave!

– Kris Hull

ABOUT THE WORLD ENGLISH BIBLE

What is the Holy Bible?

The Holy Bible is a collection of books and letters written by many people who were inspired by the Holy Spirit of God. These books tell us how we can be saved from the evil of this world and gain eternal life that is truly worth living. Although the Holy Bible contains rules of conduct, it is not just a rule book. It reveals God's heart—a Father's heart, full of love and compassion. The Holy Bible tells you what you need to know and believe to be saved from sin and evil and how to live a life that is truly worth living, no matter what your current circumstances may be.

The Holy Bible consists of two main sections: the Old Testament and the New Testament. The Old Testament records God's interaction with mankind before He sent His son to redeem us, while recording prophesy predicting that coming. The New Testament tells us of God's Son and Anointed One, Jesus, and the wonderful salvation that He purchased for us.

The same Holy Spirit who inspired the Holy Bible is living among us today, and He is happy to help you understand what He intended as you study His Word. Just ask Him, and He is more than happy to help you apply His message to your life.

The Old Testament was originally written mostly in Hebrew. The New Testament was originally written mostly in the common street Greek (not the formal Greek used for official legal matters). The Holy Bible is translated into many languages, and being translated into many more, so that everyone may have an opportunity to hear the Good News about Jesus Christ.

Why was the World English Bible translated?

There are already many good translations of the Holy Bible into contemporary English. Unfortunately, almost all of them are restricted by copyright and copyright holder policy. This restricts publication and republication of God's Word in many ways, such as in downloadable files on the Internet, use of extensive quotations in books, etc. The World English Bible was commissioned by God in response to prayer about this subject.

Because the World English Bible is in the Public Domain (not copyrighted), it can be freely copied, distributed, and redistributed without any payment of royalties. You don't even have to ask permission to do so. You may publish the whole World English Bible in book form, bind it in leather and sell it. You may incorporate it into your Bible study software. You may make and distribute audio recordings of it. You may broadcast it. All you have to do is maintain the integrity of God's Word before God, and reserve the name "World English Bible" for faithful copies of this translation.

How was the World English Bible translated?

The World English Bible is an update of the American Standard Version (ASV) of the Holy Bible, published in 1901. A custom computer program updated the archaic words and word forms to contemporary equivalents, and then a team of volunteers proofread and updated the grammar. The New Testament was updated to conform to the Majority Text reconstruction of the original Greek manuscripts, thus taking advantage of the superior access to manuscripts that we have now compared to when the original ASV was translated.

What is different about the World English Bible?

The style of the World English Bible, while fairly literally translated, is in informal, spoken English. The World English Bible is designed to sound good and be accurate when read aloud. It is not formal in its language, just as the original Greek of the New Testament was not formal. The WEB uses contractions rather freely.

The World English Bible doesn't capitalize pronouns pertaining to God. The original manuscripts made no such distinction. Hebrew has no such thing as upper and lower case, and the original Greek manuscripts were written in all upper case letters. Attempting to add in such a distinction raises some difficulties in translating dual-meaning Scriptures such as the coronation psalms.

The World English Bible main edition translates God's Proper Name in the Old Testament as "Yahweh." The Messianic Edition and the British Edition of the World English Bible translates the same name as "LORD" (all capital letters), or when used with "Lord" (mixed case, translated from "Adonai",) GOD. There are solid translational arguments for both traditions. In this printing, the name Yahweh" has been rendered as "YHWH" in small caps reflecting the 4-letter spelling of the name in Hebrew.

Because World English Bible uses the Majority Text as the basis for the New Testament, you may notice the following differences in comparing the WEB to other translations:

- The order of Matthew 23:13 and 14 is reversed in some translations.
- Luke 17:36 and Acts 15:34, which are not found in the majority of the Greek Manuscripts may be included in some other translations.
- Romans 14:24-26 in the WEB may appear as Romans 16:25-27 in other translations.

- 1 John 5:7-8 contains an addition in some translations, including the KJV. Erasmus admitted adding this text to his published Greek New Testament, even though he could at first find no Greek manuscript support for it, because he was being pressured by men to do so, and because he didn't see any doctrinal harm in it. Lots of things not written by John in this letter are true, but we decline to add them to what the Holy Spirit inspired through John.

With all of the above and some other places where lack of clarity in the original manuscripts has led to multiple possible readings, significant variants are listed in footnotes in the full WEB text. *(All footnotes have been omitted from this edition, however).* The reading that in our prayerful judgment is best is in the main text. Overall, the World English Bible isn't very much different than several other good contemporary English translations of the Holy Bible. The message of Salvation through Jesus Christ is still the same. The point of this translation was not to be very different (except for legal status), but to update the ASV for readability while retaining or improving the accuracy of that well-respected translation and retaining the public domain status of the ASV.

More Information

For answers to frequently asked questions about the World English Bible, please visit WorldEnglishBible.org.

THE BOOK OF

JOSHUA

1 HR 34 MIN

Now after the death of Moses the servant of YHWH, YHWH spoke to Joshua the son of Nun, Moses' servant, saying, "Moses my servant is dead. Now therefore arise, go across this Jordan, you and all these people, to the land which I am giving to them, even to the children of Israel. I have given you every place that the sole of your foot will tread on, as I told Moses. From the wilderness and this Lebanon even to the great river, the river Euphrates, all the land of the Hittites, and to the great sea toward the going down of the sun, shall be your border. No man will be able to stand before you all the days of your life. As I was with Moses, so I will be with you. I will not fail you nor forsake you.

"Be strong and courageous; for you shall cause this people to inherit the land which I swore to their fathers to give them. Only be strong and very courageous. Be careful to observe to do according to all the law which Moses my servant commanded you. Don't turn from it to the right hand or to the left, that you may have good success wherever you go. This book of the law shall not depart from your mouth, but you shall meditate on it day and night, that you may observe to do according to all that is written in it; for then you shall make your way prosperous, and then you shall have good success. Haven't I commanded you? Be strong and courageous. Don't be afraid. Don't be dismayed, for YHWH your God is with you wherever you go."

Then Joshua commanded the officers of the people, saying, "Pass through the middle of the camp, and command the people, saying, 'Prepare food; for within three days you are to pass over this Jordan, to go in to possess the land which YHWH your God gives you to possess.'"

Joshua spoke to the Reubenites, and to the Gadites, and to the half-tribe of Manasseh, saying, "Remember the word which Moses the servant of YHWH commanded you, saying, 'YHWH your God gives you rest, and will give you this land. Your wives, your little ones, and your livestock shall live in the land which Moses gave you beyond the Jordan; but you shall pass over before your brothers armed, all the mighty men of valor, and shall help them until YHWH has given your brothers rest, as he has given you, and they have also possessed the land which YHWH your God gives them. Then you shall return to the land of your possession and possess it, which Moses the servant of YHWH gave you beyond the Jordan toward the sunrise.'"

They answered Joshua, saying, "All that you have commanded us we will do, and wherever you send us we will go. Just as we listened to Moses in all things, so will we listen to you. Only may YHWH your God be with you, as he was with Moses. Whoever rebels against your commandment, and doesn't listen to your words in all that you command him shall himself be put to death. Only be strong and courageous."

....

Joshua the son of Nun secretly sent two men out of Shittim as spies, saying, "Go, view the land, including Jericho." They went and came into the house of a prostitute whose name was Rahab, and slept there.

The king of Jericho was told, "Behold, men of the children of Israel came in here tonight to spy out the land."

Jericho's king sent to Rahab, saying, "Bring out the men who have come to you, who have entered into your house; for they have come to spy out all the land."

The woman took the two men and hid them. Then she said, "Yes, the men came to me, but I didn't know where they came from. About the time of the shutting of the gate, when it was dark, the men went out. Where the men went, I don't know. Pursue them quickly. You may catch up with them." But she had brought them up to the roof, and hidden them under the stalks of flax which she had laid in order on the roof. The men pursued them along the way to the fords of the Jordan River. As soon as those who pursued them had gone out, they shut the gate. Before they had lain down, she came up to them on the roof. She said to the men, "I know that YHWH has given you the land, and that the fear of you has fallen upon us, and that all the inhabitants of the land melt away before you. For we have heard how YHWH dried up the water of the Red Sea before you, when you came out of Egypt; and what you did to the two kings of the Amorites, who were beyond the Jordan, to Sihon and to Og, whom you utterly destroyed. As soon as we had heard it, our hearts melted, and there wasn't any more spirit in any man, because of you: for YHWH your God, he is God in heaven above, and on earth beneath. Now therefore, please swear to me by YHWH, since I have dealt kindly with you, that you also will deal kindly with my father's house, and give me a true sign; and that you will save alive my father, my mother, my brothers, and my sisters, and all that they have, and will deliver our lives from death."

The men said to her, "Our life for yours, if you don't talk about this business of ours; and it shall be, when YHWH gives us the land, that we will deal kindly and truly with you."

Then she let them down by a cord through the window; for her house was on the side of the wall, and she lived on the wall. She said to them, "Go to the mountain, lest the pursuers find you. Hide yourselves there three days, until the pursuers have returned. Afterward, you may go your way."

The men said to her, "We will be guiltless of this your oath which you've made us to swear. Behold, when we come into the land, tie this line of scarlet thread in the window which you used to let us down. Gather to yourself into the house your father, your mother, your brothers, and all your father's household. It shall be that whoever goes out of the doors of your house into the street, his blood will be on his head, and we will be guiltless. Whoever is with you in the house, his blood shall be on our head, if any hand is on him. But if you talk about this business of ours, then we shall be guiltless of your oath which you've made us to swear."

She said, "Let it be as you have said." She sent them away, and they departed. Then she tied the scarlet line in the window.

They went and came to the mountain, and stayed there three days, until the pursuers had returned. The pursuers sought them all along the way, but didn't find them. Then the two men returned, descended from the mountain, crossed the river, and came to Joshua the son of Nun. They told him all that had happened to them. They said to Joshua, "Truly YHWH has delivered all the land into our hands. Moreover, all the inhabitants of the land melt away before us."

....

Joshua got up early in the morning; and they moved from Shittim and came to the Jordan, he and all the children of Israel. They camped there before they crossed over. After three days, the officers went through the middle of the camp; and they commanded the people, saying, "When you see the ark of YHWH your God's covenant, and the Levitical priests bearing it, then leave your place and follow it. Yet there shall be a space between you and it of about two thousand cubits by measure—don't come closer to it—that you may know the way by which you must go; for you have not passed this way before."

Joshua said to the people, "Sanctify yourselves; for tomorrow

YHWH will do wonders among you."

Joshua spoke to the priests, saying, "Take up the ark of the covenant, and cross over before the people." They took up the ark of the covenant, and went before the people.

YHWH said to Joshua, "Today I will begin to magnify you in the sight of all Israel, that they may know that as I was with Moses, so I will be with you. You shall command the priests who bear the ark of the covenant, saying, 'When you come to the brink of the waters of the Jordan, you shall stand still in the Jordan.'"

Joshua said to the children of Israel, "Come here, and hear the words of YHWH your God." Joshua said, "By this you shall know that the living God is among you, and that he will without fail drive the Canaanite, the Hittite, the Hivite, the Perizzite, the Girgashite, the Amorite, and the Jebusite out from before you. Behold, the ark of the covenant of the Lord of all the earth passes over before you into the Jordan. Now therefore take twelve men out of the tribes of Israel, for every tribe a man. It shall be that when the soles of the feet of the priests who bear the ark of YHWH, the Lord of all the earth, rest in the waters of the Jordan, that the waters of the Jordan will be cut off. The waters that come down from above shall stand in one heap."

When the people moved from their tents to pass over the Jordan, the priests who bore the ark of the covenant being before the people, and when those who bore the ark had come to the Jordan, and the feet of the priests who bore the ark had dipped in the edge of the water (for the Jordan overflows all its banks all the time of harvest), the waters which came down from above stood, and rose up in one heap a great way off, at Adam, the city that is beside Zarethan; and those that went down toward the sea of the Arabah, even the Salt Sea, were wholly cut off. Then the people passed over near Jericho. The priests who bore the ark of YHWH's covenant stood firm on dry ground in the middle of the Jordan; and all Israel crossed over on dry ground, until all the nation had passed completely over the Jordan.

When all the nation had completely crossed over the Jordan, YHWH spoke to Joshua, saying, "Take twelve men out of the people, a man out of every tribe, and command them, saying, 'Take from out of the middle of the Jordan, out of the place where the priests' feet stood firm, twelve stones, carry them over with you, and lay them down in the place where you'll camp tonight.'"

Then Joshua called the twelve men whom he had prepared of the children of Israel, a man out of every tribe. Joshua said to them, "Cross before the ark of YHWH your God into the middle of the Jordan, and each of you pick up a stone and put it on your shoulder, according to the number of the tribes of the children of Israel; that this may be a sign among you, that when your children ask in the future, saying, 'What do you mean by these stones?' then you shall tell them, 'Because the waters of the Jordan were cut off before the ark of YHWH's covenant. When it crossed over the Jordan, the waters of the Jordan were cut off. These stones shall be for a memorial to the children of Israel forever.'"

The children of Israel did as Joshua commanded, and took up twelve stones out of the middle of the Jordan, as YHWH spoke to Joshua, according to the number of the tribes of the children of Israel. They carried them over with them to the place where they camped, and laid them down there. Joshua set up twelve stones in the middle of the Jordan, in the place where the feet of the priests who bore the ark of the covenant stood; and they are there to this day. For the priests who bore the ark stood in the middle of the Jordan until everything was finished that YHWH commanded Joshua to speak to the people, according to all that Moses commanded Joshua; and the people hurried and passed over. When all the people had completely crossed over, YHWH's ark crossed over with the priests in the presence of the people.

The children of Reuben, and the children of Gad, and the half-tribe of Manasseh crossed over armed before the children of Israel, as Moses spoke to them. About forty thousand men, ready and armed for war, passed over before YHWH to battle, to the plains of Jericho. On that day, YHWH magnified Joshua in the sight of all Israel; and they feared him, as they feared Moses, all the days of his life.

YHWH spoke to Joshua, saying, "Command the priests who bear the ark of the covenant, that they come up out of the Jordan."

Joshua therefore commanded the priests, saying, "Come up out of the Jordan!" When the priests who bore the ark of YHWH's covenant had come up out of the middle of the Jordan, and the soles of the priests' feet had been lifted up to the dry ground, the waters of the Jordan returned to their place, and went over all its banks, as before. The people came up out of the Jordan on the tenth day of the first month, and encamped in Gilgal, on the east border of Jericho.

Joshua set up those twelve stones, which they took out of the

Jordan, in Gilgal. He spoke to the children of Israel, saying, "When your children ask their fathers in time to come, saying, 'What do these stones mean?' Then you shall let your children know, saying, 'Israel came over this Jordan on dry land. For YHWH your God dried up the waters of the Jordan from before you until you had crossed over, as YHWH your God did to the Red Sea, which he dried up from before us, until we had crossed over, that all the peoples of the earth may know that YHWH's hand is mighty, and that you may fear YHWH your God forever.'"

....

When all the kings of the Amorites, who were beyond the Jordan westward, and all the kings of the Canaanites, who were by the sea, heard how YHWH had dried up the waters of the Jordan from before the children of Israel until we had crossed over, their heart melted, and there was no more spirit in them, because of the children of Israel. At that time, YHWH said to Joshua, "Make flint knives, and circumcise again the sons of Israel the second time." Joshua made himself flint knives, and circumcised the sons of Israel at the hill of the foreskins. This is the reason Joshua circumcised them: all the people who came out of Egypt, who were males, even all the men of war, died in the wilderness along the way, after they came out of Egypt. For all the people who came out were circumcised; but all the people who were born in the wilderness along the way as they came out of Egypt had not been circumcised. For the children of Israel walked forty years in the wilderness until all the nation, even the men of war who came out of Egypt, were consumed, because they didn't listen to YHWH's voice. YHWH swore to them that he wouldn't let them see the land which YHWH swore to their fathers that he would give us, a land flowing with milk and honey. Their children, whom he raised up in their place, were circumcised by Joshua, for they were uncircumcised, because they had not circumcised them on the way. When they were done circumcising the whole nation, they stayed in their places in the camp until they were healed.

YHWH said to Joshua, "Today I have rolled away the reproach of Egypt from you." Therefore the name of that place was called Gilgal to this day. The children of Israel encamped in Gilgal. They kept the Passover on the fourteenth day of the month at evening in the plains of Jericho. They ate unleavened cakes and parched grain of the produce of the land on the next day after the Passover, in the same day. The manna ceased on the next day, after they had eaten of the produce of the land. The children of Israel didn't have manna any more, but they ate of the fruit of the land of Canaan that year.

When Joshua was by Jericho, he lifted up his eyes and looked, and behold, a man stood in front of him with his sword drawn in his hand. Joshua went to him and said to him, "Are you for us, or for our enemies?"

He said, "No; but I have come now as commander of YHWH's army."

Joshua fell on his face to the earth, and worshiped, and asked him, "What does my lord say to his servant?"

The prince of YHWH's army said to Joshua, "Take off your sandals, for the place on which you stand is holy." Joshua did so.

....

Now Jericho was tightly shut up because of the children of Israel. No one went out, and no one came in. YHWH said to Joshua, "Behold, I have given Jericho into your hand, with its king and the mighty men of valor. All of your men of war shall march around the city, going around the city once. You shall do this six days. Seven priests shall bear seven trumpets of rams' horns before the ark. On the seventh day, you shall march around the city seven times, and the priests shall blow the trumpets. It shall be that when they make a long blast with the ram's horn, and when you hear the sound of the trumpet, all the people shall shout with a great shout; and the city wall shall fall down flat, and the people shall go up, every man straight in front of him."

Joshua the son of Nun called the priests, and said to them, "Take up the ark of the covenant, and let seven priests bear seven trumpets of rams' horns before YHWH's ark."

They said to the people, "Advance! March around the city, and let the armed men pass on before YHWH's ark."

It was so, that when Joshua had spoken to the people, the seven priests bearing the seven trumpets of rams' horns before YHWH advanced and blew the trumpets, and the ark of YHWH's covenant followed them. The armed men went before the priests who blew the trumpets, and the ark went after them. The trumpets sounded as they went.

Joshua commanded the people, saying, "You shall not shout nor let your voice be heard, neither shall any word proceed out of your mouth until the day I tell you to shout. Then you shall shout." So he caused YHWH's ark to go around the city, circling it once. Then they came into the camp, and stayed in the camp. Joshua rose early in the morning, and the priests took up YHWH's ark. The seven priests bearing the seven trumpets of rams' horns in front of YHWH's ark went on continually, and blew the trumpets. The armed men went in front of them. The rear guard came after YHWH's ark. The trumpets sounded as they went. The second day they marched around the city once, and returned into the camp. They did this six days.

On the seventh day, they rose early at the dawning of the day, and marched around the city in the same way seven times. On this day only they marched around the city seven times. At the seventh time, when the priests blew the trumpets, Joshua said to the people, "Shout, for YHWH has given you the city! The city shall be devoted, even it and all that is in it, to YHWH. Only Rahab the prostitute shall live, she and all who are with her in the house, because she hid the messengers that we sent. But as for you, only keep yourselves from what is devoted to destruction, lest when you have devoted it, you take of the devoted thing; so you would make the camp of Israel accursed and trouble it. But all the silver, gold, and vessels of bronze and iron are holy to YHWH. They shall come into YHWH's treasury."

So the people shouted and the priests blew the trumpets. When the people heard the sound of the trumpet, the people shouted with a great shout, and the wall fell down flat, so that the people went up into the city, every man straight in front of him, and they took the city. They utterly destroyed all that was in the city, both man and woman, both young and old, and ox, sheep, and donkey, with the edge of the sword. Joshua said to the two men who had spied out the land, "Go into the prostitute's house, and bring the woman and all that she has out from there, as you swore to her." The young men who were spies went in, and brought out Rahab with her father, her mother, her brothers, and all that she had. They also brought out all of her relatives, and they set them outside of the camp of Israel. They burned the city with fire, and all that was in it. Only they put the silver, the gold, and the vessels of bronze and of iron into the treasury of YHWH's house. But Rahab the prostitute, her father's household, and all that she had, Joshua saved alive. She lives in the middle of Israel to this day, because she hid the messengers whom Joshua sent to spy out Jericho.

Joshua commanded them with an oath at that time, saying,

"Cursed is the man before YHWH who rises up and builds this city Jericho. With the loss of his firstborn he will lay its foundation, and with the loss of his youngest son he will set up its gates." So YHWH was with Joshua; and his fame was in all the land.

....

But the children of Israel committed a trespass in the devoted things; for Achan, the son of Carmi, the son of Zabdi, the son of Zerah, of the tribe of Judah, took some of the devoted things. Therefore YHWH's anger burned against the children of Israel. Joshua sent men from Jericho to Ai, which is beside Beth Aven, on the east side of Bethel, and spoke to them, saying, "Go up and spy out the land."

The men went up and spied out Ai. They returned to Joshua, and said to him, "Don't let all the people go up, but let about two or three thousand men go up and strike Ai. Don't make all the people to toil there, for there are only a few of them." So about three thousand men of the people went up there, and they fled before the men of Ai. The men of Ai struck about thirty-six men of them. They chased them from before the gate even to Shebarim, and struck them at the descent. The hearts of the people melted, and became like water. Joshua tore his clothes, and fell to the earth on his face before YHWH's ark until the evening, he and the elders of Israel; and they put dust on their heads. Joshua said, "Alas, Lord YHWH, why have you brought this people over the Jordan at all, to deliver us into the hand of the Amorites, to cause us to perish? I wish that we had been content and lived beyond the Jordan! Oh, Lord, what shall I say, after Israel has turned their backs before their enemies? For the Canaanites and all the inhabitants of the land will hear of it, and will surround us, and cut off our name from the earth. What will you do for your great name?"

YHWH said to Joshua, "Get up! Why have you fallen on your face like that? Israel has sinned. Yes, they have even transgressed my covenant which I commanded them. Yes, they have even taken some of the devoted things, and have also stolen, and also deceived. They have even put it among their own stuff. Therefore the children of Israel can't stand before their enemies. They turn their backs before their enemies, because they have become devoted for destruction. I will not be with you any more, unless you destroy the devoted things from among you. Get up! Sanctify the people, and say, 'Sanctify yourselves for tomorrow, for YHWH, the God of Israel, says, "There is a devoted thing among you, Israel. You cannot stand before your enemies until you take away the devoted thing from among you." In the morning therefore you shall be brought near by your tribes. It shall be that the tribe which YHWH selects shall come near by families. The family which YHWH selects shall come near by households. The household which YHWH selects shall come near man by man. It shall be, that he who is taken with the devoted thing shall be burned with fire, he and all that he has, because he has transgressed YHWH's covenant, and because he has done a disgraceful thing in Israel.'"

So Joshua rose up early in the morning and brought Israel near by their tribes. The tribe of Judah was selected. He brought near the family of Judah, and he selected the family of the Zerahites. He brought near the family of the Zerahites man by man, and Zabdi was selected. He brought near his household man by man, and Achan, the son of Carmi, the son of Zabdi, the son of Zerah, of the tribe of Judah, was selected. Joshua said to Achan, "My son, please give glory to YHWH, the God of Israel, and make confession to him. Tell me now what you have done! Don't hide it from me!"

Achan answered Joshua, and said, "I have truly sinned against YHWH, the God of Israel, and this is what I have done. When I saw among the plunder a beautiful Babylonian robe, two hundred shekels of silver, and a wedge of gold weighing fifty shekels, then I coveted them and took them. Behold, they are hidden in the ground in the middle of my tent, with the silver under it."

So Joshua sent messengers, and they ran to the tent. Behold, it was hidden in his tent, with the silver under it. They took them from the middle of the tent, and brought them to Joshua and to all the children of Israel. They laid them down before YHWH. Joshua, and all Israel with him, took Achan the son of Zerah, the silver, the robe, the wedge of gold, his sons, his daughters, his cattle, his donkeys, his sheep, his tent, and all that he had; and they brought them up to the valley of Achor. Joshua said, "Why have you troubled us? YHWH will trouble you today." All Israel stoned him with stones, and they burned them with fire and stoned them with stones. They raised over him a great heap of stones that remains to this day. YHWH turned from the fierceness of his anger. Therefore the name of that place was called "The valley of Achor" to this day.

....

YHWH said to Joshua, "Don't be afraid, and don't be dismayed.

Take all the warriors with you, and arise, go up to Ai. Behold, I have given into your hand the king of Ai, with his people, his city, and his land. You shall do to Ai and her king as you did to Jericho and her king, except you shall take its goods and its livestock for yourselves. Set an ambush for the city behind it."

So Joshua arose, with all the warriors, to go up to Ai. Joshua chose thirty thousand men, the mighty men of valor, and sent them out by night. He commanded them, saying, "Behold, you shall lie in ambush against the city, behind the city. Don't go very far from the city, but all of you be ready. I and all the people who are with me will approach the city. It shall happen, when they come out against us, as at the first, that we will flee before them. They will come out after us until we have drawn them away from the city; for they will say, 'They flee before us, like the first time.' So we will flee before them, and you shall rise up from the ambush, and take possession of the city; for YHWH your God will deliver it into your hand. It shall be, when you have seized the city, that you shall set the city on fire. You shall do this according to YHWH's word. Behold, I have commanded you."

Joshua sent them out; and they went to set up the ambush, and stayed between Bethel and Ai on the west side of Ai; but Joshua stayed among the people that night. Joshua rose up early in the morning, mustered the people, and went up, he and the elders of Israel, before the people to Ai. All the people, even the men of war who were with him, went up and came near, and came before the city and encamped on the north side of Ai. Now there was a valley between him and Ai. He took about five thousand men, and set them in ambush between Bethel and Ai, on the west side of the city. So they set the people, even all the army who was on the north of the city, and their ambush on the west of the city; and Joshua went that night into the middle of the valley. When the king of Ai saw it, they hurried and rose up early, and the men of the city went out against Israel to battle, he and all his people, at the time appointed, before the Arabah; but he didn't know that there was an ambush against him behind the city. Joshua and all Israel made as if they were beaten before them, and fled by the way of the wilderness. All the people who were in the city were called together to pursue after them. They pursued Joshua, and were drawn away from the city. There was not a man left in Ai or Bethel who didn't go out after Israel. They left the city open, and pursued Israel.

YHWH said to Joshua, "Stretch out the javelin that is in your hand toward Ai, for I will give it into your hand."

Joshua stretched out the javelin that was in his hand toward the city. The ambush arose quickly out of their place, and they ran as soon as he had stretched out his hand and entered into the city and took it. They hurried and set the city on fire. When the men of Ai looked behind them, they saw, and behold, the smoke of the city ascended up to heaven, and they had no power to flee this way or that way. The people who fled to the wilderness turned back on the pursuers. When Joshua and all Israel saw that the ambush had taken the city, and that the smoke of the city ascended, then they turned back and killed the men of Ai. The others came out of the city against them, so they were in the middle of Israel, some on this side, and some on that side. They struck them, so that they let none of them remain or escape. They captured the king of Ai alive, and brought him to Joshua.

When Israel had finished killing all the inhabitants of Ai in the field, in the wilderness in which they pursued them, and they had all fallen by the edge of the sword until they were consumed, all Israel returned to Ai and struck it with the edge of the sword. All that fell that day, both of men and women, were twelve thousand, even all the people of Ai. For Joshua didn't draw back his hand, with which he stretched out the javelin, until he had utterly destroyed all the inhabitants of Ai. Israel took for themselves only the livestock and the goods of that city, according to yhwh's word which he commanded Joshua. So Joshua burned Ai and made it a heap forever, even a desolation, to this day. He hanged the king of Ai on a tree until the evening. At sundown, Joshua commanded, and they took his body down from the tree and threw it at the entrance of the gate of the city, and raised a great heap of stones on it that remains to this day.

Then Joshua built an altar to yhwh, the God of Israel, on Mount Ebal, as Moses the servant of yhwh commanded the children of Israel, as it is written in the book of the law of Moses: an altar of uncut stones, on which no one had lifted up any iron. They offered burnt offerings on it to yhwh and sacrificed peace offerings. He wrote there on the stones a copy of Moses' law, which he wrote in the presence of the children of Israel. All Israel, with their elders, officers, and judges, stood on both sides of the ark before the Levitical priests, who carried the ark of yhwh's covenant, the foreigner as well as the native; half of them in front of Mount Gerizim, and half of them in front of Mount Ebal, as Moses the servant of yhwh had commanded at the first, that they should bless the people of Israel. Afterward he read all the words of the law, the blessing and the curse, according to all that is written in the book of the law. There was not a word of all that Moses commanded which Joshua didn't read before all the assembly of Israel, with the women, the little ones, and the foreigners who were among them.

....

When all the kings who were beyond the Jordan, in the hill country, and in the lowland, and on all the shore of the great sea in front of Lebanon, the Hittite, the Amorite, the Canaanite, the Perizzite, the Hivite, and the Jebusite, heard of it they gathered themselves together to fight with Joshua and with Israel, with one accord. But when the inhabitants of Gibeon heard what Joshua had done to Jericho and to Ai, they also resorted to a ruse, and went and made as if they had been ambassadors, and took old sacks on their donkeys, and old, torn-up and bound up wine skins, and old and patched sandals on their feet, and wore old garments. All the bread of their food supply was dry and moldy. They went to Joshua at the camp at Gilgal, and said to him and to the men of Israel, "We have come from a far country. Now therefore make a covenant with us."

The men of Israel said to the Hivites, "What if you live among us? How could we make a covenant with you?"

They said to Joshua, "We are your servants."

Joshua said to them, "Who are you? Where do you come from?"

They said to him, "Your servants have come from a very far country because of the name of YHWH your God; for we have heard of his fame, all that he did in Egypt, and all that he did to the two kings of the Amorites who were beyond the Jordan, to Sihon king of Heshbon and to Og king of Bashan, who was at Ashtaroth. Our elders and all the inhabitants of our country spoke to us, saying, 'Take supplies in your hand for the journey, and go to meet them. Tell them, "We are your servants. Now make a covenant with us."' This our bread we took hot for our supplies out of our houses on the day we went out to go to you; but now, behold, it is dry, and has become moldy. These wine skins, which we filled, were new; and behold, they are torn. These our garments and our sandals have become old because of the very long journey."

The men sampled their provisions, and didn't ask counsel from YHWH's mouth. Joshua made peace with them, and made a covenant with them, to let them live. The princes of the congregation swore to them. At the end of three days after they had made a covenant with them, they heard that they were their neighbors, and that they lived among them. The children of Israel traveled and came to their cities on the third day. Now their cities were Gibeon, Chephirah, Beeroth, and Kiriath Jearim. The children of Israel didn't strike them, because the princes of the congregation had sworn to them by YHWH, the God of Israel. All the congregation murmured against the princes. But all the princes said to all the congregation, "We have sworn to them by YHWH, the God of Israel. Now therefore we may not touch them. We will do this to them, and let them live; lest wrath be on us, because of the oath which we swore to them." The princes said to them, "Let them live." So they became wood cutters and drawers of water for all the congregation, as the princes had spoken to them.

Joshua called for them, and he spoke to them, saying, "Why have you deceived us, saying, 'We are very far from you,' when you live among us? Now therefore you are cursed, and some of you will never fail to be slaves, both wood cutters and drawers of water for the house of my God."

They answered Joshua, and said, "Because your servants were certainly told how YHWH your God commanded his servant Moses to give you all the land, and to destroy all the inhabitants of the land from before you. Therefore we were very afraid for our lives because of you, and have done this thing. Now, behold, we are in your hand. Do to us as it seems good and right to you to do."

He did so to them, and delivered them out of the hand of the children of Israel, so that they didn't kill them. That day Joshua made them wood cutters and drawers of water for the congregation and for YHWH's altar to this day, in the place which he should choose.

....

Now when Adoni-Zedek king of Jerusalem heard how Joshua had taken Ai, and had utterly destroyed it; as he had done to Jericho and her king, so he had done to Ai and her king; and how the inhabitants of Gibeon had made peace with Israel, and were among them, they were very afraid, because Gibeon was a great city, as one of the royal cities, and because it was greater than Ai, and all its men were mighty. Therefore Adoni-Zedek king of Jerusalem sent to Hoham king of Hebron, Piram king of Jarmuth, Japhia king of Lachish, and Debir king of Eglon, saying, "Come up to me and help me. Let's strike Gibeon; for they have made peace with Joshua and with the children of Israel." Therefore the five kings of the Amorites, the king of Jerusalem, the king of Hebron, the king of Jarmuth, the king of Lachish, and the king of Eglon, gathered themselves together and went up, they and all their armies, and encamped against Gibeon, and made war against it. The men of Gibeon sent to Joshua at the camp at Gilgal, saying, "Don't abandon your servants! Come up to us quickly and save us! Help us; for all the kings of the Amorites that dwell in the hill country have gathered together against us."

So Joshua went up from Gilgal, he, and the whole army with him, including all the mighty men of valor. YHWH said to Joshua, "Don't fear them, for I have delivered them into your hands. Not a man of them will stand before you."

Joshua therefore came to them suddenly. He marched from Gilgal all night. YHWH confused them before Israel. He killed them with a great slaughter at Gibeon, and chased them by the way of the ascent of Beth Horon, and struck them to Azekah and to Makkedah. As they fled from before Israel, while they were at the descent of Beth Horon, YHWH hurled down great stones from the sky on them to Azekah, and they died. There were more who died from the hailstones than those whom the children of Israel killed with the sword.

Then Joshua spoke to YHWH in the day when YHWH delivered up the Amorites before the children of Israel. He said in the sight of Israel, "Sun, stand still on Gibeon! You, moon, stop in the valley of Aijalon!"

The sun stood still, and the moon stayed, until the nation had avenged themselves of their enemies. Isn't this written in the book of Jashar? The sun stayed in the middle of the sky, and didn't hurry to go down about a whole day. There was no day like that before it or after it, that YHWH listened to the voice of a man; for YHWH fought for Israel.

Joshua returned, and all Israel with him, to the camp to Gilgal. These five kings fled, and hid themselves in the cave at Makkedah. Joshua was told, saying, "The five kings have been found, hidden in the cave at Makkedah."

Joshua said, "Roll large stones to cover the cave's entrance, and set men by it to guard them; but don't stay there. Pursue your enemies, and attack them from the rear. Don't allow them to enter into their cities; for YHWH your God has delivered them into your hand."

When Joshua and the children of Israel had finished killing them with a very great slaughter until they were consumed, and the remnant which remained of them had entered into the fortified cities, all the people returned to the camp to Joshua at Makkedah in peace. None moved his tongue against any of the children of Israel. Then Joshua said, "Open the cave entrance, and bring those five kings out of the cave to me."

They did so, and brought those five kings out of the cave to him: the king of Jerusalem, the king of Hebron, the king of Jarmuth, the king of Lachish, and the king of Eglon. When they brought those kings out to Joshua, Joshua called for all the men of Israel, and said to the chiefs of the men of war who went with him, "Come near. Put your feet on the necks of these kings."

They came near, and put their feet on their necks.

Joshua said to them, "Don't be afraid, nor be dismayed. Be strong and courageous, for YHWH will do this to all your enemies against whom you fight."

Afterward Joshua struck them, put them to death, and hanged them on five trees. They were hanging on the trees until the evening. At the time of the going down of the sun, Joshua commanded, and they took them down off the trees, and threw them into the cave in which they had hidden themselves, and laid great stones on the mouth of the cave, which remain to this very day.

Joshua took Makkedah on that day, and struck it with the edge of the sword, with its king. He utterly destroyed it and all the souls who were in it. He left no one remaining. He did to the king of Makkedah as he had done to the king of Jericho.

Joshua passed from Makkedah, and all Israel with him, to Libnah, and fought against Libnah. YHWH delivered it also, with its king, into the hand of Israel. He struck it with the edge of the sword, and all the souls who were in it. He left no one remaining in it. He did to its king as he had done to the king of Jericho.

Joshua passed from Libnah, and all Israel with him, to Lachish, and encamped against it, and fought against it. YHWH delivered Lachish into the hand of Israel. He took it on the second day, and struck it with the edge of the sword, with all the souls who were in it, according to all that he had done to Libnah. Then Horam king of Gezer came up to help Lachish; and Joshua struck him and his people, until he had left him no one remaining.

Joshua passed from Lachish, and all Israel with him, to Eglon; and they encamped against it and fought against it. They took it on that day, and struck it with the edge of the sword. He utterly destroyed all the souls who were in it that day, according to all that he had done to Lachish.

Joshua went up from Eglon, and all Israel with him, to Hebron; and they fought against it. They took it, and struck it with the edge of the sword, with its king and all its cities, and all the souls who were in it. He left no one remaining, according to all that he had done to Eglon; but he utterly destroyed it, and all the souls who were in it.

Joshua returned, and all Israel with him, to Debir, and fought against it. He took it, with its king and all its cities. They struck them with the edge of the sword, and utterly destroyed all the souls who were in it. He left no one remaining. As he had done to Hebron, so he did to Debir, and to its king; as he had done also to Libnah, and to its king. So Joshua struck all the land, the hill country, the South, the lowland, the slopes, and all their kings. He left no one remaining, but he utterly destroyed all that breathed, as YHWH, the God of Israel, commanded. Joshua struck them from Kadesh Barnea even to Gaza, and all the country of Goshen, even to Gibeon. Joshua took all these kings and their land at one time because YHWH, the God of Israel, fought for Israel. Joshua returned, and all Israel with him, to the camp to Gilgal.

....

When Jabin king of Hazor heard of it, he sent to Jobab king of Madon, to the king of Shimron, to the king of Achshaph, and to the kings who were on the north, in the hill country, in the Arabah south of Chinneroth, in the lowland, and in the heights of Dor on the west, to the Canaanite on the east and on the west, the Amorite, the Hittite, the Perizzite, the Jebusite in the hill country, and the Hivite under Hermon in the land of Mizpah. They went out, they and all their armies with them, many people, even as the sand that is on the seashore in multitude, with very many horses and chariots. All these kings met together; and they came and encamped together at the waters of Merom, to fight with Israel.

YHWH said to Joshua, "Don't be afraid because of them; for tomorrow at this time, I will deliver them up all slain before Israel. You shall hamstring their horses and burn their chariots with fire."

So Joshua came suddenly, with all the warriors, against them by the waters of Merom, and attacked them. YHWH delivered them into the hand of Israel, and they struck them, and chased them to great Sidon, and to Misrephoth Maim, and to the valley of Mizpah eastward. They struck them until they left them no one remaining. Joshua did to them as YHWH told him. He hamstrung their horses and burned their chariots with fire. Joshua turned back at that time, and took Hazor, and struck its king with the sword: for Hazor used to be the head of all those kingdoms. They struck all the souls who were in it with the edge of the sword, utterly destroying them. There was no one left who breathed. He burned Hazor with fire. Joshua captured all the cities of those kings, with their kings, and he struck them with the edge of the sword, and utterly destroyed them; as Moses the servant of YHWH commanded. But as for the cities that stood on their mounds, Israel burned none of them, except Hazor only. Joshua burned that. The children of Israel took all the plunder of these cities, with the livestock, as plunder for themselves; but every man they struck with the edge of the sword, until they had destroyed them. They didn't leave any who breathed.

As YHWH commanded Moses his servant, so Moses commanded Joshua. Joshua did so. He left nothing undone of all that YHWH commanded Moses. So Joshua captured all that land, the hill country, all the South, all the land of Goshen, the lowland, the Arabah, the hill country of Israel, and the lowland of the same; from Mount Halak, that goes up to Seir, even to Baal Gad in the valley of Lebanon under Mount Hermon. He took all their kings, struck them, and put them to death. Joshua made war a long time with all those kings. There was not a city that made peace with the children of Israel, except the Hivites, the inhabitants of Gibeon. They took all in battle. For it was of YHWH to harden their hearts, to come against Israel in battle, that he might utterly destroy them, that they might have no favor, but that he might destroy them, as YHWH commanded Moses. Joshua came at that time, and cut off the Anakim from the hill country, from Hebron, from Debir, from Anab, and from all the hill country of Judah, and from all the hill country of Israel: Joshua utterly destroyed them with their cities. There were none of the Anakim left in the land of the children of Israel. Only in Gaza, in Gath, and in Ashdod, did some remain. So Joshua took the whole land, according to all that YHWH spoke to Moses; and Joshua gave it for an inheritance to Israel according to their divisions by their tribes. Then the land had rest from war.

Now these are the kings of the land, whom the children of Israel struck, and possessed their land beyond the Jordan toward the sunrise, from the valley of the Arnon to Mount Hermon, and all the Arabah eastward: Sihon king of the Amorites, who lived in Heshbon, and ruled from Aroer, which is on the edge of the valley of the Arnon, and the middle of the valley, and half Gilead, even to the river Jabbok, the border of the children of Ammon; and the Arabah to the sea of Chinneroth, eastward, and to the sea of the Arabah, even the Salt Sea, eastward, the way to Beth Jeshimoth; and on the south, under the slopes of Pisgah: and the border of Og king of Bashan, of the remnant of the Rephaim, who lived at Ashtaroth and at Edrei, and ruled in Mount Hermon, and in Salecah, and in all Bashan, to the border of the Geshurites and the Maacathites, and half Gilead, the border of Sihon king of Heshbon.

Moses the servant of YHWH and the children of Israel struck them. Moses the servant of YHWH gave it for a possession to the Reubenites, and the Gadites, and the half-tribe of Manasseh. These are the kings of the land whom Joshua and the children of Israel struck beyond the Jordan westward, from Baal Gad in the valley of Lebanon even to Mount Halak, that goes up to Seir. Joshua gave it to the tribes of Israel for a possession according to their divisions; in the hill country, and in the lowland, and in the Arabah, and in the slopes, and in the wilderness, and in the South; the Hittite, the Amorite, and the Canaanite, the Perizzite, the Hivite, and the Jebusite:

the king of Jericho, one;
the king of Ai, which is beside Bethel, one;
the king of Jerusalem, one;
the king of Hebron, one;
the king of Jarmuth, one;
the king of Lachish, one;
the king of Eglon, one;
the king of Gezer, one;
the king of Debir, one;
the king of Geder, one;
the king of Hormah, one;
the king of Arad, one;
the king of Libnah, one;
the king of Adullam, one;
the king of Makkedah, one;
the king of Bethel, one;

the king of Tappuah, one;
the king of Hepher, one;
the king of Aphek, one;
the king of Lassharon, one;
the king of Madon, one;
the king of Hazor, one;
the king of Shimron Meron, one;
the king of Achshaph, one;
the king of Taanach, one;
the king of Megiddo, one;
the king of Kedesh, one;
the king of Jokneam in Carmel, one;
the king of Dor in the height of Dor, one;
the king of Goiim in Gilgal, one;
the king of Tirzah, one:
all the kings thirty-one.

....

Now Joshua was old and well advanced in years. YHWH said to him, "You are old and advanced in years, and there remains yet very much land to be possessed.

"This is the land that still remains: all the regions of the Philistines, and all the Geshurites; from the Shihor, which is before Egypt, even to the border of Ekron northward, which is counted as Canaanite; the five lords of the Philistines; the Gazites, and the Ashdodites, the Ashkelonites, the Gittites, and the Ekronites; also the Avvim, on the south; all the land of the Canaanites, and Mearah that belongs to the Sidonians, to Aphek, to the border of the Amorites; and the land of the Gebalites, and all Lebanon, toward the sunrise, from Baal Gad under Mount Hermon to the entrance of Hamath; all the inhabitants of the hill country from Lebanon to Misrephoth Maim, even all the Sidonians. I will drive them out from before the children of Israel. Just allocate it to Israel for an inheritance, as I have commanded you. Now therefore divide this land for an inheritance to the nine tribes and the half-tribe of Manasseh." With him the Reubenites and the Gadites received their inheritance, which Moses gave them, beyond the Jordan eastward, even as Moses the servant of YHWH gave them: from Aroer, that is on the edge of the valley of the Arnon, and the city that is in the middle of the valley, and all the plain of Medeba to Dibon; and all the cities of Sihon king of the

Amorites, who reigned in Heshbon, to the border of the children of Ammon; and Gilead, and the border of the Geshurites and Maacathites, and all Mount Hermon, and all Bashan to Salecah; all the kingdom of Og in Bashan, who reigned in Ashtaroth and in Edrei (who was left of the remnant of the Rephaim); for Moses attacked these, and drove them out. Nevertheless the children of Israel didn't drive out the Geshurites, nor the Maacathites: but Geshur and Maacath live within Israel to this day. Only he gave no inheritance to the tribe of Levi. The offerings of yhwh, the God of Israel, made by fire are his inheritance, as he spoke to him. Moses gave to the tribe of the children of Reuben according to their families. Their border was from Aroer, that is on the edge of the valley of the Arnon, and the city that is in the middle of the valley, and all the plain by Medeba; Heshbon, and all its cities that are in the plain; Dibon, Bamoth Baal, Beth Baal Meon, Jahaz, Kedemoth, Mephaath, Kiriathaim, Sibmah, Zereth Shahar in the mount of the valley, Beth Peor, the slopes of Pisgah, Beth Jeshimoth, all the cities of the plain, and all the kingdom of Sihon king of the Amorites, who reigned in Heshbon, whom Moses struck with the chiefs of Midian, Evi, Rekem, Zur, Hur, and Reba, the princes of Sihon, who lived in the land. The children of Israel also killed Balaam the son of Beor, the soothsayer, with the sword, among the rest of their slain.

The border of the children of Reuben was the bank of the Jordan. This was the inheritance of the children of Reuben according to their families, the cities and its villages.

Moses gave to the tribe of Gad, to the children of Gad, according to their families. Their border was Jazer, and all the cities of Gilead, and half the land of the children of Ammon, to Aroer that is near Rabbah; and from Heshbon to Ramath Mizpeh, and Betonim; and from Mahanaim to the border of Debir; and in the valley, Beth Haram, Beth Nimrah, Succoth, and Zaphon, the rest of the kingdom of Sihon king of Heshbon, the Jordan's bank, to the uttermost part of the sea of Chinnereth beyond the Jordan eastward. This is the inheritance of the children of Gad according to their families, the cities and its villages.

Moses gave an inheritance to the half-tribe of Manasseh. It was for the half-tribe of the children of Manasseh according to their families. Their border was from Mahanaim, all Bashan, all the kingdom of Og king of Bashan, and all the villages of Jair, which are in Bashan, sixty cities. Half Gilead, Ashtaroth, and Edrei, the cities of the kingdom of Og in Bashan, were for the children of Machir the son of Manasseh, even for the half of the children of Machir according to their families.

These are the inheritances which Moses distributed in the plains of Moab, beyond the Jordan at Jericho, eastward. But Moses gave no inheritance to the tribe of Levi. YHWH, the God of Israel, is their inheritance, as he spoke to them.

··

These are the inheritances which the children of Israel took in the land of Canaan, which Eleazar the priest, Joshua the son of Nun, and the heads of the fathers' houses of the tribes of the children of Israel, distributed to them, by the lot of their inheritance, as YHWH commanded by Moses, for the nine tribes, and for the half-tribe. For Moses had given the inheritance of the two tribes and the half-tribe beyond the Jordan; but to the Levites he gave no inheritance among them. For the children of Joseph were two tribes, Manasseh and Ephraim. They gave no portion to the Levites in the land, except cities to dwell in, with their pasture lands for their livestock and for their property. The children of Israel did as YHWH commanded Moses, and they divided the land.

Then the children of Judah came near to Joshua in Gilgal. Caleb the son of Jephunneh the Kenizzite said to him, "You know the thing that YHWH spoke to Moses the man of God concerning me and concerning you in Kadesh Barnea. I was forty years old when Moses the servant of YHWH sent me from Kadesh Barnea to spy out the land. I brought him word again as it was in my heart. Nevertheless, my brothers who went up with me made the heart of the people melt; but I wholly followed YHWH my God. Moses swore on that day, saying, 'Surely the land where you walked shall be an inheritance to you and to your children forever, because you have wholly followed YHWH my God.'

"Now, behold, YHWH has kept me alive, as he spoke, these forty-five years, from the time that YHWH spoke this word to Moses, while Israel walked in the wilderness. Now, behold, I am eighty-five years old, today. As yet I am as strong today as I was in the day that Moses sent me. As my strength was then, even so is my strength now for war, to go out and to come in. Now therefore give me this hill country, of which YHWH spoke in that day; for you heard in that day how the Anakim were there, and great and fortified cities. It may be that YHWH will be with me, and I shall drive them out, as YHWH said."

Joshua blessed him; and he gave Hebron to Caleb the son of Jephunneh for an inheritance. Therefore Hebron became the inheritance of Caleb the son of Jephunneh the Kenizzite to this day, because he followed YHWH, the God of Israel wholeheartedly. Now the name of Hebron before was Kiriath Arba, after the greatest man among the Anakim. Then the land had rest from war.

....

The lot for the tribe of the children of Judah according to their families was to the border of Edom, even to the wilderness of Zin southward, at the uttermost part of the south. Their south border was from the uttermost part of the Salt Sea, from the bay that looks southward; and it went out southward of the ascent of Akrabbim, and passed along to Zin, and went up by the south of Kadesh Barnea, and passed along by Hezron, went up to Addar, and turned toward Karka; and it passed along to Azmon, went out at the brook of Egypt; and the border ended at the sea. This shall be your south border. The east border was the Salt Sea, even to the end of the Jordan. The border of the north quarter was from the bay of the sea at the end of the Jordan. The border went up to Beth Hoglah, and passed along by the north of Beth Arabah; and the border went up to the stone of Bohan the son of Reuben. The border went up to Debir from the valley of Achor, and so northward, looking toward Gilgal, that faces the ascent of Adummim, which is on the south side of the river. The border passed along to the waters of En Shemesh, and ended at En Rogel. The border went up by the valley of the son of Hinnom to the side of the Jebusite (also called Jerusalem) southward; and the border went up to the top of the mountain that lies before the valley of Hinnom westward, which is at the farthest part of the valley of Rephaim northward. The border extended from the top of the mountain to the spring of the waters of Nephtoah, and went out to the cities of Mount Ephron; and the border extended to Baalah (also called Kiriath Jearim); and the border turned about from Baalah westward to Mount Seir, and passed along to the side of Mount Jearim (also called Chesalon) on the north, and went down to Beth Shemesh, and passed along by Timnah; and the border went out to the side of Ekron northward; and the border extended to Shikkeron, and passed along to Mount Baalah, and went out at Jabneel; and the goings out of the border were at the sea. The west border was to the shore of the great sea. This is the border of the children of Judah according to their families.

He gave to Caleb the son of Jephunneh a portion among the children of Judah, according to the commandment of YHWH to Joshua, even Kiriath Arba, named after the father of Anak (also called Hebron). Caleb drove out the three sons of Anak: Sheshai, and Ahiman, and Talmai, the children of Anak. He went up against the inhabitants of Debir: now the name of Debir before was Kiriath Sepher. Caleb said, "He who strikes Kiriath Sepher, and takes it, to him I will give Achsah my daughter as wife." Othniel the son of Kenaz, the brother of Caleb, took it: and he gave him Achsah his daughter as wife. When she came, she had him ask her father for a field. She got off her donkey, and Caleb said, "What do you want?"

She said, "Give me a blessing. Because you have set me in the land of the South, give me also springs of water."

So he gave her the upper springs and the lower springs.

This is the inheritance of the tribe of the children of Judah according to their families. The farthest cities of the tribe of the children of Judah toward the border of Edom in the South were Kabzeel, Eder, Jagur, Kinah, Dimonah, Adadah, Kedesh, Hazor, Ithnan, Ziph, Telem, Bealoth, Hazor Hadattah, Kerioth Hezron (also called Hazor), Amam, Shema, Moladah, Hazar Gaddah, Heshmon, Beth Pelet, Hazar Shual, Beersheba, Biziothiah, Baalah, Iim, Ezem, Eltolad, Chesil, Hormah, Ziklag, Madmannah, Sansannah, Lebaoth, Shilhim, Ain, and Rimmon. All the cities are twenty-nine, with their villages.

In the lowland, Eshtaol, Zorah, Ashnah, Zanoah, En Gannim, Tappuah, Enam, Jarmuth, Adullam, Socoh, Azekah, Shaaraim, Adithaim and Gederah (or Gederothaim); fourteen cities with their villages.

Zenan, Hadashah, Migdal Gad, Dilean, Mizpah, Joktheel, Lachish, Bozkath, Eglon, Cabbon, Lahmam, Chitlish, Gederoth, Beth Dagon, Naamah, and Makkedah; sixteen cities with their villages.

Libnah, Ether, Ashan, Iphtah, Ashnah, Nezib, Keilah, Achzib, and Mareshah; nine cities with their villages.

Ekron, with its towns and its villages; from Ekron even to the sea, all that were by the side of Ashdod, with their villages. Ashdod, its towns and its villages; Gaza, its towns and its villages; to the brook of Egypt, and the great sea with its coastline.

In the hill country, Shamir, Jattir, Socoh, Dannah, Kiriath Sannah (which is Debir), Anab, Eshtemoh, Anim, Goshen, Holon, and Giloh; eleven cities with their villages.

Arab, Dumah, Eshan, Janim, Beth Tappuah, Aphekah, Humtah, Kiriath Arba (also called Hebron), and Zior; nine cities with their villages.

Maon, Carmel, Ziph, Jutah, Jezreel, Jokdeam, Zanoah, Kain, Gibeah, and Timnah; ten cities with their villages.

Halhul, Beth Zur, Gedor, Maarath, Beth Anoth, and Eltekon; six cities with their villages. Kiriath Baal (also called Kiriath Jearim), and Rabbah; two cities with their villages.

In the wilderness, Beth Arabah, Middin, Secacah, Nibshan, the City of Salt, and En Gedi; six cities with their villages.

As for the Jebusites, the inhabitants of Jerusalem, the children of Judah couldn't drive them out; but the Jebusites live with the children of Judah at Jerusalem to this day.

....

The lot came out for the children of Joseph from the Jordan at Jericho, at the waters of Jericho on the east, even the wilderness, going up from Jericho through the hill country to Bethel. It went out from Bethel to Luz, and passed along to the border of the Archites to Ataroth; and it went down westward to the border of the Japhletites, to the border of Beth Horon the lower, and on to Gezer; and ended at the sea.

The children of Joseph, Manasseh and Ephraim, took their inheritance. This was the border of the children of Ephraim according to their families. The border of their inheritance eastward was Ataroth Addar, to Beth Horon the upper. The border went out westward at Michmethath on the north. The border turned about eastward to Taanath Shiloh, and passed along it on the east of Janoah. It went down from Janoah to Ataroth, to Naarah, reached to Jericho, and went out at the Jordan. From Tappuah the border went along westward to the brook of Kanah; and ended at the sea. This is the inheritance of the tribe of the children of Ephraim according to their families; together with the cities which were set apart for the children of Ephraim in the middle of the inheritance of the children of Manasseh, all the cities with their villages. They didn't drive out the Canaanites who lived in Gezer; but the Canaanites dwell in the territory of Ephraim to this day, and have become servants to do forced labor.

....

This was the lot for the tribe of Manasseh, for he was the first-born of Joseph. As for Machir the firstborn of Manasseh, the father of Gilead, because he was a man of war, therefore he had Gilead and Bashan. So this was for the rest of the children of Manasseh according to their families: for the children of Abiezer, for the children of Helek, for the children of Asriel, for the children of Shechem, for the children of Hepher, and for the children of Shemida. These were the male children of Manasseh the son of Joseph according to their families. But Zelophehad, the son of Hepher, the son of Gilead, the son of Machir, the son of Manasseh, had no sons, but daughters. These are the names of his daughters: Mahlah, Noah, Hoglah, Milcah, and Tirzah. They came to Eleazar the priest, and to Joshua the son of Nun, and to the princes, saying, "YHWH commanded Moses to give us an inheritance among our brothers." Therefore according to the commandment of YHWH he gave them an inheritance among the brothers of their father. Ten parts fell to Manasseh, in addition to the land of Gilead and Bashan, which is beyond the Jordan; because the daughters of Manasseh had an inheritance among his sons. The land of Gilead belonged to the rest of the sons of Manasseh. The border of Manasseh was from Asher to Michmethath, which is before Shechem. The border went along to the right hand, to the inhabitants of En Tappuah. The land of Tappuah belonged to Manasseh; but Tappuah on the border of Manasseh belonged to the children of Ephraim. The border went down to the brook of Kanah, southward of the brook. These cities belonged to Ephraim among the cities of Manasseh. The border of Manasseh was on the north side of the brook, and ended at the sea. Southward it was Ephraim's, and northward it was Manasseh's, and the sea was his border. They reached to Asher on the north, and to Issachar on the east. Manasseh had three heights in Issachar, in Asher Beth Shean and its towns, and Ibleam and its towns, and the inhabitants of Dor and its towns, and the inhabitants of Endor and its towns, and the inhabitants of Taanach and its towns, and the inhabitants of Megiddo and its towns. Yet the children of Manasseh couldn't drive out the inhabitants of those cities; but the Canaanites would dwell in that land.

When the children of Israel had grown strong, they put the Canaanites to forced labor, and didn't utterly drive them out. The children of Joseph spoke to Joshua, saying, "Why have you given me just one lot and one part for an inheritance, since we are a numerous people, because YHWH has blessed us so far?"

Joshua said to them, "If you are a numerous people, go up to the forest, and clear land for yourself there in the land of the Perizzites and of the Rephaim; since the hill country of Ephraim is too narrow for you."

The children of Joseph said, "The hill country is not enough for us. All the Canaanites who dwell in the land of the valley have chariots of iron, both those who are in Beth Shean and its towns, and those who are in the valley of Jezreel."

Joshua spoke to the house of Joseph, that is, to Ephraim and to Manasseh, saying, "You are a numerous people, and have great power. You shall not have one lot only; but the hill country shall be yours. Although it is a forest, you shall cut it down, and it's farthest extent shall be yours; for you shall drive out the Canaanites, though they have chariots of iron, and though they are strong."

....

The whole congregation of the children of Israel assembled themselves together at Shiloh, and set up the Tent of Meeting there. The land was subdued before them. Seven tribes remained among the children of Israel, which had not yet divided their inheritance. Joshua said to the children of Israel, "How long will you neglect to go in to possess the land, which YHWH, the God of your fathers, has given you? Appoint for yourselves three men from each tribe. I will send them, and they shall arise, walk through the land, and describe it according to their inheritance; then they shall come to me. They shall divide it into seven portions. Judah shall live in his borders on the south, and the house of Joseph shall live in their borders on the north. You shall survey the land into seven parts, and bring the description here to me; and I will cast lots for you here before YHWH our God. However, the Levites have no portion among you; for the priesthood of YHWH is their inheritance. Gad, Reuben, and the half-tribe of Manasseh have received their inheritance east of the Jordan, which Moses the servant of YHWH gave them."

The men arose and went. Joshua commanded those who went to survey the land, saying, "Go walk through the land, survey it, and come again to me. I will cast lots for you here before YHWH in Shiloh."

The men went and passed through the land, and surveyed it by cities into seven portions in a book. They came to Joshua to the camp at Shiloh. Joshua cast lots for them in Shiloh before YHWH.

There Joshua divided the land to the children of Israel according to their divisions.

The lot of the tribe of the children of Benjamin came up according to their families. The border of their lot went out between the children of Judah and the children of Joseph. Their border on the north quarter was from the Jordan. The border went up to the side of Jericho on the north, and went up through the hill country westward. It ended at the wilderness of Beth Aven. The border passed along from there to Luz, to the side of Luz (also called Bethel), southward. The border went down to Ataroth Addar, by the mountain that lies on the south of Beth Horon the lower. The border extended, and turned around on the west quarter southward, from the mountain that lies before Beth Horon southward; and ended at Kiriath Baal (also called Kiriath Jearim), a city of the children of Judah. This was the west quarter. The south quarter was from the farthest part of Kiriath Jearim. The border went out westward, and went out to the spring of the waters of Nephtoah. The border went down to the farthest part of the mountain that lies before the valley of the son of Hinnom, which is in the valley of Rephaim northward. It went down to the valley of Hinnom, to the side of the Jebusite southward, and went down to En Rogel. It extended northward, went out at En Shemesh, and went out to Geliloth, which is opposite the ascent of Adummim. It went down to the stone of Bohan the son of Reuben. It passed along to the side opposite the Arabah northward, and went down to the Arabah. The border passed along to the side of Beth Hoglah northward; and the border ended at the north bay of the Salt Sea, at the south end of the Jordan. This was the south border. The Jordan was its border on the east quarter. This was the inheritance of the children of Benjamin, by the borders around it, according to their families. Now the cities of the tribe of the children of Benjamin according to their families were Jericho, Beth Hoglah, Emek Keziz, Beth Arabah, Zemaraim, Bethel, Avvim, Parah, Ophrah, Chephar Ammoni, Ophni, and Geba; twelve cities with their villages. Gibeon, Ramah, Beeroth, Mizpeh, Chephirah, Mozah, Rekem, Irpeel, Taralah, Zelah, Eleph, the Jebusite (also called Jerusalem), Gibeath, and Kiriath; fourteen cities with their villages. This is the inheritance of the children of Benjamin according to their families.

....

The second lot came out for Simeon, even for the tribe of the children of Simeon according to their families. Their inheritance was in the middle of the inheritance of the children of Judah. They had for their inheritance Beersheba (or Sheba), Moladah, Hazar Shual, Balah, Ezem, Eltolad, Bethul, Hormah, Ziklag, Beth Marcaboth, Hazar Susah, Beth Lebaoth, and Sharuhen; thirteen cities with their villages; Ain, Rimmon, Ether, and Ashan; four cities with their villages; and all the villages that were around these cities to Baalath Beer, Ramah of the South. This is the inheritance of the tribe of the children of Simeon according to their families. Out of the part of the children of Judah was the inheritance of the children of Simeon; for the portion of the children of Judah was too much for them. Therefore the children of Simeon had inheritance in the middle of their inheritance.

The third lot came up for the children of Zebulun according to their families. The border of their inheritance was to Sarid. Their border went up westward, even to Maralah, and reached to Dabbesheth. It reached to the brook that is before Jokneam. It turned from Sarid eastward toward the sunrise to the border of Chisloth Tabor. It went out to Daberath, and went up to Japhia. From there it passed along eastward to Gath Hepher, to Ethkazin; and it went out at Rimmon which stretches to Neah. The border turned around it on the north to Hannathon; and it ended at the valley of Iphtah El; Kattath, Nahalal, Shimron, Idalah, and Bethlehem: twelve cities with their villages. This is the inheritance of the children of Zebulun according to their families, these cities with their villages.

The fourth lot came out for Issachar, even for the children of Issachar according to their families. Their border was to Jezreel, Chesulloth, Shunem, Hapharaim, Shion, Anaharath, Rabbith, Kishion, Ebez, Remeth, Engannim, En Haddah, and Beth Pazzez. The border reached to Tabor, Shahazumah, and Beth Shemesh. Their border ended at the Jordan: sixteen cities with their villages. This is the inheritance of the tribe of the children of Issachar according to their families, the cities with their villages.

The fifth lot came out for the tribe of the children of Asher according to their families. Their border was Helkath, Hali, Beten, Achshaph, Allammelech, Amad, Mishal. It reached to Carmel westward, and to Shihorlibnath. It turned toward the sunrise to Beth Dagon, and reached to Zebulun, and to the valley of Iphtah El northward to Beth Emek and Neiel. It went out to Cabul on the left hand, and Ebron, Rehob, Hammon, and Kanah, even to great Sidon.

The border turned to Ramah, to the fortified city of Tyre; and the border turned to Hosah. It ended at the sea by the region of Achzib; Ummah also, and Aphek, and Rehob: twenty-two cities with their villages. This is the inheritance of the tribe of the children of Asher according to their families, these cities with their villages.

The sixth lot came out for the children of Naphtali, even for the children of Naphtali according to their families. Their border was from Heleph, from the oak in Zaanannim, Adami-nekeb, and Jabneel, to Lakkum. It ended at the Jordan. The border turned westward to Aznoth Tabor, and went out from there to Hukkok. It reached to Zebulun on the south, and reached to Asher on the west, and to Judah at the Jordan toward the sunrise. The fortified cities were Ziddim, Zer, Hammath, Rakkath, Chinnereth, Adamah, Ramah, Hazor, Kedesh, Edrei, En Hazor, Iron, Migdal El, Horem, Beth Anath, and Beth Shemesh; nineteen cities with their villages. This is the inheritance of the tribe of the children of Naphtali according to their families, the cities with their villages.

The seventh lot came out for the tribe of the children of Dan according to their families. The border of their inheritance was Zorah, Eshtaol, Irshemesh, Shaalabbin, Aijalon, Ithlah, Elon, Timnah, Ekron, Eltekeh, Gibbethon, Baalath, Jehud, Bene Berak, Gath Rimmon, Me Jarkon, and Rakkon, with the border opposite Joppa. The border of the children of Dan went out beyond them; for the children of Dan went up and fought against Leshem, and took it, and struck it with the edge of the sword, and possessed it, and lived therein, and called Leshem, Dan, after the name of Dan their forefather. This is the inheritance of the tribe of the children of Dan according to their families, these cities with their villages.

So they finished distributing the land for inheritance by its borders. The children of Israel gave an inheritance to Joshua the son of Nun among them. According to YHWH's commandment, they gave him the city which he asked, even Timnathserah in the hill country of Ephraim; and he built the city, and lived there. These are the inheritances, which Eleazar the priest, Joshua the son of Nun, and the heads of the fathers' houses of the tribes of the children of Israel, distributed for inheritance by lot in Shiloh before YHWH, at the door of the Tent of Meeting. So they finished dividing the land.

....

YHWH spoke to Joshua, saying, "Speak to the children of Israel, saying, 'Assign the cities of refuge, of which I spoke to you by Moses, that the man slayer who kills any person accidentally or unintentionally may flee there. They shall be to you for a refuge from the avenger of blood. He shall flee to one of those cities, and shall stand at the entrance of the gate of the city, and declare his case in the ears of the elders of that city. They shall take him into the city with them, and give him a place, that he may live among them. If the avenger of blood pursues him, then they shall not deliver up the man slayer into his hand; because he struck his neighbor unintentionally, and didn't hate him before. He shall dwell in that city until he stands before the congregation for judgment, until the death of the high priest that shall be in those days. Then the man slayer shall return, and come to his own city, and to his own house, to the city he fled from.'"

They set apart Kedesh in Galilee in the hill country of Naphtali, Shechem in the hill country of Ephraim, and Kiriath Arba (also called Hebron) in the hill country of Judah. Beyond the Jordan at Jericho eastward, they assigned Bezer in the wilderness in the plain out of the tribe of Reuben, Ramoth in Gilead out of the tribe of Gad, and Golan in Bashan out of the tribe of Manasseh. These were the appointed cities for all the children of Israel, and for the alien who lives among them, that whoever kills any person unintentionally might flee there, and not die by the hand of the avenger of blood, until he stands trial before the congregation.

....

Then the heads of fathers' houses of the Levites came near to Eleazar the priest, and to Joshua the son of Nun, and to the heads of fathers' houses of the tribes of the children of Israel. They spoke to them at Shiloh in the land of Canaan, saying, "YHWH commanded through Moses to give us cities to dwell in, with their pasture lands for our livestock."

The children of Israel gave to the Levites out of their inheritance, according to the commandment of YHWH, these cities with their pasture lands. The lot came out for the families of the Kohathites. The children of Aaron the priest, who were of the Levites, had thirteen cities by lot out of the tribe of Judah, out of the tribe of the Simeonites, and out of the tribe of Benjamin. The rest of the children of Kohath had ten cities by lot out of the families of the tribe of Ephraim, out of the tribe of Dan, and out of the half-tribe of Manasseh. The children of Gershon had thirteen cities by lot out of the families of the tribe of Issachar, out of the tribe of Asher, out of the tribe of Naphtali, and out of the half-tribe of Manasseh in Bashan. The children of Merari according to their families had twelve cities out of the tribe of Reuben, out of the tribe of Gad, and out of the tribe of Zebulun. The children of Israel gave these cities with their pasture lands by lot to the Levites, as YHWH commanded by Moses. They gave out of the tribe of the children of Judah, and out of the tribe of the children of Simeon, these cities which are mentioned by name: and they were for the children of Aaron, of the families of the Kohathites, who were of the children of Levi; for theirs was the first lot. They gave them Kiriath Arba, named after the father of Anak (also called Hebron), in the hill country of Judah, with its pasture lands around it. But they gave the fields of the city and its villages to Caleb the son of Jephunneh for his possession. To the children of Aaron the priest they gave Hebron with its pasture lands, the city of refuge for the man slayer, Libnah with its pasture lands, Jattir with its pasture lands, Eshtemoa with its pasture lands, Holon with its pasture lands, Debir with its pasture lands, Ain with its pasture lands, Juttah with its pasture lands, and Beth Shemesh with its pasture lands: nine cities out of those two tribes. Out of the tribe of Benjamin, Gibeon with its pasture lands, Geba with its pasture lands, Anathoth with its pasture lands, and Almon with its pasture lands: four cities. All the cities of the children of Aaron, the priests, were thirteen cities with their pasture lands.

The families of the children of Kohath, the Levites, even the rest of the children of Kohath, had the cities of their lot out of the tribe of Ephraim. They gave them Shechem with its pasture lands in the hill country of Ephraim, the city of refuge for the man slayer, and Gezer with its pasture lands, Kibzaim with its pasture lands, and Beth Horon with its pasture lands: four cities. Out of the tribe of Dan, Elteke with its pasture lands, Gibbethon with its pasture lands, Aijalon with its pasture lands, Gath Rimmon with its pasture lands: four cities. Out of the half-tribe of Manasseh, Taanach with its pasture lands, and Gath Rimmon with its pasture lands: two cities. All the cities of the families of the rest of the children of Kohath were ten with their pasture lands.

They gave to the children of Gershon, of the families of the Levites, out of the half-tribe of Manasseh Golan in Bashan with its pasture lands, the city of refuge for the man slayer, and Be Eshterah with its pasture lands: two cities. Out of the tribe of Issachar, Kishion with its pasture lands, Daberath with its pasture lands, Jarmuth with its pasture lands, En Gannim with its pasture lands: four cities. Out of the tribe of Asher, Mishal with its pasture lands, Abdon with its pasture lands, Helkath with its pasture lands, and Rehob with its pasture lands: four cities. Out of the tribe of Naphtali, Kedesh in Galilee with its pasture lands, the city of refuge for the man slayer, Hammothdor with its pasture lands, and Kartan with its pasture lands: three cities. All the cities of the Gershonites according to their families were thirteen cities with their pasture lands.

To the families of the children of Merari, the rest of the Levites, out of the tribe of Zebulun, Jokneam with its pasture lands, Kartah with its pasture lands, Dimnah with its pasture lands, and Nahalal with its pasture lands: four cities. Out of the tribe of Reuben, Bezer with its pasture lands, Jahaz with its pasture lands, Kedemoth with its pasture lands, and Mephaath with its pasture lands: four cities. Out of the tribe of Gad, Ramoth in Gilead with its pasture lands, the city of refuge for the man slayer, and Mahanaim with its pasture lands, Heshbon with its pasture lands, Jazer with its pasture lands: four cities in all. All these were the cities of the children of Merari according to their families, even the rest of the families of the Levites. Their lot was twelve cities.

All the cities of the Levites among the possessions of the children of Israel were forty-eight cities with their pasture lands. Each of these cities included their pasture lands around them. It was this way with all these cities.

So YHWH gave to Israel all the land which he swore to give to their fathers. They possessed it, and lived in it. YHWH gave them rest all around, according to all that he swore to their fathers. Not a man of all their enemies stood before them. YHWH delivered all their enemies into their hand. Nothing failed of any good thing which YHWH had spoken to the house of Israel. All came to pass.

....

Then Joshua called the Reubenites, the Gadites, and the half-tribe of Manasseh, and said to them, "You have kept all that Moses the servant of YHWH commanded you, and have listened to my voice in all that I commanded you. You have not left your brothers these many days to this day, but have performed the duty of the commandment of YHWH your God. Now YHWH your God has given rest to your brothers, as he spoke to them. Therefore now return and go to your tents, to the land of your possession, which Moses the servant of YHWH gave you beyond the Jordan. Only take diligent heed to do the commandment and the law which Moses the servant of YHWH commanded you, to love YHWH your God, to walk in all his ways, to keep his commandments, to hold fast to him, and to serve him with all your heart and with all your soul."

So Joshua blessed them, and sent them away; and they went to their tents. Now to the one half-tribe of Manasseh Moses had given inheritance in Bashan; but Joshua gave to the other half among their brothers beyond the Jordan westward. Moreover when Joshua sent them away to their tents, he blessed them, and spoke to them, saying, "Return with much wealth to your tents, with very much livestock, with silver, with gold, with bronze, with iron, and with very much clothing. Divide the plunder of your enemies with your brothers."

The children of Reuben and the children of Gad and the half-tribe of Manasseh returned, and departed from the children of Israel out of Shiloh, which is in the land of Canaan, to go to the land of Gilead, to the land of their possession, which they owned, according to the commandment of YHWH by Moses. When they came to the region near the Jordan, that is in the land of Canaan, the children of Reuben and the children of Gad and the half-tribe of Manasseh built an altar there by the Jordan, a great altar to look at. The children of Israel heard this, "Behold, the children of Reuben and the children of Gad and the half-tribe of Manasseh have built an altar along the border of the land of Canaan, in the region around the Jordan, on the side that belongs to the children of Israel." When the children of Israel heard of it, the whole congregation of the children of Israel gathered themselves together at Shiloh, to go up against them to war. The children of Israel sent to the children of Reuben, and to the children of Gad, and to the half-tribe of Manasseh, into the land of Gilead, Phinehas the son of Eleazar the priest. With him were ten princes, one prince of a fathers' house for each of the tribes of Israel; and they were each head of their fathers' houses among the thousands of Israel. They came to the children of Reuben, and to the children of Gad, and to the half-tribe of Manasseh, to the land of Gilead, and they spoke with them, saying, "The whole congregation of YHWH says, 'What trespass is this that you have committed against the God of Israel, to turn away today from following YHWH, in that you have built yourselves an altar, to rebel today against YHWH? Is the iniquity of Peor too little for us, from which we have not cleansed ourselves to this day, although there came a plague on the congregation of YHWH, that you must turn away today from following YHWH? It will be, since you rebel today against YHWH, that tomorrow he will be angry with the whole congregation of Israel. However, if the land of your possession is unclean, then pass over to the land of the possession of YHWH, in which YHWH's tabernacle dwells, and take possession among us; but don't rebel against YHWH, nor rebel against us, in building an altar other than YHWH our God's altar. Didn't Achan the son of Zerah commit a trespass in the devoted thing, and wrath fell on all the congregation of Israel? That man didn't perish alone in his iniquity.'"

Then the children of Reuben and the children of Gad and the half-tribe of Manasseh answered, and spoke to the heads of the thousands of Israel, "The Mighty One, God, YHWH, the Mighty One, God, YHWH, he knows; and Israel shall know: if it was in rebellion, or if in trespass against YHWH (don't save us today), that we have built us an altar to turn away from following YHWH; or if to offer burnt offering or meal offering, or if to offer sacrifices of peace offerings, let YHWH himself require it.

"If we have not out of concern done this, and for a reason, saying, 'In time to come your children might speak to our children, saying, "What have you to do with YHWH, the God of Israel? For YHWH has made the Jordan a border between us and you, you children of Reuben and children of Gad. You have no portion in YHWH."' So your children might make our children cease from fearing YHWH.

"Therefore we said, 'Let's now prepare to build ourselves an altar, not for burnt offering, nor for sacrifice; but it will be a witness between us and you, and between our generations after us, that we may perform the service of YHWH before him with our burnt offerings, with our sacrifices, and with our peace offerings;' that your children may not tell our children in time to come, 'You have no portion in YHWH.'

"Therefore we said, 'It shall be, when they tell us or our generations this in time to come, that we shall say, "Behold the pattern of YHWH's altar, which our fathers made, not for burnt offering, nor for sacrifice; but it is a witness between us and you."'

"Far be it from us that we should rebel against YHWH, and turn away today from following YHWH, to build an altar for burnt offering, for meal offering, or for sacrifice, besides YHWH our God's altar that is before his tabernacle!"

When Phinehas the priest, and the princes of the congregation, even the heads of the thousands of Israel that were with him, heard the words that the children of Reuben and the children of Gad and the children of Manasseh spoke, it pleased them well. Phinehas the son of Eleazar the priest said to the children of Reuben, to the children of Gad, and to the children of Manasseh, "Today we know that YHWH is among us, because you have not committed this trespass against YHWH. Now you have delivered the children of Israel out of YHWH's hand." Phinehas the son of Eleazar the priest, and the princes, returned from the children of Reuben, and from the children of Gad, out of the land of Gilead, to the land of Canaan, to the children of Israel, and brought them word again. The thing pleased the children of Israel; and the children of Israel blessed God, and spoke no more of going up against them to war, to destroy the land in which the children of Reuben and the children of Gad lived. The children of Reuben and the children of Gad named the altar "A Witness Between Us that YHWH is God."

....

After many days, when YHWH had given rest to Israel from their enemies all around, and Joshua was old and well advanced in years, Joshua called for all Israel, for their elders and for their heads, and for their judges and for their officers, and said to them, "I am old and well advanced in years. You have seen all that YHWH your God has done to all these nations because of you; for it is YHWH your God who has fought for you. Behold, I have allotted to you these nations that remain, to be an inheritance for your tribes, from the Jordan, with all the nations that I have cut off, even to the great sea toward the going down of the sun. YHWH your God will thrust them out from before you, and drive them from out of your sight. You shall possess their land, as YHWH your God spoke to you.

"Therefore be very courageous to keep and to do all that is written in the book of the law of Moses, that you not turn away from it to the right hand or to the left; that you not come among these nations, these that remain among you; neither make mention of the name of their gods, nor cause to swear by them, neither serve them, nor bow down yourselves to them; but hold fast to YHWH your God, as you have done to this day.

"For YHWH has driven great and strong nations out from before you. But as for you, no man has stood before you to this day. One man of you shall chase a thousand; for it is YHWH your God who fights for you, as he spoke to you. Take good heed therefore to yourselves, that you love YHWH your God.

"But if you do at all go back, and hold fast to the remnant of these nations, even these who remain among you, and make marriages with them, and go in to them, and they to you; know for a certainty that YHWH your God will no longer drive these nations from out of your sight; but they shall be a snare and a trap to you, a scourge in your sides, and thorns in your eyes, until you perish from off this good land which YHWH your God has given you.

"Behold, today I am going the way of all the earth. You know in all your hearts and in all your souls that not one thing has failed of all the good things which YHWH your God spoke concerning you. All have happened to you. Not one thing has failed of it. It shall happen that as all the good things have come on you of which YHWH your God spoke to you, so YHWH will bring on you all the evil things, until he has destroyed you from off this good land which YHWH your God has given you, when you disobey the covenant of YHWH your God, which he commanded you, and go and serve other gods, and bow down yourselves to them. Then YHWH's anger will be kindled against you, and you will perish quickly from off the good land which he has given to you."

....

Joshua gathered all the tribes of Israel to Shechem, and called for the elders of Israel, for their heads, for their judges, and for their officers; and they presented themselves before God. Joshua said to all the people, "YHWH, the God of Israel, says, 'Your fathers lived of old time beyond the River, even Terah, the father of Abraham, and the father of Nahor. They served other gods. I took your father Abraham from beyond the River, and led him throughout all the land of Canaan, and multiplied his offspring, and gave him Isaac. I gave to Isaac Jacob and Esau: and I gave to Esau Mount Seir, to possess it. Jacob and his children went down into Egypt.

"'I sent Moses and Aaron, and I plagued Egypt, according to that which I did among them: and afterward I brought you out. I brought your fathers out of Egypt: and you came to the sea. The Egyptians pursued your fathers with chariots and with horsemen to the Red Sea. When they cried out to YHWH, he put darkness between you and the Egyptians, and brought the sea on them, and covered them; and your eyes saw what I did in Egypt. You lived in the wilderness many days.

"'I brought you into the land of the Amorites, that lived beyond the Jordan. They fought with you, and I gave them into your hand. You possessed their land, and I destroyed them from before you. Then Balak the son of Zippor, king of Moab, arose and fought against Israel. He sent and called Balaam the son of Beor to curse you, but I would not listen to Balaam; therefore he blessed you still. So I delivered you out of his hand.

"'You went over the Jordan, and came to Jericho. The men of Jericho fought against you, the Amorite, the Perizzite, the Canaanite, the Hittite, the Girgashite, the Hivite, and the Jebusite; and I delivered them into your hand. I sent the hornet before you, which drove them out from before you, even the two kings of the Amorites; not with your sword, nor with your bow. I gave you a land on which you had not labored, and cities which you didn't build, and you live in them. You eat of vineyards and olive groves which you didn't plant.'

"Now therefore fear YHWH, and serve him in sincerity and in truth. Put away the gods which your fathers served beyond the River, in Egypt; and serve YHWH. If it seems evil to you to serve YHWH, choose today whom you will serve; whether the gods which your fathers served that were beyond the River, or the gods of the Amorites, in whose land you dwell; but as for me and my house, we will serve YHWH."

The people answered, "Far be it from us that we should forsake YHWH, to serve other gods; for it is YHWH our God who brought us and our fathers up out of the land of Egypt, from the house of bondage, and who did those great signs in our sight, and preserved us in all the way in which we went, and among all the peoples through the middle of whom we passed. YHWH drove out from before us all the peoples, even the Amorites who lived in the land. Therefore we also will serve YHWH; for he is our God."

Joshua said to the people, "You can't serve YHWH, for he is a holy God. He is a jealous God. He will not forgive your disobedience nor your sins. If you forsake YHWH, and serve foreign gods, then he will turn and do you evil, and consume you, after he has done you good."

The people said to Joshua, "No, but we will serve YHWH." Joshua said to the people, "You are witnesses against yourselves that you have chosen YHWH yourselves, to serve him."

They said, "We are witnesses."

"Now therefore put away the foreign gods which are among you, and incline your heart to YHWH, the God of Israel."

The people said to Joshua, "We will serve YHWH our God, and we will listen to his voice."

So Joshua made a covenant with the people that day, and made for them a statute and an ordinance in Shechem. Joshua wrote these words in the book of the law of God; and he took a great stone, and set it up there under the oak that was by the sanctuary of YHWH. Joshua said to all the people, "Behold, this stone shall be a witness against us, for it has heard all YHWH's words which he spoke to us. It shall be therefore a witness against you, lest you deny your God." So Joshua sent the people away, each to his own inheritance.

After these things, Joshua the son of Nun, the servant of YHWH, died, being one hundred ten years old. They buried him in the border of his inheritance in Timnathserah, which is in the hill country of Ephraim, on the north of the mountain of Gaash. Israel served YHWH all the days of Joshua, and all the days of the elders who outlived Joshua, and had known all the work of YHWH, that he had worked for Israel. They buried the bones of Joseph, which the children of Israel brought up out of Egypt, in Shechem, in the parcel of ground which Jacob bought from the sons of Hamor the father of Shechem for a hundred pieces of silver. They became the inheritance of the children of Joseph. Eleazar the son of Aaron died. They buried him in the hill of Phinehas his son, which was given him in the hill country of Ephraim.

THE BOOK OF

JUDGES

1 HR 34 MIN

After the death of Joshua, the children of Israel asked of YHWH, saying, "Who should go up for us first against the Canaanites, to fight against them?"

YHWH said, "Judah shall go up. Behold, I have delivered the land into his hand."

Judah said to Simeon his brother, "Come up with me into my lot, that we may fight against the Canaanites; and I likewise will go with you into your lot." So Simeon went with him. Judah went up, and YHWH delivered the Canaanites and the Perizzites into their hand. They struck ten thousand men in Bezek. They found Adoni-Bezek in Bezek, and they fought against him. They struck the Canaanites and the Perizzites. But Adoni-Bezek fled. They pursued him, caught him, and cut off his thumbs and his big toes. Adoni-Bezek said, "Seventy kings, having their thumbs and their big toes cut off, scavenged under my table. As I have done, so God has done to me." They brought him to Jerusalem, and he died there. The children of Judah fought against Jerusalem, took it, struck it with the edge of the sword, and set the city on fire.

After that, the children of Judah went down to fight against the Canaanites who lived in the hill country, and in the South, and in the lowland. Judah went against the Canaanites who lived in Hebron. (The name of Hebron before that was Kiriath Arba.) They struck Sheshai, Ahiman, and Talmai.

From there he went against the inhabitants of Debir. (The name of Debir before that was Kiriath Sepher.) Caleb said, "I will give Achsah my daughter as wife to the man who strikes Kiriath Sepher, and takes it." Othniel the son of Kenaz, Caleb's younger brother, took it, so he gave him Achsah his daughter as his wife.

When she came, she got him to ask her father for a field. She got off her donkey; and Caleb said to her, "What would you like?"

She said to him, "Give me a blessing; because you have set me in the land of the South, give me also springs of water." Then Caleb gave her the upper springs and the lower springs. The children of the Kenite, Moses' brother-in-law, went up out of the city of palm trees with the children of Judah into the wilderness of Judah, which is in the south of Arad; and they went and lived with the people. Judah went with Simeon his brother, and they struck the Canaanites who inhabited Zephath, and utterly destroyed it. The name of the city was called Hormah. Also Judah took Gaza with its border, and Ashkelon with its border, and Ekron with its border. YHWH was with

Judah, and drove out the inhabitants of the hill country; for he could not drive out the inhabitants of the valley, because they had chariots of iron. They gave Hebron to Caleb, as Moses had said, and he drove the three sons of Anak out of there. The children of Benjamin didn't drive out the Jebusites who inhabited Jerusalem, but the Jebusites dwell with the children of Benjamin in Jerusalem to this day.

The house of Joseph also went up against Bethel, and YHWH was with them. The house of Joseph sent to spy out Bethel. (The name of the city before that was Luz.) The watchers saw a man come out of the city, and they said to him, "Please show us the entrance into the city, and we will deal kindly with you." He showed them the entrance into the city, and they struck the city with the edge of the sword; but they let the man and all his family go. The man went into the land of the Hittites, built a city, and called its name Luz, which is its name to this day.

Manasseh didn't drive out the inhabitants of Beth Shean and its towns, nor Taanach and its towns, nor the inhabitants of Dor and its towns, nor the inhabitants of Ibleam and its towns, nor the inhabitants of Megiddo and its towns; but the Canaanites would dwell in that land. When Israel had grown strong, they put the Canaanites to forced labor, and didn't utterly drive them out. Ephraim didn't drive out the Canaanites who lived in Gezer, but the Canaanites lived in Gezer among them. Zebulun didn't drive out the inhabitants of Kitron, nor the inhabitants of Nahalol; but the Canaanites lived among them, and became subject to forced labor. Asher didn't drive out the inhabitants of Acco, nor the inhabitants of Sidon, nor of Ahlab, nor of Achzib, nor of Helbah, nor of Aphik, nor of Rehob; but the Asherites lived among the Canaanites, the inhabitants of the land, for they didn't drive them out. Naphtali didn't drive out the inhabitants of Beth Shemesh, nor the inhabitants of Beth Anath; but he lived among the Canaanites, the inhabitants of the land. Nevertheless the inhabitants of Beth Shemesh and of Beth Anath became subject to forced labor. The Amorites forced the children of Dan into the hill country, for they would not allow them to come down to the valley; but the Amorites would dwell in Mount Heres, in Aijalon, and in Shaalbim. Yet the hand of the house of Joseph prevailed, so that they became subject to forced labor. The border of the Amorites was from the ascent of Akrabbim, from the rock, and upward.

....

YHWH's angel came up from Gilgal to Bochim. He said, "I brought you out of Egypt, and have brought you to the land which I swore to give your fathers. I said, 'I will never break my covenant with you. You shall make no covenant with the inhabitants of this land. You shall break down their altars.' But you have not listened to my voice. Why have you done this? Therefore I also said, 'I will not drive them out from before you; but they shall be in your sides, and their gods will be a snare to you.'"

When YHWH's angel spoke these words to all the children of Israel, the people lifted up their voice and wept. They called the name of that place Bochim, and they sacrificed there to YHWH. Now when Joshua had sent the people away, the children of Israel each went to his inheritance to possess the land. The people served YHWH all the days of Joshua, and all the days of the elders who outlived Joshua, who had seen all the great work of YHWH that he had worked for Israel. Joshua the son of Nun, the servant of YHWH, died, being one hundred ten years old. They buried him in the border of his inheritance in Timnath Heres, in the hill country of Ephraim, on the north of the mountain of Gaash. After all that generation were gathered to their fathers, another generation arose after them who didn't know YHWH, nor the work which he had done for Israel. The children of Israel did that which was evil in YHWH's sight, and served the Baals. They abandoned YHWH, the God of their fathers, who brought them out of the land of Egypt, and followed other gods, of the gods of the peoples who were around them, and bowed themselves down to them; and they provoked YHWH to anger. They abandoned YHWH, and served Baal and the Ashtaroth. YHWH's anger burned against Israel, and he delivered them into the hands of raiders who plundered them. He sold them into the hands of their enemies all around, so that they could no longer stand before their enemies. Wherever they went out, YHWH's hand was against them for evil, as YHWH had spoken, and as YHWH had sworn to them; and they were very distressed. YHWH raised up judges, who saved them out of the hand of those who plundered them. Yet they didn't listen to their judges; for they prostituted themselves to other gods, and bowed themselves down to them. They quickly turned away from the way in which their fathers walked, obeying YHWH's commandments. They didn't do so. When YHWH raised up judges for them, then YHWH was with the judge, and saved them out of the hand of their enemies all the days of the judge; for it grieved YHWH because of their groaning by reason of those who oppressed them and troubled them. But when the judge was dead, they turned back, and dealt more corruptly than their fathers in following other gods to serve them and to bow down to them. They didn't cease what they were doing, or give up their stubborn ways. YHWH's anger burned against Israel; and he said, "Because this nation transgressed my covenant which I commanded their fathers, and has not listened to my voice, I also will no longer drive out any of the nations that Joshua left when he died from before them; that by them I may test Israel, to see if they will keep YHWH's way to walk therein, as their fathers kept it, or not." So YHWH left those nations, without driving them out hastily. He didn't deliver them into Joshua's hand.

....

Now these are the nations which YHWH left, to test Israel by them, even as many as had not known all the wars of Canaan; only that the generations of the children of Israel might know, to teach them war, at least those who knew nothing of it before: the five lords of the Philistines, all the Canaanites, the Sidonians, and the Hivites who lived on Mount Lebanon, from Mount Baal Hermon to the entrance of Hamath. They were left to test Israel by them, to know whether they would listen to YHWH's commandments, which he commanded their fathers by Moses. The children of Israel lived among the Canaanites, the Hittites, the Amorites, the Perizzites, the Hivites, and the Jebusites. They took their daughters to be their wives, and gave their own daughters to their sons and served their gods. The children of Israel did that which was evil in YHWH's sight, and forgot YHWH their God, and served the Baals and the Asheroth. Therefore YHWH's anger burned against Israel, and he sold them into the hand of Cushan Rishathaim king of Mesopotamia; and the children of Israel served Cushan Rishathaim eight years. When the children of Israel cried to YHWH, YHWH raised up a savior to the children of Israel, who saved them, even Othniel the son of Kenaz, Caleb's younger brother. YHWH's Spirit came on him, and he judged Israel; and he went out to war, and YHWH delivered Cushan Rishathaim king of Mesopotamia into his hand. His hand prevailed against Cushan Rishathaim. The land had rest forty years, then Othniel the son of Kenaz died.

The children of Israel again did that which was evil in YHWH's sight, and YHWH strengthened Eglon the king of Moab against Israel, because they had done that which was evil in YHWH's sight. He gathered the children of Ammon and Amalek to himself; and he went and struck Israel, and they possessed the city of palm trees. The children of Israel served Eglon the king of Moab eighteen years. But when the children of Israel cried to YHWH, YHWH raised up a savior for them: Ehud the son of Gera, the Benjamite, a left-handed man. The children of Israel sent tribute by him to Eglon the king of Moab. Ehud made himself a sword which had two edges, a cubit in length; and he wore it under his clothing on his right thigh. He offered the tribute to Eglon king of Moab. Now Eglon was a very fat man. When Ehud had finished offering the tribute, he sent away the people who carried the tribute. But he himself turned back from the stone idols that were by Gilgal, and said, "I have a secret message for you, O king."

The king said, "Keep silence!" All who stood by him left him.

Ehud came to him; and he was sitting by himself alone in the cool upper room. Ehud said, "I have a message from God to you." He arose out of his seat. Ehud put out his left hand, and took the sword from his right thigh, and thrust it into his body. The handle also went in after the blade; and the fat closed on the blade, for he didn't draw the sword out of his body; and it came out behind. Then Ehud went out onto the porch, and shut the doors of the upper room on him, and locked them.

After he had gone, his servants came and saw that the doors of the upper room were locked. They said, "Surely he is covering his feet in the upper room." They waited until they were ashamed; and behold, he didn't open the doors of the upper room. Therefore they took the key and opened them, and behold, their lord had fallen down dead on the floor.

Ehud escaped while they waited, passed beyond the stone idols, and escaped to Seirah. When he had come, he blew a trumpet in the hill country of Ephraim; and the children of Israel went down with him from the hill country, and he led them.

He said to them, "Follow me; for YHWH has delivered your enemies the Moabites into your hand." They followed him, and took the fords of the Jordan against the Moabites, and didn't allow any man to pass over. They struck at that time about ten thousand men of Moab, every strong man and every man of valor. No man escaped. So Moab was subdued that day under the hand of Israel. Then the land had rest eighty years.

After him was Shamgar the son of Anath, who struck six hundred men of the Philistines with an ox goad. He also saved Israel.

....

The children of Israel again did that which was evil in YHWH's sight, when Ehud was dead. YHWH sold them into the hand of Jabin king of Canaan, who reigned in Hazor; the captain of whose army was Sisera, who lived in Harosheth of the Gentiles. The children of Israel cried to YHWH, for he had nine hundred chariots of iron; and he mightily oppressed the children of Israel for twenty years. Now Deborah, a prophetess, the wife of Lappidoth, judged Israel at that time. She lived under Deborah's palm tree between Ramah and Bethel in the hill country of Ephraim; and the children of Israel came up to her for judgment. She sent and called Barak the son of Abinoam out of Kedesh Naphtali, and said to him, "Hasn't YHWH, the God of Israel, commanded, 'Go and lead the way to Mount Tabor, and take with you ten thousand men of the children of Naphtali and of the children of Zebulun? I will draw to you, to the river Kishon, Sisera, the captain of Jabin's army, with his chariots and his multitude; and I will deliver him into your hand.'"

Barak said to her, "If you will go with me, then I will go; but if you will not go with me, I will not go."

She said, "I will surely go with you. Nevertheless, the journey that you take won't be for your honor; for YHWH will sell Sisera into a woman's hand." Deborah arose, and went with Barak to Kedesh.

Barak called Zebulun and Naphtali together to Kedesh. Ten thousand men followed him; and Deborah went up with him. Now Heber the Kenite had separated himself from the Kenites, even from the children of Hobab, Moses' brother-in-law, and had pitched his tent as far as the oak in Zaanannim, which is by Kedesh. They told Sisera that Barak the son of Abinoam was gone up to Mount Tabor. Sisera gathered together all his chariots, even nine hundred chariots of iron, and all the people who were with him, from Harosheth of the Gentiles, to the river Kishon.

Deborah said to Barak, "Go; for this is the day in which YHWH has delivered Sisera into your hand. Hasn't YHWH gone out before you?" So Barak went down from Mount Tabor, and ten thousand men after him. YHWH confused Sisera, all his chariots, and all his army, with the edge of the sword before Barak. Sisera abandoned his chariot and fled away on his feet. But Barak pursued the chariots and the army to Harosheth of the Gentiles; and all the army of Sisera fell by the edge of the sword. There was not a man left.

However Sisera fled away on his feet to the tent of Jael the wife of Heber the Kenite; for there was peace between Jabin the king of Hazor and the house of Heber the Kenite. Jael went out to meet Sisera, and said to him, "Turn in, my lord, turn in to me; don't be afraid." He came in to her into the tent, and she covered him with a rug.

He said to her, "Please give me a little water to drink; for I am thirsty."

She opened a container of milk, and gave him a drink, and covered him.

He said to her, "Stand in the door of the tent, and if any man comes and inquires of you, and says, 'Is there any man here?' you shall say, 'No.'"

Then Jael Heber's wife took a tent peg, and took a hammer in her hand, and went softly to him, and struck the pin into his temples, and it pierced through into the ground, for he was in a deep sleep; so he fainted and died. Behold, as Barak pursued Sisera, Jael came out to meet him, and said to him, "Come, and I will show you the man whom you seek." He came to her; and behold, Sisera lay dead, and the tent peg was in his temples. So God subdued Jabin the king of Canaan before the children of Israel on that day. The hand of the children of Israel prevailed more and more against Jabin the king of Canaan, until they had destroyed Jabin king of Canaan.

....

Then Deborah and Barak the son of Abinoam sang on that day, saying,

"Because the leaders took the lead in Israel,
  because the people offered themselves willingly,
be blessed, YHWH!

"Hear, you kings!
  Give ear, you princes!
I, even I, will sing to YHWH.
  I will sing praise to YHWH, the God of Israel.

"YHWH, when you went out of Seir,
  when you marched out of the field of Edom,
the earth trembled, the sky also dropped.
  Yes, the clouds dropped water.

The mountains quaked YHWH's presence,
    even Sinai at the presence of YHWH, the God of Israel.

"In the days of Shamgar the son of Anath,
    in the days of Jael, the highways were unoccupied.
    The travelers walked through byways.
The rulers ceased in Israel.
    They ceased until I, Deborah, arose;
    Until I arose a mother in Israel.
They chose new gods.
    Then war was in the gates.
    Was there a shield or spear seen among forty thousand in
    Israel?
My heart is toward the governors of Israel,
    who offered themselves willingly among the people.
    Bless YHWH!

"Speak, you who ride on white donkeys,
    you who sit on rich carpets,
    and you who walk by the way.
Far from the noise of archers, in the places of drawing water,
    there they will rehearse YHWH's righteous acts,
    the righteous acts of his rule in Israel.

"Then YHWH's people went down to the gates.
    'Awake, awake, Deborah!
    Awake, awake, utter a song!
    Arise, Barak, and lead away your captives, you son of Abino-
    am.'

"Then a remnant of the nobles and the people came down.
    YHWH came down for me against the mighty.
Those whose root is in Amalek came out of Ephraim,
    after you, Benjamin, among your peoples.
Governors come down out of Machir.
    Those who handle the marshal's staff came out of Zebulun.
The princes of Issachar were with Deborah.
    As was Issachar, so was Barak.
    They rushed into the valley at his feet.
By the watercourses of Reuben,

there were great resolves of heart.
Why did you sit among the sheepfolds?
  To hear the whistling for the flocks?
At the watercourses of Reuben,
  there were great searchings of heart.
Gilead lived beyond the Jordan.
   Why did Dan remain in ships?
  Asher sat still at the haven of the sea,
  and lived by his creeks.
Zebulun was a people that jeopardized their lives to the death;
  Naphtali also, on the high places of the field.

"The kings came and fought,
  then the kings of Canaan fought at Taanach by the waters of
  Megiddo.
  They took no plunder of silver.
From the sky the stars fought.
  From their courses, they fought against Sisera.
The river Kishon swept them away,
  that ancient river, the river Kishon.
  My soul, march on with strength.
Then the horse hoofs stamped because of the prancing,
  the prancing of their strong ones.
'Curse Meroz,' said YHWH's angel.
  'Curse bitterly its inhabitants,
  because they didn't come to help YHWH,
  to help YHWH against the mighty.'

"Jael shall be blessed above women,
  the wife of Heber the Kenite;
  blessed shall she be above women in the tent.
He asked for water.
  She gave him milk.
  She brought him butter in a lordly dish.
She put her hand to the tent peg,
  and her right hand to the workmen's hammer.
With the hammer she struck Sisera.
  She struck through his head.
  Yes, she pierced and struck through his temples.
At her feet he bowed, he fell, he lay.

At her feet he bowed, he fell.
Where he bowed, there he fell down dead.

"*Through the window she looked out, and cried:*
Sisera's mother looked through the lattice.
'*Why is his chariot so long in coming?*
Why do the wheels of his chariots wait?'
Her wise ladies answered her,
Yes, she returned answer to herself,
'*Have they not found, have they not divided the plunder?*
A lady, two ladies to every man;
to Sisera a plunder of dyed garments,
a plunder of dyed garments embroidered,
of dyed garments embroidered on both sides, on the necks of
the plunder?'

"*So let all your enemies perish, YHWH,*
but let those who love him be as the sun when it rises in its
strength."

Then the land had rest forty years.

....

The children of Israel did that which was evil in YHWH's sight, so YHWH delivered them into the hand of Midian seven years. The hand of Midian prevailed against Israel; and because of Midian the children of Israel made themselves the dens which are in the mountains, the caves, and the strongholds. So it was, when Israel had sown, that the Midianites, the Amalekites, and the children of the east came up against them. They encamped against them, and destroyed the increase of the earth, until you come to Gaza. They left no sustenance in Israel, and no sheep, ox, or donkey. For they came up with their livestock and their tents. They came in as locusts for multitude. Both they and their camels were without number; and they came into the land to destroy it. Israel was brought very low because of Midian; and the children of Israel cried to YHWH.

When the children of Israel cried to YHWH because of Midian, YHWH sent a prophet to the children of Israel; and he said to them, "YHWH, the God of Israel, says, 'I brought you up from Egypt, and brought you out of the house of bondage. I delivered you out of the hand of the Egyptians and out of the hand of all who oppressed you, and drove them out from before you, and gave you their land. I said to you, "I am YHWH your God. You shall not fear the gods of the Amorites, in whose land you dwell." But you have not listened to my voice.'"

YHWH's angel came and sat under the oak which was in Ophrah, that belonged to Joash the Abiezrite. His son Gideon was beating out wheat in the wine press, to hide it from the Midianites. YHWH's angel appeared to him, and said to him, "YHWH is with you, you mighty man of valor!"

Gideon said to him, "Oh, my lord, if YHWH is with us, why then has all this happened to us? Where are all his wondrous works which our fathers told us of, saying, 'Didn't YHWH bring us up from Egypt?' But now YHWH has cast us off, and delivered us into the hand of Midian."

YHWH looked at him, and said, "Go in this your might, and save Israel from the hand of Midian. Haven't I sent you?"

He said to him, "O Lord, how shall I save Israel? Behold, my family is the poorest in Manasseh, and I am the least in my father's house."

YHWH said to him, "Surely I will be with you, and you shall strike the Midianites as one man."

He said to him, "If now I have found favor in your sight, then show me a sign that it is you who talk with me. Please don't go away until I come to you, and bring out my present, and lay it before you."

He said, "I will wait until you come back."

Gideon went in and prepared a young goat and unleavened cakes of an ephah of meal. He put the meat in a basket and he put the broth in a pot, and brought it out to him under the oak, and presented it.

The angel of God said to him, "Take the meat and the unleavened cakes, and lay them on this rock, and pour out the broth."

He did so. Then YHWH's angel stretched out the end of the staff that was in his hand, and touched the meat and the unleavened cakes; and fire went up out of the rock and consumed the meat and the unleavened cakes. Then YHWH's angel departed out of his sight.

Gideon saw that he was YHWH's angel; and Gideon said, "Alas, Lord YHWH! Because I have seen YHWH's angel face to face!"

YHWH said to him, "Peace be to you! Don't be afraid. You shall not die."

Then Gideon built an altar there to YHWH, and called it "YHWH is Peace." To this day it is still in Ophrah of the Abiezrites.

That same night, YHWH said to him, "Take your father's bull, even the second bull seven years old, and throw down the altar of Baal that your father has, and cut down the Asherah that is by it. Then build an altar to YHWH your God on the top of this stronghold, in an orderly way, and take the second bull, and offer a burnt offering with the wood of the Asherah which you shall cut down."

Then Gideon took ten men of his servants, and did as YHWH had spoken to him. Because he feared his father's household and the men of the city, he could not do it by day, but he did it by night.

When the men of the city arose early in the morning, behold, the altar of Baal was broken down, and the Asherah was cut down that was by it, and the second bull was offered on the altar that was built. They said to one another, "Who has done this thing?"

When they inquired and asked, they said, "Gideon the son of Joash has done this thing."

Then the men of the city said to Joash, "Bring out your son, that he may die, because he has broken down the altar of Baal, and because he has cut down the Asherah that was by it." Joash said to all who stood against him, "Will you contend for Baal? Or will you save him? He who will contend for him, let him be put to death by morning! If he is a god, let him contend for himself, because someone has broken down his altar!" Therefore on that day he named him Jerub-Baal, saying, "Let Baal contend against him, because he has broken down his altar."

Then all the Midianites and the Amalekites and the children of the east assembled themselves together; and they passed over, and encamped in the valley of Jezreel. But YHWH's Spirit came on Gideon, and he blew a trumpet; and Abiezer was gathered together to follow him. He sent messengers throughout all Manasseh, and they also were gathered together to follow him. He sent messengers to Asher, and to Zebulun, and to Naphtali; and they came up to meet them.

Gideon said to God, "If you will save Israel by my hand, as you have spoken, behold, I will put a fleece of wool on the threshing floor. If there is dew on the fleece only, and it is dry on all the ground, then I'll know that you will save Israel by my hand, as you have spoken."

It was so; for he rose up early on the next day, and pressed the fleece together, and wrung the dew out of the fleece, a bowl full of water.

Gideon said to God, "Don't let your anger be kindled against me, and I will speak but this once. Please let me make a trial just this once with the fleece. Let it now be dry only on the fleece, and on all the ground let there be dew."

God did so that night; for it was dry on the fleece only, and there was dew on all the ground.

....

Then Jerubbaal, who is Gideon, and all the people who were with him, rose up early and encamped beside the spring of Harod. Midian's camp was on the north side of them, by the hill of Moreh, in the valley. YHWH said to Gideon, "The people who are with you are too many for me to give the Midianites into their hand, lest Israel brag against me, saying, 'My own hand has saved me.' Now therefore proclaim in the ears of the people, saying, 'Whoever is fearful and trembling, let him return and depart from Mount Gilead.'" So twenty-two thousand of the people returned, and ten thousand remained.

YHWH said to Gideon, "There are still too many people. Bring them down to the water, and I will test them for you there. It shall be, that those whom I tell you, 'This shall go with you,' shall go with you; and whoever I tell you, 'This shall not go with you,' shall not go." So he brought down the people to the water; and YHWH said to Gideon, "Everyone who laps of the water with his tongue, like a dog laps, you shall set him by himself; likewise everyone who bows down on his knees to drink." The number of those who lapped, putting their hand to their mouth, was three hundred men; but all the rest of the people bowed down on their knees to drink water. YHWH said to Gideon, "I will save you by the three hundred men who lapped, and deliver the Midianites into your hand. Let all the other people go, each to his own place."

So the people took food in their hand, and their trumpets; and he sent all the rest of the men of Israel to their own tents, but retained the three hundred men; and the camp of Midian was beneath him in the valley. That same night, YHWH said to him, "Arise, go down into the camp, for I have delivered it into your hand. But if you are afraid to go down, go with Purah your servant down to the camp. You will hear what they say; and afterward your hands will be strengthened to go down into the camp." Then went he down with Purah his servant to the outermost part of the armed men who were in the camp.

The Midianites and the Amalekites and all the children of the east lay along in the valley like locusts for multitude; and their camels were without number, as the sand which is on the seashore for multitude.

When Gideon had come, behold, there was a man telling a dream to his fellow. He said, "Behold, I dreamed a dream; and behold, a cake of barley bread tumbled into the camp of Midian, came to the tent, and struck it so that it fell, and turned it upside down, so that the tent lay flat."

His fellow answered, "This is nothing other than the sword of Gideon the son of Joash, a man of Israel. God has delivered Midian into his hand, with all the army."

It was so, when Gideon heard the telling of the dream and its interpretation, that he worshiped. Then he returned into the camp of Israel and said, "Arise, for YHWH has delivered the army of Midian into your hand!"

He divided the three hundred men into three companies, and he put into the hands of all them trumpets and empty pitchers, with torches within the pitchers.

He said to them, "Watch me, and do likewise. Behold, when I come to the outermost part of the camp, it shall be that, as I do, so you shall do. When I blow the trumpet, I and all who are with me, then blow the trumpets also on every side of all the camp, and shout, 'For YHWH and for Gideon!'"

So Gideon and the hundred men who were with him came to the outermost part of the camp in the beginning of the middle watch, when they had but newly set the watch. Then they blew the trumpets and broke in pieces the pitchers that were in their hands. The three companies blew the trumpets, broke the pitchers, and held the torches in their left hands and the trumpets in their right hands with which to blow; and they shouted, "The sword of YHWH and of Gideon!" They each stood in his place around the camp, and all the army ran; and they shouted, and put them to flight. They blew the three hundred trumpets, and YHWH set every man's sword against his fellow and against all the army; and the army fled as far as Beth Shittah toward Zererah, as far as the border of Abel Meholah, by Tabbath. The men of Israel were gathered together out of Naphtali, out of Asher, and out of all Manasseh, and pursued Midian. Gideon sent messengers throughout all the hill country of Ephraim, saying, "Come down against Midian and take the waters before them as far as Beth Barah, even the Jordan!" So all the men of Ephraim were gathered together and took the waters as far as Beth Barah, even the Jordan. They took the two princes of Midian, Oreb and Zeeb. They killed Oreb at Oreb's rock, and Zeeb they killed at Zeeb's wine press, as they pursued Midian. Then they brought the heads of Oreb and Zeeb to Gideon beyond the Jordan.

....

The men of Ephraim said to him, "Why have you treated us this way, that you didn't call us when you went to fight with Midian?" They rebuked him sharply. He said to them, "What have I now done in comparison with you? Isn't the gleaning of the grapes of Ephraim better than the vintage of Abiezer? God has delivered into your hand the princes of Midian, Oreb and Zeeb! What was I able to do in comparison with you?" Then their anger was abated toward him when he had said that.

Gideon came to the Jordan and passed over, he and the three hundred men who were with him, faint, yet pursuing. He said to the men of Succoth, "Please give loaves of bread to the people who follow me; for they are faint, and I am pursuing after Zebah and Zalmunna, the kings of Midian."

The princes of Succoth said, "Are the hands of Zebah and Zalmunna now in your hand, that we should give bread to your army?"

Gideon said, "Therefore when YHWH has delivered Zebah and Zalmunna into my hand, then I will tear your flesh with the thorns of the wilderness and with briers."

He went up there to Penuel, and spoke to them in the same way; and the men of Penuel answered him as the men of Succoth had answered. He spoke also to the men of Penuel, saying, "When I come again in peace, I will break down this tower."

Now Zebah and Zalmunna were in Karkor, and their armies with them, about fifteen thousand men, all who were left of all the army of the children of the east; for there fell one hundred twenty thousand men who drew sword. Gideon went up by the way of those who lived in tents on the east of Nobah and Jogbehah, and struck the army; for the army felt secure. Zebah and Zalmunna fled and he pursued them. He took the two kings of Midian, Zebah and Zalmunna, and confused all the army. Gideon the son of Joash returned from the battle from the ascent of Heres. He caught a young man of the men of Succoth, and inquired of him; and he described for him the princes of Succoth, and its elders, seventy-seven men. He came to the men of Succoth, and said, "See Zebah and Zalmunna, concerning whom you taunted me, saying, 'Are the hands of Zebah and Zalmunna now in your hand, that we should give bread to your men who are weary?'" He took the elders of the city, and thorns of the wilderness and briers, and with them he taught the men of Succoth. He broke down the tower of Penuel, and killed the men of the city.

Then he said to Zebah and Zalmunna, "What kind of men were they whom you killed at Tabor?"

They answered, "They were like you. They all resembled the children of a king."

He said, "They were my brothers, the sons of my mother. As YHWH lives, if you had saved them alive, I would not kill you."

He said to Jether his firstborn, "Get up and kill them!" But the youth didn't draw his sword; for he was afraid, because he was yet a youth.

Then Zebah and Zalmunna said, "You rise and fall on us; for as the man is, so is his strength." Gideon arose, and killed Zebah and Zalmunna, and took the crescents that were on their camels' necks.

Then the men of Israel said to Gideon, "Rule over us, both you, your son, and your son's son also; for you have saved us out of the hand of Midian."

Gideon said to them, "I will not rule over you, neither shall my son rule over you. YHWH shall rule over you." Gideon said to them, "I do have a request: that you would each give me the earrings of his plunder." (For they had golden earrings, because they were Ishmaelites.)

They answered, "We will willingly give them." They spread a garment, and every man threw the earrings of his plunder into it. The weight of the golden earrings that he requested was one thousand and seven hundred shekels of gold, in addition to the crescents, and the pendants, and the purple clothing that was on the kings of Midian, and in addition to the chains that were about their camels' necks. Gideon made an ephod out of it, and put it in Ophrah, his city. Then all Israel played the prostitute with it there; and it became a snare to Gideon and to his house. So Midian was subdued before the children of Israel, and they lifted up their heads no more. The land had rest forty years in the days of Gideon.

Jerubbaal the son of Joash went and lived in his own house. Gideon had seventy sons conceived from his body, for he had many wives. His concubine who was in Shechem also bore him a son, and he named him Abimelech. Gideon the son of Joash died in a good old age, and was buried in the tomb of Joash his father, in Ophrah of the Abiezrites.

As soon as Gideon was dead, the children of Israel turned again and played the prostitute following the Baals, and made Baal Berith their god. The children of Israel didn't remember YHWH their God, who had delivered them out of the hand of all their enemies on every side; neither did they show kindness to the house of Jerubbaal, that is, Gideon, according to all the goodness which he had shown to Israel.

....

Abimelech the son of Jerubbaal went to Shechem to his mother's brothers, and spoke with them and with all the family of the house of his mother's father, saying, "Please speak in the ears of all the men of Shechem, 'Is it better for you that all the sons of Jerubbaal, who are seventy persons, rule over you, or that one rule over you?' Remember also that I am your bone and your flesh."

His mother's brothers spoke of him in the ears of all the men of Shechem all these words. Their hearts inclined to follow Abimelech; for they said, "He is our brother." They gave him seventy pieces of silver out of the house of Baal Berith, with which Abimelech hired vain and reckless fellows who followed him. He went to his father's house at Ophrah, and killed his brothers the sons of Jerubbaal, being seventy persons, on one stone; but Jotham the youngest son of Jerubbaal was left, for he hid himself. All the men of Shechem assembled themselves together with all the house of Millo, and went and made Abimelech king by the oak of the pillar that was in Shechem. When they told it to Jotham, he went and stood on the top of Mount Gerizim and lifted up his voice, cried out, and said to them, "Listen to me, you men of Shechem, that God may listen to you. The trees set out to anoint a king over themselves. They said to the olive tree, 'Reign over us.'

"But the olive tree said to them, 'Should I stop producing my oil, with which they honor God and man by me, and go to wave back and forth over the trees?'

"The trees said to the fig tree, 'Come and reign over us.'

"But the fig tree said to them, 'Should I leave my sweetness, and my good fruit, and go to wave back and forth over the trees?'

"The trees said to the vine, 'Come and reign over us.'

"The vine said to them, 'Should I leave my new wine, which cheers God and man, and go to wave back and forth over the trees?'

"Then all the trees said to the bramble, 'Come and reign over us.'

"The bramble said to the trees, 'If in truth you anoint me king over you, then come and take refuge in my shade; and if not, let fire come out of the bramble, and devour the cedars of Lebanon.'

"Now therefore, if you have dealt truly and righteously, in that you have made Abimelech king, and if you have dealt well with Jerubbaal and his house, and have done to him according to the deserving of his hands (for my father fought for you, risked his life, and delivered you out of the hand of Midian; and you have risen up against my father's house today and have slain his sons, seventy persons, on one stone, and have made Abimelech, the son of his female servant, king over the men of Shechem, because he is your brother); if you then have dealt truly and righteously with Jerubbaal and with his house today, then rejoice in Abimelech, and let him also rejoice in you; but if not, let fire come out from Abimelech and devour the men of Shechem and the house of Millo; and let fire come out from the men of Shechem and from the house of Millo and devour Abimelech."

Jotham ran away and fled, and went to Beer and lived there, for fear of Abimelech his brother.

Abimelech was prince over Israel three years. Then God sent an evil spirit between Abimelech and the men of Shechem; and the men of Shechem dealt treacherously with Abimelech, that the violence done to the seventy sons of Jerubbaal might come, and that their blood might be laid on Abimelech their brother who killed them, and on the men of Shechem who strengthened his hands to kill his brothers. The men of Shechem set an ambush for him on the tops of the mountains, and they robbed all who came along that way by them; and Abimelech was told about it.

Gaal the son of Ebed came with his brothers and went over to Shechem; and the men of Shechem put their trust in him. They went out into the field, harvested their vineyards, trod the grapes, celebrated, and went into the house of their god and ate and drank, and cursed Abimelech. Gaal the son of Ebed said, "Who is Abimelech, and who is Shechem, that we should serve him? Isn't he the son of Jerubbaal? Isn't Zebul his officer? Serve the men of Hamor the father of Shechem, but why should we serve him? I wish that this people were under my hand! Then I would remove Abimelech." He said to

Abimelech, "Increase your army and come out!"

When Zebul the ruler of the city heard the words of Gaal the son of Ebed, his anger burned. He sent messengers to Abimelech craftily, saying, "Behold, Gaal the son of Ebed and his brothers have come to Shechem; and behold, they incite the city against you. Now therefore, go up by night, you and the people who are with you, and lie in wait in the field. It shall be that in the morning, as soon as the sun is up, you shall rise early and rush on the city. Behold, when he and the people who are with him come out against you, then may you do to them as you shall find occasion."

Abimelech rose up, and all the people who were with him, by night, and they laid wait against Shechem in four companies. Gaal the son of Ebed went out, and stood in the entrance of the gate of the city. Abimelech rose up, and the people who were with him, from the ambush.

When Gaal saw the people, he said to Zebul, "Behold, people are coming down from the tops of the mountains."

Zebul said to him, "You see the shadows of the mountains as if they were men."

Gaal spoke again and said, "Behold, people are coming down by the middle of the land, and one company comes by the way of the oak of Meonenim."

Then Zebul said to him, "Now where is your mouth, that you said, 'Who is Abimelech, that we should serve him?' Isn't this the people that you have despised? Please go out now and fight with them."

Gaal went out before the men of Shechem, and fought with Abimelech. Abimelech chased him, and he fled before him, and many fell wounded, even to the entrance of the gate. Abimelech lived at Arumah; and Zebul drove out Gaal and his brothers, that they should not dwell in Shechem. On the next day, the people went out into the field; and they told Abimelech. He took the people and divided them into three companies, and laid wait in the field; and he looked, and behold, the people came out of the city. So, he rose up against them and struck them. Abimelech and the companies that were with him rushed forward and stood in the entrance of the gate of the city; and the two companies rushed on all who were in the field and struck them. Abimelech fought against the city all that day; and he took the city and killed the people in it. He beat down the city and sowed it with salt.

When all the men of the tower of Shechem heard of it, they entered into the stronghold of the house of Elberith. Abimelech was told that all the men of the tower of Shechem were gathered together. Abimelech went up to Mount Zalmon, he and all the people who were with him; and Abimelech took an ax in his hand, and cut down a bough from the trees, and took it up, and laid it on his shoulder. Then he said to the people who were with him, "What you have seen me do, make haste, and do as I have done!" All the people likewise each cut down his bough, followed Abimelech, and put them at the base of the stronghold, and set the stronghold on fire over them, so that all the people of the tower of Shechem died also, about a thousand men and women. Then Abimelech went to Thebez and encamped against Thebez, and took it. But there was a strong tower within the city, and all the men and women of the city fled there, and shut themselves in, and went up to the roof of the tower. Abimelech came to the tower and fought against it, and came near to the door of the tower to burn it with fire. A certain woman cast an upper millstone on Abimelech's head, and broke his skull.

Then he called hastily to the young man, his armor bearer, and said to him, "Draw your sword and kill me, that men not say of me, 'A woman killed him.' His young man thrust him through, and he died."

When the men of Israel saw that Abimelech was dead, they each departed to his place. Thus God repaid the wickedness of Abimelech, which he did to his father in killing his seventy brothers; and God repaid all the wickedness of the men of Shechem on their heads; and the curse of Jotham the son of Jerubbaal came on them.

After Abimelech, Tola the son of Puah, the son of Dodo, a man of Issachar, arose to save Israel. He lived in Shamir in the hill country of Ephraim. He judged Israel twenty-three years, and died, and was buried in Shamir.

After him Jair, the Gileadite, arose. He judged Israel twenty-two years. He had thirty sons who rode on thirty donkey colts. They had thirty cities, which are called Havvoth Jair to this day, which are in the land of Gilead. Jair died, and was buried in Kamon.

The children of Israel again did that which was evil in YHWH's sight, and served the Baals, the Ashtaroth, the gods of Syria, the gods of Sidon, the gods of Moab, the gods of the children of Ammon, and the gods of the Philistines. They abandoned YHWH, and didn't serve him. YHWH's anger burned against Israel, and he sold them into the hand of the Philistines and into the hand of the children of Ammon. They troubled and oppressed the children of Israel that year. For eighteen years they oppressed all the children of Israel that were beyond the Jordan in the land of the Amorites, which is in Gilead. The children of Ammon passed over the Jordan to fight also against Judah, and against Benjamin, and against the house of Ephraim, so that Israel was very distressed. The children of Israel cried to YHWH, saying, "We have sinned against you, even because we have forsaken our God, and have served the Baals."

YHWH said to the children of Israel, "Didn't I save you from the Egyptians, and from the Amorites, from the children of Ammon, and from the Philistines? The Sidonians also, and the Amalekites, and the Maonites, oppressed you; and you cried to me, and I saved you out of their hand. Yet you have forsaken me and served other gods. Therefore I will save you no more. Go and cry to the gods which you have chosen. Let them save you in the time of your distress!"

The children of Israel said to YHWH, "We have sinned! Do to us whatever seems good to you; only deliver us, please, today." They put away the foreign gods from among them and served YHWH; and his soul was grieved for the misery of Israel.

Then the children of Ammon were gathered together and encamped in Gilead. The children of Israel assembled themselves together and encamped in Mizpah. The people, the princes of Gilead, said to one another, "Who is the man who will begin to fight against the children of Ammon? He shall be head over all the inhabitants of Gilead."

....

Now Jephthah the Gileadite was a mighty man of valor. He was the son of a prostitute. Gilead became the father of Jephthah. Gilead's wife bore him sons. When his wife's sons grew up, they drove Jephthah out and said to him, "You will not inherit in our father's house, for you are the son of another woman." Then Jephthah fled from his brothers and lived in the land of Tob. Outlaws joined up with Jephthah, and they went out with him.

After a while, the children of Ammon made war against Israel. When the children of Ammon made war against Israel, the elders of Gilead went to get Jephthah out of the land of Tob. They said to Jephthah, "Come and be our chief, that we may fight with the children of Ammon."

Jephthah said to the elders of Gilead, "Didn't you hate me, and drive me out of my father's house? Why have you come to me now when you are in distress?"

The elders of Gilead said to Jephthah, "Therefore we have turned again to you now, that you may go with us and fight with the children of Ammon. You will be our head over all the inhabitants of Gilead."

Jephthah said to the elders of Gilead, "If you bring me home again to fight with the children of Ammon, and YHWH delivers them before me, will I be your head?"

The elders of Gilead said to Jephthah, "YHWH will be witness between us. Surely we will do what you say."

Then Jephthah went with the elders of Gilead, and the people made him head and chief over them. Jephthah spoke all his words before YHWH in Mizpah.

Jephthah sent messengers to the king of the children of Ammon, saying, "What do you have to do with me, that you have come to me to fight against my land?"

The king of the children of Ammon answered the messengers of Jephthah, "Because Israel took away my land when he came up out of Egypt, from the Arnon even to the Jabbok, and to the Jordan. Now therefore restore that territory again peaceably."

Jephthah sent messengers again to the king of the children of Ammon; and he said to him, "Jephthah says: Israel didn't take away the land of Moab, nor the land of the children of Ammon; but when they came up from Egypt, and Israel went through the wilderness to the Red Sea, and came to Kadesh, then Israel sent messengers to the king of Edom, saying, 'Please let me pass through your land;' but the king of Edom didn't listen. In the same way, he sent to the king of Moab, but he refused; so Israel stayed in Kadesh. Then they went through the wilderness, and went around the land of Edom, and the land of Moab, and came by the east side of the land of Moab, and they encamped on the other side of the Arnon; but they didn't come within the border of Moab, for the Arnon was the border of Moab. Israel sent messengers to Sihon king of the Amorites, the king of Heshbon; and Israel said to him, 'Please let us pass through your land to my place.' But Sihon didn't trust Israel to pass through his border;

but Sihon gathered all his people together, and encamped in Jahaz, and fought against Israel. YHWH, the God of Israel, delivered Sihon and all his people into the hand of Israel, and they struck them. So Israel possessed all the land of the Amorites, the inhabitants of that country. They possessed all the border of the Amorites, from the Arnon even to the Jabbok, and from the wilderness even to the Jordan. So now YHWH, the God of Israel, has dispossessed the Amorites from before his people Israel, and should you possess them? Won't you possess that which Chemosh your god gives you to possess? So whoever YHWH our God has dispossessed from before us, them will we possess. Now are you anything better than Balak the son of Zippor, king of Moab? Did he ever strive against Israel, or did he ever fight against them? Israel lived in Heshbon and its towns, and in Aroer and its towns, and in all the cities that are along the side of the Arnon for three hundred years! Why didn't you recover them within that time? Therefore I have not sinned against you, but you do me wrong to war against me. May YHWH the Judge be judge today between the children of Israel and the children of Ammon."

However, the king of the children of Ammon didn't listen to the words of Jephthah which he sent him. Then YHWH's Spirit came on Jephthah, and he passed over Gilead and Manasseh, and passed over Mizpah of Gilead, and from Mizpah of Gilead he passed over to the children of Ammon.

Jephthah vowed a vow to YHWH, and said, "If you will indeed deliver the children of Ammon into my hand, then it shall be, that whatever comes out of the doors of my house to meet me when I return in peace from the children of Ammon, it shall be YHWH's, and I will offer it up for a burnt offering."

So Jephthah passed over to the children of Ammon to fight against them; and YHWH delivered them into his hand. He struck them from Aroer until you come to Minnith, even twenty cities, and to Abelcheramim, with a very great slaughter. So the children of Ammon were subdued before the children of Israel.

Jephthah came to Mizpah to his house; and behold, his daughter came out to meet him with tambourines and with dances. She was his only child. Besides her he had neither son nor daughter. When he saw her, he tore his clothes, and said, "Alas, my daughter! You have brought me very low, and you are one of those who trouble me; for I have opened my mouth to YHWH, and I can't go back."

She said to him, "My father, you have opened your mouth to

YHWH; do to me according to that which has proceeded out of your mouth, because YHWH has taken vengeance for you on your enemies, even on the children of Ammon." Then she said to her father, "Let this thing be done for me. Leave me alone two months, that I may depart and go down on the mountains, and bewail my virginity, I and my companions."

He said, "Go." He sent her away for two months; and she departed, she and her companions, and mourned her virginity on the mountains. At the end of two months, she returned to her father, who did with her according to his vow which he had vowed. She was a virgin. It became a custom in Israel that the daughters of Israel went yearly to celebrate the daughter of Jephthah the Gileadite four days in a year.

....

The men of Ephraim were gathered together, and passed northward; and they said to Jephthah, "Why did you pass over to fight against the children of Ammon, and didn't call us to go with you? We will burn your house around you with fire!"

Jephthah said to them, "I and my people were at great strife with the children of Ammon; and when I called you, you didn't save me out of their hand. When I saw that you didn't save me, I put my life in my hand, and passed over against the children of Ammon, and YHWH delivered them into my hand. Why then have you come up to me today, to fight against me?"

Then Jephthah gathered together all the men of Gilead, and fought with Ephraim. The men of Gilead struck Ephraim, because they said, "You are fugitives of Ephraim, you Gileadites, in the middle of Ephraim, and in the middle of Manasseh." The Gileadites took the fords of the Jordan against the Ephraimites. Whenever a fugitive of Ephraim said, "Let me go over," the men of Gilead said to him, "Are you an Ephraimite?" If he said, "No;" then they said to him, "Now say 'Shibboleth;'" and he said "Sibboleth"; for he couldn't manage to pronounce it correctly, then they seized him and killed him at the fords of the Jordan. At that time, forty-two thousand of Ephraim fell.

Jephthah judged Israel six years. Then Jephthah the Gileadite died, and was buried in the cities of Gilead.

After him Ibzan of Bethlehem judged Israel. He had thirty sons. He sent his thirty daughters outside his clan, and he brought in thirty daughters from outside his clan for his sons. He judged Israel seven years. Ibzan died, and was buried at Bethlehem.

After him, Elon the Zebulunite judged Israel; and he judged Israel ten years. Elon the Zebulunite died, and was buried in Aijalon in the land of Zebulun.

After him, Abdon the son of Hillel the Pirathonite judged Israel. He had forty sons and thirty sons' sons who rode on seventy donkey colts. He judged Israel eight years. Abdon the son of Hillel the Pirathonite died, and was buried in Pirathon in the land of Ephraim, in the hill country of the Amalekites.

....

The children of Israel again did that which was evil in YHWH's sight; and YHWH delivered them into the hand of the Philistines forty years.

There was a certain man of Zorah, of the family of the Danites, whose name was Manoah; and his wife was barren, and childless. YHWH's angel appeared to the woman, and said to her, "See now, you are barren and childless; but you shall conceive and bear a son. Now therefore please beware and drink no wine nor strong drink, and don't eat any unclean thing; for, behold, you shall conceive and give birth to a son. No razor shall come on his head, for the child shall be a Nazirite to God from the womb. He shall begin to save Israel out of the hand of the Philistines."

Then the woman came and told her husband, saying, "A man of God came to me, and his face was like the face of the angel of God, very awesome. I didn't ask him where he was from, neither did he tell me his name; but he said to me, 'Behold, you shall conceive and bear a son; and now drink no wine nor strong drink. Don't eat any unclean thing, for the child shall be a Nazirite to God from the womb to the day of his death.'"

Then Manoah entreated YHWH, and said, "Oh, Lord, please let the man of God whom you sent come again to us, and teach us what we should do to the child who shall be born."

God listened to the voice of Manoah, and the angel of God came again to the woman as she sat in the field; but Manoah, her husband, wasn't with her. The woman hurried and ran, and told her husband, saying to him, "Behold, the man who came to me that day has appeared to me,"

Manoah arose and followed his wife, and came to the man, and said to him, "Are you the man who spoke to my wife?"

He said, "I am."

Manoah said, "Now let your words happen. What shall the child's way of life and mission be?"

YHWH's angel said to Manoah, "Of all that I said to the woman let her beware. She may not eat of anything that comes of the vine, neither let her drink wine or strong drink, nor eat any unclean thing. Let her observe all that I commanded her."

Manoah said to YHWH's angel, "Please stay with us, that we may make a young goat ready for you."

YHWH's angel said to Manoah, "Though you detain me, I won't eat your bread. If you will prepare a burnt offering, you must offer it to YHWH." For Manoah didn't know that he was YHWH's angel.

Manoah said to YHWH's angel, "What is your name, that when your words happen, we may honor you?"

YHWH's angel said to him, "Why do you ask about my name, since it is incomprehensible?"

So Manoah took the young goat with the meal offering, and offered it on the rock to YHWH. Then the angel did an amazing thing as Manoah and his wife watched. For when the flame went up toward the sky from off the altar, YHWH's angel ascended in the flame of the altar. Manoah and his wife watched; and they fell on their faces to the ground. But YHWH's angel didn't appear to Manoah or to his wife any more. Then Manoah knew that he was YHWH's angel. Manoah said to his wife, "We shall surely die, because we have seen God."

But his wife said to him, "If YHWH were pleased to kill us, he wouldn't have received a burnt offering and a meal offering at our hand, and he wouldn't have shown us all these things, nor would he have told us such things as these at this time." The woman bore a son and named him Samson. The child grew, and YHWH blessed him. YHWH's Spirit began to move him in Mahaneh Dan, between Zorah and Eshtaol.

....

Samson went down to Timnah, and saw a woman in Timnah of the daughters of the Philistines. He came up, and told his father and his mother, saying, "I have seen a woman in Timnah of the daughters of the Philistines. Now therefore get her for me as my wife."

Then his father and his mother said to him, "Isn't there a woman among your brothers' daughters, or among all my people, that you go to take a wife of the uncircumcised Philistines?"

Samson said to his father, "Get her for me, for she pleases me well."

But his father and his mother didn't know that it was of YHWH; for he sought an occasion against the Philistines. Now at that time the Philistines ruled over Israel.

Then Samson went down to Timnah with his father and his mother, and came to the vineyards of Timnah; and behold, a young lion roared at him. YHWH's Spirit came mightily on him, and he tore him as he would have torn a young goat with his bare hands, but he didn't tell his father or his mother what he had done. He went down and talked with the woman, and she pleased Samson well. After a while he returned to take her, and he went over to see the carcass of the lion; and behold, there was a swarm of bees in the body of the lion, and honey. He took it into his hands, and went on, eating as he went. He came to his father and mother and gave to them, and they ate, but he didn't tell them that he had taken the honey out of the lion's body. His father went down to the woman; and Samson made a feast there, for the young men used to do so. When they saw him, they brought thirty companions to be with him.

Samson said to them, "Let me tell you a riddle now. If you can tell me the answer within the seven days of the feast, and find it out, then I will give you thirty linen garments and thirty changes of clothing; but if you can't tell me the answer, then you shall give me thirty linen garments and thirty changes of clothing."

They said to him, "Tell us your riddle, that we may hear it."

He said to them,

"*Out of the eater came out food.*
   Out of the strong came out sweetness."

They couldn't in three days declare the riddle. On the seventh day, they said to Samson's wife, "Entice your husband, that he may declare to us the riddle, lest we burn you and your father's house with fire. Have you called us to impoverish us? Isn't that so?"

Samson's wife wept before him, and said, "You just hate me, and don't love me. You've told a riddle to the children of my people, and haven't told it to me."

He said to her, "Behold, I haven't told my father or my mother, so why should I tell you?"

She wept before him the seven days, while their feast lasted; and on the seventh day, he told her, because she pressed him severely; and she told the riddle to the children of her people. The men of the city said to him on the seventh day before the sun went down, "What is sweeter than honey? What is stronger than a lion?"

He said to them,

"If you hadn't plowed with my heifer,
you wouldn't have found out my riddle."

YHWH's Spirit came mightily on him, and he went down to Ashkelon and struck thirty men of them. He took their plunder, then gave the changes of clothing to those who declared the riddle. His anger burned, and he went up to his father's house. But Samson's wife was given to his companion, who had been his friend.

....

But after a while, in the time of wheat harvest, Samson visited his wife with a young goat. He said, "I will go in to my wife's room."

But her father wouldn't allow him to go in. Her father said, "I most certainly thought that you utterly hated her; therefore I gave her to your companion. Isn't her younger sister more beautiful than she? Please, take her instead."

Samson said to them, "This time I will be blameless in the case of the Philistines when I harm them." Samson went and caught three hundred foxes, and took torches, and turned tail to tail, and put a torch in the middle between every two tails. When he had set the torches on fire, he let them go into the standing grain of the Philistines, and burned up both the shocks and the standing grain, and also the olive groves.

Then the Philistines said, "Who has done this?"

They said, "Samson, the son-in-law of the Timnite, because he has taken his wife and given her to his companion." The Philistines came up, and burned her and her father with fire.

Samson said to them, "If you behave like this, surely I will take revenge on you, and after that I will cease." He struck them hip and thigh with a great slaughter; and he went down and lived in the cave in Etam's rock. Then the Philistines went up, encamped in Judah, and spread themselves in Lehi.

The men of Judah said, "Why have you come up against us?"

They said, "We have come up to bind Samson, to do to him as he has done to us."

Then three thousand men of Judah went down to the cave in Etam's rock, and said to Samson, "Don't you know that the Philistines are rulers over us? What then is this that you have done to us?"

He said to them, "As they did to me, so I have done to them."

They said to him, "We have come down to bind you, that we may deliver you into the hand of the Philistines."

Samson said to them, "Swear to me that you will not attack me yourselves."

They spoke to him, saying, "No, but we will bind you securely and deliver you into their hands; but surely we will not kill you." They bound him with two new ropes, and brought him up from the rock.

When he came to Lehi, the Philistines shouted as they met him. Then YHWH's Spirit came mightily on him, and the ropes that were on his arms became as flax that was burned with fire; and his bands dropped from off his hands. He found a fresh jawbone of a donkey, put out his hand, took it, and struck a thousand men with it. Samson said, "With the jawbone of a donkey, heaps on heaps; with the jawbone of a donkey I have struck a thousand men." When he had finished speaking, he threw the jawbone out of his hand; and that place was called Ramath Lehi.

He was very thirsty, and called on YHWH and said, "You have given this great deliverance by the hand of your servant; and now shall I die of thirst, and fall into the hands of the uncircumcised?"

But God split the hollow place that is in Lehi, and water came out of it. When he had drunk, his spirit came again, and he revived. Therefore its name was called En Hakkore, which is in Lehi, to this day. He judged Israel twenty years in the days of the Philistines.

....

Samson went to Gaza, and saw there a prostitute, and went in to her. The Gazites were told, "Samson is here!" They surrounded him, and laid wait for him all night in the gate of the city, and were quiet all the night, saying, "Wait until morning light, then we will kill him." Samson lay until midnight, and arose at midnight, and took hold of the doors of the gate of the city, and the two posts, and plucked them up, bar and all, and put them on his shoulders, and carried them up to the top of the mountain that is before Hebron.

It came to pass afterward, that he loved a woman in the valley of Sorek, whose name was Delilah. The lords of the Philistines came up to her, and said to her, "Entice him, and see in which his great strength lies, and by what means we may prevail against him, that we may bind him to afflict him; and we will each give you eleven hundred pieces of silver."

Delilah said to Samson, "Please tell me where your great strength lies, and what you might be bound to afflict you."

Samson said to her, "If they bind me with seven green cords that were never dried, then shall I become weak, and be as another man."

Then the lords of the Philistines brought up to her seven green cords which had not been dried, and she bound him with them. Now she had an ambush waiting in the inner room. She said to him, "The Philistines are on you, Samson!" He broke the cords, as a string of tow is broken when it touches the fire. So his strength was not known.

Delilah said to Samson, "Behold, you have mocked me, and told me lies: now please tell me with which you might be bound."

He said to her, "If they only bind me with new ropes with which no work has been done, then shall I become weak, and be as another man."

So Delilah took new ropes, and bound him therewith, and said to him, "The Philistines are on you, Samson!" The ambush was waiting in the inner room. He broke them off his arms like a thread.

Delilah said to Samson, "Until now, you have mocked me and told me lies. Tell me with what you might be bound."

He said to her, "If you weave the seven locks of my head with the web."

She fastened it with the pin, and said to him, "The Philistines are on you, Samson!" He awakened out of his sleep, and plucked away the pin of the beam, and the web.

She said to him, "How can you say, 'I love you,' when your heart is not with me? You have mocked me these three times, and have not told me where your great strength lies."

When she pressed him daily with her words, and urged him, his soul was troubled to death. He told her all his heart, and said to her, "No razor has ever come on my head; for I have been a Nazirite to God from my mother's womb. If I am shaved, then my strength will go from me, and I will become weak, and be like any other man."

When Delilah saw that he had told her all his heart, she sent and called for the lords of the Philistines, saying, "Come up this once, for he has told me all his heart." Then the lords of the Philistines came up to her, and brought the money in their hand. She made him sleep on her knees; and she called for a man, and shaved off the seven locks of his head; and she began to afflict him, and his strength went from him. She said, "The Philistines are upon you, Samson!"

He awoke out of his sleep, and said, "I will go out as at other times, and shake myself free." But he didn't know that YHWH had departed from him. The Philistines laid hold on him, and put out his eyes; and they brought him down to Gaza, and bound him with fetters of bronze; and he ground at the mill in the prison. However the hair of his head began to grow again after he was shaved.

The lords of the Philistines gathered them together to offer a great sacrifice to Dagon their god, and to rejoice; for they said, "Our god has delivered Samson our enemy into our hand." When the people saw him, they praised their god; for they said, "Our god has delivered our enemy and the destroyer of our country, who has slain many of us, into our hand."

When their hearts were merry, they said, "Call for Samson, that he may entertain us." They called for Samson out of the prison; and he performed before them. They set him between the pillars; and Samson said to the boy who held him by the hand, "Allow me to feel the pillars whereupon the house rests, that I may lean on them."

Now the house was full of men and women; and all the lords of the Philistines were there; and there were on the roof about three thousand men and women, who saw while Samson performed. Samson called to YHWH, and said, "Lord YHWH, remember me, please, and strengthen me, please, only this once, God, that I may be at once avenged of the Philistines for my two eyes." Samson took hold of the two middle pillars on which the house rested, and leaned on them, the one with his right hand, and the other with his left. Samson said, "Let me die with the Philistines!" He bowed himself with all his might; and the house fell on the lords, and on all the people who were therein. So the dead that he killed at his death were more than those who he killed in his life. Then his brothers and all the house of his father came down, and took him, and brought him up, and buried him between Zorah and Eshtaol in the burial site of Manoah his father. He judged Israel twenty years.

....

There was a man of the hill country of Ephraim, whose name was Micah. He said to his mother, "The eleven hundred pieces of silver that were taken from you, about which you uttered a curse, and also spoke it in my ears, behold, the silver is with me. I took it."

His mother said, "May YHWH bless my son!"

He restored the eleven hundred pieces of silver to his mother, then his mother said, "I most certainly dedicate the silver to YHWH from my hand for my son, to make a carved image and a molten image. Now therefore I will restore it to you."

When he restored the money to his mother, his mother took two hundred pieces of silver, and gave them to a silversmith, who made a carved image and a molten image out of it. It was in the house of Micah.

The man Micah had a house of gods, and he made an ephod, and teraphim, and consecrated one of his sons, who became his priest. In those days there was no king in Israel. Everyone did that which was right in his own eyes. There was a young man out of Bethlehem Judah, of the family of Judah, who was a Levite; and he lived there. The man departed out of the city, out of Bethlehem Judah, to live where he could find a place, and he came to the hill country of Ephraim, to the house of Micah, as he traveled. Micah said to him, "Where did you come from?"

He said to him, "I am a Levite of Bethlehem Judah, and I am looking for a place to live." Micah said to him, "Dwell with me, and be to me a father and a priest, and I will give you ten pieces of silver per year, a suit of clothing, and your food." So the Levite went in. The Levite was content to dwell with the man; and the young man was to him as one of his sons. Micah consecrated the Levite, and the young man became his priest, and was in the house of Micah. Then Micah said, "Now I know that YHWH will do good to me, since I have a Levite as my priest."

In those days there was no king in Israel. In those days the tribe of the Danites sought an inheritance to dwell in; for to that day, their inheritance had not fallen to them among the tribes of Israel. The children of Dan sent five men of their family from their whole number, men of valor, from Zorah, and from Eshtaol, to spy out the land, and to search it. They said to them, "Go, explore the land!"

They came to the hill country of Ephraim, to the house of Micah, and lodged there. When they were by the house of Micah, they knew the voice of the young man the Levite; so they went over there, and said to him, "Who brought you here? What do you do in this place? What do you have here?"

He said to them, "Thus and thus has Micah dealt with me, and he has hired me, and I have become his priest."

They said to him, "Please ask counsel of God, that we may know whether our way which we go shall be prosperous."

The priest said to them, "Go in peace. Your way in which you go is before YHWH."

Then the five men departed, and came to Laish, and saw the people who were there, how they lived in safety, in the way of the Sidonians, quiet and secure; for there was no one in the land, possessing authority, that might put them to shame in anything, and they were far from the Sidonians, and had no dealings with anyone else. They came to their brothers at Zorah and Eshtaol; and their brothers asked them, "What do you say?"

They said, "Arise, and let's go up against them; for we have seen the land, and behold, it is very good. Do you stand still? Don't be slothful to go and to enter in to possess the land. When you go, you will come to an unsuspecting people, and the land is large; for God has given it into your hand, a place where there is no lack of anything that is in the earth."

The family of the Danites set out from Zorah and Eshtaol, with six hundred men armed with weapons of war. They went up and encamped in Kiriath Jearim, in Judah. Therefore they called that place Mahaneh Dan, to this day. Behold, it is behind Kiriath Jearim. They passed from there to the hill country of Ephraim, and came to the house of Micah.

Then the five men who went to spy out the country of Laish answered, and said to their brothers, "Do you know that there is in these houses an ephod, and teraphim, and a carved image, and a molten image? Now therefore consider what you have to do." They went over there, and came to the house of the young Levite man, even to the house of Micah, and asked him how he was doing. The six hundred men armed with their weapons of war, who were of the children of Dan, stood by the entrance of the gate. The five men who went to spy out the land went up, and came in there, and took the engraved image, the ephod, the teraphim, and the molten image; and the priest stood by the entrance of the gate with the six hundred men armed with weapons of war.

When these went into Micah's house, and took the engraved image, the ephod, the teraphim, and the molten image, the priest said to them, "What are you doing?"

They said to him, "Hold your peace, put your hand on your mouth, and go with us, and be to us a father and a priest. Is it better for you to be priest to the house of one man, or to be priest to a tribe and a family in Israel?"

The priest's heart was glad, and he took the ephod, the teraphim, and the engraved image, and went with the people. So they turned and departed, and put the little ones, the livestock, and the goods before them. When they were a good way from the house of Micah, the men who were in the houses near Micah's house gathered together and overtook the children of Dan. As they cried to the children of Dan, they turned their faces, and said to Micah, "What ails you, that you come with such a company?"

He said, "You have taken away my gods which I made, and the priest, and have gone away! What more do I have? How can you ask me, 'What ails you?'"

The children of Dan said to him, "Don't let your voice be heard among us, lest angry fellows fall on you, and you lose your life, with the lives of your household."

The children of Dan went their way; and when Micah saw that they were too strong for him, he turned and went back to his house. They took that which Micah had made, and the priest whom he had, and came to Laish, to a people quiet and unsuspecting, and struck them with the edge of the sword; then they burned the city with fire. There was no deliverer, because it was far from Sidon, and they had no dealings with anyone else; and it was in the valley that lies by Beth Rehob. They built the city, and lived in it. They called the name of the city Dan, after the name of Dan their father, who was born to Israel; however the name of the city used to be Laish. The children of Dan set up for themselves the engraved image; and Jonathan, the son of Gershom, the son of Moses, and his sons were priests to the tribe of the Danites until the day of the captivity of the land. So they set up for themselves Micah's engraved image which he made, and it remained all the time that God's house was in Shiloh.

....

In those days, when there was no king in Israel, there was a certain Levite living on the farther side of the hill country of Ephraim, who took for himself a concubine out of Bethlehem Judah. His concubine played the prostitute against him, and went away from him to her father's house to Bethlehem Judah, and was there for four months. Her husband arose, and went after her, to speak kindly to her, to bring her again, having his servant with him, and a couple of donkeys. She brought him into her father's house; and when the father of the young lady saw him, he rejoiced to meet him. His father-in-law, the young lady's father, kept him there; and he stayed with him three days. So they ate and drank, and stayed there.

On the fourth day, they got up early in the morning, and he rose up to depart. The young lady's father said to his son-in-law, "Strengthen your heart with a morsel of bread, and afterward you shall go your way." So they sat down, ate, and drank, both of them together. Then the young lady's father said to the man, "Please be pleased to stay all night, and let your heart be merry." The man rose up to depart; but his father-in-law urged him, and he stayed there again. He arose early in the morning on the fifth day to depart; and the young lady's father said, "Please strengthen your heart and stay until the day declines;" and they both ate.

When the man rose up to depart, he, and his concubine, and his servant, his father-in-law, the young lady's father, said to him, "Behold, now the day draws toward evening, please stay all night. Behold, the day is ending. Stay here, that your heart may be merry; and tomorrow go on your way early, that you may go home." But the man wouldn't stay that night, but he rose up and went near Jebus (also called Jerusalem). With him were a couple of saddled donkeys. His concubine also was with him.

When they were by Jebus, the day was far spent; and the servant said to his master, "Please come and let's enter into this city of the Jebusites, and stay in it."

His master said to him, "We won't enter into the city of a foreigner that is not of the children of Israel; but we will pass over to Gibeah." He said to his servant, "Come and let's draw near to one of these places; and we will lodge in Gibeah, or in Ramah." So they passed on and went their way; and the sun went down on them near Gibeah, which belongs to Benjamin. They went over there, to go in to stay in Gibeah. He went in, and sat down in the street of the city; for there was no one who took them into his house to stay.

Behold, an old man came from his work out of the field at evening. Now the man was from the hill country of Ephraim, and he lived in Gibeah; but the men of the place were Benjamites. He lifted up his eyes, and saw the wayfaring man in the street of the city; and the old man said, "Where are you going? Where did you come from?"

He said to him, "We are passing from Bethlehem Judah to the farther side of the hill country of Ephraim. I am from there, and I went to Bethlehem Judah. I am going to YHWH's house; and there is no one who has taken me into his house. Yet there is both straw and feed for our donkeys; and there is bread and wine also for me, and for your servant, and for the young man who is with your servants. There is no lack of anything."

The old man said, "Peace be to you! Just let me supply all your needs, but don't sleep in the street." So he brought him into his house, and gave the donkeys fodder. Then they washed their feet, and ate and drank. As they were making their hearts merry, behold, the men of the city, certain wicked fellows, surrounded the house, beating at the door; and they spoke to the master of the house, the old man, saying, "Bring out the man who came into your house, that we can have sex with him!"

The man, the master of the house, went out to them, and said to them, "No, my brothers, please don't act so wickedly; since this man has come into my house, don't do this folly. Behold, here is my virgin daughter and his concubine. I will bring them out now. Humble them, and do with them what seems good to you; but to this man don't do any such folly."

But the men wouldn't listen to him: so the man grabbed his concubine, and brought her out to them; and they had sex with her, and abused her all night until the morning. When the day began to dawn, they let her go. Then the woman came in the dawning of the day, and fell down at the door of the man's house where her lord was, until it was light. Her lord rose up in the morning, and opened the doors of the house, and went out to go his way; and behold, the woman his concubine had fallen down at the door of the house, with her hands on the threshold.

He said to her, "Get up, and let's get going!" but no one answered. Then he took her up on the donkey; and the man rose up, and went to his place.

When he had come into his house, he took a knife, and cut up his concubine, and divided her, limb by limb, into twelve pieces, and sent her throughout all the borders of Israel. It was so, that all who saw it said, "Such a deed has not been done or seen from the day that the children of Israel came up out of the land of Egypt to this day! Consider it, take counsel, and speak."

Then all the children of Israel went out, and the congregation was assembled as one man, from Dan even to Beersheba, with the land of Gilead, to YHWH at Mizpah. The chiefs of all the people, even of all the tribes of Israel, presented themselves in the assembly of the people of God, four hundred thousand footmen who drew sword. (Now the children of Benjamin heard that the children of Israel had gone up to Mizpah.) The children of Israel said, "Tell us, how did this wickedness happen?"

The Levite, the husband of the woman who was murdered, answered, "I came into Gibeah that belongs to Benjamin, I and my concubine, to spend the night. The men of Gibeah rose against me, and surrounded the house by night. They intended to kill me, and they raped my concubine, and she is dead. I took my concubine, and cut her in pieces, and sent her throughout all the country of the inheritance of Israel; for they have committed lewdness and folly in Israel. Behold, you children of Israel, all of you, give here your advice and counsel."

All the people arose as one man, saying, "None of us will go to his tent, neither will any of us turn to his house. But now this is the thing which we will do to Gibeah: we will go up against it by lot; and we will take ten men of one hundred throughout all the tribes of Israel, and one hundred of one thousand, and a thousand out of ten thousand, to get food for the people, that they may do, when they come to Gibeah of Benjamin, according to all the folly that they have worked in Israel." So all the men of Israel were gathered against the city, knit together as one man.

The tribes of Israel sent men through all the tribe of Benjamin, saying, "What wickedness is this that has happened among you? Now therefore deliver up the men, the wicked fellows, who are in Gibeah, that we may put them to death, and put away evil from Israel."

But Benjamin would not listen to the voice of their brothers the children of Israel. The children of Benjamin gathered themselves together out of the cities to Gibeah, to go out to battle against the children of Israel. The children of Benjamin were counted on that day out of the cities twenty-six thousand men who drew the sword, in addition to the inhabitants of Gibeah, who were counted seven hundred chosen men. Among all these soldiers there were seven hundred chosen men who were left-handed. Every one of them could sling a stone at a hair and not miss. The men of Israel, besides Benjamin, were counted four hundred thousand men who drew sword. All these were men of war.

The children of Israel arose, went up to Bethel, and asked counsel of God. They asked, "Who shall go up for us first to battle against the children of Benjamin?"

YHWH said, "Judah first."

The children of Israel rose up in the morning, and encamped against Gibeah. The men of Israel went out to battle against Benjamin; and the men of Israel set the battle in array against them at Gibeah. The children of Benjamin came out of Gibeah, and on that day destroyed twenty-two thousand of the Israelite men down to the ground. The people, the men of Israel, encouraged themselves, and set the battle again in array in the place where they set themselves in array the first day. The children of Israel went up and wept before YHWH until evening; and they asked of YHWH, saying, "Shall I again draw near to battle against the children of Benjamin my brother?"

YHWH said, "Go up against him."

The children of Israel came near against the children of Benjamin the second day. Benjamin went out against them out of Gibeah the second day, and destroyed down to the ground of the children of Israel again eighteen thousand men. All these drew the sword.

Then all the children of Israel, and all the people, went up, and came to Bethel, and wept, and sat there before YHWH, and fasted that day until evening; then they offered burnt offerings and peace offerings before YHWH. The children of Israel asked YHWH (for the ark of the covenant of God was there in those days, and Phinehas, the son of Eleazar, the son of Aaron, stood before it in those days), saying, "Shall I yet again go out to battle against the children of Benjamin my brother, or shall I cease?"

YHWH said, "Go up; for tomorrow I will deliver him into your hand."

Israel set ambushes all around Gibeah. The children of Israel went up against the children of Benjamin on the third day, and set themselves in array against Gibeah, as at other times. The children of Benjamin went out against the people, and were drawn away from the city; and they began to strike and kill of the people, as at other times, in the highways, of which one goes up to Bethel, and the other to Gibeah, in the field, about thirty men of Israel.

The children of Benjamin said, "They are struck down before us, as at the first." But the children of Israel said, "Let's flee, and draw them away from the city to the highways."

All the men of Israel rose up out of their place, and set themselves in array at Baal Tamar. Then the ambushers of Israel broke out of their place, even out of Maareh Geba. Ten thousand chosen men out of all Israel came over against Gibeah, and the battle was severe; but they didn't know that disaster was close to them. YHWH struck Benjamin before Israel; and the children of Israel destroyed of Benjamin that day twenty-five thousand one hundred men. All these drew the sword. So the children of Benjamin saw that they were struck; for the men of Israel yielded to Benjamin, because they trusted the ambushers whom they had set against Gibeah. The ambushers hurried, and rushed on Gibeah; then the ambushers spread out, and struck all the city with the edge of the sword. Now the appointed sign between the men of Israel and the ambushers was that they should make a great cloud of smoke rise up out of the city. The men of Israel turned in the battle, and Benjamin began to strike and kill of the men of Israel about thirty persons; for they said, "Surely they are struck down before us, as in the first battle." But when the cloud began to arise up out of the city in a pillar of smoke, the Benjamites looked behind them; and behold, the whole city went up in smoke to the sky. The men of Israel turned, and the men of Benjamin were dismayed; for they saw that disaster had come on them. Therefore they turned their backs before the men of Israel to the way of the wilderness; but the battle followed hard after them; and those who came out of the cities destroyed them in the middle of it. They surrounded the Benjamites, chased them, and trod them down at their resting place, as far as near Gibeah toward the sunrise. Eighteen thousand men of Benjamin fell; all these were men of valor. They turned and fled toward the wilderness to the rock of Rimmon; and they gleaned five thousand men of them in the highways, and followed hard after them to Gidom, and struck two thousand men of them. So that all who fell that day of Benjamin were twenty-five thousand men who drew the sword. All these were men of valor. But six hundred men turned and fled toward the wilderness to the rock of Rimmon, and stayed in the rock of Rimmon four months. The men of Israel turned again on the children of Benjamin, and struck them with the edge of the sword, both the entire city, and the livestock, and all that they found. Moreover they set all the cities which they found on fire.

....

Now the men of Israel had sworn in Mizpah, saying, "None of us will give his daughter to Benjamin as a wife." The people came to Bethel, and sat there until evening before God, and lifted up their voices, and wept severely. They said, "YHWH, the God of Israel, why has this happened in Israel, that there should be one tribe lacking in Israel today?"

On the next day, the people rose early, and built an altar there, and offered burnt offerings and peace offerings. The children of Israel said, "Who is there among all the tribes of Israel who didn't come up in the assembly to YHWH?" For they had made a great oath concerning him who didn't come up to YHWH to Mizpah, saying, "He shall surely be put to death." The children of Israel grieved for Benjamin their brother, and said, "There is one tribe cut off from Israel today. How shall we provide wives for those who remain, since we have sworn by YHWH that we will not give them of our daughters to wives?" They said, "What one is there of the tribes of Israel who didn't come up to YHWH to Mizpah?" Behold, no one came from Jabesh Gilead to the camp to the assembly. For when the people were counted, behold, there were none of the inhabitants of Jabesh Gilead there. The congregation sent twelve thousand of the most valiant men there, and commanded them, saying, "Go and strike the inhabitants of Jabesh Gilead with the edge of the sword, with the women and the little ones. This is the thing that you shall do: you shall utterly destroy every male, and every woman who has lain with a man." They found among the inhabitants of Jabesh Gilead four hundred young virgins, who had not known man by lying with him; and they brought them to the camp to Shiloh, which is in the land of Canaan.

The whole congregation sent and spoke to the children of Benjamin who were in the rock of Rimmon, and proclaimed peace to them. Benjamin returned at that time; and they gave them the women whom they had saved alive of the women of Jabesh Gilead. There still weren't enough for them. The people grieved for Benjamin, because YHWH had made a breach in the tribes of Israel. Then the elders of the congregation said, "How shall we provide wives for those who remain, since the women are destroyed out of Benjamin?" They said, "There must be an inheritance for those who are escaped of Benjamin, that a tribe not be blotted out from Israel. However we may not give them wives of our daughters, for the children of Israel had sworn, saying, 'Cursed is he who gives a wife to Benjamin.'" They said, "Behold, there is a feast of YHWH from year to year in Shiloh, which is on the north of Bethel, on the east side of the highway that goes up from Bethel to Shechem, and on the south of Lebonah." They commanded the children of Benjamin, saying, "Go and lie in wait in the vineyards, and see, and behold, if the daughters of Shiloh come out to dance in the dances, then come out of the vineyards, and each man catch his wife of the daughters of Shiloh, and go to the land of Benjamin. It shall be, when their fathers or their brothers come to complain to us, that we will say to them, 'Grant them graciously to us, because we didn't take for each man his wife in battle, neither did you give them to them, otherwise you would now be guilty.'"

The children of Benjamin did so, and took wives for themselves, according to their number, of those who danced, whom they carried off. They went and returned to their inheritance, built the cities, and lived in them. The children of Israel departed from there at that time, every man to his tribe and to his family, and they each went out from there to his own inheritance. In those days there was no king in Israel. Everyone did that which was right in his own eyes.

THE BOOK OF

RUTH

14 MIN

In the days when the judges judged, there was a famine in the land. A certain man of Bethlehem Judah went to live in the country of Moab, he, and his wife, and his two sons. The name of the man was Elimelech, and the name of his wife Naomi. The names of his two sons were Mahlon and Chilion, Ephrathites of Bethlehem Judah. They came into the country of Moab, and lived there. Elimelech, Naomi's husband, died; and she was left with her two sons. They took for themselves wives of the women of Moab. The name of the one was Orpah, and the name of the other was Ruth. They lived there about ten years. Mahlon and Chilion both died, and the woman was bereaved of her two children and of her husband. Then she arose with her daughters-in-law, that she might return from the country of Moab; for she had heard in the country of Moab how YHWH had visited his people in giving them bread. She went out of the place where she was, and her two daughters-in-law with her. They went on the way to return to the land of Judah. Naomi said to her two daughters-in-law, "Go, return each of you to her mother's house. May YHWH deal kindly with you, as you have dealt with the dead, and with me. May YHWH grant you that you may find rest, each of you in the house of her husband."

Then she kissed them, and they lifted up their voices, and wept. They said to her, "No, but we will return with you to your people."

Naomi said, "Go back, my daughters. Why do you want to go with me? Do I still have sons in my womb, that they may be your husbands? Go back, my daughters, go your way; for I am too old to have a husband. If I should say, 'I have hope,' if I should even have a husband tonight, and should also bear sons; would you then wait until they were grown? Would you then refrain from having husbands? No, my daughters, for it grieves me seriously for your sakes, for YHWH's hand has gone out against me."

They lifted up their voices, and wept again; then Orpah kissed her mother-in-law, but Ruth joined with her. She said, "Behold, your sister-in-law has gone back to her people, and to her god. Follow your sister-in-law."

Ruth said, "Don't urge me to leave you, and to return from following you, for where you go, I will go; and where you stay, I will stay. Your people will be my people, and your God my God. Where you die, I will die, and there I will be buried. May YHWH do so to me, and more also, if anything but death parts you and me."

When she saw that she was determined to go with her, she

stopped urging her.

So they both went until they came to Bethlehem. When they had come to Bethlehem, all the city was excited about them, and they asked, "Is this Naomi?"

She said to them, "Don't call me Naomi. Call me Mara; for the Almighty has dealt very bitterly with me. I went out full, and YHWH has brought me home again empty. Why do you call me Naomi, since YHWH has testified against me, and the Almighty has afflicted me?" So Naomi returned, and Ruth the Moabitess, her daughter-in-law, with her, who returned out of the country of Moab. They came to Bethlehem in the beginning of barley harvest.

....

Naomi had a relative of her husband's, a mighty man of wealth, of the family of Elimelech, and his name was Boaz. Ruth the Moabitess said to Naomi, "Let me now go to the field, and glean among the ears of grain after him in whose sight I find favor."

She said to her, "Go, my daughter." She went, and came and gleaned in the field after the reapers; and she happened to come to the portion of the field belonging to Boaz, who was of the family of Elimelech.

Behold, Boaz came from Bethlehem, and said to the reapers, "May YHWH be with you."

They answered him, "May YHWH bless you."

Then Boaz said to his servant who was set over the reapers, "Whose young lady is this?"

The servant who was set over the reapers answered, "It is the Moabite lady who came back with Naomi out of the country of Moab. She said, 'Please let me glean and gather after the reapers among the sheaves.' So she came, and has continued even from the morning until now, except that she rested a little in the house."

Then Boaz said to Ruth, "Listen, my daughter. Don't go to glean in another field, and don't go from here, but stay here close to my maidens. Let your eyes be on the field that they reap, and go after them. Haven't I commanded the young men not to touch you? When you are thirsty, go to the vessels, and drink from that which the young men have drawn."

Then she fell on her face, and bowed herself to the ground, and said to him, "Why have I found favor in your sight, that you should take knowledge of me, since I am a foreigner?"

Boaz answered her, "I have been told all about what you have done for your mother-in-law since the death of your husband, and how you have left your father and your mother, and the land of your birth, and have come to a people that you didn't know before. May YHWH repay your work, and a full reward be given to you from YHWH, the God of Israel, under whose wings you have come to take refuge."

Then she said, "Let me find favor in your sight, my lord, because you have comforted me, and because you have spoken kindly to your servant, though I am not as one of your servants."

At meal time Boaz said to her, "Come here, and eat some bread, and dip your morsel in the vinegar."

She sat beside the reapers, and they passed her parched grain, and she ate, and was satisfied, and left some of it. When she had risen up to glean, Boaz commanded his young men, saying, "Let her glean even among the sheaves, and don't reproach her. Also pull out some for her from the bundles, and leave it. Let her glean, and don't rebuke her."

So she gleaned in the field until evening; and she beat out that which she had gleaned, and it was about an ephah of barley. She took it up, and went into the city. Then her mother-in-law saw what she had gleaned; and she brought out and gave to her that which she had left after she had enough.

Her mother-in-law said to her, "Where have you gleaned today? Where have you worked? Blessed be he who noticed you."

She told her mother-in-law with whom she had worked, "The man's name with whom I worked today is Boaz." Naomi said to her daughter-in-law, "May he be blessed by YHWH, who has not abandoned his kindness to the living and to the dead." Naomi said to her, "The man is a close relative to us, one of our near kinsmen."

Ruth the Moabitess said, "Yes, he said to me, 'You shall stay close to my young men, until they have finished all my harvest.'"

Naomi said to Ruth her daughter-in-law, "It is good, my daughter, that you go out with his maidens, and that they not meet you in any other field." So she stayed close to the maidens of Boaz, to glean to the end of barley harvest and of wheat harvest; and she lived with her mother-in-law.

....

Naomi her mother-in-law said to her, "My daughter, shall I not seek rest for you, that it may be well with you? Now isn't Boaz our kinsman, with whose maidens you were? Behold, he will be winnowing barley tonight on the threshing floor. Therefore wash yourself, anoint yourself, get dressed, and go down to the threshing floor, but don't make yourself known to the man until he has finished eating and drinking. It shall be, when he lies down, that you shall note the place where he is lying. Then you shall go in, uncover his feet, and lay down. Then he will tell you what to do."

She said to her, "All that you say, I will do." She went down to the threshing floor, and did everything that her mother-in-law told her. When Boaz had eaten and drunk, and his heart was merry, he went to lie down at the end of the heap of grain. She came softly, uncovered his feet, and laid down. At midnight, the man was startled and turned himself; and behold, a woman lay at his feet. He said, "Who are you?"

She answered, "I am Ruth your servant. Therefore spread the corner of your garment over your servant; for you are a near kinsman."

He said, "You are blessed by YHWH, my daughter. You have shown more kindness in the latter end than at the beginning, because you didn't follow young men, whether poor or rich. Now, my daughter, don't be afraid. I will do to you all that you say; for all the city of my people knows that you are a worthy woman. Now it is true that I am a near kinsman. However, there is a kinsman nearer than I. Stay this night, and in the morning, if he will perform for you the part of a kinsman, good. Let him do the kinsman's duty. But if he will not do the duty of a kinsman for you, then I will do the duty of a kinsman for you, as YHWH lives. Lie down until the morning."

She lay at his feet until the morning, then she rose up before one could discern another. For he said, "Let it not be known that the woman came to the threshing floor." He said, "Bring the mantle that is on you, and hold it." She held it; and he measured six measures of barley, and laid it on her; then he went into the city.

When she came to her mother-in-law, she said, "How did it go, my daughter?"

She told her all that the man had done for her. She said, "He gave me these six measures of barley; for he said, 'Don't go empty to your mother-in-law.'"

Then she said, "Wait, my daughter, until you know what will happen; for the man will not rest until he has settled this today."

Now Boaz went up to the gate, and sat down there. Behold, the near kinsman of whom Boaz spoke came by. He said to him, "Come over here, friend, and sit down!" He came over, and sat down. He took ten men of the elders of the city, and said, "Sit down here," and they sat down. He said to the near kinsman, "Naomi, who has come back out of the country of Moab, is selling the parcel of land, which was our brother Elimelech's. I thought I should tell you, saying, 'Buy it before those who sit here, and before the elders of my people.' If you will redeem it, redeem it; but if you will not redeem it, then tell me, that I may know. For there is no one to redeem it besides you; and I am after you."

He said, "I will redeem it."

Then Boaz said, "On the day you buy the field from the hand of Naomi, you must buy it also from Ruth the Moabitess, the wife of the dead, to raise up the name of the dead on his inheritance."

The near kinsman said, "I can't redeem it for myself, lest I endanger my own inheritance. Take my right of redemption for yourself; for I can't redeem it."

Now this was the custom in former time in Israel concerning redeeming and concerning exchanging, to confirm all things: a man took off his sandal, and gave it to his neighbor; and this was the way of formalizing transactions in Israel. So the near kinsman said to Boaz, "Buy it for yourself," then he took off his sandal.

Boaz said to the elders, and to all the people, "You are witnesses today, that I have bought all that was Elimelech's, and all that was Chilion's and Mahlon's, from the hand of Naomi. Moreover Ruth the Moabitess, the wife of Mahlon, I have purchased to be my wife, to raise up the name of the dead on his inheritance, that the name of the dead may not be cut off from among his brothers, and from the gate of his place. You are witnesses today."

All the people who were in the gate, and the elders, said, "We are witnesses. May YHWH make the woman who has come into your house like Rachel and like Leah, which both built the house of Israel; and treat you worthily in Ephrathah, and be famous in Bethlehem. Let your house be like the house of Perez, whom Tamar bore to Judah, of the offspring which YHWH will give you by this young woman."

So Boaz took Ruth, and she became his wife; and he went in

to her, and YHWH enabled her to conceive, and she bore a son. The women said to Naomi, "Blessed be YHWH, who has not left you today without a near kinsman. Let his name be famous in Israel. He shall be to you a restorer of life, and sustain you in your old age, for your daughter-in-law, who loves you, who is better to you than seven sons, has given birth to him." Naomi took the child, and laid him in her bosom, and became nurse to it. The women, her neighbors, gave him a name, saying, "A son is born to Naomi". They named him Obed. He is the father of Jesse, the father of David.

Now this is the history of the generations of Perez: Perez became the father of Hezron, and Hezron became the father of Ram, and Ram became the father of Amminadab, and Amminadab became the father of Nahshon, and Nahshon became the father of Salmon, and Salmon became the father of Boaz, and Boaz became the father of Obed, and Obed became the father of Jesse, and Jesse became the father of David.

THE BOOK OF

SAMUEL

PART I

2 HR 3 MIN

Now there was a certain man of Ramathaim Zophim, of the hill country of Ephraim, and his name was Elkanah, the son of Jeroham, the son of Elihu, the son of Tohu, the son of Zuph, an Ephraimite. He had two wives. The name of one was Hannah, and the name of the other Peninnah. Peninnah had children, but Hannah had no children. This man went up out of his city from year to year to worship and to sacrifice to YHWH of Armies in Shiloh. The two sons of Eli, Hophni and Phinehas, priests to YHWH, were there. When the day came that Elkanah sacrificed, he gave to Peninnah his wife, and to all her sons and her daughters, portions; but to Hannah he gave a double portion, for he loved Hannah, but YHWH had shut up her womb. Her rival provoked her severely, to irritate her, because YHWH had shut up her womb. So year by year, when she went up to YHWH's house, her rival provoked her. Therefore she wept, and didn't eat. Elkanah her husband said to her, "Hannah, why do you weep? Why don't you eat? Why is your heart grieved? Am I not better to you than ten sons?"

So Hannah rose up after they had finished eating and drinking in Shiloh. Now Eli the priest was sitting on his seat by the doorpost of YHWH's temple. She was in bitterness of soul, and prayed to YHWH, weeping bitterly. She vowed a vow, and said, "YHWH of Armies, if you will indeed look at the affliction of your servant, and remember me, and not forget your servant, but will give to your servant a boy, then I will give him to YHWH all the days of his life, and no razor shall come on his head."

As she continued praying before YHWH, Eli saw her mouth. Now Hannah spoke in her heart. Only her lips moved, but her voice was not heard. Therefore Eli thought she was drunk. Eli said to her, "How long will you be drunk? Get rid of your wine!"

Hannah answered, "No, my lord, I am a woman of a sorrowful spirit. I have not been drinking wine or strong drink, but I poured out my soul before YHWH. Don't consider your servant a wicked woman; for I have been speaking out of the abundance of my complaint and my provocation."

Then Eli answered, "Go in peace; and may the God of Israel grant your petition that you have asked of him."

She said, "Let your servant find favor in your sight." So the woman went her way, and ate; and her facial expression wasn't sad any more.

They rose up in the morning early and worshiped YHWH, then

returned and came to their house to Ramah. Then Elkanah knew Hannah his wife; and YHWH remembered her.

When the time had come, Hannah conceived, and bore a son; and she named him Samuel, saying, "Because I have asked him of YHWH."

The man Elkanah, and all his house, went up to offer to YHWH the yearly sacrifice, and his vow. But Hannah didn't go up; for she said to her husband, "Not until the child is weaned; then I will bring him, that he may appear before YHWH, and stay there forever."

Elkanah her husband said to her, "Do what seems good to you. Wait until you have weaned him; only may YHWH establish his word."

So the woman waited and nursed her son, until she weaned him. When she had weaned him, she took him up with her, with three bulls, and one ephah of meal, and a container of wine, and brought him to YHWH's house in Shiloh. The child was young. They killed the bull, and brought the child to Eli. She said, "Oh, my lord, as your soul lives, my lord, I am the woman who stood by you here, praying to YHWH. I prayed for this child; and YHWH has given me my petition which I asked of him. Therefore I have also given him to YHWH. As long as he lives he is given to YHWH." He worshiped YHWH there.

....

Hannah prayed, and said:
"My heart exults in YHWH!
My horn is exalted in YHWH.
My mouth is enlarged over my enemies,
because I rejoice in your salvation.
There is no one as holy as YHWH,
For there is no one besides you,
nor is there any rock like our God.

"Don't keep talking so exceedingly proudly.
Don't let arrogance come out of your mouth,
For YHWH is a God of knowledge.
By him actions are weighed.

"The bows of the mighty men are broken.
Those who stumbled are armed with strength.
Those who were full have hired themselves out for bread.
Those who were hungry are satisfied.

Yes, the barren has borne seven.
She who has many children languishes.

"YHWH kills, and makes alive.
He brings down to Sheol, and brings up.
YHWH makes poor, and makes rich.
He brings low, he also lifts up.
He raises up the poor out of the dust.
He lifts up the needy from the dunghill,
To make them sit with princes,
and inherit the throne of glory.
For the pillars of the earth are YHWH's.
He has set the world on them.
He will keep the feet of his holy ones,
but the wicked shall be put to silence in darkness;
for no man shall prevail by strength.
Those who strive with YHWH shall be broken to pieces.
He will thunder against them in the sky.

"YHWH will judge the ends of the earth.
He will give strength to his king,
and exalt the horn of his anointed."

Elkanah went to Ramah to his house. The child served YHWH before Eli the priest. Now the sons of Eli were wicked men. They didn't know YHWH. The custom of the priests with the people was that when anyone offered a sacrifice, the priest's servant came while the meat was boiling, with a fork of three teeth in his hand; and he stabbed it into the pan, or kettle, or cauldron, or pot. The priest took all that the fork brought up for himself. They did this to all the Israelites who came there to Shiloh. Yes, before they burned the fat, the priest's servant came, and said to the man who sacrificed, "Give meat to roast for the priest; for he will not accept boiled meat from you, but raw."

If the man said to him, "Let the fat be burned first, and then take as much as your soul desires;" then he would say, "No, but you shall give it to me now; and if not, I will take it by force." The sin of the young men was very great before YHWH; for the men despised YHWH's offering. But Samuel ministered before YHWH, being a child, clothed with a linen ephod. Moreover his mother made him a little robe, and brought it to him from year to year, when she came up with her husband to offer the yearly sacrifice. Eli blessed Elkanah and his wife, and said, "May YHWH give you offspring from this woman for the petition which was asked of YHWH." Then they went to their own home. YHWH visited Hannah, and she conceived, and bore three sons and two daughters. The child Samuel grew before YHWH. Now Eli was very old; and he heard all that his sons did to all Israel, and how that they slept with the women who served at the door of the Tent of Meeting. He said to them, "Why do you do such things? For I hear of your evil dealings from all this people. No, my sons; for it is not a good report that I hear! You make YHWH's people disobey. If one man sins against another, God will judge him; but if a man sins against YHWH, who will intercede for him?" Notwithstanding, they didn't listen to the voice of their father, because YHWH intended to kill them. The child Samuel grew on, and increased in favor both with YHWH, and also with men. A man of God came to Eli, and said to him, "YHWH says, 'Did I reveal myself to the house of your father, when they were in Egypt in bondage to Pharaoh's house? Didn't I choose him out of all the tribes of Israel to be my priest, to go up to my altar, to burn incense, to wear an ephod before me? Didn't I give to the house of your father all the offerings of the children of Israel made by fire? Why do you kick at my sacrifice and at my offering, which I have commanded in my habitation, and honor your sons above me, to make yourselves fat with the best of all the offerings of Israel my people?'

"Therefore YHWH, the God of Israel, says, 'I said indeed that your house, and the house of your father, should walk before me forever.' But now YHWH says, 'Far be it from me; for those who honor me I will honor, and those who despise me will be cursed. Behold, the days come, that I will cut off your arm, and the arm of your father's house, that there will not be an old man in your house. You will see the affliction of my habitation, in all the wealth which I will give Israel; and there shall not be an old man in your house forever. The man of yours, whom I don't cut off from my altar, will consume your eyes and grieve your heart; and all the increase of your house will die in the flower of their age.

"'This will be the sign to you, that will come on your two sons, on Hophni and Phinehas: in one day they will both die. I will raise up a faithful priest for myself, that will do according to that which is in my heart and in my mind. I will build him a sure house; and he will walk before my anointed forever. It will happen, that everyone who is left in your house will come and bow down to him for a piece of silver and a loaf of bread, and will say, "Please put me into one of the priests' offices, that I may eat a morsel of bread."'"

....

The child Samuel ministered to YHWH before Eli. YHWH's word was rare in those days. There were not many visions, then. At that time, when Eli was laid down in his place (now his eyes had begun to grow dim, so that he could not see), and God's lamp hadn't yet gone out, and Samuel had laid down in YHWH's temple, where God's ark was; YHWH called Samuel; and he said, "Here I am." He ran to Eli, and said, "Here I am; for you called me."

He said, "I didn't call. Lie down again."

He went and lay down. YHWH called yet again, "Samuel!"

Samuel arose and went to Eli, and said, "Here I am; for you called me."

He answered, "I didn't call, my son. Lie down again." Now Samuel didn't yet know YHWH, neither was YHWH's word yet revealed to him. YHWH called Samuel again the third time. He arose and went to Eli, and said, "Here I am; for you called me."

Eli perceived that YHWH had called the child. Therefore Eli said to Samuel, "Go, lie down. It shall be, if he calls you, that you shall say, 'Speak, YHWH; for your servant hears.'" So Samuel went and lay down in his place. YHWH came, and stood, and called as at other times, "Samuel! Samuel!"

Then Samuel said, "Speak; for your servant hears."

YHWH said to Samuel, "Behold, I will do a thing in Israel, at which both the ears of everyone who hears it will tingle. In that day I will perform against Eli all that I have spoken concerning his house, from the beginning even to the end. For I have told him that I will judge his house forever, for the iniquity which he knew, because his sons brought a curse on themselves, and he didn't restrain them. Therefore I have sworn to the house of Eli, that the iniquity of Eli's house shall not be removed with sacrifice or offering forever."

Samuel lay until the morning, and opened the doors of YHWH's house. Samuel feared to show Eli the vision. Then Eli called Samuel, and said, "Samuel, my son!"

He said, "Here I am."

He said, "What is the thing that he has spoken to you? Please don't hide it from me. God do so to you, and more also, if you hide anything from me of all the things that he spoke to you."

Samuel told him every bit, and hid nothing from him.

He said, "It is YHWH. Let him do what seems good to him."

Samuel grew, and YHWH was with him, and let none of his words fall to the ground. All Israel from Dan even to Beersheba knew that Samuel was established to be a prophet of YHWH. YHWH appeared again in Shiloh; for YHWH revealed himself to Samuel in Shiloh by YHWH's word.

....

The word of Samuel came to all Israel.

Now Israel went out against the Philistines to battle, and encamped beside Ebenezer; and the Philistines encamped in Aphek. The Philistines put themselves in array against Israel. When they joined battle, Israel was defeated by the Philistines, who killed about four thousand men of the army in the field. When the people had come into the camp, the elders of Israel said, "Why has YHWH defeated us today before the Philistines? Let's get the ark of YHWH's covenant out of Shiloh and bring it to us, that it may come among us, and save us out of the hand of our enemies."

So the people sent to Shiloh; and they brought from there the ark of the covenant of YHWH of Armies, who sits above the cherubim: and the two sons of Eli, Hophni and Phinehas, were there with the ark of the covenant of God. When the ark of YHWH's covenant came into the camp, all Israel shouted with a great shout, so that the earth rang again. When the Philistines heard the noise of the shout, they said, "What does the noise of this great shout in the camp of the Hebrews mean?" They understood that YHWH's ark had come into the camp. The Philistines were afraid, for they said, "God has come into the camp." They said, "Woe to us! For there has not been such a thing before. Woe to us! Who shall deliver us out of the hand of these mighty gods? These are the gods that struck the Egyptians with all kinds of plagues in the wilderness. Be strong, and behave like men, O you Philistines, that you not be servants to the Hebrews, as they have been to you. Strengthen yourselves like men, and fight!" The Philistines fought, and Israel was defeated, and each man fled to his tent. There was a very great slaughter; for thirty thousand footmen of Israel fell. God's ark was taken; and the two sons of Eli, Hophni and Phinehas, were slain. A man of Benjamin ran out of the army, and came to Shiloh the same day, with his clothes torn, and with dirt on his head. When he came, behold, Eli was sitting on his seat by the road watching; for his heart trembled for God's ark. When the man came into the city and told about it, all the city cried out. When Eli heard the noise of the crying, he said, "What does the noise of this tumult mean?"

The man hurried, and came and told Eli. Now Eli was ninety-eight years old. His eyes were set, so that he could not see. The man said to Eli, "I am he who came out of the army, and I fled today out of the army."

He said, "How did the matter go, my son?"

He who brought the news answered, "Israel has fled before the Philistines, and there has been also a great slaughter among the people. Your two sons also, Hophni and Phinehas, are dead, and God's ark has been captured."

When he made mention of God's ark, Eli fell from off his seat backward by the side of the gate; and his neck broke, and he died; for he was an old man, and heavy. He had judged Israel forty years.

His daughter-in-law, Phinehas' wife, was with child, near to giving birth. When she heard the news that God's ark was taken, and that her father-in-law and her husband were dead, she bowed herself and gave birth; for her pains came on her. About the time of her death the women who stood by her said to her, "Don't be afraid; for you have given birth to a son." But she didn't answer, neither did she regard it. She named the child Ichabod, saying, "The glory has departed from Israel;" because God's ark was taken, and because of her father-in-law and her husband. She said, "The glory has departed from Israel; for God's ark has been taken."

....

Now the Philistines had taken God's ark, and they brought it from Ebenezer to Ashdod. The Philistines took God's ark, and brought it into the house of Dagon, and set it by Dagon. When the people of Ashdod arose early on the next day, behold, Dagon had fallen on his face to the ground before YHWH's ark. They took Dagon, and set him in his place again. When they arose early on the following morning, behold, Dagon had fallen on his face to the ground before YHWH's ark; and the head of Dagon and both the palms of his hands were cut off on the threshold. Only Dagon's torso was intact. Therefore neither the priests of Dagon, nor any who come into Dagon's house, step on the threshold of Dagon in Ashdod, to this day. But YHWH's hand was heavy on the people of Ashdod, and he destroyed them, and struck them with tumors, even Ashdod and its borders.

When the men of Ashdod saw that it was so, they said, "The ark of the God of Israel shall not stay with us; for his hand is severe on us, and on Dagon our god." They sent therefore and gathered together all the lords of the Philistines, and said, "What shall we do with the ark of the God of Israel?"

They answered, "Let the ark of the God of Israel be carried over to Gath." They carried the ark of the God of Israel there. It was so, that after they had carried it there, YHWH's hand was against the city with a very great confusion; and he struck the men of the city, both small and great so that tumors broke out on them. So they sent God's ark to Ekron.

As God's ark came to Ekron, the Ekronites cried out, saying, "They have brought the ark of the God of Israel here to us, to kill us and our people." They sent therefore and gathered together all the lords of the Philistines, and they said, "Send the ark of the God of Israel away, and let it go again to its own place, that it not kill us and our people." For there was a deadly confusion throughout all the city. The hand of God was very heavy there. The men who didn't die were struck with the tumors; and the cry of the city went up to heaven.

....

YHWH's ark was in the country of the Philistines seven months. The Philistines called for the priests and the diviners, saying, "What shall we do with YHWH's ark? Show us how we should send it to its place."

They said, "If you send away the ark of the God of Israel, don't send it empty; but by all means return a trespass offering to him. Then you will be healed, and it will be known to you why his hand is not removed from you."

Then they said, "What should the trespass offering be which we shall return to him?"

They said, "Five golden tumors, and five golden mice, for the number of the lords of the Philistines; for one plague was on you all, and on your lords. Therefore you shall make images of your tumors, and images of your mice that mar the land; and you shall give glory to the God of Israel. Perhaps he will release his hand from you, from your gods, and from your land. Why then do you harden your hearts, as the Egyptians and Pharaoh hardened their hearts? When he had worked wonderfully among them, didn't they let the people go, and they departed?

"Now therefore take and prepare yourselves a new cart, and two milk cows, on which there has come no yoke; and tie the cows to the cart, and bring their calves home from them; and take YHWH's ark, and lay it on the cart. Put the jewels of gold, which you return him for a trespass offering, in a coffer by its side; and send it away, that it may go. Behold; if it goes up by the way of its own border to Beth Shemesh, then he has done us this great evil; but if not, then we shall know that it is not his hand that struck us. It was a chance that happened to us."

The men did so, and took two milk cows, and tied them to the cart, and shut up their calves at home. They put YHWH's ark on the cart, and the coffer with the golden mice and the images of their tumors. The cows took the straight way by the way to Beth Shemesh. They went along the highway, lowing as they went, and didn't turn away to the right hand or to the left; and the lords of the Philistines went after them to the border of Beth Shemesh. The people of Beth Shemesh were reaping their wheat harvest in the valley; and they lifted up their eyes, and saw the ark, and rejoiced to see it. The cart came into the field of Joshua of Beth Shemesh, and stood there, where there was a great stone. Then they split the wood of the cart, and offered up the cows for a burnt offering to YHWH. The Levites took down YHWH's ark, and the box that was with it, in which the jewels of gold were, and put them on the great stone; and the men of Beth Shemesh offered burnt offerings and sacrificed sacrifices the same day to YHWH. When the five lords of the Philistines had seen it, they returned to Ekron the same day. These are the golden tumors which the Philistines returned for a trespass offering to YHWH: for Ashdod one, for Gaza one, for Ashkelon one, for Gath one, for Ekron one; and the golden mice, according to the number of all the cities of the Philistines belonging to the five lords, both of fortified cities and of country villages, even to the great stone, on which they set down YHWH's ark. That stone remains to this day in the field of Joshua of Beth Shemesh. He struck of the men of Beth Shemesh, because they had looked into YHWH's ark, he struck fifty thousand seventy of the men. Then the people mourned, because YHWH had struck the people with a great slaughter. The men of Beth Shemesh said, "Who is able to stand before YHWH, this holy God? To whom shall he go up from us?"

They sent messengers to the inhabitants of Kiriath Jearim, saying, "The Philistines have brought back YHWH's ark. Come down, and bring it up to yourselves."

....

The men of Kiriath Jearim came, and took YHWH's ark, and brought it into Abinadab's house on the hill, and consecrated Eleazar his son to keep YHWH's ark. From the day that the ark stayed in Kiriath Jearim, the time was long; for it was twenty years; and all the house of Israel lamented after YHWH. Samuel spoke to all the house of Israel, saying, "If you are returning to YHWH with all your heart, then put away the foreign gods and the Ashtaroth from among you, and direct your hearts to YHWH, and serve him only; and he will deliver you out of the hand of the Philistines." Then the children of Israel removed the Baals and the Ashtaroth, and served YHWH only. Samuel said, "Gather all Israel to Mizpah, and I will pray to YHWH for you." They gathered together to Mizpah, and drew water, and poured it out before YHWH, and fasted on that day, and said there, "We have sinned against YHWH." Samuel judged the children of Israel in Mizpah. When the Philistines heard that the children of Israel were gathered together at Mizpah, the lords of the Philistines went up against Israel. When the children of Israel heard it, they were afraid of the Philistines. The children of Israel said to Samuel, "Don't stop crying to YHWH our God for us, that he will save us out of the hand of the Philistines." Samuel took a suckling lamb, and offered it for a whole burnt offering to YHWH. Samuel cried to YHWH for Israel; and YHWH answered him. As Samuel was offering up the burnt offering, the Philistines came near to battle against Israel; but YHWH thundered with a great thunder on that day on the Philistines, and confused them; and they were struck down before Israel. The men of Israel went out of Mizpah, and pursued the Philistines, and struck them, until they came under Beth Kar.

Then Samuel took a stone, and set it between Mizpah and Shen, and called its name Ebenezer, saying, "YHWH helped us until now." So the Philistines were subdued, and they stopped coming within the border of Israel. YHWH's hand was against the Philistines all the days of Samuel.

The cities which the Philistines had taken from Israel were restored to Israel, from Ekron even to Gath; and Israel recovered its border out of the hand of the Philistines. There was peace between Israel and the Amorites.

Samuel judged Israel all the days of his life. He went from year to year in a circuit to Bethel, Gilgal, and Mizpah; and he judged Israel in all those places. His return was to Ramah, for his house was there; and he judged Israel there; and he built an altar to YHWH there.

....

When Samuel was old, he made his sons judges over Israel. Now the name of his firstborn was Joel; and the name of his second, Abijah. They were judges in Beersheba. His sons didn't walk in his ways, but turned away after dishonest gain, took bribes, and perverted justice. Then all the elders of Israel gathered themselves together and came to Samuel to Ramah. They said to him, "Behold, you are old, and your sons don't walk in your ways. Now make us a king to judge us like all the nations." But the thing displeased Samuel, when they said, "Give us a king to judge us."

Samuel prayed to YHWH. YHWH said to Samuel, "Listen to the voice of the people in all that they tell you; for they have not rejected you, but they have rejected me as the king over them. According to all the works which they have done since the day that I brought them up out of Egypt even to this day, in that they have forsaken me, and served other gods, so they also do to you. Now therefore listen to their voice. However you shall protest solemnly to them, and shall show them the way of the king who will reign over them."

Samuel told all YHWH's words to the people who asked him for a king. He said, "This will be the way of the king who shall reign over you: he will take your sons, and appoint them as his servants, for his chariots, and to be his horsemen; and they will run before his chariots. He will appoint them to him for captains of thousands, and captains of fifties; and he will assign some to plow his ground, and to reap his harvest, and to make his instruments of war, and the instruments of his chariots. He will take your daughters to be perfumers, to be cooks, and to be bakers. He will take your fields, your vineyards, and your olive groves, even their best, and give them to his servants. He will take one tenth of your seed, and of your vineyards, and give it to his officers, and to his servants. He will take your male servants, your female servants, your best young men, and your donkeys, and assign them to his own work. He will take one tenth of your flocks; and you will be his servants. You will cry out in that day because of your king whom you will have chosen for yourselves; and YHWH will not answer you in that day."

But the people refused to listen to the voice of Samuel; and they said, "No; but we will have a king over us, that we also may be like all the nations, and that our king may judge us, and go out before us, and fight our battles."

Samuel heard all the words of the people, and he rehearsed them in the ears of YHWH. YHWH said to Samuel, "Listen to their voice, and make them a king."

Samuel said to the men of Israel, "Everyone go to your own city."

....

Now there was a man of Benjamin, whose name was Kish, the son of Abiel, the son of Zeror, the son of Becorath, the son of Aphiah, the son of a Benjamite, a mighty man of valor. He had a son, whose name was Saul, an impressive young man; and there was not among the children of Israel a better person than he. From his shoulders and upward he was taller than any of the people.

The donkeys of Kish, Saul's father, were lost. Kish said to Saul his son, "Now take one of the servants with you, and arise, go look for the donkeys." He passed through the hill country of Ephraim, and passed through the land of Shalishah, but they didn't find them. Then they passed through the land of Shaalim, and they weren't there. Then he passed through the land of the Benjamites, but they didn't find them.

When they had come to the land of Zuph, Saul said to his servant who was with him, "Come! Let's return, lest my father stop caring about the donkeys, and be anxious for us."

The servant said to him, "Behold now, there is a man of God in this city, and he is a man who is held in honor. All that he says surely happens. Now let's go there. Perhaps he can tell us which way to go."

Then Saul said to his servant, "But, behold, if we go, what should we bring the man? For the bread is spent in our sacks, and there is not a present to bring to the man of God. What do we have?"

The servant answered Saul again, and said, "Behold, I have in my hand the fourth part of a shekel of silver. I will give that to the man of God, to tell us our way." (In earlier times in Israel, when a man went to inquire of God, he said, "Come! Let's go to the seer;" for he who is now called a prophet was before called a seer.)

Then Saul said to his servant, "Well said. Come! Let's go." So they went to the city where the man of God was. As they went up the ascent to the city, they found young maidens going out to draw water, and said to them, "Is the seer here?"

They answered them, and said, "He is. Behold, he is before you. Hurry now, for he has come today into the city; for the people have a sacrifice today in the high place. As soon as you have come into the city, you will immediately find him, before he goes up to the high place to eat; for the people will not eat until he comes, because he blesses the sacrifice. Afterwards those who are invited eat. Now therefore go up; for at this time you will find him."

They went up to the city. As they came within the city, behold, Samuel came out toward them, to go up to the high place.

Now YHWH had revealed to Samuel a day before Saul came, saying, "Tomorrow about this time I will send you a man out of the land of Benjamin, and you shall anoint him to be prince over my people Israel. He will save my people out of the hand of the Philistines; for I have looked upon my people, because their cry has come to me."

When Samuel saw Saul, YHWH said to him, "Behold, the man of whom I spoke to you! He will have authority over my people."

Then Saul approached Samuel in the gateway, and said, "Please tell me where the seer's house is."

Samuel answered Saul, and said, "I am the seer. Go up before me to the high place, for you are to eat with me today. In the morning I will let you go, and will tell you all that is in your heart. As for your donkeys who were lost three days ago, don't set your mind on them; for they have been found. For whom is all that is desirable in Israel? Is it not for you, and for all your father's house?"

Saul answered, "Am I not a Benjamite, of the smallest of the tribes of Israel? And my family the least of all the families of the tribe of Benjamin? Why then do you speak to me like this?"

Samuel took Saul and his servant, and brought them into the guest room, and made them sit in the best place among those who were invited, who were about thirty persons. Samuel said to the cook, "Bring the portion which I gave you, of which I said to you, 'Set it aside.'" The cook took up the thigh, and that which was on it, and set it before Saul. Samuel said, "Behold, that which has been reserved! Set it before yourself and eat; because it has been kept for you for the appointed time, for I said, 'I have invited the people.'" So Saul ate with Samuel that day.

When they had come down from the high place into the city,

he talked with Saul on the housetop. They arose early; and about daybreak, Samuel called to Saul on the housetop, saying, "Get up, that I may send you away." Saul arose, and they both went outside, he and Samuel, together. As they were going down at the end of the city, Samuel said to Saul, "Tell the servant to go on ahead of us." He went ahead, then Samuel said, "But stand still first, that I may cause you to hear God's message."

....

Then Samuel took the vial of oil, and poured it on his head, and kissed him, and said, "Hasn't YHWH anointed you to be prince over his inheritance? When you have departed from me today, then you will find two men by Rachel's tomb, on the border of Benjamin at Zelzah. They will tell you, 'The donkeys which you went to look for have been found; and behold, your father has stopped caring about the donkeys, and is anxious for you, saying, "What shall I do for my son?"'

"Then you will go on forward from there, and you will come to the oak of Tabor. Three men will meet you there going up to God to Bethel, one carrying three young goats, and another carrying three loaves of bread, and another carrying a container of wine. They will greet you, and give you two loaves of bread, which you shall receive from their hand.

"After that you will come to the hill of God, where the garrison of the Philistines is; and it will happen, when you have come there to the city, that you will meet a band of prophets coming down from the high place with a lute, a tambourine, a pipe, and a harp before them; and they will be prophesying. Then YHWH's Spirit will come mightily on you, and you will prophesy with them, and will be turned into another man. Let it be, when these signs have come to you, that you do what is appropriate for the occasion; for God is with you.

"Go down ahead of me to Gilgal; and behold, I will come down to you, to offer burnt offerings, and to sacrifice sacrifices of peace offerings. Wait seven days, until I come to you, and show you what you are to do." It was so, that when he had turned his back to go from Samuel, God gave him another heart; and all those signs happened that day. When they came there to the hill, behold, a band of prophets met him; and the Spirit of God came mightily on him, and he prophesied among them. When all who knew him before saw that, behold, he prophesied with the prophets, then the people said to one another, "What is this that has come to the son of Kish? Is Saul also among the prophets?"

One of the same place answered, "Who is their father?" Therefore it became a proverb, "Is Saul also among the prophets?" When he had finished prophesying, he came to the high place.

Saul's uncle said to him and to his servant, "Where did you go?"

He said, "To seek the donkeys. When we saw that they were not found, we came to Samuel."

Saul's uncle said, "Please tell me what Samuel said to you."

Saul said to his uncle, "He told us plainly that the donkeys were found." But concerning the matter of the kingdom, of which Samuel spoke, he didn't tell him.

Samuel called the people together to YHWH to Mizpah; and he said to the children of Israel, "YHWH, the God of Israel, says 'I brought Israel up out of Egypt, and I delivered you out of the hand of the Egyptians, and out of the hand of all the kingdoms that oppressed you.' But you have today rejected your God, who himself saves you out of all your calamities and your distresses; and you have said to him, 'No! Set a king over us.' Now therefore present yourselves before YHWH by your tribes, and by your thousands."

So Samuel brought all the tribes of Israel near, and the tribe of Benjamin was chosen. He brought the tribe of Benjamin near by their families; and the family of the Matrites was chosen. Then Saul the son of Kish was chosen; but when they looked for him, he could not be found. Therefore they asked of YHWH further, "Is there yet a man to come here?"

YHWH answered, "Behold, he has hidden himself among the baggage."

They ran and got him there. When he stood among the people, he was higher than any of the people from his shoulders and upward. Samuel said to all the people, "Do you see him whom YHWH has chosen, that there is no one like him among all the people?"

All the people shouted, and said, "Long live the king!"

Then Samuel told the people the regulations of the kingdom, and wrote it in a book, and laid it up before YHWH. Samuel sent all the people away, every man to his house. Saul also went to his house to Gibeah; and the army went with him, whose hearts God had touched. But certain worthless fellows said, "How could this man save us?" They despised him, and brought him no present. But he held his peace.

....

Then Nahash the Ammonite came up, and encamped against Jabesh Gilead: and all the men of Jabesh said to Nahash, "Make a covenant with us, and we will serve you." Nahash the Ammonite said to them, "On this condition I will make it with you, that all your right eyes be gouged out. I will make this dishonor all Israel."

The elders of Jabesh said to him, "Give us seven days, that we may send messengers to all the borders of Israel; and then, if there is no one to save us, we will come out to you." Then the messengers came to Gibeah of Saul, and spoke these words in the ears of the people, then all the people lifted up their voice, and wept.

Behold, Saul came following the oxen out of the field; and Saul said, "What ails the people that they weep?" They told him the words of the men of Jabesh. God's Spirit came mightily on Saul when he heard those words, and his anger burned hot. He took a yoke of oxen, and cut them in pieces, and sent them throughout all the borders of Israel by the hand of messengers, saying, "Whoever doesn't come out after Saul and after Samuel, so shall it be done to his oxen." The dread of YHWH fell on the people, and they came out as one man. He counted them in Bezek; and the children of Israel were three hundred thousand, and the men of Judah thirty thousand. They said to the messengers who came, "Tell the men of Jabesh Gilead, 'Tomorrow, by the time the sun is hot, you will be rescued.'" The messengers came and told the men of Jabesh; and they were glad. Therefore the men of Jabesh said, "Tomorrow we will come out to you, and you shall do with us all that seems good to you." On the next day, Saul put the people in three companies; and they came into the middle of the camp in the morning watch, and struck the Ammonites until the heat of the day. Those who remained were scattered, so that no two of them were left together. The people said to Samuel, "Who is he who said, 'Shall Saul reign over us?' Bring those men, that we may put them to death!"

Saul said, "No man shall be put to death today; for today YHWH has rescued Israel." Then Samuel said to the people, "Come! Let's go to Gilgal, and renew the kingdom there." All the people went to Gilgal; and there they made Saul king before YHWH in Gilgal. There they offered sacrifices of peace offerings before YHWH; and there Saul and all the men of Israel rejoiced greatly.

Samuel said to all Israel, "Behold, I have listened to your voice in all that you said to me, and have made a king over you. Now, behold, the king walks before you. I am old and gray-headed. Behold, my sons are with you. I have walked before you from my youth to this day. Here I am. Witness against me before YHWH, and before his anointed. Whose ox have I taken? Whose donkey have I taken? Whom have I defrauded? Whom have I oppressed? Of whose hand have I taken a bribe to make me blind my eyes? I will restore it to you."

They said, "You have not defrauded us, nor oppressed us, neither have you taken anything from anyone's hand."

He said to them, "YHWH is witness against you, and his anointed is witness today, that you have not found anything in my hand."

They said, "He is witness." Samuel said to the people, "It is YHWH who appointed Moses and Aaron, and that brought your fathers up out of the land of Egypt. Now therefore stand still, that I may plead with you before YHWH concerning all the righteous acts of YHWH, which he did to you and to your fathers.

"When Jacob had come into Egypt, and your fathers cried to YHWH, then YHWH sent Moses and Aaron, who brought your fathers out of Egypt, and made them to dwell in this place.

"But they forgot YHWH their God; and he sold them into the hand of Sisera, captain of the army of Hazor, and into the hand of the Philistines, and into the hand of the king of Moab; and they fought against them. They cried to YHWH, and said, 'We have sinned, because we have forsaken YHWH, and have served the Baals and the Ashtaroth: but now deliver us out of the hand of our enemies, and we will serve you.' YHWH sent Jerubbaal, Bedan, Jephthah, and Samuel, and delivered you out of the hand of your enemies on every side; and you lived in safety.

"When you saw that Nahash the king of the children of Ammon came against you, you said to me, 'No, but a king shall reign over us;' when YHWH your God was your king. Now therefore see the king whom you have chosen, and whom you have asked for. Behold, YHWH has set a king over you. If you will fear YHWH, and serve him, and listen to his voice, and not rebel against the commandment of YHWH, then both you and also the king who reigns over you are followers of YHWH your God. But if you will not listen to YHWH's voice, but rebel against the commandment of YHWH, then YHWH's hand will be against you, as it was against your fathers.

"Now therefore stand still and see this great thing, which YHWH will do before your eyes. Isn't it wheat harvest today? I will call to YHWH, that he may send thunder and rain; and you will know and see that your wickedness is great, which you have done in YHWH's sight, in asking for a king."

So Samuel called to YHWH; and YHWH sent thunder and rain that day. Then all the people greatly feared YHWH and Samuel.

All the people said to Samuel, "Pray for your servants to YHWH your God, that we not die; for we have added to all our sins this evil, to ask for a king."

Samuel said to the people, "Don't be afraid. You have indeed done all this evil; yet don't turn away from following YHWH, but serve YHWH with all your heart. Don't turn away to go after vain things which can't profit or deliver, for they are vain. For YHWH will not forsake his people for his great name's sake, because it has pleased YHWH to make you a people for himself. Moreover as for me, far be it from me that I should sin against YHWH in ceasing to pray for you: but I will instruct you in the good and the right way. Only fear YHWH, and serve him in truth with all your heart; for consider what great things he has done for you. But if you keep doing evil, you will be consumed, both you and your king."

....

Saul was thirty years old when he became king, and he reigned over Israel forty-two years. Saul chose for himself three thousand men of Israel, of which two thousand were with Saul in Michmash and in the Mount of Bethel, and one thousand were with Jonathan in Gibeah of Benjamin. He sent the rest of the people to their own tents. Jonathan struck the garrison of the Philistines that was in Geba, and the Philistines heard of it. Saul blew the trumpet throughout all the land, saying, "Let the Hebrews hear!" All Israel heard that Saul had struck the garrison of the Philistines, and also that Israel was considered an abomination to the Philistines. The people were gathered together after Saul to Gilgal. The Philistines assembled themselves together to fight with Israel, thirty thousand chariots, and six thousand horsemen, and people as the sand which is on the seashore in multitude. They came up and encamped in Michmash, eastward of Beth Aven. When the men of Israel saw that they were in trouble (for the people were distressed), then the people hid themselves in caves, in thickets, in rocks, in tombs, and in pits. Now some of the Hebrews had gone over the Jordan to the land of Gad and Gilead; but as for Saul, he was yet in Gilgal, and all the people followed him trembling. He stayed seven days, according to the time set by Samuel; but Samuel didn't come to Gilgal, and the people were scattering from him. Saul said, "Bring the burnt offering to me here, and the peace offerings." He offered the burnt offering.

It came to pass that as soon as he had finished offering the burnt offering, behold, Samuel came; and Saul went out to meet him, that he might greet him. Samuel said, "What have you done?"

Saul said, "Because I saw that the people were scattered from me, and that you didn't come within the days appointed, and that the Philistines assembled themselves together at Michmash; therefore I said, 'Now the Philistines will come down on me to Gilgal, and I haven't entreated the favor of YHWH.' I forced myself therefore, and offered the burnt offering."

Samuel said to Saul, "You have done foolishly. You have not kept the commandment of YHWH your God, which he commanded you; for now YHWH would have established your kingdom on Israel forever. But now your kingdom will not continue. YHWH has sought for himself a man after his own heart, and YHWH has appointed him to be prince over his people, because you have not kept that which YHWH commanded you."

Samuel arose, and went from Gilgal to Gibeah of Benjamin. Saul counted the people who were present with him, about six hundred men. Saul, and Jonathan his son, and the people who were present with them, stayed in Geba of Benjamin; but the Philistines encamped in Michmash. The raiders came out of the camp of the Philistines in three companies: one company turned to the way that leads to Ophrah, to the land of Shual; another company turned the way to Beth Horon; and another company turned the way of the border that looks down on the valley of Zeboim toward the wilderness. Now there was no blacksmith found throughout all the land of Israel; for the Philistines said, "Lest the Hebrews make themselves swords or spears"; but all the Israelites went down to the Philistines, each man to sharpen his own plowshare, mattock, ax, and sickle. The price was one payim each to sharpen mattocks, plowshares, pitchforks, axes, and goads. So it came to pass in the day of battle, that neither sword nor spear was found in the hand of any of the people who were with

Saul and Jonathan; but Saul and Jonathan his son had them. The garrison of the Philistines went out to the pass of Michmash.

....

Now it fell on a day, that Jonathan the son of Saul said to the young man who bore his armor, "Come! Let's go over to the Philistines' garrison that is on the other side." But he didn't tell his father. Saul stayed in the uttermost part of Gibeah under the pomegranate tree which is in Migron: and the people who were with him were about six hundred men; including Ahijah, the son of Ahitub, Ichabod's brother, the son of Phinehas, the son of Eli, the priest of YHWH in Shiloh, wearing an ephod. The people didn't know that Jonathan was gone. Between the passes, by which Jonathan sought to go over to the Philistines' garrison, there was a rocky crag on the one side, and a rocky crag on the other side: and the name of the one was Bozez, and the name of the other Seneh. The one crag rose up on the north in front of Michmash, and the other on the south in front of Geba. Jonathan said to the young man who bore his armor, "Come! Let's go over to the garrison of these uncircumcised. It may be that YHWH will work for us; for there is no restraint on YHWH to save by many or by few." His armor bearer said to him, "Do all that is in your heart. Turn and, behold, I am with you according to your heart." Then Jonathan said, "Behold, we will pass over to the men, and we will reveal ourselves to them. If they say this to us, 'Wait until we come to you!' then we will stand still in our place, and will not go up to them. But if they say this, 'Come up to us!' then we will go up; for YHWH has delivered them into our hand. This shall be the sign to us."

Both of them revealed themselves to the garrison of the Philistines: and the Philistines said, "Behold, the Hebrews are coming out of the holes where they had hidden themselves!" The men of the garrison answered Jonathan and his armor bearer, and said, "Come up to us, and we will show you something!"

Jonathan said to his armor bearer, "Come up after me; for YHWH has delivered them into the hand of Israel." Jonathan climbed up on his hands and on his feet, and his armor bearer after him: and they fell before Jonathan; and his armor bearer killed them after him. That first slaughter, which Jonathan and his armor bearer made, was about twenty men, within as it were half a furrow's length in an acre of land. There was a trembling in the camp, in the field, and among all the people; the garrison, and the raiders, also trembled; and the earth quaked, so there was an exceedingly great trembling. The watchmen of Saul in Gibeah of Benjamin looked; and behold, the multitude melted away and scattered. Then Saul said to the people who were with him, "Count now, and see who is missing from us." When they had counted, behold, Jonathan and his armor bearer were not there.

Saul said to Ahijah, "Bring God's ark here." For God's ark was with the children of Israel at that time. While Saul talked to the priest, the tumult that was in the camp of the Philistines went on and increased; and Saul said to the priest, "Withdraw your hand!"

Saul and all the people who were with him were gathered together, and came to the battle; and behold, they were all striking each other with their swords in very great confusion. Now the Hebrews who were with the Philistines before, and who went up with them into the camp, from all around, even they also turned to be with the Israelites who were with Saul and Jonathan. Likewise all the men of Israel who had hidden themselves in the hill country of Ephraim, when they heard that the Philistines fled, even they also followed hard after them in the battle. So YHWH saved Israel that day; and the battle passed over by Beth Aven.

The men of Israel were distressed that day; for Saul had adjured the people, saying, "Cursed is the man who eats any food until it is evening, and I am avenged of my enemies." So none of the people tasted food.

All the people came into the forest; and there was honey on the ground. When the people had come to the forest, behold, honey was dripping, but no one put his hand to his mouth; for the people feared the oath. But Jonathan didn't hear when his father commanded the people with the oath. Therefore he put out the end of the rod that was in his hand, and dipped it in the honeycomb, and put his hand to his mouth; and his eyes brightened. Then one of the people answered, and said, "Your father directly commanded the people with an oath, saying, 'Cursed is the man who eats food today.'" So the people were faint.

Then Jonathan said, "My father has troubled the land. Please look how my eyes have brightened, because I tasted a little of this honey. How much more, if perhaps the people had eaten freely today of the plunder of their enemies which they found? For now there has been no great slaughter among the Philistines." They struck the Philistines that day from Michmash to Aijalon. The people were very faint; and the people pounced on the plunder, and took sheep, cattle, and calves, and killed them on the ground; and the people ate them with the blood. Then they told Saul, saying, "Behold, the people are sinning against YHWH, in that they eat meat with the blood."

He said, "You have dealt treacherously. Roll a large stone to me today!" Saul said, "Disperse yourselves among the people, and tell them, 'Every man bring me here his ox, and every man his sheep, and kill them here, and eat; and don't sin against YHWH in eating meat with the blood.'" All the people brought every man his ox with him that night, and killed them there.

Saul built an altar to YHWH. This was the first altar that he built to YHWH. Saul said, "Let's go down after the Philistines by night, and take plunder among them until the morning light, and let's not leave a man of them."

They said, "Do whatever seems good to you."

Then the priest said, "Let's draw near here to God."

Saul asked counsel of God, "Shall I go down after the Philistines? Will you deliver them into the hand of Israel?" But he didn't answer him that day. Saul said, "Draw near here, all you chiefs of the people; and know and see in which this sin has been today. For, as YHWH lives, who saves Israel, though it is in Jonathan my son, he shall surely die." But there was not a man among all the people who answered him. Then he said to all Israel, "You be on one side, and I and Jonathan my son will be on the other side."

The people said to Saul, "Do what seems good to you."

Therefore Saul said to YHWH, the God of Israel, "Show the right." Jonathan and Saul were chosen, but the people escaped.

Saul said, "Cast lots between me and Jonathan my son."

Jonathan was selected.

Then Saul said to Jonathan, "Tell me what you have done!"

Jonathan told him, and said, "I certainly did taste a little honey with the end of the rod that was in my hand; and behold, I must die."

Saul said, "God do so and more also; for you shall surely die, Jonathan."

The people said to Saul, "Shall Jonathan die, who has worked this great salvation in Israel? Far from it! As YHWH lives, there shall not one hair of his head fall to the ground; for he has worked with God today!" So the people rescued Jonathan, that he didn't die. Then Saul went up from following the Philistines; and the Philistines went to their own place.

Now when Saul had taken the kingdom over Israel, he fought against all his enemies on every side, against Moab, and against the children of Ammon, and against Edom, and against the kings of Zobah, and against the Philistines. Wherever he turned himself, he defeated them. He did valiantly, and struck the Amalekites, and delivered Israel out of the hands of those who plundered them. Now the sons of Saul were Jonathan, Ishvi, and Malchishua; and the names of his two daughters were these: the name of the firstborn Merab, and the name of the younger Michal. The name of Saul's wife was Ahinoam the daughter of Ahimaaz. The name of the captain of his army was Abner the son of Ner, Saul's uncle. Kish was the father of Saul; and Ner the father of Abner was the son of Abiel. There was severe war against the Philistines all the days of Saul; and when Saul saw any mighty man, or any valiant man, he took him into his service.

....

Samuel said to Saul, "YHWH sent me to anoint you to be king over his people, over Israel. Now therefore listen to the voice of YHWH's words. YHWH of Armies says, 'I remember what Amalek did to Israel, how he set himself against him on the way, when he came up out of Egypt. Now go and strike Amalek, and utterly destroy all that they have, and don't spare them; but kill both man and woman, infant and nursing baby, ox and sheep, camel and donkey.'"

Saul summoned the people, and counted them in Telaim, two hundred thousand footmen, and ten thousand men of Judah. Saul came to the city of Amalek, and set an ambush in the valley. Saul said to the Kenites, "Go, depart, go down from among the Amalekites, lest I destroy you with them; for you showed kindness to all the children of Israel, when they came up out of Egypt." So the Kenites departed from among the Amalekites.

Saul struck the Amalekites, from Havilah as you go to Shur, that is before Egypt. He took Agag the king of the Amalekites alive, and utterly destroyed all the people with the edge of the sword. But Saul and the people spared Agag, and the best of the sheep, of the cattle, and of the fat calves, and the lambs, and all that was good, and were not willing to utterly destroy them; but everything that was vile and refuse, that they destroyed utterly. Then YHWH's word came to Samuel, saying, "It grieves me that I have set up Saul to be king; for he has turned back from following me, and has not performed my commandments." Samuel was angry; and he cried to YHWH all night.

Samuel rose early to meet Saul in the morning; and Samuel was told, saying, "Saul came to Carmel, and behold, he set up a monument for himself, and turned, and passed on, and went down to Gilgal."

Samuel came to Saul; and Saul said to him, "You are blessed by YHWH! I have performed the commandment of YHWH."

Samuel said, "Then what does this bleating of the sheep in my ears, and the lowing of the cattle which I hear mean?"

Saul said, "They have brought them from the Amalekites; for the people spared the best of the sheep and of the cattle, to sacrifice to YHWH your God. We have utterly destroyed the rest."

Then Samuel said to Saul, "Stay, and I will tell you what YHWH said to me last night."

He said to him, "Say on."

Samuel said, "Though you were little in your own sight, weren't you made the head of the tribes of Israel? YHWH anointed you king over Israel; and YHWH sent you on a journey, and said, 'Go, and utterly destroy the sinners the Amalekites, and fight against them until they are consumed.' Why then didn't you obey YHWH's voice, but took the plunder, and did that which was evil in YHWH's sight?"

Saul said to Samuel, "But I have obeyed YHWH's voice, and have gone the way which YHWH sent me, and have brought Agag the king of Amalek, and have utterly destroyed the Amalekites. But the people took of the plunder, sheep and cattle, the chief of the devoted things, to sacrifice to YHWH your God in Gilgal."

Samuel said, "Has YHWH as great delight in burnt offerings and sacrifices, as in obeying YHWH's voice? Behold, to obey is better than sacrifice, and to listen than the fat of rams. For rebellion is as the sin of witchcraft, and stubbornness is as idolatry and teraphim. Because you have rejected YHWH's word, he has also rejected you from being king."

Saul said to Samuel, "I have sinned; for I have transgressed the commandment of YHWH, and your words, because I feared the people, and obeyed their voice. Now therefore, please pardon my sin, and turn again with me, that I may worship YHWH."

Samuel said to Saul, "I will not return with you; for you have rejected YHWH's word, and YHWH has rejected you from being king over Israel." As Samuel turned around to go away, Saul grabbed the skirt of his robe, and it tore. Samuel said to him, "YHWH has torn the kingdom of Israel from you today, and has given it to a neighbor of yours who is better than you. Also the Strength of Israel will not lie nor repent; for he is not a man, that he should repent."

Then he said, "I have sinned; yet please honor me now before the elders of my people, and before Israel, and come back with me, that I may worship YHWH your God."

So Samuel went back with Saul; and Saul worshiped YHWH. Then Samuel said, "Bring Agag the king of the Amalekites here to me!"

Agag came to him cheerfully. Agag said, "Surely the bitterness of death is past."

Samuel said, "As your sword has made women childless, so your mother will be childless among women!" Then Samuel cut Agag in pieces before YHWH in Gilgal.

Then Samuel went to Ramah; and Saul went up to his house to Gibeah of Saul. Samuel came no more to see Saul until the day of his death; for Samuel mourned for Saul: and YHWH grieved that he had made Saul king over Israel.

....

YHWH said to Samuel, "How long will you mourn for Saul, since I have rejected him from being king over Israel? Fill your horn with oil, and go. I will send you to Jesse the Bethlehemite; for I have provided a king for myself among his sons."

Samuel said, "How can I go? If Saul hears it, he will kill me."

YHWH said, "Take a heifer with you, and say, I have come to sacrifice to YHWH. Call Jesse to the sacrifice, and I will show you what you shall do. You shall anoint to me him whom I name to you."

Samuel did that which YHWH spoke, and came to Bethlehem. The elders of the city came to meet him trembling, and said, "Do you come peaceably?"

He said, "Peaceably; I have come to sacrifice to YHWH. Sanctify yourselves, and come with me to the sacrifice." He sanctified Jesse and his sons, and called them to the sacrifice. When they had come, he looked at Eliab, and said, "Surely YHWH's anointed is before him."

But YHWH said to Samuel, "Don't look on his face, or on the height of his stature, because I have rejected him; for I don't see as man sees. For man looks at the outward appearance, but YHWH looks at the heart." Then Jesse called Abinadab, and made him pass before Samuel. He said, "YHWH has not chosen this one, either." Then Jesse made Shammah to pass by. He said, "YHWH has not chosen this one, either." Jesse made seven of his sons to pass before Samuel. Samuel said to Jesse, "YHWH has not chosen these." Samuel said to Jesse, "Are all your children here?"

He said, "There remains yet the youngest. Behold, he is keeping the sheep."

Samuel said to Jesse, "Send and get him, for we will not sit down until he comes here."

He sent, and brought him in. Now he was ruddy, with a handsome face and good appearance. YHWH said, "Arise! Anoint him, for this is he."

Then Samuel took the horn of oil, and anointed him in the middle of his brothers. Then YHWH's Spirit came mightily on David from that day forward. So Samuel rose up and went to Ramah. Now YHWH's Spirit departed from Saul, and an evil spirit from YHWH troubled him. Saul's servants said to him, "See now, an evil spirit from God troubles you. Let our lord now command your servants who are in front of you to seek out a man who is a skillful player on the harp. Then when the evil spirit from God is on you, he will play with his hand, and you will be well."

Saul said to his servants, "Provide me now a man who can play well, and bring him to me."

Then one of the young men answered, and said, "Behold, I have seen a son of Jesse the Bethlehemite who is skillful in playing, a mighty man of valor, a man of war, prudent in speech, and a handsome person; and YHWH is with him."

Therefore Saul sent messengers to Jesse, and said, "Send me David your son, who is with the sheep."

Jesse took a donkey loaded with bread, and a container of wine, and a young goat, and sent them by David his son to Saul. David came to Saul, and stood before him. He loved him greatly; and he became his armor bearer. Saul sent to Jesse, saying, "Please let David stand before me; for he has found favor in my sight." When the spirit from God was on Saul, David took the harp, and played with his hand; so Saul was refreshed, and was well, and the evil spirit departed from him.

....

Now the Philistines gathered together their armies to battle; and they were gathered together at Socoh, which belongs to Judah, and encamped between Socoh and Azekah, in Ephesdammim. Saul and the men of Israel were gathered together, and encamped in the valley of Elah, and set the battle in array against the Philistines. The Philistines stood on the mountain on the one side, and Israel stood on the mountain on the other side: and there was a valley between them. A champion out of the camp of the Philistines named Goliath, of Gath, whose height was six cubits and a span went out. He had a helmet of bronze on his head, and he wore a coat of mail; and the weight of the coat was five thousand shekels of bronze. He had bronze shin armor on his legs, and a bronze javelin between his shoulders. The staff of his spear was like a weaver's beam; and his spear's head weighed six hundred shekels of iron. His shield bearer went before him. He stood and cried to the armies of Israel, and said to them, "Why have you come out to set your battle in array? Am I not a Philistine, and you servants to Saul? Choose a man for yourselves, and let him come down to me. If he is able to fight with me and kill me, then will we be your servants; but if I prevail against him and kill him, then you will be our servants and serve us." The Philistine said, "I defy the armies of Israel today! Give me a man, that we may fight together!"

When Saul and all Israel heard those words of the Philistine, they were dismayed, and greatly afraid. Now David was the son of that Ephrathite of Bethlehem Judah, whose name was Jesse; and he had eight sons. The man was an elderly old man in the days of Saul. The three oldest sons of Jesse had gone after Saul to the battle: and the names of his three sons who went to the battle were Eliab the firstborn, and next to him Abinadab, and the third Shammah. David was the youngest; and the three oldest followed Saul. Now David went back and forth from Saul to feed his father's sheep at Bethlehem. The Philistine came near morning and evening, and presented himself forty days. Jesse said to David his son, "Now take for your brothers an ephah of this parched grain, and these ten loaves, and carry them quickly to the camp to your brothers; and bring these ten cheeses to the captain of their thousand, and see how your brothers are doing, and bring back news." Now Saul, and they, and all the men of Israel, were in the valley of Elah, fighting with the Philistines. David rose up early in the morning, and left the sheep with a keeper, and took and went, as Jesse had commanded him. He came to the place of the wagons, as the army which was going out to the fight shouted for the battle. Israel and the Philistines put the battle in array, army against army. David left his baggage in the hand of the keeper of the baggage, and ran to the army, and came and greeted his brothers. As he talked with them, behold, the champion, the Philistine of Gath, Goliath by name, came up out of the ranks of the Philistines, and said the same words; and David heard them. All the men of Israel, when they saw the man, fled from him, and were terrified. The men of Israel said, "Have you seen this man who has come up? He has surely come up to defy Israel. The king will give great riches to the man who kills him, and will give him his daughter, and make his father's house free in Israel."

David spoke to the men who stood by him, saying, "What shall be done to the man who kills this Philistine, and takes away the reproach from Israel? For who is this uncircumcised Philistine, that he should defy the armies of the living God?"

The people answered him in this way, saying, "So shall it be done to the man who kills him."

Eliab his oldest brother heard when he spoke to the men; and Eliab's anger burned against David, and he said, "Why have you come down? With whom have you left those few sheep in the wilderness? I know your pride, and the naughtiness of your heart; for you have come down that you might see the battle."

David said, "What have I now done? Is there not a cause?" He turned away from him toward another, and spoke like that again; and the people answered him again the same way. When the words were heard which David spoke, they rehearsed them before Saul; and he sent for him. David said to Saul, "Let no man's heart fail because of him. Your servant will go and fight with this Philistine."

Saul said to David, "You are not able to go against this Philistine to fight with him; for you are but a youth, and he a man of war from his youth."

David said to Saul, "Your servant was keeping his father's sheep; and when a lion or a bear came, and took a lamb out of the flock, I went out after him, and struck him, and rescued it out of his mouth. When he arose against me, I caught him by his beard, and struck him, and killed him. Your servant struck both the lion and the bear. This uncircumcised Philistine shall be as one of them, since he has defied the armies of the living God." David said, "YHWH who delivered me out of the paw of the lion, and out of the paw of the bear, he will deliver me out of the hand of this Philistine."

Saul said to David, "Go! YHWH will be with you." Saul dressed David with his clothing. He put a helmet of bronze on his head, and he clad him with a coat of mail. David strapped his sword on his clothing, and he tried to move; for he had not tested it. David said to Saul, "I can't go with these; for I have not tested them." Then David took them off.

He took his staff in his hand, and chose for himself five smooth stones out of the brook, and put them in the pouch of his shepherd's bag which he had. His sling was in his hand; and he came near to the Philistine. The Philistine walked and came near to David; and the man who bore the shield went before him. When the Philistine looked around, and saw David, he disdained him; for he was but a youth, and ruddy, and had a good looking face. The Philistine said to David, "Am I a dog, that you come to me with sticks?" The Philistine cursed David by his gods. The Philistine said to David, "Come to me, and I will give your flesh to the birds of the sky, and to the animals of the field."

Then David said to the Philistine, "You come to me with a sword, with a spear, and with a javelin; but I come to you in the name of YHWH of Armies, the God of the armies of Israel, whom you have defied. Today, YHWH will deliver you into my hand. I will strike you, and take your head from off you. I will give the dead bodies of the army of the Philistines today to the birds of the sky, and to the wild animals of the earth; that all the earth may know that there is a God in Israel, and that all this assembly may know that YHWH doesn't save with sword and spear; for the battle is YHWH's, and he will give you into our hand."

When the Philistine arose, and walked and came near to meet David, David hurried, and ran toward the army to meet the Philistine. David put his hand in his bag, took a stone, and slung it, and struck the Philistine in his forehead. The stone sank into his forehead, and he fell on his face to the earth. So David prevailed over the Philistine with a sling and with a stone, and struck the Philistine, and killed him; but there was no sword in the hand of David. Then David ran, stood over the Philistine, took his sword, drew it out of its sheath, killed him, and cut off his head with it. When the Philistines saw that their champion was dead, they fled. The men of Israel and of Judah arose and shouted, and pursued the Philistines as far as Gai and to the gates of Ekron. The wounded of the Philistines fell down by the way to Shaaraim, even to Gath and to Ekron. The children of Israel returned from chasing after the Philistines and they plundered their camp. David took the head of the Philistine, and brought it to Jerusalem; but he put his armor in his tent. When Saul saw David go out against the Philistine, he said to Abner, the captain of the army, "Abner, whose son is this youth?"

Abner said, "As your soul lives, O king, I can't tell."

The king said, "Inquire whose son the young man is!"

As David returned from the slaughter of the Philistine, Abner took him and brought him before Saul with the head of the Philistine in his hand. Saul said to him, "Whose son are you, you young man?"

David answered, "I am the son of your servant Jesse the Bethlehemite."

....

When he had finished speaking to Saul, the soul of Jonathan was knit with the soul of David, and Jonathan loved him as his own soul. Saul took him that day, and wouldn't let him go home to his father's house any more. Then Jonathan and David made a covenant, because he loved him as his own soul. Jonathan stripped himself of the robe that was on him, and gave it to David, and his clothing, even including his sword, his bow, and his sash. David went out wherever Saul sent him, and behaved himself wisely; and Saul set him over the men of war. It was good in the sight of all the people, and also in the sight of Saul's servants.

As they came, when David returned from the slaughter of the Philistine, the women came out of all the cities of Israel, singing and dancing, to meet king Saul, with tambourines, with joy, and with instruments of music. The women sang to one another as they played, and said,

"*Saul has slain his thousands,*
and David his ten thousands."

Saul was very angry, and this saying displeased him. He said, "They have credited David with ten thousands, and they have only credited me with thousands. What can he have more but the kingdom?" Saul watched David from that day and forward. On the next day, an evil spirit from God came mightily on Saul, and he prophesied in the middle of the house. David played with his hand, as he did day by day. Saul had his spear in his hand; and Saul threw the spear, for he said, "I will pin David to the wall!" David escaped from his presence twice. Saul was afraid of David, because YHWH was with him, and had departed from Saul. Therefore Saul removed him from his presence, and made him his captain over a thousand; and he went out and came in before the people.

David behaved himself wisely in all his ways; and YHWH was with him. When Saul saw that he behaved himself very wisely, he stood in awe of him. But all Israel and Judah loved David; for he went out and came in before them. Saul said to David, "Behold, my elder daughter Merab, I will give her to you as wife. Only be valiant for me, and fight YHWH's battles." For Saul said, "Don't let my hand be on him, but let the hand of the Philistines be on him." David said to Saul, "Who am I, and what is my life, or my father's family in Israel, that I should be son-in-law to the king?"

But at the time when Merab, Saul's daughter, should have been given to David, she was given to Adriel the Meholathite as wife. Michal, Saul's daughter, loved David; and they told Saul, and the thing pleased him. Saul said, I will give her to him, that she may be a snare to him, and that the hand of the Philistines may be against him. Therefore Saul said to David, "You shall today be my son-in-law a second time." Saul commanded his servants, "Talk with David secretly, and say, 'Behold, the king has delight in you, and all his servants love you. Now therefore be the king's son-in-law.'"

Saul's servants spoke those words in the ears of David. David said, "Does it seem to you a light thing to be the king's son-in-law, since I am a poor man, and little known?"

The servants of Saul told him, saying, "David spoke like this."

Saul said, "Tell David, 'The king desires no dowry except one hundred foreskins of the Philistines, to be avenged of the king's enemies.'" Now Saul thought he would make David fall by the hand of the Philistines. When his servants told David these words, it pleased David well to be the king's son-in-law. Before the deadline, David arose and went, he and his men, and killed two hundred men of the Philistines. Then David brought their foreskins, and they gave them in full number to the king, that he might be the king's son-in-law. Then Saul gave him Michal his daughter as wife. Saul saw and knew that YHWH was with David; and Michal, Saul's daughter, loved him. Saul was even more afraid of David; and Saul was David's enemy continually. Then the princes of the Philistines went out; and as often as they went out, David behaved himself more wisely than all the servants of Saul, so that his name was highly esteemed.

....

Saul spoke to Jonathan his son, and to all his servants, that they should kill David. But Jonathan, Saul's son, greatly delighted in David. Jonathan told David, saying, "Saul my father seeks to kill you. Now therefore, please take care of yourself in the morning, and live in a secret place, and hide yourself. I will go out and stand beside my father in the field where you are, and I will talk with my father about you; and if I see anything, I will tell you."

Jonathan spoke good of David to Saul his father, and said to him, "Don't let the king sin against his servant, against David; because he has not sinned against you, and because his works have been very good toward you; for he put his life in his hand, and struck the Philistine, and YHWH worked a great victory for all Israel. You saw it, and rejoiced. Why then will you sin against innocent blood, to kill David without a cause?"

Saul listened to the voice of Jonathan: and Saul swore, "As YHWH lives, he shall not be put to death."

Jonathan called David, and Jonathan showed him all those things. Then Jonathan brought David to Saul, and he was in his presence, as before. There was war again. David went out, and fought with the Philistines, and killed them with a great slaughter; and they fled before him.

An evil spirit from YHWH was on Saul, as he sat in his house with his spear in his hand; and David was playing with his hand. Saul sought to pin David to the wall with the spear; but he slipped away out of Saul's presence, and he stuck the spear into the wall. David fled, and escaped that night. Saul sent messengers to David's house, to watch him, and to kill him in the morning. Michal, David's wife, told him, saying, "If you don't save your life tonight, tomorrow you will be killed." So Michal let David down through the window. He went away, fled, and escaped. Michal took the teraphim, and laid it in the bed, and put a pillow of goats' hair at its head, and covered it with clothes. When Saul sent messengers to take David, she said, "He is sick."

Saul sent the messengers to see David, saying, "Bring him up to me in the bed, that I may kill him." When the messengers came in, behold, the teraphim was in the bed, with the pillow of goats' hair at its head.

Saul said to Michal, "Why have you deceived me like this and let my enemy go, so that he has escaped?"

Michal answered Saul, "He said to me, 'Let me go! Why should I kill you?'"

Now David fled and escaped, and came to Samuel at Ramah, and told him all that Saul had done to him. He and Samuel went and lived in Naioth. Saul was told, saying, "Behold, David is at Naioth in Ramah."

Saul sent messengers to seize David: and when they saw the company of the prophets prophesying, and Samuel standing as head over them, God's Spirit came on Saul's messengers, and they also prophesied. When Saul was told, he sent other messengers, and they also prophesied. Saul sent messengers again the third time, and they also prophesied. Then he also went to Ramah, and came to the great well that is in Secu: and he asked, "Where are Samuel and David?"

One said, "Behold, they are at Naioth in Ramah."

He went there to Naioth in Ramah. Then God's Spirit came on him also, and he went on, and prophesied, until he came to Naioth in Ramah. He also stripped off his clothes, and he also prophesied before Samuel, and lay down naked all that day and all that night. Therefore they say, "Is Saul also among the prophets?"

....

David fled from Naioth in Ramah, and came and said before Jonathan, "What have I done? What is my iniquity? What is my sin before your father, that he seeks my life?"

He said to him, "Far from it; you will not die. Behold, my father does nothing either great or small, but that he discloses it to me. Why would my father hide this thing from me? It is not so."

David swore moreover, and said, "Your father knows well that I have found favor in your eyes; and he says, 'Don't let Jonathan know this, lest he be grieved;' but truly as YHWH lives, and as your soul lives, there is but a step between me and death."

Then Jonathan said to David, "Whatever your soul desires, I will even do it for you."

David said to Jonathan, "Behold, tomorrow is the new moon, and I should not fail to dine with the king; but let me go, that I may hide myself in the field to the third day at evening. If your father misses me at all, then say, 'David earnestly asked leave of me that he might run to Bethlehem his city; for it is the yearly sacrifice there for all the family.' If he says, 'It is well,' your servant shall have peace; but if he is angry, then know that evil is determined by him. Therefore deal kindly with your servant; for you have brought your servant into a covenant of YHWH with you; but if there is iniquity in me, kill me yourself; for why should you bring me to your father?"

Jonathan said, "Far be it from you; for if I should at all know that evil were determined by my father to come on you, then wouldn't I tell you that?"

Then David said to Jonathan, "Who will tell me if your father answers you roughly?"

Jonathan said to David, "Come! Let's go out into the field." They both went out into the field. Jonathan said to David, "By YHWH, the God of Israel, when I have sounded my father about this time tomorrow, or the third day, behold, if there is good toward David, won't I then send to you, and disclose it to you? YHWH do so to Jonathan, and more also, should it please my father to do you evil, if I don't disclose it to you, and send you away, that you may go in peace. May YHWH be with you, as he has been with my father. You shall not only show me the loving kindness of YHWH while I still live, that I not die; but you shall also not cut off your kindness from my house forever; no, not when YHWH has cut off every one of the enemies of David from the surface of the earth." So Jonathan made a covenant with David's house, saying, "YHWH will require it at the hand of David's enemies." Jonathan caused David to swear again, for the love that he had to him; for he loved him as he loved his own soul. Then Jonathan said to him, "Tomorrow is the new moon, and you will be missed, because your seat will be empty. When you have stayed three days, go down quickly, and come to the place where you hid yourself when this started, and remain by the stone Ezel. I will shoot three arrows on its side, as though I shot at a mark. Behold, I will send the boy, saying, 'Go, find the arrows!' If I tell the boy, 'Behold, the arrows are on this side of you. Take them;' then come; for there is peace to you and no danger, as YHWH lives. But if I say this to the boy, 'Behold, the arrows are beyond you;' then go your way; for YHWH has sent you away. Concerning the matter which you and I have spoken of, behold, YHWH is between you and me forever."

So David hid himself in the field. When the new moon had come, the king sat himself down to eat food. The king sat on his seat, as at other times, even on the seat by the wall; and Jonathan stood up, and Abner sat by Saul's side, but David's place was empty. Nevertheless Saul didn't say anything that day, for he thought, "Something has happened to him. He is not clean. Surely he is not clean."

On the next day after the new moon, the second day, David's place was empty. Saul said to Jonathan his son, "Why doesn't the son of Jesse come to eat, either yesterday, or today?"

Jonathan answered Saul, "David earnestly asked permission of me to go to Bethlehem. He said, 'Please let me go, for our family has a sacrifice in the city. My brother has commanded me to be there. Now, if I have found favor in your eyes, please let me go away and see my brothers.' Therefore he has not come to the king's table."

Then Saul's anger burned against Jonathan, and he said to him, "You son of a perverse rebellious woman, don't I know that you have chosen the son of Jesse to your own shame, and to the shame of your mother's nakedness? For as long as the son of Jesse lives on the earth, you will not be established, nor will your kingdom. Therefore now send and bring him to me, for he shall surely die!"

Jonathan answered Saul his father, and said to him, "Why should he be put to death? What has he done?"

Saul cast his spear at him to strike him. By this Jonathan knew that his father was determined to put David to death. So Jonathan arose from the table in fierce anger, and ate no food the second day of the month; for he was grieved for David, because his father had treated him shamefully. In the morning, Jonathan went out into the field at the time appointed with David, and a little boy with him. He said to his boy, "Run, find now the arrows which I shoot." As the boy ran, he shot an arrow beyond him. When the boy had come to the place of the arrow which Jonathan had shot, Jonathan cried after the boy, and said, "Isn't the arrow beyond you?" Jonathan cried after the boy, "Go fast! Hurry! Don't delay!" Jonathan's boy gathered up the arrows, and came to his master. But the boy didn't know anything. Only Jonathan and David knew the matter. Jonathan gave his weapons to his boy, and said to him, "Go, carry them to the city."

As soon as the boy was gone, David arose out of the south, and fell on his face to the ground, and bowed himself three times. They kissed one another, and wept one with another, and David wept the most. Jonathan said to David, "Go in peace, because we have both sworn in YHWH's name, saying, 'YHWH is between me and you, and between my offspring and your offspring, forever.'" He arose and departed; and Jonathan went into the city.

....

Then David came to Nob to Ahimelech the priest. Ahimelech came to meet David trembling, and said to him, "Why are you alone, and no man with you?" David said to Ahimelech the priest,

"The king has commanded me to do something, and has said to me, 'Let no one know anything about the business about which I send you, and what I have commanded you. I have sent the young men to a certain place.' Now therefore what is under your hand? Please give me five loaves of bread in my hand, or whatever is available."

The priest answered David, and said, "I have no common bread, but there is holy bread; if only the young men have kept themselves from women."

David answered the priest, and said to him, "Truly, women have been kept from us as usual these three days. When I came out, the vessels of the young men were holy, though it was only a common journey. How much more then today shall their vessels be holy?" So the priest gave him holy bread; for there was no bread there but the show bread that was taken from before YHWH, to put hot bread in the day when it was taken away.

Now a certain man of the servants of Saul was there that day, detained before YHWH; and his name was Doeg the Edomite, the best of the herdsmen who belonged to Saul. David said to Ahimelech, "Isn't there here under your hand spear or sword? For I have neither brought my sword nor my weapons with me, because the king's business required haste."

The priest said, "Behold, the sword of Goliath the Philistine, whom you killed in the valley of Elah, is here wrapped in a cloth behind the ephod. If you would like to take that, take it; for there is no other except that here."

David said, "There is none like that. Give it to me."

David arose, and fled that day for fear of Saul, and went to Achish the king of Gath. The servants of Achish said to him, "Isn't this David the king of the land? Didn't they sing to one another about him in dances, saying,

'Saul has slain his thousands,
    and David his ten thousands?'"

David laid up these words in his heart, and was very afraid of Achish the king of Gath. He changed his behavior before them, and pretended to be insane in their hands, and scribbled on the doors of the gate, and let his spittle fall down on his beard. Then Achish said to his servants, "Look, you see the man is insane. Why then have you brought him to me? Do I lack madmen, that you have brought this fellow to play the madman in my presence? Should this fellow come into my house?"

David therefore departed from there, and escaped to Adullam's cave. When his brothers and all his father's house heard it, they went down there to him. Everyone who was in distress, everyone who was in debt, and everyone who was discontented, gathered themselves to him; and he became captain over them. There were with him about four hundred men. David went from there to Mizpeh of Moab, and he said to the king of Moab, "Please let my father and my mother come out with you, until I know what God will do for me." He brought them before the king of Moab; and they lived with him all the time that David was in the stronghold. The prophet Gad said to David, "Don't stay in the stronghold. Depart, and go into the land of Judah."

Then David departed, and came into the forest of Hereth. Saul heard that David was discovered, with the men who were with him. Now Saul was sitting in Gibeah, under the tamarisk tree in Ramah, with his spear in his hand, and all his servants were standing around him. Saul said to his servants who stood around him, "Hear now, you Benjamites! Will the son of Jesse give everyone of you fields and vineyards? Will he make you all captains of thousands and captains of hundreds, that all of you have conspired against me, and there is no one who discloses to me when my son makes a treaty with the son of Jesse, and there is none of you who is sorry for me, or discloses to me that my son has stirred up my servant against me, to lie in wait, as it is today?"

Then Doeg the Edomite, who stood by the servants of Saul, answered and said, "I saw the son of Jesse coming to Nob, to Ahimelech the son of Ahitub. He inquired of YHWH for him, gave him food, and gave him the sword of Goliath the Philistine."

Then the king sent to call Ahimelech the priest, the son of Ahitub, and all his father's house, the priests who were in Nob; and they all came to the king. Saul said, "Hear now, you son of Ahitub."

He answered, "Here I am, my lord."

Saul said to him, "Why have you conspired against me, you and the son of Jesse, in that you have given him bread, and a sword, and have inquired of God for him, that he should rise against me, to lie in wait, as it is today?"

Then Ahimelech answered the king, and said, "Who among all your servants is so faithful as David, who is the king's son-in-law, captain of your body guard, and honored in your house? Have I today begun to inquire of God for him? Be it far from me! Don't let the king impute anything to his servant, nor to all the house of my father; for your servant knows nothing of all this, less or more."

The king said, "You shall surely die, Ahimelech, you, and all your father's house." The king said to the guard who stood about him, "Turn, and kill the priests of YHWH; because their hand also is with David, and because they knew that he fled, and didn't disclose it to me." But the servants of the king wouldn't put out their hand to fall on the priests of YHWH.

The king said to Doeg, "Turn and attack the priests!"

Doeg the Edomite turned, and he attacked the priests, and he killed on that day eighty-five people who wore a linen ephod. He struck Nob, the city of the priests, with the edge of the sword, both men and women, children and nursing babies, and cattle and donkeys and sheep, with the edge of the sword. One of the sons of Ahimelech, the son of Ahitub, named Abiathar, escaped, and fled after David. Abiathar told David that Saul had slain YHWH's priests.

David said to Abiathar, "I knew on that day, when Doeg the Edomite was there, that he would surely tell Saul. I am responsible for the death of all the persons of your father's house. Stay with me. Don't be afraid, for he who seeks my life seeks your life. For you will be safe with me."

....

David was told, "Behold, the Philistines are fighting against Keilah, and are robbing the threshing floors."

Therefore David inquired of YHWH, saying, "Shall I go and strike these Philistines?"

YHWH said to David, "Go strike the Philistines, and save Keilah."

David's men said to him, "Behold, we are afraid here in Judah. How much more then if we go to Keilah against the armies of the Philistines?"

Then David inquired of YHWH yet again. YHWH answered him, and said, "Arise, go down to Keilah; for I will deliver the Philistines into your hand."

David and his men went to Keilah, and fought with the Philistines, and brought away their livestock, and killed them with a great slaughter. So David saved the inhabitants of Keilah. When Abiathar the son of Ahimelech fled to David to Keilah, he came down with an ephod in his hand.

Saul was told that David had come to Keilah. Saul said, "God has delivered him into my hand; for he is shut in by entering into a town that has gates and bars." Saul summoned all the people to war, to go down to Keilah, to besiege David and his men. David knew that Saul was devising mischief against him; and he said to Abiathar the priest, "Bring the ephod here." Then David said, "O YHWH, the God of Israel, your servant has surely heard that Saul seeks to come to Keilah, to destroy the city for my sake. Will the men of Keilah deliver me up into his hand? Will Saul come down, as your servant has heard? YHWH, the God of Israel, I beg you, tell your servant."

YHWH said, "He will come down."

Then David said, "Will the men of Keilah deliver me and my men into the hand of Saul?"

YHWH said, "They will deliver you up."

Then David and his men, who were about six hundred, arose and departed out of Keilah, and went wherever they could go. Saul was told that David was escaped from Keilah; and he gave up going there. David stayed in the wilderness in the strongholds, and remained in the hill country in the wilderness of Ziph. Saul sought him every day, but God didn't deliver him into his hand. David saw that Saul had come out to seek his life. David was in the wilderness of Ziph in the wood.

Jonathan, Saul's son, arose, and went to David into the woods, and strengthened his hand in God. He said to him, "Don't be afraid; for the hand of Saul my father won't find you; and you will be king over Israel, and I will be next to you; and Saul my father knows that also." They both made a covenant before YHWH. Then David stayed in the woods, and Jonathan went to his house.

Then the Ziphites came up to Saul to Gibeah, saying, "Doesn't David hide himself with us in the strongholds in the woods, in the hill of Hachilah, which is on the south of the desert? Now therefore, O king, come down. According to all the desire of your soul to come down; and our part will be to deliver him up into the king's hand."

Saul said, "You are blessed by YHWH; for you have had compassion on me. Please go make yet more sure, and know and see his place where his haunt is, and who has seen him there; for I have been told that he is very cunning. See therefore, and take knowledge of all the lurking places where he hides himself, and come again to me with certainty, and I will go with you. It shall happen, if he is in the land, that I will search him out among all the thousands of Judah."

They arose, and went to Ziph before Saul: but David and his men were in the wilderness of Maon, in the Arabah on the south of the desert. Saul and his men went to seek him. When David was told, he went down to the rock, and stayed in the wilderness of Maon. When Saul heard that, he pursued David in the wilderness of Maon. Saul went on this side of the mountain, and David and his men on that side of the mountain; and David hurried to get away for fear of Saul; for Saul and his men surrounded David and his men to take them. But a messenger came to Saul, saying, "Hurry and come; for the Philistines have made a raid on the land!" So Saul returned from pursuing David, and went against the Philistines. Therefore they called that place Sela Hammahlekoth.

David went up from there, and lived in the strongholds of En Gedi.

....

When Saul had returned from following the Philistines, he was told, "Behold, David is in the wilderness of En Gedi." Then Saul took three thousand chosen men out of all Israel, and went to seek David and his men on the rocks of the wild goats. He came to the sheep pens by the way, where there was a cave; and Saul went in to relieve himself. Now David and his men were staying in the innermost parts of the cave. David's men said to him, "Behold, the day of which YHWH said to you, 'Behold, I will deliver your enemy into your hand, and you shall do to him as it shall seem good to you.'" Then David arose, and cut off the skirt of Saul's robe secretly. Afterward, David's heart struck him, because he had cut off Saul's skirt. He said to his men, "YHWH forbid that I should do this thing to my lord, YHWH's anointed, to stretch out my hand against him, since he is YHWH's anointed." So David checked his men with these words, and didn't allow them to rise against Saul. Saul rose up out of the cave, and went on his way. David also arose afterward, and went out the cave, and cried after Saul, saying, "My lord the king!"

When Saul looked behind him, David bowed with his face to the earth, and showed respect. David said to Saul, "Why do you listen to men's words, saying, 'Behold, David seeks to harm you?' Behold, today your eyes have seen how YHWH had delivered you today into my hand in the cave. Some urged me to kill you; but I spared you; and I said, I will not stretch out my hand against my lord;

for he is yhwh's anointed. Moreover, my father, behold, yes, see the skirt of your robe in my hand; for in that I cut off the skirt of your robe, and didn't kill you, know and see that there is neither evil nor disobedience in my hand, and I have not sinned against you, though you hunt for my life to take it. May yhwh judge between me and you, and may yhwh avenge me of you; but my hand will not be on you. As the proverb of the ancients says, 'Out of the wicked comes wickedness;' but my hand will not be on you. Against whom has the king of Israel come out? Whom do you pursue? A dead dog? A flea? May yhwh therefore be judge, and give sentence between me and you, and see, and plead my cause, and deliver me out of your hand."

It came to pass, when David had finished speaking these words to Saul, that Saul said, "Is that your voice, my son David?" Saul lifted up his voice, and wept. He said to David, "You are more righteous than I; for you have done good to me, whereas I have done evil to you. You have declared today how you have dealt well with me, because when yhwh had delivered me up into your hand, you didn't kill me. For if a man finds his enemy, will he let him go away unharmed? Therefore may yhwh reward you good for that which you have done to me today. Now, behold, I know that you will surely be king, and that the kingdom of Israel will be established in your hand. Swear now therefore to me by yhwh, that you will not cut off my offspring after me, and that you will not destroy my name out of my father's house."

David swore to Saul. Saul went home, but David and his men went up to the stronghold.

....

Samuel died; and all Israel gathered themselves together, and mourned for him, and buried him at his house at Ramah.

Then David arose, and went down to the wilderness of Paran. There was a man in Maon, whose possessions were in Carmel; and the man was very great. He had three thousand sheep and a thousand goats; and he was shearing his sheep in Carmel. Now the name of the man was Nabal; and the name of his wife Abigail. This woman was intelligent and had a beautiful face; but the man was surly and evil in his doings. He was of the house of Caleb. David heard in the wilderness that Nabal was shearing his sheep. David sent ten young men, and David said to the young men, "Go up to Carmel, and go to Nabal, and greet him in my name. Tell him, 'Long life to you! Peace be to you! Peace be to your house! Peace be to all that you have! Now I have heard that you have shearers. Your shepherds have now been with us, and we didn't harm them. Nothing was missing from them all the time they were in Carmel. Ask your young men, and they will tell you. Therefore let the young men find favor in your eyes; for we come on a good day. Please give whatever comes to your hand, to your servants, and to your son David.'"

When David's young men came, they spoke to Nabal all those words in the name of David, and waited.

Nabal answered David's servants, and said, "Who is David? Who is the son of Jesse? There are many servants who break away from their masters these days. Shall I then take my bread, my water, and my meat that I have killed for my shearers, and give it to men who I don't know where they come from?"

So David's young men turned on their way, and went back, and came and told him all these words.

David said to his men, "Every man put on his sword!"

Every man put on his sword. David also put on his sword. About four hundred men followed David, and two hundred stayed by the baggage. But one of the young men told Abigail, Nabal's wife, saying, "Behold, David sent messengers out of the wilderness to Greet our master; and he insulted them. But the men were very good to us, and we were not harmed, and we didn't miss anything, as long as we went with them, when we were in the fields. They were a wall to us both by night and by day, all the while we were with them keeping the sheep. Now therefore know and consider what you will do; for evil is determined against our master, and against all his house; for he is such a worthless fellow that one can't speak to him."

Then Abigail hurried and took two hundred loaves of bread, two containers of wine, five sheep ready dressed, five seahs of parched grain, one hundred clusters of raisins, and two hundred cakes of figs, and laid them on donkeys. She said to her young men, "Go on before me. Behold, I am coming after you." But she didn't tell her husband, Nabal. As she rode on her donkey, and came down by the covert of the mountain, that behold, David and his men came down toward her, and she met them.

Now David had said, "Surely in vain I have kept all that this fellow has in the wilderness, so that nothing was missed of all that pertained to him. He has returned me evil for good. God do so to the enemies of David, and more also, if I leave of all that belongs to him by the morning light so much as one who urinates on a wall."

When Abigail saw David, she hurried and got off her donkey, and fell before David on her face, and bowed herself to the ground. She fell at his feet, and said, "On me, my lord, on me be the blame! Please let your servant speak in your ears. Hear the words of your servant. Please don't let my lord pay attention to this worthless fellow, Nabal; for as his name is, so is he. Nabal is his name, and folly is with him; but I, your servant, didn't see my lord's young men, whom you sent. Now therefore, my lord, as YHWH lives, and as your soul lives, since YHWH has withheld you from blood guiltiness, and from avenging yourself with your own hand, now therefore let your enemies, and those who seek evil to my lord, be as Nabal. Now this present which your servant has brought to my lord, let it be given to the young men who follow my lord. Please forgive the trespass of your servant. For YHWH will certainly make my lord a sure house, because my lord fights YHWH's battles. Evil will not be found in you all your days. Though men may rise up to pursue you, and to seek your soul, yet the soul of my lord will be bound in the bundle of life with YHWH your God. He will sling out the souls of your enemies, as from the hollow of a sling. It will come to pass, when YHWH has done to my lord according to all the good that he has spoken concerning you, and has appointed you prince over Israel, that this shall be no grief to you, nor offense of heart to my lord, either that you have shed blood without cause, or that my lord has avenged himself. When YHWH has dealt well with my lord, then remember your servant."

David said to Abigail, "Blessed is YHWH, the God of Israel, who sent you today to meet me! Blessed is your discretion, and blessed are you, who have kept me today from blood guiltiness, and from avenging myself with my own hand. For indeed, as YHWH, the God of Israel, lives, who has withheld me from harming you, unless you had hurried and come to meet me, surely there wouldn't have been left to Nabal by the morning light so much as one who urinates on a wall."

So David received from her hand that which she had brought him. Then he said to her, "Go up in peace to your house. Behold, I have listened to your voice, and have granted your request."

Abigail came to Nabal; and behold, he held a feast in his house, like the feast of a king. Nabal's heart was merry within him, for he was very drunk. Therefore she told him nothing until the morning light. In the morning, when the wine had gone out of Nabal, his wife told him these things, and his heart died within him, and he became as a stone. About ten days later, YHWH struck Nabal, so that he died. When David heard that Nabal was dead, he said, "Blessed is YHWH, who has pleaded the cause of my reproach from the hand of Nabal, and has kept back his servant from evil. YHWH has returned the evil-doing of Nabal on his own head." David sent and spoke concerning Abigail, to take her to himself as wife. When David's servants had come to Abigail to Carmel, they spoke to her, saying, "David has sent us to you, to take you to him as wife."

She arose, and bowed herself with her face to the earth, and said, "Behold, your servant is a servant to wash the feet of the servants of my lord." Abigail hurried, and arose, and rode on a donkey, with five ladies of hers who followed her; and she went after the messengers of David, and became his wife. David also took Ahinoam of Jezreel; and they both became his wives. Now Saul had given Michal his daughter, David's wife, to Palti the son of Laish, who was of Gallim.

....

The Ziphites came to Saul to Gibeah, saying, "Doesn't David hide himself in the hill of Hachilah, which is before the desert?" Then Saul arose, and went down to the wilderness of Ziph, having three thousand chosen men of Israel with him, to seek David in the wilderness of Ziph. Saul encamped in the hill of Hachilah, which is before the desert, by the way. But David stayed in the wilderness, and he saw that Saul came after him into the wilderness. David therefore sent out spies, and understood that Saul had certainly come. Then David arose, and came to the place where Saul had encamped; and David saw the place where Saul lay, with Abner the son of Ner, the captain of his army. Saul lay within the place of the wagons, and the people were encamped around him.

Then David answered and said to Ahimelech the Hittite, and to Abishai the son of Zeruiah, brother of Joab, saying, "Who will go down with me to Saul to the camp?"

Abishai said, "I will go down with you." So David and Abishai came to the people by night: and, behold, Saul lay sleeping within the place of the wagons, with his spear stuck in the ground at his head; and Abner and the people lay around him. Then Abishai said to David, "God has delivered up your enemy into your hand today. Now therefore please let me strike him with the spear to the earth at one stroke, and I will not strike him the second time."

David said to Abishai, "Don't destroy him; for who can stretch out his hand against YHWH's anointed, and be guiltless?" David said, "As YHWH lives, YHWH will strike him; or his day shall come to die; or he shall go down into battle and perish. YHWH forbid that I should stretch out my hand against YHWH's anointed; but now please take the spear that is at his head, and the jar of water, and let's go."

So David took the spear and the jar of water from Saul's head; and they went away: and no man saw it, or knew it, nor did any awake; for they were all asleep, because a deep sleep from YHWH had fallen on them. Then David went over to the other side, and stood on the top of the mountain afar off; a great space being between them; and David cried to the people, and to Abner the son of Ner, saying, "Don't you answer, Abner?"

Then Abner answered, "Who are you who cries to the king?"

David said to Abner, "Aren't you a man? Who is like you in Israel? Why then have you not kept watch over your lord, the king? For one of the people came in to destroy the king your lord. This thing isn't good that you have done. As YHWH lives, you are worthy to die, because you have not kept watch over your lord, YHWH's anointed. Now see where the king's spear is, and the jar of water that was at his head."

Saul knew David's voice, and said, "Is this your voice, my son David?"

David said, "It is my voice, my lord, O king." He said, "Why does my lord pursue his servant? For what have I done? What evil is in my hand? Now therefore, please let my lord the king hear the words of his servant. If it is so that YHWH has stirred you up against me, let him accept an offering. But if it is the children of men, they are cursed before YHWH; for they have driven me out today that I shouldn't cling to YHWH's inheritance, saying, 'Go, serve other gods!' Now therefore, don't let my blood fall to the earth away from the presence of YHWH; for the king of Israel has come out to seek a flea, as when one hunts a partridge in the mountains."

Then Saul said, "I have sinned. Return, my son David; for I will no more do you harm, because my life was precious in your eyes today. Behold, I have played the fool, and have erred exceedingly."

David answered, "Behold the spear, O king! Then let one of the young men come over and get it. YHWH will render to every man his righteousness and his faithfulness; because YHWH delivered you into my hand today, and I wouldn't stretch out my hand against YHWH's anointed. Behold, as your life was respected today in my eyes, so let my life be respected in YHWH's eyes, and let him deliver me out of all oppression."

Then Saul said to David, "You are blessed, my son David. You will both do mightily, and will surely prevail." So David went his way, and Saul returned to his place.

....

David said in his heart, "I will now perish one day by the hand of Saul. There is nothing better for me than that I should escape into the land of the Philistines; and Saul will despair of me, to seek me any more in all the borders of Israel. So shall I escape out of his hand." David arose, and passed over, he and the six hundred men who were with him, to Achish the son of Maoch, king of Gath. David lived with Achish at Gath, he and his men, every man with his household, even David with his two wives, Ahinoam the Jezreelitess, and Abigail the Carmelitess, Nabal's wife. Saul was told that David had fled to Gath: and he sought no more again for him. David said to Achish, "If now I have found favor in your eyes, let them give me a place in one of the cities in the country, that I may dwell there. For why should your servant dwell in the royal city with you?" Then Achish gave him Ziklag that day: therefore Ziklag belongs to the kings of Judah to this day. The number of the days that David lived in the country of the Philistines was a full year and four months. David and his men went up and raided the Geshurites, the Girzites, and the Amalekites; for those were the inhabitants of the land, who were of old, on the way to Shur, even to the land of Egypt. David struck the land, and saved no man or woman alive, and took away the sheep, the cattle, the donkeys, the camels, and the clothing. Then he returned, and came to Achish.

Achish said, "Against whom have you made a raid today?"

David said, "Against the South of Judah, against the South of the Jerahmeelites, and against the South of the Kenites." David saved neither man nor woman alive, to bring them to Gath, saying, "Lest they should tell about us, saying, 'David did this, and this has been his way all the time he has lived in the country of the Philistines.'"

Achish believed David, saying, "He has made his people Israel utterly to abhor him. Therefore he will be my servant forever."

....

In those days, the Philistines gathered their armies together for warfare, to fight with Israel. Achish said to David, "Know assuredly that you will go out with me in the army, you and your men."

David said to Achish, "Therefore you will know what your servant can do."

Achish said to David, "Therefore I will make you my bodyguard forever."

Now Samuel was dead, and all Israel had mourned for him, and buried him in Ramah, even in his own city. Saul had sent away those who had familiar spirits and the wizards out of the land. The Philistines gathered themselves together, and came and encamped in Shunem; and Saul gathered all Israel together, and they encamped in Gilboa. When Saul saw the army of the Philistines, he was afraid, and his heart trembled greatly. When Saul inquired of YHWH, YHWH didn't answer him by dreams, by Urim, or by prophets. Then Saul said to his servants, "Seek for me a woman who has a familiar spirit, that I may go to her, and inquire of her."

His servants said to him, "Behold, there is a woman who has a familiar spirit at Endor."

Saul disguised himself and put on other clothing, and went, he and two men with him, and they came to the woman by night. Then he said, "Please consult for me by the familiar spirit, and bring me up whomever I shall name to you."

The woman said to him, "Behold, you know what Saul has done, how he has cut off those who have familiar spirits, and the wizards, out of the land. Why then do you lay a snare for my life, to cause me to die?"

Saul swore to her by YHWH, saying, "As YHWH lives, no punishment will happen to you for this thing."

Then the woman said, "Whom shall I bring up to you?"

He said, "Bring Samuel up for me."

When the woman saw Samuel, she cried with a loud voice; and the woman spoke to Saul, saying, "Why have you deceived me? For you are Saul!"

The king said to her, "Don't be afraid! What do you see?"

The woman said to Saul, "I see a god coming up out of the earth."

He said to her, "What does he look like?"

She said, "An old man comes up. He is covered with a robe." Saul perceived that it was Samuel, and he bowed with his face to the ground, and showed respect.

Samuel said to Saul, "Why have you disturbed me, to bring me up?"

Saul answered, "I am very distressed; for the Philistines make war against me, and God has departed from me, and answers me no more, by prophets, or by dreams. Therefore I have called you, that you may make known to me what I shall do."

Samuel said, "Why then do you ask me, since YHWH has departed from you and has become your adversary? YHWH has done to you as he spoke by me. YHWH has torn the kingdom out of your hand, and given it to your neighbor, even to David. Because you didn't obey YHWH's voice, and didn't execute his fierce wrath on Amalek, therefore YHWH has done this thing to you today. Moreover YHWH will deliver Israel also with you into the hand of the Philistines; and tomorrow you and your sons will be with me. YHWH will deliver the army of Israel also into the hand of the Philistines."

Then Saul fell immediately his full length on the earth, and was terrified, because of Samuel's words. There was no strength in him; for he had eaten no bread all day long or all night long.

The woman came to Saul, and saw that he was very troubled, and said to him, "Behold, your servant has listened to your voice, and I have put my life in my hand, and have listened to your words which you spoke to me. Now therefore, please listen also to the voice of your servant, and let me set a morsel of bread before you. Eat, that you may have strength, when you go on your way."

But he refused, and said, "I will not eat." But his servants, together with the woman, constrained him; and he listened to their voice. So he arose from the earth and sat on the bed. The woman had a fattened calf in the house. She hurried and killed it; and she took flour, and kneaded it, and baked unleavened bread of it. She brought it before Saul, and before his servants; and they ate. Then they rose up, and went away that night.

....

Now the Philistines gathered together all their armies to Aphek; and the Israelites encamped by the spring which is in Jezreel. The lords of the Philistines passed on by hundreds and by thousands; and David and his men passed on in the rear with Achish.

Then the princes of the Philistines said, "What about these Hebrews?"

Achish said to the princes of the Philistines, "Isn't this David, the servant of Saul the king of Israel, who has been with me these days, or rather these years? I have found no fault in him since he fell away until today."

But the princes of the Philistines were angry with him; and the princes of the Philistines said to him, "Make the man return, that he may go back to his place where you have appointed him, and let him not go down with us to battle, lest in the battle he become an adversary to us. For with what should this fellow reconcile himself to his lord? Should it not be with the heads of these men? Isn't this David, of whom people sang to one another in dances, saying,

> 'Saul has slain his thousands,
> and David his ten thousands?'"

Then Achish called David, and said to him, "As YHWH lives, you have been upright, and your going out and your coming in with me in the army is good in my sight; for I have not found evil in you since the day of your coming to me to this day. Nevertheless, the lords don't favor you. Therefore now return, and go in peace, that you not displease the lords of the Philistines."

David said to Achish, "But what have I done? What have you found in your servant so long as I have been before you to this day, that I may not go and fight against the enemies of my lord the king?"

Achish answered David, "I know that you are good in my sight, as an angel of God. Notwithstanding the princes of the Philistines have said, 'He shall not go up with us to the battle.' Therefore now rise up early in the morning with the servants of your lord who have come with you; and as soon as you are up early in the morning, and have light, depart."

So David rose up early, he and his men, to depart in the morning, to return into the land of the Philistines, and the Philistines went up to Jezreel.

....

When David and his men had come to Ziklag on the third day, the Amalekites had made a raid on the South, and on Ziklag, and had struck Ziklag, and burned it with fire, and had taken captive the women and all who were in it, both small and great. They didn't kill any, but carried them off, and went their way. When David and his men came to the city, behold, it was burned with fire; and their wives, their sons, and their daughters were taken captive. Then David and the people who were with him lifted up their voice and wept until they had no more power to weep. David's two wives were taken captive, Ahinoam the Jezreelitess, and Abigail the wife of Nabal the Carmelite. David was greatly distressed; for the people spoke of stoning him, because the souls of all the people were grieved, every man for his sons and for his daughters; but David strengthened himself in YHWH his God. David said to Abiathar the priest, the son of Ahimelech, "Please bring the ephod here to me."

Abiathar brought the ephod to David. David inquired of YHWH, saying, "If I pursue after this troop, will I overtake them?"

He answered him, "Pursue; for you will surely overtake them, and will without fail recover all."

So David went, he and the six hundred men who were with him, and came to the brook Besor, where those who were left behind stayed. But David pursued, he and four hundred men; for two hundred stayed behind, who were so faint that they couldn't go over the brook Besor. They found an Egyptian in the field, and brought him to David, and gave him bread, and he ate; and they gave him water to drink. They gave him a piece of a cake of figs, and two clusters of raisins. When he had eaten, his spirit came again to him; for he had eaten no bread, and drank no water for three days and three nights. David asked him, "To whom do you belong? Where are you from?"

He said, "I am a young man of Egypt, servant to an Amalekite; and my master left me, because three days ago I got sick. We made a raid on the South of the Cherethites, and on that which belongs to Judah, and on the South of Caleb; and we burned Ziklag with fire."

David said to him, "Will you bring me down to this troop?"

He said, "Swear to me by God that you will not kill me and not deliver me up into the hands of my master, and I will bring you down to this troop."

When he had brought him down, behold, they were spread around over all the ground, eating, drinking, and dancing, because of all the great plunder that they had taken out of the land of the Philistines, and out of the land of Judah. David struck them from the twilight even to the evening of the next day. Not a man of them escaped from there, except four hundred young men, who rode on camels and fled. David recovered all that the Amalekites had taken, and David rescued his two wives. There was nothing lacking to them, neither small nor great, neither sons nor daughters, neither plunder, nor anything that they had taken to them. David brought back all. David took all the flocks and the herds, which they drove before those other livestock, and said, "This is David's plunder."

David came to the two hundred men, who were so faint that they could not follow David, whom also they had made to stay at the brook Besor; and they went out to meet David, and to meet the people who were with him. When David came near to the people, he greeted them. Then all the wicked men and worthless fellows, of those who went with David, answered and said, "Because they didn't go with us, we will not give them anything of the plunder that we have recovered, except to every man his wife and his children, that he may lead them away, and depart."

Then David said, "Do not do so, my brothers, with that which YHWH has given to us, who has preserved us, and delivered the troop that came against us into our hand. Who will listen to you in this matter? For as his share is who goes down to the battle, so shall his share be who stays with the baggage. They shall share alike." It was so from that day forward, that he made it a statute and an ordinance for Israel to this day. When David came to Ziklag, he sent some of the plunder to the elders of Judah, even to his friends, saying, "Behold, a present for you from the plunder of YHWH's enemies." He sent it to those who were in Bethel, to those who were in Ramoth of the South, to those who were in Jattir, to those who were in Aroer, to those who were in Siphmoth, to those who were in Eshtemoa, to those who were in Racal, to those who were in the cities of the Jerahmeelites, to those who were in the cities of the Kenites, to those who were in Hormah, to those who were in Borashan, to those who were in Athach, to those who were in Hebron, and to all the places where David himself and his men used to stay.

....

Now the Philistines fought against Israel; and the men of Israel fled from before the Philistines, and fell down slain on Mount Gilboa. The Philistines overtook Saul and on his sons; and the Philistines killed Jonathan, Abinadab, and Malchishua, the sons of Saul. The battle went hard against Saul, and the archers overtook him; and he was greatly distressed by reason of the archers. Then Saul said to his armor bearer, "Draw your sword, and thrust me through with it, lest these uncircumcised come and thrust me through, and abuse me!" But his armor bearer would not; for he was terrified. Therefore Saul took his sword, and fell on it. When his armor bearer saw that Saul was dead, he likewise fell on his sword, and died with him. So

Saul died, and his three sons, and his armor bearer, and all his men, that same day together.

When the men of Israel who were on the other side of the valley, and those who were beyond the Jordan, saw that the men of Israel fled, and that Saul and his sons were dead, they abandoned the cities and fled; and the Philistines came and lived in them. On the next day, when the Philistines came to strip the slain, they found Saul and his three sons fallen on Mount Gilboa. They cut off his head, stripped off his armor, and sent into the land of the Philistines all around, to carry the news to the house of their idols, and to the people. They put his armor in the house of the Ashtaroth, and they fastened his body to the wall of Beth Shan. When the inhabitants of Jabesh Gilead heard what the Philistines had done to Saul, all the valiant men arose, went all night, and took the body of Saul and the bodies of his sons from the wall of Beth Shan; and they came to Jabesh, and burned them there. They took their bones and buried them under the tamarisk tree in Jabesh, and fasted seven days.

THE BOOK OF

SAMUEL

PART II

1 HR 43 MIN

After the death of Saul, when David had returned from the slaughter of the Amalekites, and David had stayed two days in Ziklag; on the third day, behold, a man came out of the camp from Saul, with his clothes torn, and earth on his head. When he came to David, he fell to the earth, and showed respect.

David said to him, "Where do you come from?"

He said to him, "I have escaped out of the camp of Israel."

David said to him, "How did it go? Please tell me."

He answered, "The people have fled from the battle, and many of the people also have fallen and are dead. Saul and Jonathan his son are dead also."

David said to the young man who told him, "How do you know that Saul and Jonathan his son are dead?"

The young man who told him said, "As I happened by chance on Mount Gilboa, behold, Saul was leaning on his spear; and behold, the chariots and the horsemen followed close behind him. When he looked behind him, he saw me, and called to me. I answered, 'Here I am.' He said to me, 'Who are you?' I answered him, 'I am an Amalekite.' He said to me, 'Please stand beside me, and kill me; for anguish has taken hold of me, because my life lingers in me.' So I stood beside him and killed him, because I was sure that he could not live after he had fallen. I took the crown that was on his head and the bracelet that was on his arm, and have brought them here to my lord."

Then David took hold on his clothes, and tore them; and all the men who were with him did likewise. They mourned, wept, and fasted until evening, for Saul, and for Jonathan his son, and for the people of YHWH, and for the house of Israel; because they had fallen by the sword. David said to the young man who told him, "Where are you from?"

He answered, "I am the son of a foreigner, an Amalekite."

David said to him, "Why were you not afraid to stretch out your hand to destroy YHWH's anointed?" David called one of the young men, and said, "Go near, and cut him down!" He struck him so that he died. David said to him, "Your blood be on your head; for your mouth has testified against you, saying, 'I have slain YHWH's anointed.'"

David lamented with this lamentation over Saul and over Jonathan his son (and he commanded them to teach the children of Judah the song of the bow; behold, it is written in the book of Jashar):

"Your glory, Israel, was slain on your high places!
How the mighty have fallen!
Don't tell it in Gath.
Don't publish it in the streets of Ashkelon,
lest the daughters of the Philistines rejoice,
lest the daughters of the uncircumcised triumph.
You mountains of Gilboa,
let there be no dew or rain on you, and no fields of offerings;
For there the shield of the mighty was defiled and cast away,
The shield of Saul was not anointed with oil.
From the blood of the slain,
from the fat of the mighty,
Jonathan's bow didn't turn back.
Saul's sword didn't return empty.
Saul and Jonathan were lovely and pleasant in their lives.
In their death, they were not divided.
They were swifter than eagles.
They were stronger than lions.
You daughters of Israel, weep over Saul,
who clothed you delicately in scarlet,
who put ornaments of gold on your clothing.
How the mighty have fallen in the middle of the battle!
Jonathan was slain on your high places.
I am distressed for you, my brother Jonathan.
You have been very pleasant to me.
Your love to me was wonderful,
passing the love of women.
How the mighty have fallen,
and the weapons of war have perished!"

After this, David inquired of YHWH, saying, "Shall I go up into any of the cities of Judah?"

YHWH said to him, "Go up."

David said, "Where shall I go up?"

He said, "To Hebron."

So David went up there with his two wives, Ahinoam the Jezreelitess, and Abigail the wife of Nabal the Carmelite. David brought up his men who were with him, every man with his household. They lived in the cities of Hebron. The men of Judah came, and there they anointed David king over the house of Judah. They told David, "The men of Jabesh Gilead were those who buried Saul." David sent messengers to the men of Jabesh Gilead, and said to them, "Blessed are you by YHWH, that you have shown this kindness to your lord, even to Saul, and have buried him. Now may YHWH show loving kindness and truth to you. I also will reward you for this kindness, because you have done this thing. Now therefore let your hands be strong, and be valiant; for Saul your lord is dead, and also the house of Judah have anointed me king over them."

Now Abner the son of Ner, captain of Saul's army, had taken Ishbosheth the son of Saul, and brought him over to Mahanaim; and he made him king over Gilead, and over the Ashurites, and over Jezreel, and over Ephraim, and over Benjamin, and over all Israel. Ishbosheth, Saul's son, was forty years old when he began to reign over Israel, and he reigned two years. But the house of Judah followed David. The time that David was king in Hebron over the house of Judah was seven years and six months. Abner the son of Ner, and the servants of Ishbosheth the son of Saul, went out from Mahanaim to Gibeon. Joab the son of Zeruiah and David's servants went out, and met them by the pool of Gibeon; and they sat down, the one on the one side of the pool, and the other on the other side of the pool. Abner said to Joab, "Please let the young men arise and play before us!"

Joab said, "Let them arise!" Then they arose and went over by number: twelve for Benjamin and for Ishbosheth the son of Saul, and twelve of David's servants. They each caught his opponent by the head, and thrust his sword in his fellow's side; so they fell down together: therefore that place in Gibeon was called Helkath Hazzurim. The battle was very severe that day; and Abner was beaten, and the men of Israel, before David's servants. The three sons of Zeruiah were there, Joab, and Abishai, and Asahel: and Asahel was as light of foot as a wild gazelle. Asahel pursued Abner; and in going he didn't turn to the right hand or to the left from following Abner. Then Abner looked behind him, and said, "Is that you, Asahel?"

He answered, "It is."

Abner said to him, "Turn away to your right hand or to your left, and grab one of the young men, and take his armor." But Asahel would not turn away from following him. Abner said again to Asahel, "Turn away from following me. Why should I strike you to the ground? How then could I look Joab your brother in the face?" However he refused to turn away. Therefore Abner with the back end of the spear struck him in the body, so that the spear came out behind him; and he fell down there, and died in the same place. As many as came to the place where Asahel fell down and died stood still. But Joab and Abishai pursued Abner. The sun went down when they had come to the hill of Ammah, that lies before Giah by the way of the wilderness of Gibeon. The children of Benjamin gathered themselves together after Abner, and became one band, and stood on the top of a hill. Then Abner called to Joab, and said, "Shall the sword devour forever? Don't you know that it will be bitterness in the latter end? How long will it be then, before you ask the people to return from following their brothers?"

Joab said, "As God lives, if you had not spoken, surely then in the morning the people would have gone away, and not each followed his brother." So Joab blew the trumpet; and all the people stood still, and pursued Israel no more, and they fought no more. Abner and his men went all that night through the Arabah; and they passed over the Jordan, and went through all Bithron, and came to Mahanaim. Joab returned from following Abner; and when he had gathered all the people together, nineteen men of David's and Asahel were missing. But David's servants had struck Benjamin and of Abner's men so that three hundred sixty men died. They took up Asahel, and buried him in the tomb of his father, which was in Bethlehem. Joab and his men went all night, and the day broke on them at Hebron.

....

Now there was long war between Saul's house and David's house. David grew stronger and stronger, but Saul's house grew weaker and weaker. Sons were born to David in Hebron. His firstborn was Amnon, of Ahinoam the Jezreelitess; and his second, Chileab, of Abigail the wife of Nabal the Carmelite; and the third, Absalom the son of Maacah the daughter of Talmai king of Geshur; and the fourth, Adonijah the son of Haggith; and the fifth, Shephatiah the son of Abital; and the sixth, Ithream, of Eglah, David's wife. These were born to David in Hebron.

While there was war between Saul's house and David's house, Abner made himself strong in Saul's house. Now Saul had a concubine, whose name was Rizpah, the daughter of Aiah; and Ishbosheth said to Abner, "Why have you gone in to my father's concubine?"

Then Abner was very angry about Ishbosheth's words, and said, "Am I a dog's head that belongs to Judah? Today I show kindness to

Saul's house your father, to his brothers, and to his friends, and have not delivered you into the hand of David; and yet you charge me today with a fault concerning this woman! God do so to Abner, and more also, if, as YHWH has sworn to David, I don't do even so to him; to transfer the kingdom from Saul's house, and to set up David's throne over Israel and over Judah, from Dan even to Beersheba."

He could not answer Abner another word, because he was afraid of him.

Abner sent messengers to David on his behalf, saying, "Whose is the land?" and saying, "Make your alliance with me, and behold, my hand will be with you, to bring all Israel around to you."

He said, "Good. I will make a treaty with you, but one thing I require of you. That is, you will not see my face unless you first bring Michal, Saul's daughter, when you come to see my face."

David sent messengers to Ishbosheth, Saul's son, saying, "Deliver me my wife Michal, whom I was given to marry for one hundred foreskins of the Philistines."

Ishbosheth sent and took her from her husband, even from Paltiel the son of Laish. Her husband went with her, weeping as he went, and followed her to Bahurim. Then Abner said to him, "Go! Return!" and he returned. Abner had communication with the elders of Israel, saying, "In times past, you sought for David to be king over you. Now then do it; for YHWH has spoken of David, saying, 'By the hand of my servant David, I will save my people Israel out of the hand of the Philistines, and out of the hand of all their enemies.'"

Abner also spoke in the ears of Benjamin: and Abner went also to speak in the ears of David in Hebron all that seemed good to Israel, and to the whole house of Benjamin. So Abner came to David to Hebron, and twenty men with him. David made Abner and the men who were with him a feast. Abner said to David, "I will arise and go, and will gather all Israel to my lord the king, that they may make a covenant with you, and that you may reign over all that your soul desires." David sent Abner away; and he went in peace.

Behold, David's servants and Joab came from a raid, and brought in a great plunder with them; but Abner was not with David in Hebron; for he had sent him away, and he had gone in peace. When Joab and all the army who was with him had come, they told Joab, "Abner the son of Ner came to the king, and he has sent him away, and he has gone in peace."

Then Joab came to the king, and said, "What have you done?

Behold, Abner came to you. Why is it that you have sent him away, and he is already gone? You know Abner the son of Ner. He came to deceive you, and to know your going out and your coming in, and to know all that you do."

When Joab had come out from David, he sent messengers after Abner, and they brought him back from the well of Sirah; but David didn't know it. When Abner was returned to Hebron, Joab took him aside into the middle of the gate to speak with him quietly, and struck him there in the body, so that he died, for the blood of Asahel his brother. Afterward, when David heard it, he said, "I and my kingdom are guiltless before YHWH forever of the blood of Abner the son of Ner. Let it fall on the head of Joab, and on all his father's house. Let there not fail from the house of Joab one who has a discharge, or who is a leper, or who leans on a staff, or who falls by the sword, or who lacks bread." So Joab and Abishai his brother killed Abner, because he had killed their brother Asahel at Gibeon in the battle. David said to Joab, and to all the people who were with him, "Tear your clothes, and clothe yourselves with sackcloth, and mourn in front of Abner." King David followed the bier. They buried Abner in Hebron; and the king lifted up his voice, and wept at Abner's grave; and all the people wept. The king lamented for Abner, and said, "Should Abner die as a fool dies? Your hands weren't bound, and your feet weren't put into fetters. As a man falls before the children of iniquity, so you fell."

All the people wept again over him. All the people came to urge David to eat bread while it was yet day; but David swore, saying, "God do so to me, and more also, if I taste bread, or anything else, until the sun goes down."

All the people took notice of it, and it pleased them; as whatever the king did pleased all the people. So all the people and all Israel understood that day that it was not of the king to kill Abner the son of Ner. The king said to his servants, "Don't you know that a prince and a great man has fallen today in Israel? I am weak today, though anointed king. These men, the sons of Zeruiah are too hard for me. May YHWH reward the evildoer according to his wickedness."

....

When Saul's son heard that Abner was dead in Hebron, his hands became feeble, and all the Israelites were troubled. Saul's son had two men who were captains of raiding bands. The name of one was Baanah, and the name of the other Rechab, the sons of Rimmon the Beerothite, of the children of Benjamin (for Beeroth also is considered a part of Benjamin: and the Beerothites fled to Gittaim, and have lived as foreigners there until today). Now Jonathan, Saul's son, had a son who was lame in his feet. He was five years old when the news came about Saul and Jonathan out of Jezreel; and his nurse picked him up and fled. As she hurried to flee, he fell and became lame. His name was Mephibosheth. The sons of Rimmon the Beerothite, Rechab and Baanah, went and came at about the heat of the day to the house of Ishbosheth, as he took his rest at noon. They came there into the middle of the house, as though they would have fetched wheat; and they struck him in the body: and Rechab and Baanah his brother escaped. Now when they came into the house, as he lay on his bed in his bedroom, they struck him, killed him, beheaded him, and took his head, and went by the way of the Arabah all night. They brought the head of Ishbosheth to David to Hebron, and said to the king, "Behold, the head of Ishbosheth, the son of Saul, your enemy, who sought your life! YHWH has avenged my lord the king today of Saul, and of his offspring."

David answered Rechab and Baanah his brother, the sons of Rimmon the Beerothite, and said to them, "As YHWH lives, who has redeemed my soul out of all adversity, when someone told me, 'Behold, Saul is dead,' thinking that he brought good news, I seized him and killed him in Ziklag, which was the reward I gave him for his news. How much more, when wicked men have slain a righteous person in his own house on his bed, should I not now require his blood from your hand, and rid the earth of you?" David commanded his young men, and they killed them, cut off their hands and their feet, and hanged them up beside the pool in Hebron. But they took the head of Ishbosheth, and buried it in Abner's grave in Hebron.

....

Then all the tribes of Israel came to David at Hebron, and spoke, saying, "Behold, we are your bone and your flesh. In times past, when Saul was king over us, it was you who led Israel out and in. YHWH said to you, 'You will be shepherd of my people Israel, and you will be prince over Israel.'" So all the elders of Israel came to the king to Hebron, and king David made a covenant with them in Hebron before YHWH; and they anointed David king over Israel.

David was thirty years old when he began to reign, and he

reigned forty years. In Hebron he reigned over Judah seven years and six months; and in Jerusalem he reigned thirty-three years over all Israel and Judah. The king and his men went to Jerusalem against the Jebusites, the inhabitants of the land, who spoke to David, saying, "The blind and the lame will keep you out of here;" thinking, "David can't come in here." Nevertheless David took the stronghold of Zion. This is David's city. David said on that day, "Whoever strikes the Jebusites, let him go up to the watercourse and strike those lame and blind, who are hated by David's soul." Therefore they say, "The blind and the lame can't come into the house."

David lived in the stronghold, and called it David's city. David built around from Millo and inward. David grew greater and greater; for YHWH, the God of Armies, was with him. Hiram king of Tyre sent messengers to David, with cedar trees, carpenters, and masons; and they built David a house. David perceived that YHWH had established him king over Israel, and that he had exalted his kingdom for his people Israel's sake. David took more concubines and wives for himself out of Jerusalem, after he had come from Hebron; and more sons and daughters were born to David. These are the names of those who were born to him in Jerusalem: Shammua, Shobab, Nathan, Solomon, Ibhar, Elishua, Nepheg, Japhia, Elishama, Eliada, and Eliphelet.

When the Philistines heard that they had anointed David king over Israel, all the Philistines went up to seek David, but David heard about it and went down to the stronghold. Now the Philistines had come and spread themselves in the valley of Rephaim. David inquired of YHWH, saying, "Shall I go up against the Philistines? Will you deliver them into my hand?"

YHWH said to David, "Go up; for I will certainly deliver the Philistines into your hand."

David came to Baal Perazim, and David struck them there. Then he said, "YHWH has broken my enemies before me, like the breach of waters." Therefore he called the name of that place Baal Perazim. They left their images there; and David and his men took them away.

The Philistines came up yet again, and spread themselves in the valley of Rephaim. When David inquired of YHWH, he said, "You shall not go up. Circle around behind them, and attack them in front of the mulberry trees. When you hear the sound of marching in the tops of the mulberry trees, then stir yourself up; for then YHWH has gone out before you to strike the army of the Philistines."

David did so, as YHWH commanded him, and struck the Philistines all the way from Geba to Gezer.

....

David again gathered together all the chosen men of Israel, thirty thousand. David arose, and went with all the people who were with him, from Baale Judah, to bring up from there God's ark, which is called by the Name, even the name of YHWH of Armies who sits above the cherubim. They set God's ark on a new cart, and brought it out of Abinadab's house that was on the hill; and Uzzah and Ahio, the sons of Abinadab, drove the new cart. They brought it out of Abinadab's house, which was in the hill, with God's ark; and Ahio went before the ark. David and all the house of Israel played before YHWH with all kinds of instruments made of cypress wood, with harps, with stringed instruments, with tambourines, with castanets, and with cymbals. When they came to the threshing floor of Nacon, Uzzah reached for God's ark, and took hold of it; for the cattle stumbled. YHWH's anger burned against Uzzah; and God struck him there for his error; and he died there by God's ark. David was displeased, because YHWH had broken out against Uzzah; and he called that place Perez Uzzah, to this day. David was afraid of YHWH that day; and he said, "How could YHWH's ark come to me?" So David would not move YHWH's ark to be with him in David's city; but David carried it aside into Obed-Edom the Gittite's house. YHWH's ark remained in Obed-Edom the Gittite's house three months; and YHWH blessed Obed-Edom and all his house. King David was told, "YHWH has blessed the house of Obed-Edom, and all that belongs to him, because of God's ark."

So David went and brought up God's ark from the house of Obed-Edom into David's city with joy. When those who bore YHWH's ark had gone six paces, he sacrificed an ox and a fattened calf. David danced before YHWH with all his might; and David was clothed in a linen ephod. So David and all the house of Israel brought up YHWH's ark with shouting, and with the sound of the trumpet.

As YHWH's ark came into David's city, Michal the daughter of Saul looked out through the window, and saw king David leaping and dancing before YHWH; and she despised him in her heart. They brought in YHWH's ark, and set it in its place, in the middle of the tent that David had pitched for it; and David offered burnt offerings and peace offerings before YHWH. When David had finished offering the burnt offering and the peace offerings, he blessed the people in the name of YHWH of Armies. He gave to all the people, even among the whole multitude of Israel, both to men and women, to everyone a portion of bread, dates, and raisins. So all the people departed, each to his own house. Then David returned to bless his household. Michal the daughter of Saul came out to meet David, and said, "How glorious the king of Israel was today, who uncovered himself today in the eyes of his servants' maids, as one of the vain fellows shamelessly uncovers himself!"

David said to Michal, "It was before YHWH, who chose me above your father, and above all his house, to appoint me prince over the people of YHWH, over Israel. Therefore I will celebrate before YHWH. I will be yet more vile than this, and will be worthless in my own sight. But the maids of whom you have spoken will honor me."

Michal the daughter of Saul had no child to the day of her death.

....

When the king lived in his house, and YHWH had given him rest from all his enemies all around, the king said to Nathan the prophet, "See now, I dwell in a house of cedar, but God's ark dwells within curtains."

Nathan said to the king, "Go, do all that is in your heart; for YHWH is with you."

That same night, YHWH's word came to Nathan, saying, "Go and tell my servant David, 'YHWH says, "Should you build me a house for me to dwell in? For I have not lived in a house since the day that I brought the children of Israel up out of Egypt, even to this day, but have moved around in a tent and in a tabernacle. In all places in which I have walked with all the children of Israel, did I say a word to any of the tribes of Israel, whom I commanded to be shepherd of my people Israel, saying, 'Why have you not built me a house of cedar?'"' Now therefore tell my servant David this, 'YHWH of Armies says, "I took you from the sheep pen, from following the sheep, to be prince over my people, over Israel. I have been with you wherever you went, and have cut off all your enemies from before you. I will make you a great name, like the name of the great ones who are in the earth. I will appoint a place for my people Israel, and will plant them, that they may dwell in their own place, and be moved no more. The children of wickedness will not afflict them any more, as at the first, and as from the day that I commanded judges to be over my people

Israel. I will cause you to rest from all your enemies. Moreover YHWH tells you that YHWH will make you a house. When your days are fulfilled, and you sleep with your fathers, I will set up your offspring after you, who will proceed out of your body, and I will establish his kingdom. He will build a house for my name, and I will establish the throne of his kingdom forever. I will be his father, and he will be my son. If he commits iniquity, I will chasten him with the rod of men, and with the stripes of the children of men; but my loving kindness will not depart from him, as I took it from Saul, whom I put away before you. Your house and your kingdom will be made sure forever before you. Your throne will be established forever."'" Nathan spoke to David all these words, and according to all this vision.

Then David the king went in, and sat before YHWH; and he said, "Who am I, Lord YHWH, and what is my house, that you have brought me this far? This was yet a small thing in your eyes, Lord YHWH; but you have spoken also of your servant's house for a great while to come; and this among men, Lord YHWH! What more can David say to you? For you know your servant, Lord YHWH. For your word's sake, and according to your own heart, you have worked all this greatness, to make your servant know it. Therefore you are great, YHWH God. For there is no one like you, neither is there any God besides you, according to all that we have heard with our ears. What one nation in the earth is like your people, even like Israel, whom God went to redeem to himself for a people, and to make himself a name, and to do great things for you, and awesome things for your land, before your people, whom you redeemed to yourself out of Egypt, from the nations and their gods? You established for yourself your people Israel to be your people forever; and you, YHWH, became their God. Now, YHWH God, the word that you have spoken concerning your servant, and concerning his house, confirm it forever, and do as you have spoken. Let your name be magnified forever, saying, 'YHWH of Armies is God over Israel; and the house of your servant David will be established before you.' For you, YHWH of Armies, the God of Israel, have revealed to your servant, saying, 'I will build you a house.' Therefore your servant has found in his heart to pray this prayer to you.

"Now, O Lord YHWH, you are God, and your words are truth, and you have promised this good thing to your servant. Now therefore let it please you to bless the house of your servant, that it may continue forever before you; for you, Lord YHWH, have spoken it.

Let the house of your servant be blessed forever with your blessing."

....

After this, David struck the Philistines and subdued them; and David took the bridle of the mother city out of the hand of the Philistines. He struck Moab, and measured them with the line, making them to lie down on the ground; and he measured two lines to put to death, and one full line to keep alive. The Moabites became servants to David, and brought tribute. David struck also Hadadezer the son of Rehob, king of Zobah, as he went to recover his dominion at the River. David took from him one thousand seven hundred horsemen and twenty thousand footmen. David hamstrung all the chariot horses, but reserved of them for one hundred chariots. When the Syrians of Damascus came to help Hadadezer king of Zobah, David struck twenty two thousand men of the Syrians. Then David put garrisons in Syria of Damascus; and the Syrians became servants to David, and brought tribute. YHWH gave victory to David wherever he went. David took the shields of gold that were on the servants of Hadadezer, and brought them to Jerusalem. From Betah and from Berothai, cities of Hadadezer, king David took a great quantity of bronze. When Toi king of Hamath heard that David had struck all the army of Hadadezer, then Toi sent Joram his son to king David, to greet him, and to bless him, because he had fought against Hadadezer and struck him; for Hadadezer had wars with Toi. Joram brought with him vessels of silver, vessels of gold, and vessels of bronze. King David also dedicated these to YHWH, with the silver and gold that he dedicated of all the nations which he subdued; of Syria, of Moab, of the children of Ammon, of the Philistines, of Amalek, and of the plunder of Hadadezer, son of Rehob, king of Zobah.

David earned a reputation when he returned from striking down eighteen thousand men of the Syrians in the Valley of Salt. He put garrisons in Edom. Throughout all Edom, he put garrisons, and all the Edomites became servants to David. YHWH gave victory to David wherever he went. David reigned over all Israel; and David executed justice and righteousness for all his people. Joab the son of Zeruiah was over the army, Jehoshaphat the son of Ahilud was recorder, Zadok the son of Ahitub and Ahimelech the son of Abiathar were priests, Seraiah was scribe, Benaiah the son of Jehoiada was over the Cherethites and the Pelethites, and David's sons were chief ministers.

....

David said, "Is there yet any who is left of Saul's house, that I may show him kindness for Jonathan's sake?" There was of Saul's house a servant whose name was Ziba, and they called him to David; and the king said to him, "Are you Ziba?"

He said, "I am your servant."

The king said, "Is there not yet any of Saul's house, that I may show the kindness of God to him?"

Ziba said to the king, "Jonathan still has a son, who is lame in his feet."

The king said to him, "Where is he?"

Ziba said to the king, "Behold, he is in the house of Machir the son of Ammiel, in Lo Debar."

Then king David sent, and brought him out of the house of Machir the son of Ammiel, from Lo Debar. Mephibosheth, the son of Jonathan, the son of Saul, came to David, and fell on his face, and showed respect. David said, "Mephibosheth."

He answered, "Behold, your servant!"

David said to him, "Don't be afraid; for I will surely show you kindness for Jonathan your father's sake, and will restore to you all the land of Saul your father. You will eat bread at my table continually."

He bowed down, and said, "What is your servant, that you should look at such a dead dog as I am?" Then the king called to Ziba, Saul's servant, and said to him, "All that belonged to Saul and to all his house I have given to your master's son. Till the land for him, you, your sons, and your servants. Bring in the harvest, that your master's son may have bread to eat; but Mephibosheth your master's son will always eat bread at my table."

Now Ziba had fifteen sons and twenty servants. Then Ziba said to the king, "According to all that my lord the king commands his servant, so your servant will do." So Mephibosheth ate at the king's table, like one of the king's sons. Mephibosheth had a young son, whose name was Mica. All that lived in Ziba's house were servants to Mephibosheth. So Mephibosheth lived in Jerusalem; for he ate continually at the king's table. He was lame in both his feet.

....

After this, the king of the children of Ammon died, and Hanun his son reigned in his place. David said, "I will show kindness to Hanun the son of Nahash, as his father showed kindness to me."

So David sent by his servants to comfort him concerning his father. David's servants came into the land of the children of Ammon.

But the princes of the children of Ammon said to Hanun their lord, "Do you think that David honors your father, in that he has sent comforters to you? Hasn't David sent his servants to you to search the city, to spy it out, and to overthrow it?"

So Hanun took David's servants, shaved off one half of their beards, and cut off their garments in the middle, even to their buttocks, and sent them away. When they told David this, he sent to meet them, for the men were greatly ashamed. The king said, "Wait at Jericho until your beards have grown, and then return."

When the children of Ammon saw that they had become odious to David, the children of Ammon sent and hired the Syrians of Beth Rehob, and the Syrians of Zobah, twenty thousand footmen, and the king of Maacah with one thousand men, and the men of Tob twelve thousand men. When David heard of it, he sent Joab, and all the army of the mighty men. The children of Ammon came out, and put the battle in array at the entrance of the gate. The Syrians of Zobah and of Rehob, and the men of Tob and Maacah, were by themselves in the field. Now when Joab saw that the battle was set against him before and behind, he chose of all the choice men of Israel, and put them in array against the Syrians. The rest of the people he committed into the hand of Abishai his brother; and he put them in array against the children of Ammon. He said, "If the Syrians are too strong for me, then you shall help me; but if the children of Ammon are too strong for you, then I will come and help you. Be courageous, and let's be strong for our people, and for the cities of our God; and may YHWH do what seems good to him." So Joab and the people who were with him came near to the battle against the Syrians, and they fled before him. When the children of Ammon saw that the Syrians had fled, they likewise fled before Abishai, and entered into the city. Then Joab returned from the children of Ammon, and came to Jerusalem. When the Syrians saw that they were defeated by Israel, they gathered themselves together. Hadadezer sent, and brought out the Syrians who were beyond the River: and they came to Helam, with Shobach the captain of the army of Hadadezer at their head. David was told that; and he gathered all Israel together, passed over the Jordan, and came to Helam. The Syrians set themselves in array against David, and fought with him. The Syrians fled before Israel; and David killed seven hundred charioteers of the Syrians, and forty thousand horsemen, and struck Shobach the captain of their army, so that he died there. When all the kings who were servants to Hadadezer saw that they were defeated before Israel, they made peace with Israel, and served them. So the Syrians were afraid to help the children of Ammon any more.

....

At the return of the year, at the time when kings go out, David sent Joab, and his servants with him, and all Israel; and they destroyed the children of Ammon, and besieged Rabbah. But David stayed at Jerusalem. At evening, David arose from his bed and walked on the roof of the king's house. From the roof, he saw a woman bathing, and the woman was very beautiful to look at. David sent and inquired after the woman. One said, "Isn't this Bathsheba, the daughter of Eliam, Uriah the Hittite's wife?"

David sent messengers, and took her; and she came in to him, and he lay with her (for she was purified from her uncleanness); and she returned to her house. The woman conceived; and she sent and told David, and said, "I am with child."

David sent to Joab, "Send me Uriah the Hittite." Joab sent Uriah to David. When Uriah had come to him, David asked him how Joab did, and how the people fared, and how the war prospered. David said to Uriah, "Go down to your house and wash your feet." Uriah departed out of the king's house, and a gift from the king was sent after him. But Uriah slept at the door of the king's house with all the servants of his lord, and didn't go down to his house. When they had told David, saying, "Uriah didn't go down to his house," David said to Uriah, "Haven't you come from a journey? Why didn't you go down to your house?"

Uriah said to David, "The ark, Israel, and Judah, are staying in tents; and my lord Joab and the servants of my lord, are encamped in the open field. Shall I then go into my house to eat and to drink, and to lie with my wife? As you live, and as your soul lives, I will not do this thing!"

David said to Uriah, "Stay here today also, and tomorrow I will let you depart." So Uriah stayed in Jerusalem that day, and the next day. When David had called him, he ate and drank before him; and he made him drunk. At evening, he went out to lie on his bed with the servants of his lord, but didn't go down to his house. In the morning, David wrote a letter to Joab, and sent it by the hand of Uriah. He wrote in the letter, saying, "Send Uriah to the forefront of the hottest battle, and retreat from him, that he may be struck, and die."

When Joab kept watch on the city, he assigned Uriah to the place where he knew that valiant men were. The men of the city went out, and fought with Joab. Some of the people fell, even of David's servants; and Uriah the Hittite died also. Then Joab sent and told David all the things concerning the war; and he commanded the messenger, saying, "When you have finished telling all the things concerning the war to the king, it shall be that, if the king's wrath arise, and he asks you, 'Why did you go so near to the city to fight? Didn't you know that they would shoot from the wall? Who struck Abimelech the son of Jerubbesheth? Didn't a woman cast an upper millstone on him from the wall, so that he died at Thebez? Why did you go so near the wall?' then you shall say, 'Your servant Uriah the Hittite is also dead.'"

So the messenger went, and came and showed David all that Joab had sent him for. The messenger said to David, "The men prevailed against us, and came out to us into the field, and we were on them even to the entrance of the gate. The shooters shot at your servants from off the wall; and some of the king's servants are dead, and your servant Uriah the Hittite is also dead."

Then David said to the messenger, "Tell Joab, 'Don't let this thing displease you, for the sword devours one as well as another. Make your battle stronger against the city, and overthrow it.' Encourage him."

When Uriah's wife heard that Uriah her husband was dead, she mourned for her husband. When the mourning was past, David sent and took her home to his house, and she became his wife, and bore him a son. But the thing that David had done displeased YHWH.

....

YHWH sent Nathan to David. He came to him, and said to him, "There were two men in one city; the one rich, and the other poor. The rich man had very many flocks and herds, but the poor man had nothing, except one little ewe lamb, which he had bought and raised. It grew up together with him, and with his children. It ate of his own food, drank of his own cup, and lay in his bosom, and was like a daughter to him. A traveler came to the rich man, and he spared to take of his own flock and of his own herd, to prepare for the wayfaring man who had come to him, but took the poor man's lamb, and prepared it for the man who had come to him."

David's anger burned hot against the man, and he said to Nathan, "As YHWH lives, the man who has done this deserves to die! He must restore the lamb fourfold, because he did this thing, and because he had no pity!"

Nathan said to David, "You are the man. This is what YHWH, the God of Israel, says: 'I anointed you king over Israel, and I delivered you out of the hand of Saul. I gave you your master's house, and your master's wives into your bosom, and gave you the house of Israel and of Judah; and if that would have been too little, I would have added to you many more such things. Why have you despised YHWH's word, to do that which is evil in his sight? You have struck Uriah the Hittite with the sword, and have taken his wife to be your wife, and have slain him with the sword of the children of Ammon. Now therefore the sword will never depart from your house, because you have despised me, and have taken Uriah the Hittite's wife to be your wife.'

"This is what YHWH says: 'Behold, I will raise up evil against you out of your own house; and I will take your wives before your eyes, and give them to your neighbor, and he will lie with your wives in the sight of this sun. For you did this secretly, but I will do this thing before all Israel, and before the sun.'"

David said to Nathan, "I have sinned against YHWH."

Nathan said to David, "YHWH also has put away your sin. You will not die. However, because by this deed you have given great occasion to YHWH's enemies to blaspheme, the child also who is born to you will surely die." Nathan departed to his house.

YHWH struck the child that Uriah's wife bore to David, and it was very sick. David therefore begged God for the child; and David fasted, and went in, and lay all night on the ground. The elders of his house arose beside him, to raise him up from the earth: but he would not, and he didn't eat bread with them. On the seventh day, the child died. David's servants were afraid to tell him that the child was dead, for they said, "Behold, while the child was yet alive, we spoke to him, and he didn't listen to our voice. How will he then harm himself, if we tell him that the child is dead?"

But when David saw that his servants were whispering together, David perceived that the child was dead; and David said to his servants, "Is the child dead?"

They said, "He is dead."

Then David arose from the earth, and washed, and anointed himself, and changed his clothing; and he came into YHWH's house, and worshiped. Then he came to his own house; and when he requested, they set bread before him, and he ate. Then his servants said to him, "What is this that you have done? You fasted and wept for the child while he was alive, but when the child was dead, you rose up and ate bread."

He said, "While the child was yet alive, I fasted and wept; for I said, 'Who knows whether YHWH will not be gracious to me, that the child may live?' But now he is dead, why should I fast? Can I bring him back again? I will go to him, but he will not return to me."

David comforted Bathsheba his wife, and went in to her, and lay with her. She bore a son, and he called his name Solomon. YHWH loved him; and he sent by the hand of Nathan the prophet, and he named him Jedidiah, for YHWH's sake.

Now Joab fought against Rabbah of the children of Ammon, and took the royal city. Joab sent messengers to David, and said, "I have fought against Rabbah. Yes, I have taken the city of waters. Now therefore gather the rest of the people together, and encamp against the city, and take it; lest I take the city, and it be called by my name."

David gathered all the people together, and went to Rabbah, and fought against it, and took it. He took the crown of their king from off his head; and its weight was a talent of gold, and in it were precious stones; and it was set on David's head. He brought a great quantity of plunder out of the city. He brought out the people who were in it, and put them under saws, under iron picks, under axes of iron, and made them pass through the brick kiln; and he did so to all the cities of the children of Ammon. Then David and all the people returned to Jerusalem.

....

After this, Absalom the son of David had a beautiful sister, whose name was Tamar; and Amnon the son of David loved her. Amnon was so troubled that he became sick because of his sister Tamar; for she was a virgin; and it seemed hard to Amnon to do anything to her. But Amnon had a friend, whose name was Jonadab, the son of Shimeah, David's brother; and Jonadab was a very subtle man. He said to him, "Why, son of the king, are you so sad from day to day? Won't you tell me?"

Amnon said to him, "I love Tamar, my brother Absalom's sister."

Jonadab said to him, "Lay down on your bed, and pretend to be sick. When your father comes to see you, tell him, 'Please let my sister Tamar come and give me bread to eat, and prepare the food in my sight, that I may see it, and eat it from her hand.'"

So Amnon lay down and faked being sick. When the king came to see him, Amnon said to the king, "Please let my sister Tamar come, and make me a couple of cakes in my sight, that I may eat from her hand."

Then David sent home to Tamar, saying, "Go now to your brother Amnon's house, and prepare food for him." So Tamar went to her brother Amnon's house; and he was lying down. She took dough, and kneaded it, made cakes in his sight, and baked the cakes. She took the pan, and poured them out before him; but he refused to eat. Amnon said, "Have all men leave me." Then every man went out from him. Amnon said to Tamar, "Bring the food into the room, that I may eat from your hand." Tamar took the cakes which she had made, and brought them into the room to Amnon her brother. When she had brought them near to him to eat, he took hold of her, and said to her, "Come, lie with me, my sister!"

She answered him, "No, my brother, do not force me! For no such thing ought to be done in Israel. Don't you do this folly. As for me, where would I carry my shame? And as for you, you will be as one of the fools in Israel. Now therefore, please speak to the king; for he will not withhold me from you."

However he would not listen to her voice; but being stronger than she, he forced her, and lay with her. Then Amnon hated her with exceedingly great hatred; for the hatred with which he hated her was greater than the love with which he had loved her. Amnon said to her, "Arise, be gone!"

She said to him, "Not so, because this great wrong in sending me away is worse than the other that you did to me!"

But he would not listen to her. Then he called his servant who ministered to him, and said, "Now put this woman out from me, and bolt the door after her."

She had a garment of various colors on her; for the king's daughters who were virgins dressed in such robes. Then his servant brought her out and bolted the door after her. Tamar put ashes on her head, and tore her garment of various colors that was on her; and she laid her hand on her head, and went her way, crying aloud as she went. Absalom her brother said to her, "Has Amnon your brother been with you? But now hold your peace, my sister. He is your brother. Don't take this thing to heart."

So Tamar remained desolate in her brother Absalom's house. But when king David heard of all these things, he was very angry. Absalom spoke to Amnon neither good nor bad; for Absalom hated Amnon, because he had forced his sister Tamar. After two full years, Absalom had sheep shearers in Baal Hazor, which is beside Ephraim: and Absalom invited all the king's sons. Absalom came to the king, and said, "See now, your servant has sheep shearers. Please let the king and his servants go with your servant."

The king said to Absalom, "No, my son, let's not all go, lest we be burdensome to you." He pressed him; however he would not go, but blessed him.

Then Absalom said, "If not, please let my brother Amnon go with us."

The king said to him, "Why should he go with you?"

But Absalom pressed him, and he let Amnon and all the king's sons go with him. Absalom commanded his servants, saying, "Mark now, when Amnon's heart is merry with wine; and when I tell you, 'Strike Amnon,' then kill him. Don't be afraid. Haven't I commanded you? Be courageous, and be valiant!"

The servants of Absalom did to Amnon as Absalom had commanded. Then all the king's sons arose, and every man got up on his mule, and fled. While they were on the way, the news came to David, saying, "Absalom has slain all the king's sons, and there is not one of them left!"

Then the king arose, and tore his garments, and lay on the earth; and all his servants stood by with their clothes torn. Jonadab, the son of Shimeah, David's brother, answered, "Don't let my lord suppose that they have killed all the young men the king's sons; for Amnon only is dead; for by the appointment of Absalom this has been determined from the day that he forced his sister Tamar. Now therefore don't let my lord the king take the thing to his heart, to think that all the king's sons are dead; for only Amnon is dead." But Absalom fled. The young man who kept the watch lifted up his eyes, and looked, and behold, many people were coming by way of the hillside behind him. Jonadab said to the king, "Behold, the king's sons are coming! It is as your servant said." As soon as he had finished speaking, behold, the king's sons came, and lifted up their voice, and wept. The king also and all his servants wept bitterly. But Absalom fled, and went to

Talmai the son of Ammihur, king of Geshur. David mourned for his son every day. So Absalom fled, and went to Geshur, and was there three years. King David longed to go out to Absalom; for he was comforted concerning Amnon, since he was dead.

....

Now Joab the son of Zeruiah perceived that the king's heart was toward Absalom. Joab sent to Tekoa, and brought a wise woman from there, and said to her, "Please act like a mourner, and put on mourning clothing, please, and don't anoint yourself with oil, but be as a woman who has mourned a long time for the dead. Go in to the king, and speak like this to him." So Joab put the words in her mouth.

When the woman of Tekoa spoke to the king, she fell on her face to the ground, showed respect, and said, "Help, O king!"

The king said to her, "What ails you?"

She answered, "Truly I am a widow, and my husband is dead. Your servant had two sons, and they both fought together in the field, and there was no one to part them, but the one struck the other, and killed him. Behold, the whole family has risen against your servant, and they say, 'Deliver him who struck his brother, that we may kill him for the life of his brother whom he killed, and so destroy the heir also.' Thus they would quench my coal which is left, and would leave to my husband neither name nor remainder on the surface of the earth."

The king said to the woman, "Go to your house, and I will give a command concerning you."

The woman of Tekoa said to the king, "My lord, O king, may the iniquity be on me, and on my father's house; and may the king and his throne be guiltless."

The king said, "Whoever says anything to you, bring him to me, and he will not bother you any more."

Then she said, "Please let the king remember YHWH your God, that the avenger of blood destroy not any more, lest they destroy my son."

He said, "As YHWH lives, not one hair of your son shall fall to the earth."

Then the woman said, "Please let your servant speak a word to my lord the king."

He said, "Say on."

The woman said, "Why then have you devised such a thing against the people of God? For in speaking this word the king is as one who is guilty, in that the king does not bring home again his banished one. For we must die, and are like water spilled on the ground, which can't be gathered up again; neither does God take away life, but devises means, that he who is banished not be an outcast from him. Now therefore seeing that I have come to speak this word to my lord the king, it is because the people have made me afraid. Your servant said, 'I will now speak to the king; it may be that the king will perform the request of his servant.' For the king will hear, to deliver his servant out of the hand of the man who would destroy me and my son together out of the inheritance of God. Then your servant said, 'Please let the word of my lord the king bring rest; for as an angel of God, so is my lord the king to discern good and bad. May YHWH, your God, be with you.'"

Then the king answered the woman, "Please don't hide anything from me that I ask you."

The woman said, "Let my lord the king now speak."

The king said, "Is the hand of Joab with you in all this?"

The woman answered, "As your soul lives, my lord the king, no one can turn to the right hand or to the left from anything that my lord the king has spoken; for your servant Joab urged me, and he put all these words in the mouth of your servant. Your servant Joab has done this thing to change the face of the matter. My lord is wise, according to the wisdom of an angel of God, to know all things that are in the earth."

The king said to Joab, "Behold now, I have done this thing. Go therefore, and bring the young man Absalom back."

Joab fell to the ground on his face, showed respect, and blessed the king. Joab said, "Today your servant knows that I have found favor in your sight, my lord, king, in that the king has performed the request of his servant."

So Joab arose and went to Geshur, and brought Absalom to Jerusalem. The king said, "Let him return to his own house, but let him not see my face." So Absalom returned to his own house, and didn't see the king's face. Now in all Israel there was no one to be so much praised as Absalom for his beauty. From the sole of his foot even to the crown of his head there was no defect in him. When he cut the hair of his head (now it was at every year's end that he cut it; because it was heavy on him, therefore he cut it); he weighed the hair of his head at two hundred shekels, after the king's weight. Three sons were born to Absalom, and one daughter, whose name was Tamar. She was a woman with a beautiful face. Absalom lived two full years in Jerusalem, and he didn't see the king's face. Then Absalom sent for Joab, to send him to the king, but he would not come to him. Then he sent again a second time, but he would not come. Therefore he said to his servants, "Behold, Joab's field is near mine, and he has barley there. Go and set it on fire." So Absalom's servants set the field on fire.

Then Joab arose, and came to Absalom to his house, and said to him, "Why have your servants set my field on fire?"

Absalom answered Joab, "Behold, I sent to you, saying, 'Come here, that I may send you to the king, to say, "Why have I come from Geshur? It would be better for me to be there still. Now therefore let me see the king's face, and if there is iniquity in me, let him kill me."'"

So Joab came to the king, and told him; and when he had called for Absalom, he came to the king, and bowed himself on his face to the ground before the king; and the king kissed Absalom.

....

After this, Absalom prepared a chariot and horses for himself, and fifty men to run before him. Absalom rose up early, and stood beside the way of the gate. When any man had a suit which should come to the king for judgment, then Absalom called to him, and said, "What city are you from?"

He said, "Your servant is of one of the tribes of Israel."

Absalom said to him, "Behold, your matters are good and right; but there is no man deputized by the king to hear you." Absalom said moreover, "Oh that I were made judge in the land, that every man who has any suit or cause might come to me, and I would do him justice!" It was so, that when any man came near to bow down to him, he stretched out his hand, and took hold of him, and kissed him. Absalom did this sort of thing to all Israel who came to the king for judgment. So Absalom stole the hearts of the men of Israel. At the end of forty years, Absalom said to the king, "Please let me go and pay my vow, which I have vowed to YHWH, in Hebron. For your servant vowed a vow while I stayed at Geshur in Syria, saying, 'If YHWH shall indeed bring me again to Jerusalem, then I will serve YHWH.'"

The king said to him, "Go in peace."

So he arose, and went to Hebron. But Absalom sent spies throughout all the tribes of Israel, saying, "As soon as you hear the sound of the trumpet, then you shall say, 'Absalom is king in Hebron!'"

Two hundred men went with Absalom out of Jerusalem, who were invited, and went in their simplicity; and they didn't know anything. Absalom sent for Ahithophel the Gilonite, David's counselor, from his city, even from Giloh, while he was offering the sacrifices. The conspiracy was strong; for the people increased continually with Absalom. A messenger came to David, saying, "The hearts of the men of Israel are after Absalom."

David said to all his servants who were with him at Jerusalem, "Arise! Let's flee; or else none of us will escape from Absalom. Hurry to depart, lest he overtake us quickly, and bring down evil on us, and strike the city with the edge of the sword."

The king's servants said to the king, "Behold, your servants are ready to do whatever my lord the king chooses."

The king went out, and all his household after him. The king left ten women, who were concubines, to keep the house. The king went out, and all the people after him; and they stayed in Beth Merhak. All his servants passed on beside him; and all the Cherethites, and all the Pelethites, and all the Gittites, six hundred men who came after him from Gath, passed on before the king. Then the king said to Ittai the Gittite, "Why do you also go with us? Return, and stay with the king; for you are a foreigner, and also an exile. Return to your own place. Whereas you came but yesterday, should I today make you go up and down with us, since I go where I may? Return, and take back your brothers. Mercy and truth be with you."

Ittai answered the king, and said, "As YHWH lives, and as my lord the king lives, surely in what place my lord the king is, whether for death or for life, your servant will be there also."

David said to Ittai, "Go and pass over." Ittai the Gittite passed over, and all his men, and all the little ones who were with him. All the country wept with a loud voice, and all the people passed over. The king also himself passed over the brook Kidron, and all the people passed over, toward the way of the wilderness. Behold, Zadok also came, and all the Levites with him, bearing the ark of the covenant of God; and they set down God's ark; and Abiathar went up, until all the people finished passing out of the city. The king said to Zadok, "Carry God's ark back into the city. If I find favor in YHWH's eyes, he will bring me again, and show me both it, and his habitation; but if he says, 'I have no delight in you;' behold, here I am. Let him do to me as seems good to him." The king said also to Zadok the priest, "Aren't you a seer? Return into the city in peace, and your two sons with you, Ahimaaz your son, and Jonathan the son of Abiathar. Behold, I will stay at the fords of the wilderness, until word comes from you to inform me." Zadok therefore and Abiathar carried God's ark to Jerusalem again; and they stayed there. David went up by the ascent of the Mount of Olives, and wept as he went up; and he had his head covered, and went barefoot. All the people who were with him each covered his head, and they went up, weeping as they went up.

Someone told David, saying, "Ahithophel is among the conspirators with Absalom."

David said, "YHWH, please turn the counsel of Ahithophel into foolishness."

When David had come to the top, where God was worshiped, behold, Hushai the Archite came to meet him with his tunic torn, and earth on his head. David said to him, "If you pass on with me, then you will be a burden to me; but if you return to the city, and tell Absalom, 'I will be your servant, O king. As I have been your father's servant in time past, so I will now be your servant; then will you defeat for me the counsel of Ahithophel.' Don't you have Zadok and Abiathar the priests there with you? Therefore whatever you hear out of the king's house, tell it to Zadok and Abiathar the priests. Behold, they have there with them their two sons, Ahimaaz, Zadok's son, and Jonathan, Abiathar's son. Send to me everything that you shall hear by them."

So Hushai, David's friend, came into the city; and Absalom came into Jerusalem.

....

When David was a little past the top, behold, Ziba the servant of Mephibosheth met him with a couple of donkeys saddled, and on them two hundred loaves of bread, and one hundred clusters of raisins, and one hundred summer fruits, and a container of wine. The king said to Ziba, "What do you mean by these?"

Ziba said, "The donkeys are for the king's household to ride on; and the bread and summer fruit for the young men to eat; and the wine, that those who are faint in the wilderness may drink."

The king said, "Where is your master's son?"

Ziba said to the king, "Behold, he is staying in Jerusalem; for he said, 'Today the house of Israel will restore me the kingdom of my father.'"

Then the king said to Ziba, "Behold, all that belongs to Mephibosheth is yours."

Ziba said, "I bow down. Let me find favor in your sight, my lord, O king."

When king David came to Bahurim, behold, a man of the family of Saul's house came out, whose name was Shimei, the son of Gera. He came out and cursed as he came. He cast stones at David, and at all the servants of king David, and all the people and all the mighty men were on his right hand and on his left. Shimei said when he cursed, "Be gone, be gone, you man of blood, and wicked fellow! YHWH has returned on you all the blood of Saul's house, in whose place you have reigned! YHWH has delivered the kingdom into the hand of Absalom your son! Behold, you are caught by your own mischief, because you are a man of blood!"

Then Abishai the son of Zeruiah said to the king, "Why should this dead dog curse my lord the king? Please let me go over and take off his head." The king said, "What have I to do with you, you sons of Zeruiah? Because he curses, and because YHWH has said to him, 'Curse David;' who then shall say, 'Why have you done so?'"

David said to Abishai, and to all his servants, "Behold, my son, who came out of my bowels, seeks my life. How much more this Benjamite, now? Leave him alone, and let him curse; for YHWH has invited him. It may be that YHWH will look on the wrong done to me, and that YHWH will repay me good for the cursing of me today." So David and his men went by the way; and Shimei went along on the hillside opposite him, and cursed as he went, threw stones at him, and threw dust. The king, and all the people who were with him, came weary; and he refreshed himself there.

Absalom and all the people, the men of Israel, came to Jerusalem, and Ahithophel with him. When Hushai the Archite, David's friend, had come to Absalom, Hushai said to Absalom, "Long live the king! Long live the king!"

Absalom said to Hushai, "Is this your kindness to your friend? Why didn't you go with your friend?"

Hushai said to Absalom, "No; but whomever YHWH, and this people, and all the men of Israel have chosen, I will be his, and I will stay with him. Again, whom should I serve? Shouldn't I serve in the presence of his son? As I have served in your father's presence, so I will be in your presence."

Then Absalom said to Ahithophel, "Give your counsel what we shall do."

Ahithophel said to Absalom, "Go in to your father's concubines that he has left to keep the house. Then all Israel will hear that you are abhorred by your father. Then the hands of all who are with you will be strong."

So they spread a tent for Absalom on the top of the house, and Absalom went in to his father's concubines in the sight of all Israel. The counsel of Ahithophel, which he gave in those days, was as if a man inquired at the inner sanctuary of God. All the counsel of Ahithophel both was like this with David and with Absalom.

....

Moreover Ahithophel said to Absalom, "Let me now choose twelve thousand men, and I will arise and pursue after David tonight. I will come on him while he is weary and exhausted, and will make him afraid. All the people who are with him will flee. I will strike the king only, and I will bring back all the people to you. The man whom you seek is as if all returned. All the people shall be in peace."

The saying pleased Absalom well, and all the elders of Israel. Then Absalom said, "Now call Hushai the Archite also, and let's hear likewise what he says."

When Hushai had come to Absalom, Absalom spoke to him, saying, "Ahithophel has spoken like this. Shall we do what he says? If not, speak up."

Hushai said to Absalom, "The counsel that Ahithophel has given this time is not good." Hushai said moreover, "You know your father and his men, that they are mighty men, and they are fierce in their minds, like a bear robbed of her cubs in the field. Your father is a man of war, and will not lodge with the people. Behold, he is now hidden in some pit, or in some other place. It will happen, when some of them have fallen at the first, that whoever hears it will say, 'There is a slaughter among the people who follow Absalom!' Even he who is valiant, whose heart is as the heart of a lion, will utterly melt; for all Israel knows that your father is a mighty man, and those who are with him are valiant men. But I counsel that all Israel be gathered together to you, from Dan even to Beersheba, as the sand that is by the sea for multitude; and that you go to battle in your own person. So we will come on him in some place where he will be found, and we will light on him as the dew falls on the ground, then we will not leave so much as one of him and of all the men who are with him. Moreover, if he has gone into a city, then all Israel will bring ropes to that city, and we will draw it into the river, until there isn't one small stone found there."

Absalom and all the men of Israel said, "The counsel of Hushai the Archite is better than the counsel of Ahithophel." For YHWH had ordained to defeat the good counsel of Ahithophel, to the intent that YHWH might bring evil on Absalom. Then Hushai said to Zadok and to Abiathar the priests, "Ahithophel counseled Absalom and the elders of Israel that way; and I have counseled this way. Now therefore send quickly, and tell David, saying, 'Don't lodge tonight at the fords of the wilderness, but by all means pass over; lest the king be swallowed up, and all the people who are with him.'"

Now Jonathan and Ahimaaz were staying by En Rogel; and a female servant used to go and tell them; and they went and told king David. For they might not be seen to come into the city. But a boy saw them, and told Absalom. Then they both went away quickly, and came to the house of a man in Bahurim, who had a well in his court; and they went down there. The woman took and spread the covering over the well's mouth, and spread out crushed grain on it; and nothing was known. Absalom's servants came to the woman to the house; and they said, "Where are Ahimaaz and Jonathan?"

The woman said to them, "They have gone over the brook of water."

When they had sought and could not find them, they returned to Jerusalem. After they had departed, they came up out of the well, and went and told king David; and they said to David, "Arise and pass quickly over the water; for thus has Ahithophel counseled against you."

Then David arose, and all the people who were with him, and they passed over the Jordan. By the morning light there lacked not one of them who had not gone over the Jordan. When Ahithophel saw that his counsel was not followed, he saddled his donkey, arose, and went home, to his city, and set his house in order, and hanged himself; and he died, and was buried in the tomb of his father. Then David came to Mahanaim. Absalom passed over the Jordan, he and all the men of Israel with him. Absalom set Amasa over the army instead of Joab. Now Amasa was the son of a man whose name was Ithra the Israelite, who went in to Abigail the daughter of Nahash, sister to Zeruiah, Joab's mother. Israel and Absalom encamped in the land of Gilead. When David had come to Mahanaim, Shobi the son of Nahash of Rabbah of the children of Ammon, and Machir the son of Ammiel of Lodebar, and Barzillai the Gileadite of Rogelim, brought beds, basins, earthen vessels, wheat, barley, meal, parched grain, beans, lentils, roasted grain, honey, butter, sheep, and cheese of the herd, for David, and for the people who were with him, to eat; for they said, "The people are hungry, weary, and thirsty in the wilderness."

....

David counted the people who were with him, and set captains of thousands and captains of hundreds over them. David sent the people out, a third part under the hand of Joab, and a third part under the hand of Abishai the son of Zeruiah, Joab's brother, and a third part under the hand of Ittai the Gittite. The king said to the people, "I will also surely go out with you myself."

But the people said, "You shall not go out; for if we flee away, they will not care for us; neither if half of us die, will they care for us. But you are worth ten thousand of us. Therefore now it is better that you are ready to help us out of the city."

The king said to them, "I will do what seems best to you."

The king stood beside the gate, and all the people went out by hundreds and by thousands. The king commanded Joab and Abishai and Ittai, saying, "Deal gently for my sake with the young man, even with Absalom." All the people heard when the king commanded all the captains concerning Absalom.

So the people went out into the field against Israel; and the battle was in the forest of Ephraim. The people of Israel were struck there before David's servants, and there was a great slaughter there that day of twenty thousand men. For the battle was there spread over the surface of all the country, and the forest devoured more people that day than the sword devoured. Absalom happened to meet David's servants. Absalom was riding on his mule, and the mule went under the thick boughs of a great oak, and his head caught hold of the oak, and he was taken up between the sky and earth; and the mule that was under him went on. A certain man saw it, and told Joab, and said, "Behold, I saw Absalom hanging in an oak."

Joab said to the man who told him, "Behold, you saw it, and why didn't you strike him there to the ground? I would have given you ten pieces of silver, and a sash."

The man said to Joab, "Though I should receive a thousand pieces of silver in my hand, I still wouldn't stretch out my hand against the king's son; for in our hearing the king commanded you and Abishai and Ittai, saying, 'Beware that no one touch the young man Absalom.' Otherwise if I had dealt falsely against his life (and there is no matter hidden from the king), then you yourself would have set yourself against me."

Then Joab said, "I'm not going to wait like this with you." He took three darts in his hand, and thrust them through the heart of Absalom, while he was yet alive in the middle of the oak. Ten young men who bore Joab's armor surrounded and struck Absalom, and killed him. Joab blew the trumpet, and the people returned from pursuing after Israel; for Joab held the people back. They took Absalom and cast him into a great pit in the forest, and raised over him a very great heap of stones. Then all Israel fled, each to his own tent. Now Absalom in his lifetime had taken and reared up for himself the pillar which is in the king's valley, for he said, "I have no son to keep my name in memory." He called the pillar after his own name. It is called Absalom's monument, to this day.

Then Ahimaaz the son of Zadok said, "Let me now run and carry the king news, how YHWH has avenged him of his enemies."

Joab said to him, "You must not be the bearer of news today, but you must carry news another day. But today you must carry no news, because the king's son is dead."

Then Joab said to the Cushite, "Go, tell the king what you have seen!" The Cushite bowed himself to Joab, and ran.

Then Ahimaaz the son of Zadok said yet again to Joab, "But come what may, please let me also run after the Cushite."

Joab said, "Why do you want to run, my son, since you will have no reward for the news?"

"But come what may," he said, "I will run."

He said to him, "Run!" Then Ahimaaz ran by the way of the Plain, and outran the Cushite.

Now David was sitting between the two gates; and the watchman went up to the roof of the gate to the wall, and lifted up his eyes, and looked, and, behold, a man running alone. The watchman cried, and told the king. The king said, "If he is alone, there is news in his mouth." He came closer and closer.

The watchman saw another man running; and the watchman called to the gatekeeper, and said, "Behold, a man running alone!"

The king said, "He also brings news."

The watchman said, "I think the running of the first one is like the running of Ahimaaz the son of Zadok."

The king said, "He is a good man, and comes with good news."

Ahimaaz called, and said to the king, "All is well." He bowed himself before the king with his face to the earth, and said, "Blessed is YHWH your God, who has delivered up the men who lifted up their hand against my lord the king!"

The king said, "Is it well with the young man Absalom?"

Ahimaaz answered, "When Joab sent the king's servant, even me your servant, I saw a great tumult, but I don't know what it was."

The king said, "Come and stand here." He came, and stood still.

Behold, the Cushite came. The Cushite said, "News for my lord the king, for YHWH has avenged you today of all those who rose up against you."

The king said to the Cushite, "Is it well with the young man Absalom?"

The Cushite answered, "May the enemies of my lord the king, and all who rise up against you to do you harm, be as that young man is."

The king was much moved, and went up to the room over the gate, and wept. As he went, he said, "My son Absalom! My son, my son Absalom! I wish I had died for you, Absalom, my son, my son!"

....

Joab was told, "Behold, the king weeps and mourns for Absalom." The victory that day was turned into mourning among all the people; for the people heard it said that day, "The king grieves for his son."

The people sneaked into the city that day, as people who are ashamed steal away when they flee in battle. The king covered his face, and the king cried with a loud voice, "My son Absalom, Absalom, my son, my son!"

Joab came into the house to the king, and said, "Today you have shamed the faces of all your servants, who today have saved your life, and the lives of your sons and of your daughters, and the lives of your wives, and the lives of your concubines; in that you love those who hate you, and hate those who love you. For you have declared today that princes and servants are nothing to you. For today I perceive that if Absalom had lived, and all we had died today, then it would have pleased you well. Now therefore arise, go out, and speak to comfort your servants; for I swear by YHWH, if you don't go out, not a man will stay with you this night. That would be worse to you than all the evil that has happened to you from your youth until now."

Then the king arose, and sat in the gate. They told to all the people, saying, "Behold, the king is sitting in the gate." All the people came before the king. Now Israel had fled every man to his tent. All the people were at strife throughout all the tribes of Israel, saying, "The king delivered us out of the hand of our enemies, and he saved us out of the hand of the Philistines; and now he has fled out of the land from Absalom. Absalom, whom we anointed over us, is dead in battle. Now therefore why don't you speak a word of bringing the king back?"

King David sent to Zadok and to Abiathar the priests, saying, "Speak to the elders of Judah, saying, 'Why are you the last to bring the king back to his house? Since the speech of all Israel has come to the king, to return him to his house. You are my brothers. You are my bone and my flesh. Why then are you the last to bring back the king?' Say to Amasa, 'Aren't you my bone and my flesh? God do so to me, and more also, if you aren't captain of the army before me continually instead of Joab.'" He bowed the heart of all the men of Judah, even as one man; so that they sent to the king, saying, "Return, you and all your servants."

So the king returned, and came to the Jordan. Judah came to Gilgal, to go to meet the king, to bring the king over the Jordan. Shimei the son of Gera, the Benjamite, who was of Bahurim, hurried and came down with the men of Judah to meet king David. There were a thousand men of Benjamin with him, and Ziba the servant of Saul's house, and his fifteen sons and his twenty servants with him; and they went through the Jordan in the presence of the king. A ferry boat went to bring over the king's household, and to do what he thought good. Shimei the son of Gera fell down before the king, when he had come over the Jordan. He said to the king, "Don't let my lord impute iniquity to me, or remember that which your servant did perversely the day that my lord the king went out of Jerusalem, that the king should take it to his heart. For your servant knows that I have sinned. Therefore behold, I have come today as the first of all the house of Joseph to go down to meet my lord the king."

But Abishai the son of Zeruiah answered, "Shouldn't Shimei be put to death for this, because he cursed YHWH's anointed?"

David said, "What have I to do with you, you sons of Zeruiah, that you should be adversaries to me today? Shall any man be put to death today in Israel? For don't I know that I am king over Israel today?" The king said to Shimei, "You will not die." The king swore to him.

Mephibosheth the son of Saul came down to meet the king; and he had neither groomed his feet, nor trimmed his beard, nor washed his clothes, from the day the king departed until the day he came home in peace. When he had come to Jerusalem to meet the king, the king said to him, "Why didn't you go with me, Mephibosheth?"

He answered, "My lord, O king, my servant deceived me. For your servant said, 'I will saddle a donkey for myself, that I may ride on it and go with the king,' because your servant is lame. He has slandered your servant to my lord the king, but my lord the king is as an angel of God. Therefore do what is good in your eyes. For all my father's house were but dead men before my lord the king; yet you set your servant among those who ate at your own table. What right therefore have I yet that I should cry any more to the king?"

The king said to him, "Why do you speak any more of your matters? I say, you and Ziba divide the land."

Mephibosheth said to the king, "Yes, let him take all, because my lord the king has come in peace to his own house." Barzillai the Gileadite came down from Rogelim; and he went over the Jordan with the king, to conduct him over the Jordan. Now Barzillai was a very aged man, even eighty years old. He had provided the king with sustenance while he stayed at Mahanaim; for he was a very great man. The king said to Barzillai, "Come over with me, and I will sustain you with me in Jerusalem." Barzillai said to the king, "How many are the days of the years of my life, that I should go up with the king to Jerusalem? I am eighty years old, today. Can I discern between good and bad? Can your servant taste what I eat or what I drink? Can I hear the voice of singing men and singing women any more? Why then should your servant be a burden to my lord the king? Your servant would but just go over the Jordan with the king. Why should the king repay me with such a reward? Please let your servant turn back again, that I may die in my own city, by the grave of my father and my mother. But behold, your servant Chimham; let him go over with my lord the king; and do to him what shall seem good to you."

The king answered, "Chimham shall go over with me, and I will do to him that which shall seem good to you. Whatever you request of me, that I will do for you."

All the people went over the Jordan, and the king went over. Then the king kissed Barzillai, and blessed him; and he returned to his own place. So the king went over to Gilgal, and Chimham went over with him. All the people of Judah brought the king over, and also half the people of Israel. Behold, all the men of Israel came to the king, and said to the king, "Why have our brothers the men of Judah stolen you away, and brought the king, and his household, over the Jordan, and all David's men with him?"

All the men of Judah answered the men of Israel, "Because the king is a close relative to us. Why then are you angry about this matter? Have we eaten at all at the king's cost? Or has he given us any gift?"

The men of Israel answered the men of Judah, and said, "We have ten parts in the king, and we have also more claim to David than you. Why then did you despise us, that our advice should not be first had in bringing back our king?" The words of the men of Judah were fiercer than the words of the men of Israel.

....

There happened to be there a wicked fellow, whose name was Sheba, the son of Bichri, a Benjamite; and he blew the trumpet, and said, "We have no portion in David, neither have we inheritance in the son of Jesse. Every man to his tents, Israel!"

So all the men of Israel went up from following David, and followed Sheba the son of Bichri; but the men of Judah joined with their king, from the Jordan even to Jerusalem. David came to his house at Jerusalem; and the king took the ten women his concubines, whom he had left to keep the house, and put them in custody, and provided them with sustenance, but didn't go in to them. So they were shut up to the day of their death, living in widowhood.

Then the king said to Amasa, "Call me the men of Judah together within three days, and be here present."

So Amasa went to call the men of Judah together; but he stayed longer than the set time which he had appointed him. David said to Abishai, "Now Sheba the son of Bichri will do us more harm than Absalom did. Take your lord's servants, and pursue after him, lest he get himself fortified cities, and escape out of our sight."

Joab's men went out after him, and the Cherethites and the Pelethites, and all the mighty men; and they went out of Jerusalem, to pursue Sheba the son of Bichri. When they were at the great stone which is in Gibeon, Amasa came to meet them. Joab was clothed in his apparel of war that he had put on, and on it was a sash with a sword fastened on his waist in its sheath; and as he went along it fell out. Joab said to Amasa, "Is it well with you, my brother?" Joab took Amasa by the beard with his right hand to kiss him. But Amasa took no heed to the sword that was in Joab's hand. So he struck him with it in the body, and shed out his bowels to the ground, and didn't strike him again; and he died. Joab and Abishai his brother pursued Sheba the son of Bichri. One of Joab's young men stood by him, and said, "He who favors Joab, and he who is for David, let him follow Joab!"

Amasa lay wallowing in his blood in the middle of the highway. When the man saw that all the people stood still, he carried Amasa out of the highway into the field, and cast a garment over him, when he saw that everyone who came by him stood still. When he was removed out of the highway, all the people went on after Joab, to pursue Sheba the son of Bichri. He went through all the tribes of Israel to Abel, and to Beth Maacah, and all the Berites. They were gathered together, and went also after him. They came and besieged him in Abel of Beth Maacah, and they cast up a mound against the city, and it stood against the rampart; and all the people who were with Joab battered the wall, to throw it down. Then a wise woman cried out of the city, "Hear, hear! Please say to Joab, 'Come near here, that I may speak with you.'" He came near to her; and the woman said, "Are you Joab?"

He answered, "I am."

Then she said to him, "Hear the words of your servant."

He answered, "I'm listening."

Then she spoke, saying, "They used to say in old times, 'They shall surely ask counsel at Abel;' and so they settled a matter. I am among those who are peaceable and faithful in Israel. You seek to destroy a city and a mother in Israel. Why will you swallow up YHWH's inheritance?"

Joab answered, "Far be it, far be it from me, that I should swallow up or destroy. The matter is not so. But a man of the hill country of Ephraim, Sheba the son of Bichri by name, has lifted up his hand against the king, even against David. Just deliver him, and I will depart from the city."

The woman said to Joab, "Behold, his head will be thrown to you over the wall."

Then the woman went to all the people in her wisdom. They cut off the head of Sheba the son of Bichri, and threw it out to Joab. He blew the trumpet, and they were dispersed from the city, every man to his tent. Then Joab returned to Jerusalem to the king. Now Joab was over all the army of Israel, Benaiah the son of Jehoiada was over the Cherethites and over the Pelethites, Adoram was over the men subject to forced labor, Jehoshaphat the son of Ahilud was the recorder, Sheva was scribe, and Zadok and Abiathar were priests, and Ira the Jairite was chief minister to David.

....

There was a famine in the days of David for three years, year after year; and David sought the face of YHWH. YHWH said, "It is for Saul, and for his bloody house, because he put the Gibeonites to death."

The king called the Gibeonites, and said to them (now the Gibeonites were not of the children of Israel, but of the remnant of the Amorites, and the children of Israel had sworn to them; and Saul sought to kill them in his zeal for the children of Israel and Judah); and David said to the Gibeonites, "What should I do for you? And with what should I make atonement, that you may bless YHWH's inheritance?"

The Gibeonites said to him, "It is no matter of silver or gold between us and Saul, or his house; neither is it for us to put any man to death in Israel."

He said, "I will do for you whatever you say."

They said to the king, "The man who consumed us, and who devised against us, that we should be destroyed from remaining in any of the borders of Israel, let seven men of his sons be delivered to us, and we will hang them up to YHWH in Gibeah of Saul, the chosen of YHWH."

The king said, "I will give them."

But the king spared Mephibosheth, the son of Jonathan the son of Saul, because of YHWH's oath that was between them, between David and Jonathan the son of Saul. But the king took the two sons of Rizpah the daughter of Aiah, whom she bore to Saul, Armoni and Mephibosheth; and the five sons of Michal the daughter of Saul, whom she bore to Adriel the son of Barzillai the Meholathite. He delivered them into the hands of the Gibeonites, and they hanged them on the mountain before YHWH, and all seven of them fell together. They were put to death in the days of harvest, in the first days, at the beginning of barley harvest. Rizpah the daughter of Aiah took sackcloth, and spread it for herself on the rock, from the beginning of harvest until water poured on them from the sky. She allowed neither the birds of the sky to rest on them by day, nor the animals of the field by night. David was told what Rizpah the daughter of Aiah, the concubine of Saul, had done. So David went and took the bones of Saul and the bones of Jonathan his son from the men of Jabesh Gilead, who had stolen them from the street of Beth Shan, where the Philistines had hanged them, in the day that the Philistines killed Saul in Gilboa; and he brought up from there the bones of Saul and the bones of Jonathan his son. They also gathered the bones of those who were hanged. They buried the bones of Saul and Jonathan his son in the country of Benjamin in Zela, in the tomb of Kish his father: and they performed all that the king commanded. After that, God answered prayer for the land.

The Philistines had war again with Israel; and David went down, and his servants with him, and fought against the Philistines. David grew faint; and Ishbibenob, who was of the sons of the giant, the weight of whose spear was three hundred shekels of bronze in weight, he being armed with a new sword, thought he would kill David. But Abishai the son of Zeruiah helped him, and struck the Philistine, and killed him. Then the men of David swore to him, saying, "Don't go out with us to battle any more, so that you don't quench the lamp of Israel."

After this, there was again war with the Philistines at Gob. Then Sibbecai the Hushathite killed Saph, who was of the sons of the giant. There was again war with the Philistines at Gob; and Elhanan the son of Jaare-Oregim the Bethlehemite killed Goliath the Gittite's brother, the staff of whose spear was like a weaver's beam. There was again war at Gath, where there was a man of great stature, who had six fingers on every hand, and six toes on every foot, twenty four in count; and he also was born to the giant. When he defied Israel, Jonathan the son of Shimei, David's brother, killed him. These four were born to the giant in Gath; and they fell by the hand of David, and by the hand of his servants.

David spoke to YHWH the words of this song in the day that YHWH delivered him out of the hand of all his enemies, and out of the hand of Saul, and he said:

"*YHWH is my rock,*
my fortress,
and my deliverer, even mine;
God is my rock in whom I take refuge;
my shield, and the horn of my salvation,
my high tower, and my refuge.
My savior, you save me from violence.
I call on YHWH, who is worthy to be praised;
So shall I be saved from my enemies.
For the waves of death surrounded me.
The floods of ungodliness made me afraid.
The cords of Sheol were around me.
The snares of death caught me.
In my distress, I called on YHWH.
Yes, I called to my God.
He heard my voice out of his temple.
My cry came into his ears.
Then the earth shook and trembled.
The foundations of heaven quaked and were shaken,
because he was angry.
Smoke went up out of his nostrils.
Consuming fire came out of his mouth.
Coals were kindled by it.
He bowed the heavens also, and came down.
Thick darkness was under his feet.
He rode on a cherub, and flew.
Yes, he was seen on the wings of the wind.
He made darkness a shelter around himself:
gathering of waters, and thick clouds of the skies.
At the brightness before him,
coals of fire were kindled.
YHWH thundered from heaven.
The Most High uttered his voice.
He sent out arrows, and scattered them;
lightning, and confused them.
Then the channels of the sea appeared.
The foundations of the world were laid bare by YHWH's rebuke,

at the blast of the breath of his nostrils.
He sent from on high and he took me.
He drew me out of many waters.
He delivered me from my strong enemy,
from those who hated me, for they were too mighty for me.
They came on me in the day of my calamity,
but YHWH was my support.
He also brought me out into a large place.
He delivered me, because he delighted in me.
YHWH rewarded me according to my righteousness.
He rewarded me according to the cleanness of my hands.
For I have kept YHWH's ways,
and have not wickedly departed from my God.
For all his ordinances were before me.
As for his statutes, I didn't depart from them.
I was also perfect toward him.
I kept myself from my iniquity.
Therefore YHWH has rewarded me according to my righteousness,
According to my cleanness in his eyesight.
With the merciful you will show yourself merciful.
With the perfect man you will show yourself perfect.
With the pure you will show yourself pure.
With the crooked you will show yourself shrewd.
You will save the afflicted people,
But your eyes are on the arrogant, that you may bring them
down.
For you are my lamp, YHWH.
YHWH will light up my darkness.
For by you, I run against a troop.
By my God, I leap over a wall.
As for God, his way is perfect.
YHWH's word is tested.
He is a shield to all those who take refuge in him.
For who is God, besides YHWH?
Who is a rock, besides our God?
God is my strong fortress.
He makes my way perfect.
He makes his feet like hinds' feet,
and sets me on my high places.
He teaches my hands to war,

so that my arms bend a bow of bronze.
You have also given me the shield of your salvation.
Your gentleness has made me great.
You have enlarged my steps under me.
My feet have not slipped.
I have pursued my enemies and destroyed them.
I didn't turn again until they were consumed.
I have consumed them,
and struck them through,
so that they can't arise.
Yes, they have fallen under my feet.
For you have armed me with strength for the battle.
You have subdued under me those who rose up against me.
You have also made my enemies turn their backs to me,
that I might cut off those who hate me.
They looked, but there was no one to save;
even to YHWH, but he didn't answer them.
Then I beat them as small as the dust of the earth.
I crushed them as the mire of the streets, and spread them
abroad.
You also have delivered me from the strivings of my people.
You have kept me to be the head of the nations.
A people whom I have not known will serve me.
The foreigners will submit themselves to me.
As soon as they hear of me, they will obey me.
The foreigners will fade away,
and will come trembling out of their close places.
YHWH lives!
Blessed be my rock!
Exalted be God, the rock of my salvation,
even the God who executes vengeance for me,
who brings down peoples under me,
who brings me away from my enemies.
Yes, you lift me up above those who rise up against me.
You deliver me from the violent man.
Therefore I will give thanks to you, YHWH, among the nations,
and will sing praises to your name.
He gives great deliverance to his king,
and shows loving kindness to his anointed,
to David and to his offspring, forever more."

Now these are the last words of David.

David the son of Jesse says,
the man who was raised on high says,
the anointed of the God of Jacob,
the sweet psalmist of Israel:
"YHWH's Spirit spoke by me.
His word was on my tongue.
The God of Israel said,
the Rock of Israel spoke to me,
'One who rules over men righteously,
who rules in the fear of God,
shall be as the light of the morning, when the sun rises,
a morning without clouds,
when the tender grass springs out of the earth,
through clear shining after rain.'
Isn't my house so with God?
Yet he has made with me an everlasting covenant,
ordered in all things, and sure,
for it is all my salvation, and all my desire,
although he doesn't make it grow.
But all the ungodly will be as thorns to be thrust away,
because they can't be taken with the hand,
But the man who touches them must be armed with iron and the
staff of a spear.
They will be utterly burned with fire in their place."

These are the names of the mighty men whom David had: Josheb Basshebeth a Tahchemonite, chief of the captains; he was called Adino the Eznite, who killed eight hundred at one time. After him was Eleazar the son of Dodai the son of an Ahohite, one of the three mighty men with David, when they defied the Philistines who were there gathered together to battle, and the men of Israel had gone away. He arose and struck the Philistines until his hand was weary, and his hand froze to the sword; and YHWH worked a great victory that day; and the people returned after him only to take plunder. After him was Shammah the son of Agee a Hararite. The Philistines had gathered together into a troop, where there was a plot of ground full of lentils; and the people fled from the Philistines. But he stood in the middle of the plot and defended it, and killed the Philistines;

and YHWH worked a great victory. Three of the thirty chief men went down, and came to David in the harvest time to the cave of Adullam; and the troop of the Philistines was encamped in the valley of Rephaim. David was then in the stronghold; and the garrison of the Philistines was then in Bethlehem. David longed, and said, "Oh that someone would give me water to drink from the well of Bethlehem, which is by the gate!"

The three mighty men broke through the army of the Philistines, and drew water out of the well of Bethlehem that was by the gate, and took it and brought it to David; but he would not drink of it, but poured it out to YHWH. He said, "Be it far from me, YHWH, that I should do this! Isn't this the blood of the men who risked their lives to go?" Therefore he would not drink it. The three mighty men did these things.

Abishai, the brother of Joab, the son of Zeruiah, was chief of the three. He lifted up his spear against three hundred and killed them, and had a name among the three. Wasn't he most honorable of the three? Therefore he was made their captain. However he wasn't included as one of the three. Benaiah the son of Jehoiada, the son of a valiant man of Kabzeel, who had done mighty deeds, killed the two sons of Ariel of Moab. He also went down and killed a lion in the middle of a pit in a time of snow. He killed a huge Egyptian, and the Egyptian had a spear in his hand; but he went down to him with a staff, and plucked the spear out of the Egyptian's hand, and killed him with his own spear. Benaiah the son of Jehoiada did these things, and had a name among the three mighty men. He was more honorable than the thirty, but he didn't attain to the three. David set him over his guard. Asahel the brother of Joab was one of the thirty: Elhanan the son of Dodo of Bethlehem, Shammah the Harodite, Elika the Harodite, Helez the Paltite, Ira the son of Ikkesh the Tekoite, Abiezer the Anathothite, Mebunnai the Hushathite, Zalmon the Ahohite, Maharai the Netophathite, Heleb the son of Baanah the Netophathite, Ittai the son of Ribai of Gibeah of the children of Benjamin, Benaiah a Pirathonite, Hiddai of the brooks of Gaash. Abialbon the Arbathite, Azmaveth the Barhumite, Eliahba the Shaalbonite, the sons of Jashen, Jonathan, Shammah the Hararite, Ahiam the son of Sharar the Ararite, Eliphelet the son of Ahasbai, the son of the Maacathite, Eliam the son of Ahithophel the Gilonite, Hezro the Carmelite, Paarai the Arbite, Igal the son of Nathan of Zobah, Bani the Gadite, Zelek the Ammonite, Naharai the Beerothite, armor bearers to Joab the son of Zeruiah, Ira the Ithrite, Gareb the Ithrite, and Uriah the Hittite: thirty-seven in all.

....

Again YHWH's anger burned against Israel, and he moved David against them, saying, "Go, count Israel and Judah." The king said to Joab the captain of the army, who was with him, "Now go back and forth through all the tribes of Israel, from Dan even to Beersheba, and count the people, that I may know the sum of the people."

Joab said to the king, "Now may YHWH your God add to the people, however many they may be, one hundred times; and may the eyes of my lord the king see it. But why does my lord the king delight in this thing?"

Notwithstanding, the king's word prevailed against Joab, and against the captains of the army. Joab and the captains of the army went out from the presence of the king to count the people of Israel. They passed over the Jordan, and encamped in Aroer, on the right side of the city that is in the middle of the valley of Gad, and to Jazer; then they came to Gilead, and to the land of Tahtim Hodshi; and they came to Dan Jaan, and around to Sidon, and came to the stronghold of Tyre, and to all the cities of the Hivites, and of the Canaanites; and they went out to the south of Judah, at Beersheba. So when they had gone back and forth through all the land, they came to Jerusalem at the end of nine months and twenty days. Joab gave up the sum of the counting of the people to the king: and there were in Israel eight hundred thousand valiant men who drew the sword; and the men of Judah were five hundred thousand men. David's heart struck him after he had counted the people. David said to YHWH, "I have sinned greatly in that which I have done. But now, YHWH, put away, I beg you, the iniquity of your servant; for I have done very foolishly."

When David rose up in the morning, YHWH's word came to the prophet Gad, David's seer, saying, "Go and speak to David, 'YHWH says, "I offer you three things. Choose one of them, that I may do it to you."'"

So Gad came to David, and told him, and said to him, "Shall seven years of famine come to you in your land? Or will you flee three months before your foes while they pursue you? Or shall there be three days' pestilence in your land? Now answer, and consider what answer I shall return to him who sent me."

David said to Gad, "I am in distress. Let us fall now into YHWH's hand; for his mercies are great. Let me not fall into man's hand."

So YHWH sent a pestilence on Israel from the morning even to the appointed time; and seventy thousand men died of the people from Dan even to Beersheba. When the angel stretched out his hand toward Jerusalem to destroy it, YHWH relented of the disaster, and said to the angel who destroyed the people, "It is enough. Now withdraw your hand." YHWH's angel was by the threshing floor of Araunah the Jebusite.

David spoke to YHWH when he saw the angel who struck the people, and said, "Behold, I have sinned, and I have done perversely; but these sheep, what have they done? Please let your hand be against me, and against my father's house."

Gad came that day to David, and said to him, "Go up, build an altar to YHWH on the threshing floor of Araunah the Jebusite."

David went up according to the saying of Gad, as YHWH commanded. Araunah looked out, and saw the king and his servants coming on toward him. Then Araunah went out, and bowed himself before the king with his face to the ground. Araunah said, "Why has my lord the king come to his servant?"

David said, "To buy your threshing floor, to build an altar to YHWH, that the plague may be stopped from afflicting the people."

Araunah said to David, "Let my lord the king take and offer up what seems good to him. Behold, the cattle for the burnt offering, and the threshing instruments and the yokes of the oxen for the wood. All this, O king, does Araunah give to the king." Araunah said to the king, "May YHWH your God accept you."

The king said to Araunah, "No; but I will most certainly buy it from you for a price. I will not offer burnt offerings to YHWH my God which cost me nothing." So David bought the threshing floor and the oxen for fifty shekels of silver. David built an altar to YHWH there, and offered burnt offerings and peace offerings. So YHWH was entreated for the land, and the plague was removed from Israel.

THE BOOK OF

KINGS

PART I

2 HR 4 MIN

Now king David was old and advanced in years; and they covered him with clothes, but he couldn't keep warm. Therefore his servants said to him, "Let a young virgin be sought for my lord the king. Let her stand before the king, and cherish him; and let her lie in your bosom, that my lord the king may keep warm." So they sought for a beautiful young lady throughout all the borders of Israel, and found Abishag the Shunammite, and brought her to the king. The young lady was very beautiful; and she cherished the king, and served him; but the king didn't know her intimately.

Then Adonijah the son of Haggith exalted himself, saying, "I will be king." Then he prepared him chariots and horsemen, and fifty men to run before him. His father had not displeased him at any time in saying, "Why have you done so?" and he was also a very handsome man; and he was born after Absalom. He conferred with Joab the son of Zeruiah, and with Abiathar the priest; and they followed Adonijah and helped him. But Zadok the priest, Benaiah the son of Jehoiada, Nathan the prophet, Shimei, Rei, and the mighty men who belonged to David, were not with Adonijah. Adonijah killed sheep, cattle, and fatlings by the stone of Zoheleth, which is beside En Rogel; and he called all his brothers, the king's sons, and all the men of Judah, the king's servants; but he didn't call Nathan the prophet, and Benaiah, and the mighty men, and Solomon his brother. Then Nathan spoke to Bathsheba the mother of Solomon, saying, "Haven't you heard that Adonijah the son of Haggith reigns, and David our lord doesn't know it? Now therefore come, please let me give you counsel, that you may save your own life, and your son Solomon's life. Go in to king David, and tell him, 'Didn't you, my lord, king, swear to your servant, saying, "Assuredly Solomon your son shall reign after me, and he shall sit on my throne?" Why then does Adonijah reign?' Behold, while you are still talking there with the king, I will also come in after you and confirm your words."

Bathsheba went in to the king in his room. The king was very old; and Abishag the Shunammite was serving the king. Bathsheba bowed, and showed respect to the king. The king said, "What would you like?"

She said to him, "My lord, you swore by YHWH your God to your servant, 'Assuredly Solomon your son shall reign after me, and he shall sit on my throne.' Now, behold, Adonijah reigns; and you, my lord the king, don't know it. He has slain cattle and fatlings and sheep in abundance, and has called all the sons of the king, Abiathar the priest, and Joab the captain of the army; but he hasn't called Solomon your servant. You, my lord the king, the eyes of all Israel are on you, that you should tell them who will sit on the throne of my lord the king after him. Otherwise it will happen, when my lord the king sleeps with his fathers, that I and my son Solomon will be considered criminals."

Behold, while she was still talking with the king, Nathan the prophet came in. They told the king, saying, "Behold, Nathan the prophet!"

When he had come in before the king, he bowed himself before the king with his face to the ground. Nathan said, "My lord, king, have you said, 'Adonijah shall reign after me, and he shall sit on my throne?' For he has gone down today, and has slain cattle, fatlings, and sheep in abundance, and has called all the king's sons, the captains of the army, and Abiathar the priest. Behold, they are eating and drinking before him, and saying, 'Long live king Adonijah!' But he hasn't called me, even me your servant, Zadok the priest, Benaiah the son of Jehoiada, and your servant Solomon. Was this thing done by my lord the king, and you haven't shown to your servants who should sit on the throne of my lord the king after him?"

Then king David answered, "Call Bathsheba in to me." She came into the king's presence and stood before the king. The king swore, and said, "As YHWH lives, who has redeemed my soul out of all adversity, most certainly as I swore to you by YHWH, the God of Israel, saying, 'Assuredly Solomon your son shall reign after me, and he shall sit on my throne in my place;' I will most certainly do this today."

Then Bathsheba bowed with her face to the earth, and showed respect to the king, and said, "Let my lord king David live forever!"

King David said, "Call to me Zadok the priest, Nathan the prophet, and Benaiah the son of Jehoiada." They came before the king. The king said to them, "Take with you the servants of your lord, and cause Solomon my son to ride on my own mule, and bring him down to Gihon. Let Zadok the priest and Nathan the prophet anoint him there king over Israel. Blow the trumpet, and say, 'Long live king Solomon!' Then come up after him, and he shall come and sit on my throne; for he shall be king in my place. I have appointed him to be prince over Israel and over Judah."

Benaiah the son of Jehoiada answered the king, and said, "Amen. May YHWH, the God of my lord the king, say so. As YHWH has been with my lord the king, even so may he be with Solomon, and make his throne greater than the throne of my lord king David."

So Zadok the priest, Nathan the prophet, Benaiah the son of Jehoiada, and the Cherethites and the Pelethites went down and had Solomon ride on king David's mule, and brought him to Gihon. Zadok the priest took the horn of oil from the Tent, and anointed Solomon. They blew the trumpet; and all the people said, "Long live king Solomon!"

All the people came up after him, and the people piped with pipes, and rejoiced with great joy, so that the earth shook with their sound. Adonijah and all the guests who were with him heard it as they had finished eating. When Joab heard the sound of the trumpet, he said, "Why is this noise of the city being in an uproar?"

While he yet spoke, behold, Jonathan the son of Abiathar the priest came; and Adonijah said, "Come in; for you are a worthy man, and bring good news."

Jonathan answered Adonijah, "Most certainly our lord king David has made Solomon king. The king has sent with him Zadok the priest, Nathan the prophet, Benaiah the son of Jehoiada, and the Cherethites and the Pelethites; and they have caused him to ride on the king's mule. Zadok the priest and Nathan the prophet have anointed him king in Gihon. They have come up from there rejoicing, so that the city rang again. This is the noise that you have heard. Also, Solomon sits on the throne of the kingdom. Moreover the king's servants came to bless our lord king David, saying, 'May your God make the name of Solomon better than your name, and make his throne greater than your throne;' and the king bowed himself on the bed. Also thus said the king, 'Blessed be YHWH, the God of Israel, who has given one to sit on my throne today, my eyes even seeing it.'"

All the guests of Adonijah were afraid, and rose up, and each man went his way. Adonijah was afraid because of Solomon; and he arose, and went, and hung onto the horns of the altar. Solomon was told, "Behold, Adonijah fears king Solomon; for, behold, he is hanging onto the horns of the altar, saying, 'Let king Solomon swear to me first that he will not kill his servant with the sword.'"

Solomon said, "If he shows himself a worthy man, not a hair of his shall fall to the earth; but if wickedness is found in him, he shall die."

So king Solomon sent, and they brought him down from the altar. He came and bowed down to king Solomon; and Solomon said to him, "Go to your house."

....

Now the days of David came near that he should die; and he commanded Solomon his son, saying, "I am going the way of all the earth. You be strong therefore, and show yourself a man; and keep the instruction of YHWH your God, to walk in his ways, to keep his statutes, his commandments, his ordinances, and his testimonies, according to that which is written in the law of Moses, that you may prosper in all that you do, and wherever you turn yourself. Then YHWH may establish his word which he spoke concerning me, saying, 'If your children are careful of their way, to walk before me in truth with all their heart and with all their soul, there shall not fail you,' he said, 'a man on the throne of Israel.'

"Moreover you know also what Joab the son of Zeruiah did to me, even what he did to the two captains of the armies of Israel, to Abner the son of Ner, and to Amasa the son of Jether, whom he killed, and shed the blood of war in peace, and put the blood of war on his sash that was around his waist, and in his sandals that were on his feet. Do therefore according to your wisdom, and don't let his gray head go down to Sheol in peace. But show kindness to the sons of Barzillai the Gileadite, and let them be among those who eat at your table; for so they came to me when I fled from Absalom your brother.

"Behold, there is with you Shimei the son of Gera, the Benjamite, of Bahurim, who cursed me with a grievous curse in the day when I went to Mahanaim; but he came down to meet me at the Jordan, and I swore to him by YHWH, saying, 'I will not put you to death with the sword.' Now therefore don't hold him guiltless, for you are a wise man; and you will know what you ought to do to him, and you shall bring his gray head down to Sheol with blood."

David slept with his fathers, and was buried in David's city. The days that David reigned over Israel were forty years; he reigned seven years in Hebron, and he reigned thirty-three years in Jerusalem. Solomon sat on David his father's throne; and his kingdom was firmly established.

Then Adonijah the son of Haggith came to Bathsheba the mother of Solomon. She said, "Do you come peaceably?"

He said, "Peaceably. He said moreover, I have something to tell you."

She said, "Say on."

He said, "You know that the kingdom was mine, and that all Israel set their faces on me, that I should reign. However the kingdom is turned around, and has become my brother's; for it was his from YHWH. Now I ask one petition of you. Don't deny me."

She said to him, "Say on." He said, "Please speak to Solomon the king (for he will not tell you 'no'), that he give me Abishag the Shunammite as wife."

Bathsheba said, "All right. I will speak for you to the king."

Bathsheba therefore went to king Solomon, to speak to him for Adonijah. The king rose up to meet her, and bowed himself to her, and sat down on his throne, and caused a throne to be set for the king's mother; and she sat on his right hand. Then she said, "I ask one small petition of you; don't deny me."

The king said to her, "Ask on, my mother; for I will not deny you."

She said, "Let Abishag the Shunammite be given to Adonijah your brother as wife."

King Solomon answered his mother, "Why do you ask Abishag the Shunammite for Adonijah? Ask for him the kingdom also; for he is my elder brother; even for him, and for Abiathar the priest, and for Joab the son of Zeruiah." Then king Solomon swore by YHWH, saying, "God do so to me, and more also, if Adonijah has not spoken this word against his own life. Now therefore as YHWH lives, who has established me, and set me on my father David's throne, and who has made me a house as he promised, surely Adonijah shall be put to death today."

King Solomon sent Benaiah the son of Jehoiada; and he fell on him, so that he died. To Abiathar the priest the king said, "Go to Anathoth, to your own fields; for you are worthy of death. But I will not at this time put you to death, because you bore the Lord YHWH's ark before David my father, and because you were afflicted in all in which my father was afflicted." So Solomon thrust Abiathar out from being priest to YHWH, that he might fulfill YHWH's word, which he spoke concerning the house of Eli in Shiloh.

This news came to Joab; for Joab had followed Adonijah, although he didn't follow Absalom. Joab fled to YHWH's Tent, and held onto the horns of the altar. King Solomon was told, "Joab has fled to YHWH's Tent, and behold, he is by the altar." Then Solomon sent Benaiah the son of Jehoiada, saying, "Go, fall on him."

Benaiah came to YHWH's Tent, and said to him, "The king says, 'Come out!'"

He said, "No; but I will die here."

Benaiah brought the king word again, saying, "This is what Joab said, and this is how he answered me."

The king said to him, "Do as he has said, and fall on him, and bury him; that you may take away the blood, which Joab shed without cause, from me and from my father's house. YHWH will return his blood on his own head, because he fell on two men more righteous and better than he, and killed them with the sword, and my father David didn't know it: Abner the son of Ner, captain of the army of Israel, and Amasa the son of Jether, captain of the army of Judah. So their blood will return on the head of Joab, and on the head of his offspring forever. But for David, for his offspring, for his house, and for his throne, there will be peace forever from YHWH."

Then Benaiah the son of Jehoiada went up and fell on him, and killed him; and he was buried in his own house in the wilderness. The king put Benaiah the son of Jehoiada in his place over the army; and the king put Zadok the priest in the place of Abiathar. The king sent and called for Shimei, and said to him, "Build yourself a house in Jerusalem, and live there, and don't go anywhere else. For on the day you go out and pass over the brook Kidron, know for certain that you will surely die. Your blood will be on your own head."

Shimei said to the king, "What you say is good. As my lord the king has said, so will your servant do." Shimei lived in Jerusalem many days.

At the end of three years, two of Shimei's slaves ran away to Achish, son of Maacah, king of Gath. They told Shimei, saying, "Behold, your slaves are in Gath."

Shimei arose, saddled his donkey, and went to Gath to Achish, to seek his slaves; and Shimei went, and brought his slaves from Gath. Solomon was told that Shimei had gone from Jerusalem to Gath, and had come again.

The king sent and called for Shimei, and said to him, "Didn't I adjure you by YHWH, and warn you, saying, 'Know for certain, that on the day you go out, and walk anywhere else, you shall surely die?' You said to me, 'The saying that I have heard is good.' Why then have you not kept the oath of YHWH, and the commandment that I have instructed you with?" The king said moreover to Shimei, "You know in your heart all the wickedness that you did to David my father. Therefore YHWH will return your wickedness on your own head. But king Solomon will be blessed, and David's throne will be established before YHWH forever." So the king commanded Benaiah the son of Jehoiada; and he went out, and fell on him, so that he died. The kingdom was established in the hand of Solomon.

....

Solomon made an alliance with Pharaoh king of Egypt, and took Pharaoh's daughter, and brought her into David's city, until he had finished building his own house, YHWH's house, and the wall around Jerusalem. However the people sacrificed in the high places, because there was not yet a house built for YHWH's name. Solomon loved YHWH, walking in the statutes of David his father; except that he sacrificed and burned incense in the high places. The king went to Gibeon to sacrifice there; for that was the great high place. Solomon offered a thousand burnt offerings on that altar. In Gibeon, YHWH appeared to Solomon in a dream by night; and God said, "Ask for what I should give you."

Solomon said, "You have shown to your servant David my father great loving kindness, because he walked before you in truth, in righteousness, and in uprightness of heart with you. You have kept for him this great loving kindness, that you have given him a son to sit on his throne, as it is today. Now, YHWH my God, you have made your servant king instead of David my father. I am just a little child. I don't know how to go out or come in. Your servant is among your people which you have chosen, a great people, that can't be numbered or counted for multitude. Give your servant therefore an understanding heart to judge your people, that I may discern between good and evil; for who is able to judge this great people of yours?"

This request pleased the Lord, that Solomon had asked this thing. God said to him, "Because you have asked this thing, and have not asked for yourself long life, nor have you asked for riches for yourself, nor have you asked for the life of your enemies, but have asked for yourself understanding to discern justice; behold, I have done according to your word. Behold, I have given you a wise and understanding heart; so that there has been no one like you before you, and after you none will arise like you. I have also given you that which you have not asked, both riches and honor, so that there will not be any among the kings like you for all your days. If you will walk in my ways, to keep my statutes and my commandments, as your father David walked, then I will lengthen your days."

Solomon awoke; and behold, it was a dream. Then he came to Jerusalem, and stood before the ark of YHWH's covenant, and offered up burnt offerings, offered peace offerings, and made a feast for all his servants.

Then two women who were prostitutes came to the king, and stood before him. The one woman said, "Oh, my lord, I and this woman dwell in one house. I delivered a child with her in the house. The third day after I delivered, this woman delivered also. We were together. There was no stranger with us in the house, just us two in the house. This woman's child died in the night, because she lay on it. She arose at midnight, and took my son from beside me, while your servant slept, and laid it in her bosom, and laid her dead child in my bosom. When I rose in the morning to nurse my child, behold, it was dead; but when I had looked at it in the morning, behold, it was not my son, whom I bore."

The other woman said, "No; but the living one is my son, and the dead one is your son."

The first one said, "No; but the dead one is your son, and the living one is my son." They argued like this before the king.

Then the king said, "One says, 'This is my son who lives, and your son is the dead;' and the other says, 'No; but your son is the dead one, and my son is the living one.'"

The king said, "Get me a sword." So they brought a sword before the king.

The king said, "Divide the living child in two, and give half to the one, and half to the other."

Then the woman whose the living child was spoke to the king, for her heart yearned over her son, and she said, "Oh, my lord, give her the living child, and in no way kill him!"

But the other said, "He shall be neither mine nor yours. Divide him."

Then the king answered, "Give her the living child, and definitely do not kill him. She is his mother."

All Israel heard of the judgment which the king had judged; and they feared the king; for they saw that the wisdom of God was in him, to do justice.

....

King Solomon was king over all Israel. These were the princes whom he had: Azariah the son of Zadok, the priest; Elihoreph and Ahijah, the sons of Shisha, scribes; Jehoshaphat the son of Ahilud, the recorder; Benaiah the son of Jehoiada was over the army; Zadok and Abiathar were priests; Azariah the son of Nathan was over the officers; Zabud the son of Nathan was chief minister, the king's friend; Ahishar was over the household; and Adoniram the son of Abda was over the men subject to forced labor.

Solomon had twelve officers over all Israel, who provided food for the king and his household. Each man had to make provision for a month in the year. These are their names: Ben Hur, in the hill country of Ephraim; Ben Deker, in Makaz, in Shaalbim, Beth Shemesh, and Elon Beth Hanan; Ben Hesed, in Arubboth (Socoh and all the land of Hepher belonged to him); Ben Abinadab, in all the height of Dor (he had Taphath, Solomon's daughter, as wife); Baana the son of Ahilud, in Taanach and Megiddo, and all Beth Shean which is beside Zarethan, beneath Jezreel, from Beth Shean to Abel Meholah, as far as beyond Jokmeam; Ben Geber, in Ramoth Gilead (the towns of Jair the son of Manasseh, which are in Gilead, belonged to him; and the region of Argob, which is in Bashan, sixty great cities with walls and bronze bars, belonged to him); Ahinadab the son of Iddo, in Mahanaim; Ahimaaz, in Naphtali (he also took Basemath the daughter of Solomon as wife); Baana the son of Hushai, in Asher and Bealoth; Jehoshaphat the son of Paruah, in Issachar; Shimei the son of Ela, in Benjamin; Geber the son of Uri, in the land of Gilead, the country of Sihon king of the Amorites and of Og king of Bashan; and he was the only officer who was in the land.

Judah and Israel were numerous as the sand which is by the sea in multitude, eating and drinking and making merry. Solomon ruled over all the kingdoms from the River to the land of the Philistines, and to the border of Egypt. They brought tribute and served Solomon all the days of his life. Solomon's provision for one day was thirty cors of fine flour, sixty measures of meal, ten head of fat cattle, twenty head of cattle out of the pastures, and one hundred sheep, in addition to deer, and gazelles, and roebucks, and fattened fowl. For he had dominion over all on this side the River, from Tiphsah even to Gaza, over all the kings on this side the River: and he had peace on all sides around him. Judah and Israel lived safely, every man under his vine and under his fig tree, from Dan even to Beersheba, all the days of Solomon. Solomon had forty thousand stalls of horses for his chariots, and twelve thousand horsemen. Those officers provided food for king Solomon, and for all who came to king Solomon's table, every man in his month. They let nothing be lacking. They also brought Barley and straw for the horses and swift steeds to the place where the officers were, each man according to his duty. God gave Solomon abundant wisdom and understanding, and very great understanding, even as the sand that is on the seashore. Solomon's wisdom excelled the wisdom of all the children of the east and all the wisdom of Egypt. For he was wiser than all men; than Ethan the Ezrahite, Heman, Calcol, and Darda, the sons of Mahol: and his fame was in all the nations all around. He spoke three thousand proverbs; and his songs numbered one thousand five. He spoke of trees, from the cedar that is in Lebanon even to the hyssop that grows out of the wall; he also spoke of animals, of birds, of creeping things, and of fish. People of all nations came to hear the wisdom of Solomon, sent by all kings of the earth, who had heard of his wisdom.

....

Hiram king of Tyre sent his servants to Solomon; for he had heard that they had anointed him king in the place of his father, and Hiram had always loved David. Solomon sent to Hiram, saying, "You know that David my father could not build a house for the name of YHWH his God because of the wars which were around him on every side, until YHWH put his enemies under the soles of his feet. But now YHWH my God has given me rest on every side. There is no enemy and no evil occurrence. Behold, I intend to build a house for the name of YHWH my God, as YHWH spoke to David my father, saying, 'Your son, whom I will set on your throne in your place shall build the house for my name.' Now therefore command that cedar trees be cut for me out of Lebanon. My servants will be with your servants; and I will give you wages for your servants according to all that you say. For you know that there is nobody among us who knows how to cut timber like the Sidonians."

When Hiram heard the words of Solomon, he rejoiced greatly, and said, "Blessed is YHWH today, who has given to David a wise son to rule over this great people." Hiram sent to Solomon, saying, "I have heard the message which you have sent to me. I will do all your desire concerning timber of cedar, and concerning cypress timber. My servants will bring them down from Lebanon to the sea. I will make them into rafts to go by sea to the place that you specify to me, and will cause them to be broken up there, and you will receive them.

You will accomplish my desire, in giving food for my household."

So Hiram gave Solomon cedar timber and cypress timber according to all his desire. Solomon gave Hiram twenty thousand cors of wheat for food to his household, and twenty cors of pure oil. Solomon gave this to Hiram year by year. YHWH gave Solomon wisdom, as he promised him. There was peace between Hiram and Solomon, and the two of them made a treaty together. King Solomon raised a levy out of all Israel; and the levy was thirty thousand men. He sent them to Lebanon, ten thousand a month by courses; for a month they were in Lebanon, and two months at home; and Adoniram was over the men subject to forced labor. Solomon had seventy thousand who bore burdens, and eighty thousand who were stone cutters in the mountains; besides Solomon's chief officers who were over the work, three thousand and three hundred, who ruled over the people who labored in the work. The king commanded, and they cut out large stones, costly stones, to lay the foundation of the house with worked stone. Solomon's builders and Hiram's builders and the Gebalites cut them, and prepared the timber and the stones to build the house.

....

In the four hundred and eightieth year after the children of Israel had come out of the land of Egypt, in the fourth year of Solomon's reign over Israel, in the month Ziv, which is the second month, he began to build YHWH's house. The house which king Solomon built for YHWH had a length of sixty cubits, and its width twenty, and its height thirty cubits. The porch in front of the temple of the house had a length of twenty cubits, which was along the width of the house. Ten cubits was its width in front of the house. He made windows of fixed lattice work for the house. Against the wall of the house, he built floors all around, against the walls of the house all around, both of the temple and of the inner sanctuary; and he made side rooms all around. The lowest floor was five cubits wide, and the middle was six cubits wide, and the third was seven cubits wide; for on the outside he made offsets in the wall of the house all around, that the beams should not be inserted into the walls of the house. The house, when it was under construction, was built of stone prepared at the quarry; and no hammer or ax or any tool of iron was heard in the house while it was under construction. The door for the middle side rooms was in the right side of the house. They went up by winding stairs into the middle floor, and out of the middle into the third. So he built the house, and finished it; and he covered the house with beams and planks of cedar. He built the floors all along the house, each five cubits high; and they rested on the house with timber of cedar.

YHWH's word came to Solomon, saying, "Concerning this house which you are building, if you will walk in my statutes, and execute my ordinances, and keep all my commandments to walk in them; then I will establish my word with you, which I spoke to David your father. I will dwell among the children of Israel, and will not forsake my people Israel."

So Solomon built the house, and finished it. He built the walls of the house within with boards of cedar: from the floor of the house to the walls of the ceiling, he covered them on the inside with wood; and he covered the floor of the house with cypress boards. He built twenty cubits on the back part of the house with boards of cedar from the floor to the ceiling. He built them for it within, for an inner sanctuary, even for the most holy place. In front of the temple sanctuary was forty cubits. There was cedar on the house within, carved with buds and open flowers. All was cedar. No stone was visible. He prepared an inner sanctuary in the middle of the house within, to set the ark of YHWH's covenant there. Within the inner sanctuary was twenty cubits in length, and twenty cubits in width, and twenty cubits in its height; and he overlaid it with pure gold; and he covered the altar with cedar. So Solomon overlaid the house within with pure gold. He drew chains of gold across before the inner sanctuary, and he overlaid it with gold. He overlaid the whole house with gold, until all the house was finished. He also overlaid the whole altar that belonged to the inner sanctuary with gold. In the inner sanctuary he made two cherubim of olive wood, each ten cubits high. Five cubits was the one wing of the cherub, and five cubits the other wing of the cherub. From the tip of one wing to the tip of the other was ten cubits. The other cherub was ten cubits. Both the cherubim were of one measure and one form. One cherub was ten cubits high, and so was the other cherub. He set the cherubim within the inner house. The wings of the cherubim were stretched out, so that the wing of the one touched the one wall, and the wing of the other cherub touched the other wall; and their wings touched one another in the middle of the house. He overlaid the cherubim with gold. He carved all the walls of the house around with carved figures of cherubim, palm trees, and open flowers, inside and outside. He overlaid the floor of the house with gold, inside and outside. For the entrance of the inner sanctuary, he made doors of olive wood. The lintel and door posts were a fifth part of the wall. So he made two doors of olive wood; and he carved on them carvings of cherubim, palm trees, and open flowers, and overlaid them with gold. He spread the gold on the cherubim and on the palm trees. He also did so for the entrance of the temple door posts of olive wood, out of a fourth part of the wall; and two doors of cypress wood. The two leaves of the one door were folding, and the two leaves of the other door were folding. He carved cherubim, palm trees, and open flowers; and he overlaid them with gold fitted on the engraved work. He built the inner court with three courses of cut stone and a course of cedar beams. The foundation of YHWH's house was laid in the fourth year, in the month Ziv. In the eleventh year, in the month Bul, which is the eighth month, the house was finished throughout all its parts, and according to all its specifications. So he spent seven years building it.

....

Solomon was building his own house thirteen years, and he finished all his house. For he built the House of the Forest of Lebanon. Its length was one hundred cubits, its width fifty cubits, and its height thirty cubits, on four rows of cedar pillars, with cedar beams on the pillars. It was covered with cedar above over the forty-five beams, that were on the pillars, fifteen in a row. There were beams in three rows, and window was facing window in three ranks. All the doors and posts were made square with beams: and window was facing window in three ranks. He made the porch of pillars. Its length was fifty cubits and its width thirty cubits; with a porch before them, and pillars and a threshold before them. He made the porch of the throne where he was to judge, even the porch of judgment; and it was covered with cedar from floor to floor. His house where he was to dwell, the other court within the porch, was of the like work. He made also a house for Pharaoh's daughter (whom Solomon had taken as wife), like this porch. All these were of costly stones, even of cut stone, according to measure, sawed with saws, inside and outside, even from the foundation to the coping, and so on the outside to the great court. The foundation was of costly stones, even great stones, stones of ten cubits, and stones of eight cubits. Above were costly stones, even cut stone, according to measure, and cedar wood. The great court around had three courses of cut stone, and a course of cedar beams; like the inner court of YHWH's house and the porch of the house. King Solomon sent and brought Hiram out of Tyre. He was the son of a widow of the tribe of Naphtali, and his father was a man of Tyre, a worker in bronze; and he was filled with wisdom and understanding and skill, to work all works in bronze. He came to king Solomon, and performed all his work. For he fashioned the two pillars of bronze, eighteen cubits high apiece; and a line of twelve cubits encircled either of them. He made two capitals of molten bronze, to set on the tops of the pillars. The height of the one capital was five cubits, and the height of the other capital was five cubits. There were nets of checker work, and wreaths of chain work, for the capitals which were on the top of the pillars; seven for the one capital, and seven for the other capital. So he made the pillars; and there were two rows around on the one network, to cover the capitals that were on the top of the pillars: and he did so for the other capital. The capitals that were on the top of the pillars in the porch were of lily work, four cubits. There were capitals above also on the two pillars, close by the belly which was beside the network. There were two hundred pomegranates in rows around the other capital. He set up the pillars at the porch of the temple. He set up the right pillar, and called its name Jachin; and he set up the left pillar, and called its name Boaz. On the top of the pillars was lily work: so the work of the pillars was finished. He made the molten sea of ten cubits from brim to brim, round in shape. Its height was five cubits; and a line of thirty cubits encircled it. Under its brim around there were buds which encircled it for ten cubits, encircling the sea. The buds were in two rows, cast when it was cast. It stood on twelve oxen, three looking toward the north, and three looking toward the west, and three looking toward the south, and three looking toward the east; and the sea was set on them above, and all their hindquarters were inward. It was a hand width thick. Its brim was worked like the brim of a cup, like the flower of a lily. It held two thousand baths. He made the ten bases of bronze. The length of one base was four cubits, four cubits its width, and three cubits its height. The work of the bases was like this: they had panels; and there were panels between the ledges; and on the panels that were between the ledges were lions, oxen, and cherubim; and on the ledges there was a pedestal above; and beneath the lions and oxen were wreaths of hanging work. Every base had four bronze wheels, and axles of bronze; and the four feet of it had supports. The supports were cast beneath the basin, with wreaths at the side of each. Its mouth within the capital and above was a cubit. Its mouth was round after the work of a pedestal, a cubit and a half; and also on its mouth were engravings, and their panels were square, not round. The four wheels were underneath the panels; and the axles of the wheels were in the base. The height of a wheel was a cubit and half a cubit. The work of the wheels was like the work of a chariot wheel. Their axles, and their rims, and their spokes, and their naves, were all of cast metal. There were four supports at the four corners of each base. Its supports were of the base itself. In the top of the base there was a round band half a cubit high; and on the top of the base its supports and its panels were the same. On the plates of its supports, and on its panels, he engraved cherubim, lions, and palm trees, each in its space, with wreaths all around. He made the ten bases in this way: all of them had one casting, one measure, and one form. He made ten basins of bronze. One basin contained forty baths; and every basin was four cubits; and on every one of the ten bases one basin. He set the bases, five on the right side of the house, and five on the left side of the house. He set the sea on the right side of the house eastward and toward the south. Hiram made the pots, the shovels, and the basins. So Hiram finished doing all the work that he worked for king Solomon in YHWH's house: the two pillars; the two bowls of the capitals that were on the top of the pillars; the two networks to cover the two bowls of the capitals that were on the top of the pillars; the four hundred pomegranates for the two networks; two rows of pomegranates for each network, to cover the two bowls of the capitals that were on the pillars; the ten bases; the ten basins on the bases; the one sea; the twelve oxen under the sea; the pots; the shovels; and the basins: even all these vessels, which Hiram made for king Solomon, in YHWH's house, were of burnished bronze. The king cast them in the plain of the Jordan, in the clay ground between Succoth and Zarethan. Solomon left all the vessels unweighed, because there were so many of them. The weight of the bronze could not be determined. Solomon made all the vessels that were in YHWH's house: the golden altar and the table that the show bread was on, of gold; and the lamp stands, five on the right side, and five on the left, before the inner sanctuary, of pure gold; and the flowers, the lamps, and the tongs, of gold; the cups, the snuffers, the basins, the spoons, and the fire pans, of pure gold; and the hinges, both for the doors of the inner house, the most holy place, and for the doors of the house, of the temple, of gold. Thus all the work that king Solomon did in YHWH's house was finished. Solomon brought in the things which David his father had dedicated, the silver, the gold, and the vessels, and put them in the treasuries of YHWH's house.

....

Then Solomon assembled the elders of Israel, with all the heads of the tribes, the princes of the fathers' households of the children of Israel, to king Solomon in Jerusalem, to bring up the ark of YHWH's covenant out of David's city, which is Zion. All the men of Israel assembled themselves to king Solomon at the feast, in the month Ethanim, which is the seventh month. All the elders of Israel came, and the priests picked up the ark. They brought up YHWH's ark, the Tent of Meeting, and all the holy vessels that were in the Tent. The priests and the Levites brought these up. King Solomon and all the congregation of Israel, who were assembled to him, were with him before the ark, sacrificing sheep and cattle, that could not be counted or numbered for multitude. The priests brought in the ark of YHWH's covenant to its place, into the inner sanctuary of the house, to the most holy place, even under the cherubim's wings. For the cherubim spread their wings out over the place of the ark, and the cherubim covered the ark and its poles above. The poles were so long that the ends of the poles were seen from the holy place before the inner sanctuary; but they were not seen outside. They are there to this day. There was nothing in the ark except the two stone tablets which Moses put there at Horeb, when YHWH made a covenant with the children of Israel, when they came out of the land of Egypt. It came to pass, when the priests had come out of the holy place, that the cloud filled YHWH's house, so that the priests could not stand to minister by reason of the cloud; for YHWH's glory filled YHWH's house. Then Solomon said, "YHWH has said that he would dwell in the thick darkness. I have surely built you a house of habitation, a place for you to dwell in forever."

The king turned his face around, and blessed all the assembly of Israel; and all the assembly of Israel stood. He said, "Blessed is YHWH, the God of Israel, who spoke with his mouth to David your father, and has with his hand fulfilled it, saying, 'Since the day that I brought my people Israel out of Egypt, I chose no city out of all the tribes of Israel to build a house, that my name might be there; but I chose David to be over my people Israel.'

"Now it was in the heart of David my father to build a house for the name of YHWH, the God of Israel. But YHWH said to David my father, 'Whereas it was in your heart to build a house for my name, you did well that it was in your heart. Nevertheless, you shall not build the house; but your son who shall come out of your body, he shall build the house for my name.' YHWH has established his word that he spoke; for I have risen up in the place of David my father, and I sit on the throne of Israel, as YHWH promised, and have built the house for the name of YHWH, the God of Israel. There I have set a place for the ark, in which is YHWH's covenant, which he made with our fathers, when he brought them out of the land of Egypt."

Solomon stood before YHWH's altar in the presence of all the assembly of Israel, and spread out his hands toward heaven; and he said, "YHWH, the God of Israel, there is no God like you, in heaven above, or on earth beneath; who keeps covenant and loving kindness with your servants, who walk before you with all their heart; who has kept with your servant David my father that which you promised him. Yes, you spoke with your mouth, and have fulfilled it with your hand, as it is today. Now therefore, may YHWH, the God of Israel, keep with your servant David my father that which you have promised him, saying, 'There shall not fail from you a man in my sight to sit on the throne of Israel, if only your children take heed to their way, to walk before me as you have walked before me.'

"Now therefore, God of Israel, please let your word be verified, which you spoke to your servant David my father. But will God in very deed dwell on the earth? Behold, heaven and the heaven of heavens can't contain you; how much less this house that I have built! Yet have respect for the prayer of your servant, and for his supplication, YHWH my God, to listen to the cry and to the prayer which your servant prays before you today; that your eyes may be open toward this house night and day, even toward the place of which you have said, 'My name shall be there;' to listen to the prayer which your servant prays toward this place. Listen to the supplication of your servant, and of your people Israel, when they pray toward this place. Yes, hear in heaven, your dwelling place; and when you hear, forgive.

"If a man sins against his neighbor, and an oath is laid on him to cause him to swear, and he comes and swears before your altar in this house; then hear in heaven, and act, and judge your servants, condemning the wicked, to bring his way on his own head, and justifying the righteous, to give him according to his righteousness.

"When your people Israel are struck down before the enemy, because they have sinned against you; if they turn again to you, and confess your name, and pray and make supplication to you in this house; then hear in heaven, and forgive the sin of your people Israel, and bring them again to the land which you gave to their fathers.

"When the sky is shut up, and there is no rain, because they have sinned against you; if they pray toward this place, and confess your name, and turn from their sin, when you afflict them, then hear in heaven, and forgive the sin of your servants, and of your people Israel, when you teach them the good way in which they should walk; and send rain on your land, which you have given to your people for an inheritance.

"If there is famine in the land, if there is pestilence, if there is blight, mildew, locust or caterpillar; if their enemy besieges them in the land of their cities; whatever plague, whatever sickness there is; whatever prayer and supplication is made by any man, or by all your people Israel, who shall each know the plague of his own heart, and spread out his hands toward this house, then hear in heaven, your dwelling place, and forgive, and act, and give to every man according to all his ways, whose heart you know (for you, even you only, know the hearts of all the children of men); that they may fear you all the days that they live in the land which you gave to our fathers.

"Moreover concerning the foreigner, who is not of your people Israel, when he comes out of a far country for your name's sake (for they shall hear of your great name, and of your mighty hand, and of your outstretched arm); when he comes and prays toward this house; hear in heaven, your dwelling place, and do according to all that the foreigner calls to you for; that all the peoples of the earth may know your name, to fear you, as do your people Israel, and that they may know that this house which I have built is called by your name.

"If your people go out to battle against their enemy, by whatever way you shall send them, and they pray to YHWH toward the city which you have chosen, and toward the house which I have built for your name; then hear in heaven their prayer and their supplication, and maintain their cause. If they sin against you (for there is no man who doesn't sin), and you are angry with them, and deliver them to the enemy, so that they carry them away captive to the land of the enemy, far off or near; yet if they repent in the land where they are carried captive, and turn again, and make supplication to you in the land of those who carried them captive, saying, 'We have sinned, and have done perversely; we have dealt wickedly;' if they return to you with all their heart and with all their soul in the land of their enemies, who carried them captive, and pray to you toward their land, which you gave to their fathers, the city which you have chosen, and the house which I have built for your name; then hear their prayer and their supplication in heaven, your dwelling place, and maintain their cause; and forgive your people who have sinned against you, and all their transgressions in which they have transgressed against you; and give them compassion before those who carried them captive, that they may have compassion on them (for they are your people, and your inheritance, which you brought out of Egypt, from the middle of the iron furnace); that your eyes may be open to the supplication of your servant, and to the supplication of your people Israel, to listen to them whenever they cry to you. For you separated them from among all the peoples of the earth, to be your inheritance, as you spoke by Moses your servant, when you brought our fathers out of Egypt, Lord YHWH."

It was so, that when Solomon had finished praying all this prayer and supplication to YHWH, he arose from before YHWH's altar, from kneeling on his knees with his hands spread out toward heaven. He stood, and blessed all the assembly of Israel with a loud voice, saying, "Blessed be YHWH, who has given rest to his people Israel, according to all that he promised. There has not failed one word of all his good promise, which he promised by Moses his servant. May YHWH our God be with us, as he was with our fathers. Let him not leave us or forsake us; that he may incline our hearts to him, to walk in all his ways, and to keep his commandments, and his statutes, and his ordinances, which he commanded our fathers. Let these my words, with which I have made supplication before YHWH, be near to YHWH our God day and night, that he may maintain the cause of his servant, and the cause of his people Israel, as every day requires; that all the peoples of the earth may know that YHWH himself is God. There is no one else.

"Let your heart therefore be perfect with YHWH our God, to walk in his statutes, and to keep his commandments, as it is today."

The king, and all Israel with him, offered sacrifice before YHWH. Solomon offered for the sacrifice of peace offerings, which he offered to YHWH, twenty two thousand head of cattle, and one hundred twenty thousand sheep. So the king and all the children of Israel dedicated YHWH's house. The same day the king made the middle of the court holy that was before YHWH's house; for there he offered the burnt offering, and the meal offering, and the fat of the peace offerings, because the bronze altar that was before YHWH was too little to receive the burnt offering, the meal offering, and the fat of the peace offerings. So Solomon held the feast at that time, and all Israel with him, a great assembly, from the entrance of Hamath to the brook of Egypt, before YHWH our God, seven days and seven more days, even fourteen days. On the eighth day he sent the people away; and they blessed the king, and went to their tents joyful and glad in their hearts for all the goodness that YHWH had shown to David his servant, and to Israel his people.

....

When Solomon had finished the building of YHWH's house, the king's house, and all Solomon's desire which he was pleased to do, YHWH appeared to Solomon the second time, as he had appeared to him at Gibeon. YHWH said to him, "I have heard your prayer and your supplication, that you have made before me. I have made this house holy, which you have built, to put my name there forever; and my eyes and my heart shall be there perpetually. As for you, if you will walk before me, as David your father walked, in integrity of heart, and in uprightness, to do according to all that I have commanded you, and will keep my statutes and my ordinances; then I will establish the throne of your kingdom over Israel forever, as I promised to David your father, saying, 'There shall not fail from you a man on the throne of Israel.' But if you turn away from following me, you or your children, and not keep my commandments and my statutes which I have set before you, but go and serve other gods, and worship them; then I will cut off Israel out of the land which I have given them; and I will cast this house, which I have made holy for my name, out of my sight; and Israel will be a proverb and a byword among all peoples. Though this house is so high, yet everyone who passes by it will be astonished and hiss; and they will say, 'Why has YHWH done this to this land, and to this house?' and they will answer, 'Because they abandoned YHWH their God, who brought their fathers out of the land of Egypt, and embraced other gods, and worshiped them, and served them. Therefore YHWH has brought all this evil on them.'"

At the end of twenty years, in which Solomon had built the two houses, YHWH's house and the king's house (now Hiram the king of

Tyre had furnished Solomon with cedar trees and cypress trees, and with gold, according to all his desire), King Solomon gave Hiram twenty cities in the land of Galilee. Hiram came out of Tyre to see the cities which Solomon had given him; and they didn't please him. He said, "What cities are these which you have given me, my brother?" He called them the land of Cabul to this day. Hiram sent to the king one hundred twenty talents of gold.

This is the reason of the levy which king Solomon raised, to build YHWH's house, his own house, Millo, Jerusalem's wall, Hazor, Megiddo, and Gezer. Pharaoh king of Egypt had gone up, taken Gezer, burned it with fire, killed the Canaanites who lived in the city, and given it for a wedding gift to his daughter, Solomon's wife. Solomon built in the land Gezer, Beth Horon the lower, Baalath, Tamar in the wilderness, all the storage cities that Solomon had, the cities for his chariots, the cities for his horsemen, and that which Solomon desired to build for his pleasure in Jerusalem, and in Lebanon, and in all the land of his dominion. As for all the people who were left of the Amorites, the Hittites, the Perizzites, the Hivites, and the Jebusites, who were not of the children of Israel; their children who were left after them in the land, whom the children of Israel were not able utterly to destroy, of them Solomon raised a levy of bondservants to this day. But of the children of Israel Solomon made no bondservants; but they were the men of war, his servants, his princes, his captains, and rulers of his chariots and of his horsemen. These were the five hundred fifty chief officers who were over Solomon's work, who ruled over the people who labored in the work. But Pharaoh's daughter came up out of David's city to her house which Solomon had built for her. Then he built Millo. Solomon offered burnt offerings and peace offerings on the altar which he built to YHWH three times per year, burning incense with them, on the altar that was before YHWH. So he finished the house. King Solomon made a fleet of ships in Ezion Geber, which is beside Eloth, on the shore of the Red Sea, in the land of Edom. Hiram sent in the fleet his servants, sailors who had knowledge of the sea, with the servants of Solomon. They came to Ophir, and fetched from there gold, four hundred and twenty talents, and brought it to king Solomon.

....

When the queen of Sheba heard of the fame of Solomon concerning YHWH's name, she came to test him with hard questions. She came to Jerusalem with a very great caravan, with camels that bore spices, very much gold, and precious stones; and when she had come to Solomon, she talked with him about all that was in her heart. Solomon answered all her questions. There wasn't anything hidden from the king which he didn't tell her. When the queen of Sheba had seen all the wisdom of Solomon, the house that he had built, the food of his table, the sitting of his servants, the attendance of his officials, their clothing, his cup bearers, and his ascent by which he went up to YHWH's house; there was no more spirit in her. She said to the king, "It was a true report that I heard in my own land of your acts, and of your wisdom. However I didn't believe the words until I came and my eyes had seen it. Behold, not even half was told me! Your wisdom and prosperity exceed the fame which I heard. Happy are your men, happy are these your servants, who stand continually before you, who hear your wisdom. Blessed is YHWH your God, who delighted in you, to set you on the throne of Israel. Because YHWH loved Israel forever, therefore he made you king, to do justice and righteousness." She gave the king one hundred twenty talents of gold, and a very great quantity of spices, and precious stones. Never again was there such an abundance of spices as these which the queen of Sheba gave to king Solomon.

The fleet of Hiram that brought gold from Ophir, also brought in from Ophir great quantities of almug trees and precious stones. The king made of the almug trees pillars for YHWH's house, and for the king's house, harps also and stringed instruments for the singers; no such almug trees came or were seen, to this day. King Solomon gave to the queen of Sheba all her desire, whatever she asked, in addition to that which Solomon gave her of his royal bounty. So she turned and went to her own land, she and her servants. Now the weight of gold that came to Solomon in one year was six hundred sixty-six talents of gold, in addition to that which the traders brought, and the traffic of the merchants, and of all the kings of the mixed people, and of the governors of the country. King Solomon made two hundred bucklers of beaten gold; six hundred shekels of gold went to one buckler. he made three hundred shields of beaten gold; three minas of gold went to one shield; and the king put them in the House of the Forest of Lebanon. Moreover the king made a great throne of ivory, and overlaid it with the finest gold. There were six steps to the throne, and the top of the throne was round behind; and there were armrests on either side by the place of the seat, and two lions standing beside the armrests. Twelve lions stood there on the one side and on the other on the six steps. Nothing like it was made in any kingdom. All king Solomon's drinking vessels were of gold, and all the vessels of the House of the Forest of Lebanon were of pure gold. None were of silver, because it was considered of little value in the days of Solomon. For the king had a fleet of Tarshish at sea with Hiram's fleet. Once every three years the fleet of Tarshish came, bringing gold, silver, ivory, apes, and peacocks. So king Solomon exceeded all the kings of the earth in riches and in wisdom. All the earth sought the presence of Solomon, to hear his wisdom, which God had put in his heart. Year after year, every man brought his tribute, vessels of silver, vessels of gold, clothing, armor, spices, horses, and mules. Solomon gathered together chariots and horsemen. He had one thousand four hundred chariots, and twelve thousand horsemen, that he kept in the chariot cities and with the king at Jerusalem. The king made silver as common as stones in Jerusalem, and cedars as common as the sycamore trees that are in the lowland. The horses which Solomon had were brought out of Egypt. The king's merchants received them in droves, each drove at a price. A chariot came up and went out of Egypt for six hundred shekels of silver, and a horse for one hundred fifty shekels; and so they exported them to all the kings of the Hittites, and to the kings of Syria.

....

Now king Solomon loved many foreign women, together with the daughter of Pharaoh, women of the Moabites, Ammonites, Edomites, Sidonians, and Hittites; of the nations concerning which YHWH said to the children of Israel, "You shall not go among them, neither shall they come among you; for surely they will turn away your heart after their gods." Solomon joined to these in love. He had seven hundred wives, princesses, and three hundred concubines. His wives turned his heart away. When Solomon was old, his wives turned away his heart after other gods; and his heart was not perfect with YHWH his God, as the heart of David his father was. For Solomon went after Ashtoreth the goddess of the Sidonians, and after Milcom the abomination of the Ammonites. Solomon did that which was evil in YHWH's sight, and didn't go fully after YHWH, as David his father did. Then Solomon built a high place for Chemosh the abomination of Moab, on the mountain that is before Jerusalem, and for Molech the abomination of the children of Ammon. So he did for all his foreign wives, who burned incense and sacrificed to their gods. YHWH was angry with Solomon, because his heart was turned away from YHWH, the God of Israel, who had appeared to him twice, and had commanded him concerning this thing, that he should not go after other gods; but he didn't keep that which YHWH commanded. Therefore YHWH said to Solomon, "Because this is done by you, and you have not kept my covenant and my statutes, which I have commanded you, I will surely tear the kingdom from you, and will give it to your servant. Nevertheless, I will not do it in your days, for David your father's sake; but I will tear it out of your son's hand. However I will not tear away all the kingdom; but I will give one tribe to your son, for David my servant's sake, and for Jerusalem's sake which I have chosen."

YHWH raised up an adversary to Solomon: Hadad the Edomite. He was one of the king's offspring in Edom. For when David was in Edom, and Joab the captain of the army had gone up to bury the slain, and had struck every male in Edom (for Joab and all Israel remained there six months, until he had cut off every male in Edom); Hadad fled, he and certain Edomites of his father's servants with him, to go into Egypt, when Hadad was still a little child. They arose out of Midian, and came to Paran; and they took men with them out of Paran, and they came to Egypt, to Pharaoh king of Egypt, who gave him a house, and appointed him food, and gave him land. Hadad found great favor in the sight of Pharaoh, so that he gave him as wife the sister of his own wife, the sister of Tahpenes the queen. The sister of Tahpenes bore him Genubath his son, whom Tahpenes weaned in Pharaoh's house; and Genubath was in Pharaoh's house among the sons of Pharaoh. When Hadad heard in Egypt that David slept with his fathers, and that Joab the captain of the army was dead, Hadad said to Pharaoh, "Let me depart, that I may go to my own country."

Then Pharaoh said to him, "But what have you lacked with me, that behold, you seek to go to your own country?"

He answered, "Nothing, however only let me depart."

God raised up an adversary to him, Rezon the son of Eliada, who had fled from his lord Hadadezer king of Zobah. He gathered men to himself, and became captain over a troop, when David killed them of Zobah. They went to Damascus, and lived there, and reigned in Damascus. He was an adversary to Israel all the days of Solomon, in addition to the mischief of Hadad. He abhorred Israel, and reigned over Syria. Jeroboam the son of Nebat, an Ephraimite of Zeredah, a servant of Solomon, whose mother's name was Zeruah, a widow, also lifted up his hand against the king. This was the reason why he lifted up his hand against the king: Solomon built Millo, and repaired the breach of his father David's city. The man Jeroboam was a mighty man of valor; and Solomon saw the young man that he was industrious, and he put him in charge of all the labor of the house of Joseph. At that time, when Jeroboam went out of Jerusalem, the prophet Ahijah the Shilonite found him on the way. Now Ahijah had clad himself with a new garment; and the two of them were alone in the field. Ahijah took the new garment that was on him, and tore it in twelve pieces. He said to Jeroboam, "Take ten pieces; for YHWH, the God of Israel, says, 'Behold, I will tear the kingdom out of the hand of Solomon, and will give ten tribes to you (but he shall have one tribe, for my servant David's sake and for Jerusalem's sake, the city which I have chosen out of all the tribes of Israel); because that they have forsaken me, and have worshiped Ashtoreth the goddess of the Sidonians, Chemosh the god of Moab, and Milcom the god of the children of Ammon. They have not walked in my ways, to do that which is right in my eyes, and to keep my statutes and my ordinances, as David his father did.

"'However I will not take the whole kingdom out of his hand; but I will make him prince all the days of his life, for David my servant's sake whom I chose, who kept my commandments and my statutes; but I will take the kingdom out of his son's hand, and will give it to you, even ten tribes. I will give one tribe to his son, that David my servant may have a lamp always before me in Jerusalem, the city which I have chosen for myself to put my name there. I will take you, and you shall reign according to all that your soul desires, and shall be king over Israel. It shall be, if you will listen to all that I command you, and will walk in my ways, and do that which is right in my eyes, to keep my statutes and my commandments, as David my servant did; that I will be with you, and will build you a sure house, as I built for David, and will give Israel to you. I will afflict the offspring of David for this, but not forever.'"

Therefore Solomon sought to kill Jeroboam; but Jeroboam arose, and fled into Egypt, to Shishak king of Egypt, and was in Egypt until the death of Solomon. Now the rest of the acts of Solomon, and all that he did, and his wisdom, aren't they written in the book of the acts of Solomon? The time that Solomon reigned in Jerusalem over all Israel was forty years. Solomon slept with his fathers, and was buried in his father David's city; and Rehoboam his son reigned in his place.

....

Rehoboam went to Shechem, for all Israel had come to Shechem to make him king. When Jeroboam the son of Nebat heard of it (for he was yet in Egypt, where he had fled from the presence of king Solomon, and Jeroboam lived in Egypt, and they sent and called him), Jeroboam and all the assembly of Israel came, and spoke to Rehoboam, saying, "Your father made our yoke difficult. Now therefore make the hard service of your father, and his heavy yoke which he put on us, lighter, and we will serve you."

He said to them, "Depart for three days, then come back to me."

So the people departed.

King Rehoboam took counsel with the old men, who had stood before Solomon his father while he yet lived, saying, "What counsel do you give me to answer these people?"

They replied, "If you will be a servant to this people today, and will serve them, and answer them with good words, then they will be your servants forever."

But he abandoned the counsel of the old men which they had given him, and took counsel with the young men who had grown up with him, who stood before him. He said to them, "What counsel do you give, that we may answer these people, who have spoken to me, saying, 'Make the yoke that your father put on us lighter?'"

The young men who had grown up with him said to him, "Tell these people who spoke to you, saying, 'Your father made our yoke heavy, but make it lighter to us;' tell them, 'My little finger is thicker than my father's waist. Now my father burdened you with a heavy yoke, but I will add to your yoke. My father chastised you with whips, but I will chastise you with scorpions.'"

So Jeroboam and all the people came to Rehoboam the third day, as the king asked, saying, "Come to me again the third day." The king answered the people roughly, and abandoned the counsel of the old men which they had given him, and spoke to them according to the counsel of the young men, saying, "My father made your yoke heavy, but I will add to your yoke. My father chastised you with whips, but I will chastise you with scorpions."

So the king didn't listen to the people; for it was a thing brought about from YHWH, that he might establish his word, which YHWH spoke by Ahijah the Shilonite to Jeroboam the son of Nebat. When all Israel saw that the king didn't listen to them, the people answered the king, saying, "What portion have we in David? We don't have an inheritance in the son of Jesse. To your tents, Israel! Now see to your own house, David." So Israel departed to their tents.

But as for the children of Israel who lived in the cities of Judah, Rehoboam reigned over them. Then king Rehoboam sent Adoram, who was over the men subject to forced labor; and all Israel stoned him to death with stones. King Rehoboam hurried to get himself up to his chariot, to flee to Jerusalem. So Israel rebelled against David's house to this day. When all Israel heard that Jeroboam had returned, they sent and called him to the congregation, and made him king over all Israel. There was no one who followed David's house, except for the tribe of Judah only. When Rehoboam had come to Jerusalem, he assembled all the house of Judah and the tribe of Benjamin, a hundred and eighty thousand chosen men, who were warriors, to fight against the house of Israel, to bring the kingdom again to Rehoboam the son of Solomon. But the word of God came to Shemaiah the man of God, saying, "Speak to Rehoboam the son of Solomon, king of Judah, and to all the house of Judah and Benjamin, and to the rest of the people, saying, 'YHWH says, "You shall not go up or fight against your brothers, the children of Israel. Everyone return to his house; for this thing is from me."'" So they listened to YHWH's word, and returned and went their way, according to YHWH's word.

Then Jeroboam built Shechem in the hill country of Ephraim, and lived in it; and he went out from there, and built Penuel. Jeroboam said in his heart, "Now the kingdom will return to David's house. If this people goes up to offer sacrifices in YHWH's house at Jerusalem, then the heart of this people will turn again to their lord, even to Rehoboam king of Judah; and they will kill me, and return to Rehoboam king of Judah." So the king took counsel, and made two calves of gold; and he said to them, "It is too much for you to go up to Jerusalem. Look and behold your gods, Israel, which brought you up out of the land of Egypt!" He set the one in Bethel, and the other he put in Dan. This thing became a sin; for the people went even as far as Dan to worship before the one there. He made houses of high places, and made priests from among all the people, who were not of the sons of Levi. Jeroboam ordained a feast in the eighth month, on the fifteenth day of the month, like the feast that is in Judah, and he went up to the altar. He did so in Bethel, sacrificing to the calves that he had made, and he placed in Bethel the priests of the high places that he had made. He went up to the altar which he had made in Bethel on the fifteenth day in the eighth month, even in the month which he had devised of his own heart; and he ordained a feast for the children of Israel, and went up to the altar, to burn incense.

....

Behold, a man of God came out of Judah by YHWH's word to Bethel; and Jeroboam was standing by the altar to burn incense. He cried against the altar by YHWH's word, and said, "Altar! Altar! YHWH says: 'Behold, a son will be born to David's house, Josiah by name. On you he will sacrifice the priests of the high places who burn incense on you, and they will burn men's bones on you.'" He gave a sign the same day, saying, "This is the sign which YHWH has spoken: Behold, the altar will be split apart, and the ashes that are on it will be poured out."

When the king heard the saying of the man of God, which he cried against the altar in Bethel, Jeroboam put out his hand from the altar, saying, "Seize him!" His hand, which he put out against him, dried up, so that he could not draw it back again to himself. The altar was also split apart, and the ashes poured out from the altar, according to the sign which the man of God had given by YHWH's word. The king answered the man of God, "Now intercede for the favor of YHWH your God, and pray for me, that my hand may be restored me again."

The man of God interceded with YHWH, and the king's hand was restored to him again, and became as it was before.

The king said to the man of God, "Come home with me, and refresh yourself, and I will give you a reward."

The man of God said to the king, "Even if you gave me half of your house, I would not go in with you, neither would I eat bread nor drink water in this place; for so was it commanded me by YHWH's word, saying, 'You shall eat no bread, drink no water, and don't return by the way that you came.'" So he went another way, and didn't return by the way that he came to Bethel.

Now an old prophet lived in Bethel, and one of his sons came and told him all the works that the man of God had done that day in Bethel. They also told their father the words which he had spoken to the king.

Their father said to them, "Which way did he go?" Now his sons had seen which way the man of God went, who came from Judah. He said to his sons, "Saddle the donkey for me." So they saddled the donkey for him; and he rode on it. He went after the man of God, and found him sitting under an oak. He said to him, "Are you the man of God who came from Judah?"

He said, "I am." Then he said to him, "Come home with me, and eat bread."

He said, "I may not return with you, nor go in with you. I will not eat bread or drink water with you in this place. For it was said to me by YHWH's word, 'You shall eat no bread or drink water there, and don't turn again to go by the way that you came.'"

He said to him, "I also am a prophet as you are; and an angel spoke to me by YHWH's word, saying, 'Bring him back with you into your house, that he may eat bread and drink water.'" He lied to him.

So he went back with him, ate bread in his house, and drank water. As they sat at the table, YHWH's word came to the prophet who brought him back; and he cried out to the man of God who came from Judah, saying, "YHWH says, 'Because you have been disobedient to YHWH's mouth, and have not kept the commandment which YHWH your God commanded you, but came back, and have eaten bread and drank water in the place of which he said to you, "Eat no bread, and drink no water;" your body will not come to the tomb of your fathers.'"

After he had eaten bread, and after he drank, he saddled the donkey for the prophet whom he had brought back. When he had gone, a lion met him by the way and killed him. His body was thrown on the path, and the donkey stood by it. The lion also stood by the body. Behold, men passed by, and saw the body thrown on the path, and the lion standing by the body; and they came and told it in the city where the old prophet lived. When the prophet who brought him back from the way heard of it, he said, "It is the man of God who was disobedient to YHWH's mouth. Therefore YHWH has delivered him to the lion, which has mauled him and slain him, according to YHWH's word, which he spoke to him." He said to his sons, saying, "Saddle the donkey for me," and they saddled it. He went and found his body thrown on the path, and the donkey and the lion standing by the body. The lion had not eaten the body, nor mauled the donkey. The prophet took up the body of the man of God, and laid it on the donkey, and brought it back. He came to the city of the old prophet to mourn, and to bury him. He laid his body in his own grave; and they mourned over him, saying, "Alas, my brother!"

After he had buried him, he spoke to his sons, saying, "When I am dead, bury me in the tomb in which the man of God is buried. Lay my bones beside his bones. For the saying which he cried by YH-WH's word against the altar in Bethel, and against all the houses of the high places which are in the cities of Samaria, will surely happen."

After this thing Jeroboam didn't return from his evil way, but again made priests of the high places from among all the people. Whoever wanted to, he consecrated him, that there might be priests of the high places. This thing became sin to the house of Jeroboam, even to cut it off, and to destroy it from off the surface of the earth.

At that time Abijah the son of Jeroboam became sick. Jeroboam said to his wife, "Please get up and disguise yourself, so that you won't be recognized as Jeroboam's wife. Go to Shiloh. Behold, Ahijah the prophet is there, who said that I would be king over this people. Take with you ten loaves of bread, some cakes, and a jar of honey, and go to him. He will tell you what will become of the child."

Jeroboam's wife did so, and arose, and went to Shiloh, and came to Ahijah's house. Now Ahijah could not see; for his eyes were set by reason of his age. YHWH said to Ahijah, "Behold, Jeroboam's wife is coming to inquire of you concerning her son; for he is sick. Tell her such and such; for it will be, when she comes in, that she will pretend to be another woman."

So when Ahijah heard the sound of her feet as she came in at the door, he said, "Come in, Jeroboam's wife! Why do you pretend to be another? For I am sent to you with heavy news. Go, tell Jeroboam, 'YHWH, the God of Israel, says: "Because I exalted you from among the people, and made you prince over my people Israel, and tore the kingdom away from David's house, and gave it you; and yet you have not been as my servant David, who kept my commandments, and who followed me with all his heart, to do that only which was right in my eyes, but have done evil above all who were before you, and have gone and made for yourself other gods, molten images, to provoke me to anger, and have cast me behind your back; therefore, behold, I will bring evil on the house of Jeroboam, and will cut off from Jeroboam everyone who urinates on a wall, he who is shut up and he who is left at large in Israel, and will utterly sweep away the house of Jeroboam, as a man sweeps away dung, until it is all gone. The dogs will eat he who belongs to Jeroboam who dies in the city; and the birds of the sky will eat he who dies in the field: for YHWH has spoken it.'" Arise therefore, and go to your house. When your feet enter into the city, the child will die. All Israel will mourn for him and bury him; for he only of Jeroboam will come to the grave, because in him there is found some good thing toward YHWH, the God of Israel, in the house of Jeroboam. Moreover YHWH will raise up a king for himself over Israel, who will cut off the house of Jeroboam. This is the day! What? Even now. For YHWH will strike Israel, as a reed is shaken in the water; and he will root up Israel out of this good land which he gave to their fathers, and will scatter them beyond the River, because they have made their Asherah poles, provoking YHWH to anger. He will give Israel up because of the sins of Jeroboam, which he has sinned, and with which he has made Israel to sin.'"

Jeroboam's wife arose and departed, and came to Tirzah. As she came to the threshold of the house, the child died. All Israel buried him and mourned for him, according to YHWH's word, which he spoke by his servant Ahijah the prophet. The rest of the acts of Jeroboam, how he fought, and how he reigned, behold, they are written in the book of the chronicles of the kings of Israel. The days which Jeroboam reigned were twenty two years, then he slept with his fathers, and Nadab his son reigned in his place.

Rehoboam the son of Solomon reigned in Judah. Rehoboam was forty-one years old when he began to reign, and he reigned seventeen years in Jerusalem, the city which YHWH had chosen out of all the tribes of Israel, to put his name there. His mother's name was Naamah the Ammonitess. Judah did that which was evil in YHWH's sight, and they provoked him to jealousy with their sins which they committed, above all that their fathers had done. For they also built for themselves high places, sacred pillars, and Asherah poles on every high hill and under every green tree. There were also sodomites in the land. They did according to all the abominations of the nations which YHWH drove out before the children of Israel. In the fifth year of king Rehoboam, Shishak king of Egypt came up against Jerusalem, and he took away the treasures of YHWH's house, and the treasures of the king's house. He even took away all of it, including all the gold shields which Solomon had made. King Rehoboam made shields of bronze in their place, and committed them to the hands of the captains of the guard, who kept the door of the king's house. It was so, that as often as the king went into YHWH's house, the guard bore them, and brought them back into the guard room.

Now the rest of the acts of Rehoboam, and all that he did, aren't they written in the book of the chronicles of the kings of Judah? There was war between Rehoboam and Jeroboam continually. Rehoboam slept with his fathers, and was buried with his fathers in David's city. His mother's name was Naamah the Ammonitess. Abijam his son reigned in his place.

....

Now in the eighteenth year of king Jeroboam the son of Nebat, Abijam began to reign over Judah. He reigned three years in Jerusalem. His mother's name was Maacah the daughter of Abishalom. He walked in all the sins of his father, which he had done before him; and his heart was not perfect with YHWH his God, as the heart of David his father. Nevertheless for David's sake, YHWH his God gave him a lamp in Jerusalem, to set up his son after him, and to establish Jerusalem; because David did that which was right in YHWH's eyes, and didn't turn away from anything that he commanded him all the days of his life, except only in the matter of Uriah the Hittite. Now there was war between Rehoboam and Jeroboam all the days of his life. The rest of the acts of Abijam, and all that he did, aren't they written in the book of the chronicles of the kings of Judah? There was war between Abijam and Jeroboam. Abijam slept with his fathers, and they buried him in David's city; and Asa his son reigned in his place.

In the twentieth year of Jeroboam king of Israel, Asa began to reign over Judah. He reigned forty-one years in Jerusalem. His mother's name was Maacah the daughter of Abishalom. Asa did that which was right in YHWH's eyes, as David his father did. He put away the sodomites out of the land, and removed all the idols that his fathers had made. He also removed Maacah his mother from being queen, because she had made an abominable image for an Asherah. Asa cut down her image and burned it at the brook Kidron. But the high places were not taken away. Nevertheless the heart of Asa was perfect with YHWH all his days. He brought into YHWH's house the things that his father had dedicated, and the things that he himself had dedicated: silver, gold, and utensils. There was war between Asa and Baasha king of Israel all their days. Baasha king of Israel went up against Judah, and built Ramah, that he might not allow anyone to go out or come in to Asa king of Judah. Then Asa took all the silver and the gold that was left in the treasures of YHWH's house, and the treasures of the king's house, and delivered it into the hand of his servants. Then King Asa sent them to Ben Hadad, the son of Tabrimmon, the son of Hezion, king of Syria, who lived at Damascus, saying, "There is a treaty between me and you, between my father and your father. Behold, I have sent to you a present of silver and gold. Go, break your treaty with Baasha king of Israel, that he may depart from me."

Ben Hadad listened to king Asa, and sent the captains of his armies against the cities of Israel, and struck Ijon, and Dan, and Abel Beth Maacah, and all Chinneroth, with all the land of Naphtali. When Baasha heard of it, he stopped building Ramah, and lived in Tirzah. Then king Asa made a proclamation to all Judah. No one was exempted. They carried away the stones of Ramah, and its timber, with which Baasha had built; and king Asa used it to build Geba of Benjamin, and Mizpah. Now the rest of all the acts of Asa, and all his might, and all that he did, and the cities which he built, aren't they written in the book of the chronicles of the kings of Judah? But in the time of his old age he was diseased in his feet. Asa slept with his fathers, and was buried with his fathers in his father David's city; and Jehoshaphat his son reigned in his place.

Nadab the son of Jeroboam began to reign over Israel in the second year of Asa king of Judah; and he reigned over Israel two years. He did that which was evil in YHWH's sight, and walked in the way of his father, and in his sin with which he made Israel to sin. Baasha the son of Ahijah, of the house of Issachar, conspired against him; and Baasha struck him at Gibbethon, which belonged to the Philistines; for Nadab and all Israel were besieging Gibbethon. Even in the third year of Asa king of Judah, Baasha killed him, and reigned in his place. As soon as he was king, he struck all the house of Jeroboam. He didn't leave to Jeroboam any who breathed, until he had destroyed him; according to the saying of YHWH, which he spoke by his servant Ahijah the Shilonite; for the sins of Jeroboam which he sinned, and with which he made Israel to sin, because of his provocation with which he provoked YHWH, the God of Israel, to anger. Now the rest of the acts of Nadab, and all that he did, aren't they written in the book of the chronicles of the kings of Israel? There was war between Asa and Baasha king of Israel all their days.

In the third year of Asa king of Judah, Baasha the son of Ahijah began to reign over all Israel in Tirzah for twenty-four years. He did that which was evil in YHWH's sight, and walked in the way of Jeroboam, and in his sin with which he made Israel to sin.

....

YHWH's word came to Jehu the son of Hanani against Baasha, saying, "Because I exalted you out of the dust, and made you prince over my people Israel, and you have walked in the way of Jeroboam, and have made my people Israel to sin, to provoke me to anger with their sins; behold, I will utterly sweep away Baasha and his house; and I will make your house like the house of Jeroboam the son of Nebat. The dogs will eat Baasha's descendants who die in the city; and he who dies of his in the field, the birds of the sky will eat."

Now the rest of the acts of Baasha, and what he did, and his might, aren't they written in the book of the chronicles of the kings of Israel? Baasha slept with his fathers, and was buried in Tirzah; and Elah his son reigned in his place.

Moreover YHWH's word came by the prophet Jehu the son of Hanani against Baasha and against his house, both because of all the evil that he did in YHWH's sight, to provoke him to anger with the work of his hands, in being like the house of Jeroboam, and because he struck him.

In the twenty-sixth year of Asa king of Judah, Elah the son of Baasha began to reign over Israel in Tirzah for two years. His servant Zimri, captain of half his chariots, conspired against him. Now he was in Tirzah, drinking himself drunk in the house of Arza, who was over the household in Tirzah; and Zimri went in and struck him, and killed him, in the twenty-seventh year of Asa king of Judah, and reigned in his place.

When he began to reign, as soon as he sat on his throne, he attacked all the house of Baasha. He didn't leave him a single one who urinates on a wall among his relatives or his friends. Thus Zimri destroyed all the house of Baasha, according to YHWH's word, which he spoke against Baasha by Jehu the prophet, for all the sins of Baasha, and the sins of Elah his son, which they sinned, and with which they made Israel to sin, to provoke YHWH, the God of Israel, to anger with their vanities. Now the rest of the acts of Elah, and all that he did, aren't they written in the book of the chronicles of the kings of Israel? In the twenty-seventh year of Asa king of Judah, Zimri reigned seven days in Tirzah. Now the people were encamped against Gibbethon, which belonged to the Philistines. The people who were encamped heard that Zimri had conspired, and had also killed the king. Therefore all Israel made Omri, the captain of the army, king over Israel that day in the camp. Omri went up from Gibbethon, and all Israel with him, and they besieged Tirzah. When Zimri saw that the city was taken, he went into the fortified part of the king's house, and burned the king's house over him with fire, and died, for his sins which he sinned in doing that which was evil in YHWH's sight, in walking in the way of Jeroboam, and in his sin which he did, to make Israel to sin. Now the rest of the acts of Zimri, and his treason that he committed, aren't they written in the book of the chronicles of the kings of Israel?

Then the people of Israel were divided into two parts: half of the people followed Tibni the son of Ginath, to make him king; and half followed Omri. But the people who followed Omri prevailed against the people who followed Tibni the son of Ginath; so Tibni died, and Omri reigned. In the thirty-first year of Asa king of Judah, Omri began to reign over Israel for twelve years. He reigned six years in Tirzah. He bought the hill Samaria of Shemer for two talents of silver; and he built on the hill, and called the name of the city which he built Samaria, after the name of Shemer, the owner of the hill. Omri did that which was evil in YHWH's sight, and dealt wickedly above all who were before him. For he walked in all the way of Jeroboam the son of Nebat, and in his sins with which he made Israel to sin, to provoke YHWH, the God of Israel, to anger with their vanities. Now the rest of the acts of Omri which he did, and his might that he showed, aren't they written in the book of the chronicles of the kings of Israel? So Omri slept with his fathers, and was buried in Samaria; and Ahab his son reigned in his place.

In the thirty-eighth year of Asa king of Judah, Ahab the son of Omri began to reign over Israel. Ahab the son of Omri reigned over Israel in Samaria twenty-two years. Ahab the son of Omri did that which was evil in YHWH's sight above all that were before him. As if it had been a light thing for him to walk in the sins of Jeroboam the son of Nebat, he took as wife Jezebel the daughter of Ethbaal king of the Sidonians, and went and served Baal, and worshiped him. He raised up an altar for Baal in the house of Baal, which he had built in Samaria. Ahab made the Asherah; and Ahab did more yet to provoke YHWH, the God of Israel, to anger than all the kings of Israel who were before him. In his days Hiel the Bethelite built Jericho. He laid its foundation with the loss of Abiram his firstborn, and set up its gates with the loss of his youngest son Segub, according to YHWH's word, which he spoke by Joshua the son of Nun.

....

Elijah the Tishbite, who was one of the settlers of Gilead, said to Ahab, "As YHWH, the God of Israel, lives, before whom I stand, there shall not be dew nor rain these years, but according to my word."

Then YHWH's word came to him, saying, "Go away from here, turn eastward, and hide yourself by the brook Cherith, that is before the Jordan. You shall drink from the brook. I have commanded the ravens to feed you there." So he went and did according to YHWH's word; for he went and lived by the brook Cherith that is before the Jordan. The ravens brought him bread and meat in the morning, and bread and meat in the evening; and he drank from the brook. After a while, the brook dried up, because there was no rain in the land.

YHWH's word came to him, saying, "Arise, go to Zarephath, which belongs to Sidon, and stay there. Behold, I have commanded a widow there to sustain you."

So he arose and went to Zarephath; and when he came to the gate of the city, behold, a widow was there gathering sticks. He called to her, and said, "Please get me a little water in a jar, that I may drink."

As she was going to get it, he called to her, and said, "Please bring me a morsel of bread in your hand."

She said, "As YHWH your God lives, I don't have a cake, but a handful of meal in a jar, and a little oil in a jar. Behold, I am gathering two sticks, that I may go in and bake it for me and my son, that we may eat it, and die."

Elijah said to her, "Don't be afraid. Go and do as you have said; but make me a little cake from it first, and bring it out to me, and afterward make some for you and for your son. For YHWH, the God of Israel says, 'The jar of meal will not run out, and the jar of oil will not fail, until the day that YHWH sends rain on the earth.'"

She went and did according to the saying of Elijah; and she, and he, and her house, ate many days. The jar of meal didn't run out, and the jar of oil didn't fail, according to YHWH's word, which he spoke by Elijah. After these things, the son of the woman, the mistress of the house, became sick; and his sickness was so severe that there was no breath left in him. She said to Elijah, "What have I to do with you, you man of God? You have come to me to bring my sin to memory, and to kill my son!"

He said to her, "Give me your son." He took him out of her bosom, and carried him up into the room where he stayed, and laid him on his own bed. He cried to YHWH, and said, "YHWH my God, have you also brought evil on the widow with whom I am staying, by killing her son?"

He stretched himself on the child three times, and cried to YHWH, and said, "YHWH my God, please let this child's soul come into him again."

YHWH listened to the voice of Elijah; and the soul of the child came into him again, and he revived. Elijah took the child, and brought him down out of the room into the house, and delivered him to his mother; and Elijah said, "Behold, your son lives."

The woman said to Elijah, "Now I know that you are a man of God, and that YHWH's word in your mouth is truth."

....

After many days, YHWH's word came to Elijah, in the third year, saying, "Go, show yourself to Ahab; and I will send rain on the earth."

Elijah went to show himself to Ahab. The famine was severe in Samaria. Ahab called Obadiah, who was over the household. (Now Obadiah feared YHWH greatly; for when Jezebel cut off YHWH's prophets, Obadiah took one hundred prophets, and hid them by fifty in a cave, and fed them with bread and water.) Ahab said to Obadiah, "Go through the land, to all the springs of water, and to all the brooks. Perhaps we may find grass and save the horses and mules alive, that we not lose all the animals."

So they divided the land between them to pass throughout it. Ahab went one way by himself, and Obadiah went another way by himself. As Obadiah was on the way, behold, Elijah met him. He recognized him, and fell on his face, and said, "Is it you, my lord Elijah?"

He answered him, "It is I. Go, tell your lord, 'Behold, Elijah is here!'"

He said, "How have I sinned, that you would deliver your servant into the hand of Ahab, to kill me? As YHWH your God lives, there is no nation or kingdom where my lord has not sent to seek you. When they said, 'He is not here,' he took an oath of the kingdom and nation, that they didn't find you. Now you say, 'Go, tell your lord, "Behold, Elijah is here."' It will happen, as soon as I leave you, that YHWH's Spirit will carry you I don't know where; and so when I come and tell Ahab, and he can't find you, he will kill me. But I, your servant, have feared YHWH from my youth. Wasn't it told my lord what I did when Jezebel killed YHWH's prophets, how I hid one hundred men of YHWH's prophets with fifty to a cave, and fed them with bread and water? Now you say, 'Go, tell your lord, "Behold, Elijah is here".' He will kill me."

Elijah said, "As YHWH of Armies lives, before whom I stand, I will surely show myself to him today." So Obadiah went to meet Ahab, and told him; and Ahab went to meet Elijah. When Ahab saw Elijah, Ahab said to him, "Is that you, you troubler of Israel?"

He answered, "I have not troubled Israel; but you, and your father's house, in that you have forsaken YHWH's commandments, and you have followed the Baals. Now therefore send, and gather to me all Israel to Mount Carmel, and four hundred fifty of the prophets of Baal, and four hundred of the prophets of the Asherah, who eat at Jezebel's table."

So Ahab sent to all the children of Israel, and gathered the prophets together to Mount Carmel. Elijah came near to all the people, and said, "How long will you waver between the two sides? If YHWH is God, follow him; but if Baal, then follow him."

The people didn't say a word.

Then Elijah said to the people, "I, even I only, am left as a prophet of YHWH; but Baal's prophets are four hundred fifty men. Let them therefore give us two bulls; and let them choose one bull for themselves, and cut it in pieces, and lay it on the wood, and put no fire under; and I will dress the other bull, and lay it on the wood, and put no fire under it. You call on the name of your god, and I will call on YHWH's name. The God who answers by fire, let him be God."

All the people answered, "What you say is good."

Elijah said to the prophets of Baal, "Choose one bull for yourselves, and dress it first; for you are many; and call on the name of your god, but put no fire under it."

They took the bull which was given them, and they dressed it, and called on the name of Baal from morning even until noon, saying, "Baal, hear us!" But there was no voice, and nobody answered. They leaped about the altar which was made. At noon, Elijah mocked them, and said, "Cry aloud; for he is a god. Either he is deep in thought, or he has gone somewhere, or he is on a journey, or perhaps he sleeps and must be awakened."

They cried aloud, and cut themselves in their way with knives and lances, until the blood gushed out on them. When midday was past, they prophesied until the time of the evening offering; but there was no voice, no answer, and nobody paid attention.

Elijah said to all the people, "Come near to me!"; and all the people came near to him. He repaired YHWH's altar that had been thrown down. Elijah took twelve stones, according to the number of the tribes of the sons of Jacob, to whom YHWH's word came, saying, "Israel shall be your name." With the stones he built an altar in YHWH's name. He made a trench around the altar, large enough to contain two seahs of seed. He put the wood in order, and cut the bull in pieces, and laid it on the wood. He said, "Fill four jars with water, and pour it on the burnt offering, and on the wood." He said, "Do it a second time;" and they did it the second time. He said, "Do it a third time;" and they did it the third time. The water ran around the altar; and he also filled the trench with water.

At the time of the evening offering, Elijah the prophet came near, and said, "YHWH, the God of Abraham, of Isaac, and of Israel, let it be known today that you are God in Israel, and that I am your servant, and that I have done all these things at your word. Hear me, YHWH, hear me, that this people may know that you, YHWH, are God, and that you have turned their heart back again."

Then YHWH's fire fell, and consumed the burnt offering, the wood, the stones, and the dust, and licked up the water that was in the trench. When all the people saw it, they fell on their faces. They said, "YHWH, he is God! YHWH, he is God!"

Elijah said to them, "Seize the prophets of Baal! Don't let one of them escape!"

They seized them; and Elijah brought them down to the brook Kishon, and killed them there. Elijah said to Ahab, "Get up, eat and drink; for there is the sound of abundance of rain."

So Ahab went up to eat and to drink. Elijah went up to the top of Carmel; and he bowed himself down on the earth, and put his face between his knees. He said to his servant, "Go up now, and look toward the sea."

He went up, and looked, and said, "There is nothing."

He said, "Go again" seven times.

On the seventh time, he said, "Behold, a small cloud, like a man's hand, is rising out of the sea."

He said, "Go up, tell Ahab, 'Get ready and go down, so that the rain doesn't stop you.'"

In a little while, the sky grew black with clouds and wind, and there was a great rain. Ahab rode, and went to Jezreel. YHWH's hand was on Elijah; and he tucked his cloak into his belt and ran before Ahab to the entrance of Jezreel.

....

Ahab told Jezebel all that Elijah had done, and how he had killed all the prophets with the sword. Then Jezebel sent a messenger to Elijah, saying, "So let the gods do to me, and more also, if I don't make your life as the life of one of them by tomorrow about this time!"

When he saw that, he arose, and ran for his life, and came to Beersheba, which belongs to Judah, and left his servant there. But he himself went a day's journey into the wilderness, and came and sat down under a juniper tree. Then he requested for himself that he might die, and said, "It is enough. Now, O YHWH, take away my life; for I am not better than my fathers."

He lay down and slept under a juniper tree; and behold, an angel touched him, and said to him, "Arise and eat!"

He looked, and behold, there was at his head a cake baked on the coals, and a jar of water. He ate and drank, and lay down again. YHWH's angel came again the second time, and touched him, and said, "Arise and eat, because the journey is too great for you."

He arose, and ate and drank, and went in the strength of that food forty days and forty nights to Horeb, God's Mountain. He came to a cave there, and camped there; and behold, YHWH's word came to him, and he said to him, "What are you doing here, Elijah?"

He said, "I have been very jealous for YHWH, the God of Armies; for the children of Israel have forsaken your covenant, thrown down your altars, and killed your prophets with the sword. I, even I only, am left; and they seek my life, to take it away."

He said, "Go out, and stand on the mountain before YHWH."

Behold, YHWH passed by, and a great and strong wind tore the mountains, and broke in pieces the rocks before YHWH; but YHWH was not in the wind. After the wind there was an earthquake; but YHWH was not in the earthquake. After the earthquake a fire passed; but YHWH was not in the fire. After the fire, there was a still small voice. When Elijah heard it, he wrapped his face in his mantle, went out, and stood in the entrance of the cave. Behold, a voice came to him, and said, "What are you doing here, Elijah?"

He said, "I have been very jealous for YHWH, the God of Armies;

for the children of Israel have forsaken your covenant, thrown down your altars, and killed your prophets with the sword. I, even I only, am left; and they seek my life, to take it away."

YHWH said to him, "Go, return on your way to the wilderness of Damascus. When you arrive, anoint Hazael to be king over Syria. Anoint Jehu the son of Nimshi to be king over Israel; and anoint Elisha the son of Shaphat of Abel Meholah to be prophet in your place. He who escapes from the sword of Hazael, Jehu will kill; and he who escapes from the sword of Jehu, Elisha will kill. Yet I reserved seven thousand in Israel, all the knees of which have not bowed to Baal, and every mouth which has not kissed him."

So he departed from there, and found Elisha the son of Shaphat, who was plowing with twelve yoke of oxen before him, and he with the twelfth. Elijah went over to him, and put his mantle on him. Elisha left the oxen, and ran after Elijah, and said, "Let me please kiss my father and my mother, and then I will follow you."

He said to him, "Go back again; for what have I done to you?"

He returned from following him, and took the yoke of oxen, and killed them, and boiled their meat with the instruments of the oxen, and gave to the people, and they ate. Then he arose, and went after Elijah, and served him.

....

Ben Hadad the king of Syria gathered all his army together; and there were thirty-two kings with him, with horses and chariots. He went up and besieged Samaria, and fought against it. He sent messengers to Ahab king of Israel, into the city, and said to him, "Ben Hadad says, 'Your silver and your gold is mine. Your wives also and your children, even the best, are mine.'"

The king of Israel answered, "It is according to your saying, my lord, O king. I am yours, and all that I have."

The messengers came again, and said, "Ben Hadad says, 'I sent indeed to you, saying, "You shall deliver me your silver, and your gold, and your wives, and your children; but I will send my servants to you tomorrow about this time, and they will search your house, and the houses of your servants; whatever is pleasant in your eyes, they will put it in their hand, and take it away."'"

Then the king of Israel called all the elders of the land, and said, "Please notice how this man seeks mischief; for he sent to me for my wives, and for my children, and for my silver, and for my gold; and

I didn't deny him."

All the elders and all the people said to him, "Don't listen, and don't consent."

Therefore he said to the messengers of Ben Hadad, "Tell my lord the king, 'All that you sent for to your servant at the first I will do; but this thing I cannot do.'"

The messengers departed, and brought him back the message. Ben Hadad sent to him, and said, "The gods do so to me, and more also, if the dust of Samaria will be enough for handfuls for all the people who follow me."

The king of Israel answered, "Tell him, 'Don't let him who puts on his armor brag like he who takes it off.'"

When Ben Hadad heard this message, as he was drinking, he and the kings, in the pavilions, he said to his servants, "Prepare to attack!" They prepared to attack the city.

Behold, a prophet came near to Ahab king of Israel, and said, "YHWH says, 'Have you seen all this great multitude? Behold, I will deliver it into your hand today. Then you will know that I am YHWH.'"

Ahab said, "By whom?"

He said, "YHWH says, 'By the young men of the princes of the provinces.'"

Then he said, "Who shall begin the battle?"

He answered, "You."

Then he mustered the young men of the princes of the provinces, and they were two hundred and thirty-two. After them, he mustered all the people, even all the children of Israel, being seven thousand. They went out at noon. But Ben Hadad was drinking himself drunk in the pavilions, he and the kings, the thirty-two kings who helped him. The young men of the princes of the provinces went out first; and Ben Hadad sent out, and they told him, saying, "Men are coming out from Samaria."

He said, "If they have come out for peace, take them alive; or if they have come out for war, take them alive."

So these went out of the city, the young men of the princes of the provinces, and the army which followed them. They each killed his man. The Syrians fled, and Israel pursued them. Ben Hadad the king of Syria escaped on a horse with horsemen. The king of Israel went out, and struck the horses and chariots, and killed the Syrians with a great slaughter. The prophet came near to the king of Israel, and said to him, "Go, strengthen yourself, and mark, and see what you do; for at the return of the year the king of Syria will come up against you."

The servants of the king of Syria said to him, "Their god is a god of the hills; therefore they were stronger than we. But let's fight against them in the plain, and surely we will be stronger than they. Do this thing: take the kings away, every man out of his place, and put captains in their place. Muster an army, like the army that you have lost, horse for horse, and chariot for chariot. We will fight against them in the plain, and surely we will be stronger than they are."

He listened to their voice, and did so. At the return of the year, Ben Hadad mustered the Syrians, and went up to Aphek, to fight against Israel. The children of Israel were mustered and given provisions, and went against them. The children of Israel encamped before them like two little flocks of young goats; but the Syrians filled the country. A man of God came near and spoke to the king of Israel, and said, "YHWH says, 'Because the Syrians have said, "YHWH is a god of the hills, but he is not a god of the valleys;" therefore I will deliver all this great multitude into your hand, and you shall know that I am YHWH.'"

They encamped opposite each other for seven days. So it was, that in the seventh day the battle was joined; and the children of Israel killed one hundred thousand footmen of the Syrians in one day. But the rest fled to Aphek, into the city; and the wall fell on twenty-seven thousand men who were left. Ben Hadad fled, and came into the city, into an inner room. His servants said to him, "See now, we have heard that the kings of the house of Israel are merciful kings. Please let us put sackcloth on our bodies, and ropes on our heads, and go out to the king of Israel. Maybe he will save your life."

So they put sackcloth on their bodies and ropes on their heads, and came to the king of Israel, and said, "Your servant Ben Hadad says, 'Please let me live.'"

He said, "Is he still alive? He is my brother."

Now the men observed diligently, and hurried to take this phrase; and they said, "Your brother Ben Hadad."

Then he said, "Go, bring him."

Then Ben Hadad came out to him; and he caused him to come up into the chariot. Ben Hadad said to him, "The cities which my father took from your father I will restore. You shall make streets for yourself in Damascus, as my father made in Samaria."

"I", said Ahab, "will let you go with this covenant." So he made a covenant with him, and let him go.

A certain man of the sons of the prophets said to his fellow by YHWH's word, "Please strike me!"

The man refused to strike him. Then he said to him, "Because you have not obeyed YHWH's voice, behold, as soon as you have departed from me, a lion will kill you." As soon as he had departed from him, a lion found him and killed him.

Then he found another man, and said, "Please strike me."

The man struck him and wounded him. So the prophet departed, and waited for the king by the way, and disguised himself with his headband over his eyes. As the king passed by, he cried to the king; and he said, "Your servant went out into the middle of the battle; and behold, a man came over, and brought a man to me, and said, 'Guard this man! If by any means he is missing, then your life shall be for his life, or else you shall pay a talent of silver.' As your servant was busy here and there, he was gone."

The king of Israel said to him, "So shall your judgment be. You yourself have decided it."

He hurried, and took the headband away from his eyes; and the king of Israel recognized that he was one of the prophets. He said to him, "YHWH says, 'Because you have let go out of your hand the man whom I had devoted to destruction, therefore your life will take the place of his life, and your people take the place of his people.'"

The king of Israel went to his house sullen and angry, and came to Samaria.

....

After these things, Naboth the Jezreelite had a vineyard, which was in Jezreel, next to the palace of Ahab king of Samaria. Ahab spoke to Naboth, saying, "Give me your vineyard, that I may have it for a garden of herbs, because it is near my house; and I will give you for it a better vineyard than it. Or, if it seems good to you, I will give you its worth in money."

Naboth said to Ahab, "May YHWH forbid me, that I should give the inheritance of my fathers to you!"

Ahab came into his house sullen and angry because of the word which Naboth the Jezreelite had spoken to him; for he had said, "I will not give you the inheritance of my fathers." He laid himself down on his bed, and turned away his face, and would eat no bread.

But Jezebel his wife came to him, and said to him, "Why is your spirit so sad, that you eat no bread?"

He said to her, "Because I spoke to Naboth the Jezreelite, and said to him, 'Give me your vineyard for money; or else, if it pleases you, I will give you another vineyard for it.' He answered, 'I will not give you my vineyard.'"

Jezebel his wife said to him, "Do you now govern the kingdom of Israel? Arise, and eat bread, and let your heart be merry. I will give you the vineyard of Naboth the Jezreelite." So she wrote letters in Ahab's name, and sealed them with his seal, and sent the letters to the elders and to the nobles who were in his city, who lived with Naboth. She wrote in the letters, saying, "Proclaim a fast, and set Naboth on high among the people. Set two men, wicked fellows, before him, and let them testify against him, saying, 'You cursed God and the king!' Then carry him out, and stone him to death."

The men of his city, even the elders and the nobles who lived in his city, did as Jezebel had instructed them in the letters which she had written and sent to them. They proclaimed a fast, and set Naboth on high among the people. The two men, the wicked fellows, came in and sat before him. The wicked fellows testified against him, even against Naboth, in the presence of the people, saying, "Naboth cursed God and the king!" Then they carried him out of the city and stoned him to death with stones. Then they sent to Jezebel, saying, "Naboth has been stoned, and is dead."

When Jezebel heard that Naboth had been stoned, and was dead, Jezebel said to Ahab, "Arise, take possession of the vineyard of Naboth the Jezreelite, which he refused to give you for money; for Naboth is not alive, but dead."

When Ahab heard that Naboth was dead, Ahab rose up to go down to the vineyard of Naboth the Jezreelite, to take possession of it.

YHWH's word came to Elijah the Tishbite, saying, "Arise, go down to meet Ahab king of Israel, who dwells in Samaria. Behold, he is in the vineyard of Naboth, where he has gone down to take possession of it. You shall speak to him, saying, 'YHWH says, "Have you killed and also taken possession?"' You shall speak to him, saying, 'YHWH says, "In the place where dogs licked the blood of Naboth, dogs will lick your blood, even yours."'"

Ahab said to Elijah, "Have you found me, my enemy?"

He answered, "I have found you, because you have sold yourself to do that which is evil in YHWH's sight. Behold, I will bring evil on you, and will utterly sweep you away and will cut off from Ahab everyone who urinates against a wall, and him who is shut up and him who is left at large in Israel. I will make your house like the house of Jeroboam the son of Nebat, and like the house of Baasha the son of Ahijah for the provocation with which you have provoked me to anger, and have made Israel to sin." YHWH also spoke of Jezebel, saying, "The dogs will eat Jezebel by the rampart of Jezreel. The dogs will eat he who dies of Ahab in the city; and the birds of the sky will eat he who dies in the field."

But there was no one like Ahab, who sold himself to do that which was evil in YHWH's sight, whom Jezebel his wife stirred up. He did very abominably in following idols, according to all that the Amorites did, whom YHWH cast out before the children of Israel. When Ahab heard those words, he tore his clothes, and put sackcloth on his flesh, and fasted, and lay in sackcloth, and went softly.

YHWH's word came to Elijah the Tishbite, saying, "See how Ahab humbles himself before me? Because he humbles himself before me, I will not bring the evil in his days; but I will bring the evil on his house in his son's day."

....

They continued three years without war between Syria and Israel. In the third year, Jehoshaphat the king of Judah came down to the king of Israel. The king of Israel said to his servants, "You know that Ramoth Gilead is ours, and we do nothing, and don't take it out of the hand of the king of Syria?" He said to Jehoshaphat, "Will you go with me to battle to Ramoth Gilead?"

Jehoshaphat said to the king of Israel, "I am as you are, my people as your people, my horses as your horses." Jehoshaphat said to the king of Israel, "Please inquire first for YHWH's word."

Then the king of Israel gathered the prophets together, about four hundred men, and said to them, "Should I go against Ramoth Gilead to battle, or should I refrain?"

They said, "Go up; for the Lord will deliver it into the hand of the king."

But Jehoshaphat said, "Isn't there here a prophet of YHWH, that we may inquire of him?"

The king of Israel said to Jehoshaphat, "There is yet one man by whom we may inquire of YHWH, Micaiah the son of Imlah; but I hate him, for he does not prophesy good concerning me, but evil."

Jehoshaphat said, "Don't let the king say so."

Then the king of Israel called an officer, and said, "Quickly get Micaiah the son of Imlah."

Now the king of Israel and Jehoshaphat the king of Judah were sitting each on his throne, arrayed in their robes, in an open place at the entrance of the gate of Samaria; and all the prophets were prophesying before them. Zedekiah the son of Chenaanah made himself horns of iron, and said, "YHWH says, 'With these you will push the Syrians, until they are consumed.'" All the prophets prophesied so, saying, "Go up to Ramoth Gilead, and prosper; for YHWH will deliver it into the hand of the king."

The messenger who went to call Micaiah spoke to him, saying, "See now, the prophets declare good to the king with one mouth. Please let your word be like the word of one of them, and speak good."

Micaiah said, "As YHWH lives, what YHWH says to me, that I will speak."

When he had come to the king, the king said to him, "Micaiah, shall we go to Ramoth Gilead to battle, or shall we forbear?"

He answered him, "Go up and prosper; and YHWH will deliver it into the hand of the king." The king said to him, "How many times do I have to adjure you that you speak to me nothing but the truth in YHWH's name?"

He said, "I saw all Israel scattered on the mountains, as sheep that have no shepherd. YHWH said, 'These have no master. Let them each return to his house in peace.'"

The king of Israel said to Jehoshaphat, "Didn't I tell you that he would not prophesy good concerning me, but evil?"

Micaiah said, "Therefore hear YHWH's word. I saw YHWH sitting on his throne, and all the army of heaven standing by him on his right hand and on his left. YHWH said, 'Who will entice Ahab, that he may go up and fall at Ramoth Gilead?' One said one thing; and another said another.

A spirit came out and stood before YHWH, and said, 'I will entice him.'

YHWH said to him, 'How?'

He said, 'I will go out and will be a lying spirit in the mouth of all his prophets.'

He said, 'You will entice him, and will also prevail. Go out and

252

do so.' Now therefore, behold, YHWH has put a lying spirit in the mouth of all these your prophets; and YHWH has spoken evil concerning you."

Then Zedekiah the son of Chenaanah came near, and struck Micaiah on the cheek, and said, "Which way did YHWH's Spirit go from me to speak to you?"

Micaiah said, "Behold, you will see on that day, when you go into an inner room to hide yourself."

The king of Israel said, "Take Micaiah, and carry him back to Amon the governor of the city, and to Joash the king's son. Say, 'The king says, "Put this fellow in the prison, and feed him with bread of affliction and with water of affliction, until I come in peace."'"

Micaiah said, "If you return at all in peace, YHWH has not spoken by me." He said, "Listen, all you people!"

So the king of Israel and Jehoshaphat the king of Judah went up to Ramoth Gilead. The king of Israel said to Jehoshaphat, "I will disguise myself, and go into the battle; but you put on your robes." The king of Israel disguised himself, and went into the battle.

Now the king of Syria had commanded the thirty-two captains of his chariots, saying, "Don't fight with small nor great, except only with the king of Israel."

When the captains of the chariots saw Jehoshaphat, they said, "Surely that is the king of Israel!" and they came over to fight against him. Jehoshaphat cried out. When the captains of the chariots saw that it was not the king of Israel, they turned back from pursuing him. A certain man drew his bow at random, and struck the king of Israel between the joints of the armor. Therefore he said to the driver of his chariot, "Turn your hand, and carry me out of the battle; for I am severely wounded." The battle increased that day. The king was propped up in his chariot facing the Syrians, and died at evening. The blood ran out of the wound into the bottom of the chariot. A cry went throughout the army about the going down of the sun, saying, "Every man to his city, and every man to his country!"

So the king died, and was brought to Samaria; and they buried the king in Samaria. They washed the chariot by the pool of Samaria; and the dogs licked up his blood where the prostitutes washed themselves; according to YHWH's word which he spoke.

Now the rest of the acts of Ahab, and all that he did, and the ivory house which he built, and all the cities that he built, aren't they written in the book of the chronicles of the kings of Israel? So Ahab slept with his fathers; and Ahaziah his son reigned in his place.

Jehoshaphat the son of Asa began to reign over Judah in the fourth year of Ahab king of Israel. Jehoshaphat was thirty-five years old when he began to reign; and he reigned twenty-five years in Jerusalem. His mother's name was Azubah the daughter of Shilhi. He walked in all the way of Asa his father. He didn't turn away from it, doing that which was right in YHWH's eyes. However the high places were not taken away. The people still sacrificed and burned incense on the high places. Jehoshaphat made peace with the king of Israel. Now the rest of the acts of Jehoshaphat, and his might that he showed, and how he fought, aren't they written in the book of the chronicles of the kings of Judah? The remnant of the sodomites, that remained in the days of his father Asa, he put away out of the land. There was no king in Edom. A deputy ruled. Jehoshaphat made ships of Tarshish to go to Ophir for gold, but they didn't go; for the ships wrecked at Ezion Geber. Then Ahaziah the son of Ahab said to Jehoshaphat, "Let my servants go with your servants in the ships." But Jehoshaphat would not. Jehoshaphat slept with his fathers, and was buried with his fathers in his father David's city. Jehoram his son reigned in his place.

Ahaziah the son of Ahab began to reign over Israel in Samaria in the seventeenth year of Jehoshaphat king of Judah, and he reigned two years over Israel. He did that which was evil in YHWH's sight, and walked in the way of his father, and in the way of his mother, and in the way of Jeroboam the son of Nebat, in which he made Israel to sin. He served Baal and worshiped him, and provoked YHWH, the God of Israel, to anger in all the ways that his father had done so.

THE BOOK OF

KINGS

PART II

2 HR 3 MIN

Moab rebelled against Israel after the death of Ahab. Ahaziah fell down through the lattice in his upper room that was in Samaria, and was sick. So he sent messengers, and said to them, "Go, inquire of Baal Zebub, the god of Ekron, whether I will recover of this sickness."

But YHWH's angel said to Elijah the Tishbite, "Arise, go up to meet the messengers of the king of Samaria, and tell them, 'Is it because there is no God in Israel, that you go to inquire of Baal Zebub, the god of Ekron? Now therefore YHWH says, "You will not come down from the bed where you have gone up, but you will surely die."'" Then Elijah departed.

The messengers returned to him, and he said to them, "Why is it that you have returned?"

They said to him, "A man came up to meet us, and said to us, 'Go, return to the king who sent you, and tell him, "YHWH says, 'Is it because there is no God in Israel, that you send to inquire of Baal Zebub, the god of Ekron? Therefore you will not come down from the bed where you have gone up, but you will surely die.'"'"

He said to them, "What kind of man was he who came up to meet you, and told you these words?"

They answered him, "He was a hairy man, and wearing a leather belt around his waist."

He said, "It's Elijah the Tishbite."

Then the king sent a captain of fifty with his fifty to him. He went up to him; and behold, he was sitting on the top of the hill. He said to him, "Man of God, the king has said, 'Come down!'"

Elijah answered to the captain of fifty, "If I am a man of God, then let fire come down from the sky, and consume you and your fifty!" Then fire came down from the sky, and consumed him and his fifty.

Again he sent to him another captain of fifty with his fifty. He answered him, "Man of God, the king has said, 'Come down quickly!'"

Elijah answered them, "If I am a man of God, then let fire come down from the sky, and consume you and your fifty!" Then God's fire came down from the sky, and consumed him and his fifty.

Again he sent the captain of a third fifty with his fifty. The third captain of fifty went up, and came and fell on his knees before Elijah, and begged him, and said to him, "Man of God, please let my life, and the life of these fifty of your servants, be precious in your sight.

Behold, fire came down from the sky, and consumed the last two captains of fifty with their fifties. But now let my life be precious in your sight."

YHWH's angel said to Elijah, "Go down with him. Don't be afraid of him."

Then he arose, and went down with him to the king. He said to him, "YHWH says, 'Because you have sent messengers to inquire of Baal Zebub, the god of Ekron, is it because there is no God in Israel to inquire of his word? Therefore you will not come down from the bed where you have gone up, but you will surely die.'"

So he died according to YHWH's word which Elijah had spoken. Jehoram began to reign in his place in the second year of Jehoram the son of Jehoshaphat king of Judah, because he had no son. Now the rest of the acts of Ahaziah which he did, aren't they written in the book of the chronicles of the kings of Israel?

....

When YHWH was about to take Elijah up by a whirlwind into heaven, Elijah went with Elisha from Gilgal. Elijah said to Elisha, "Please wait here, for YHWH has sent me as far as Bethel."

Elisha said, "As YHWH lives, and as your soul lives, I will not leave you." So they went down to Bethel.

The sons of the prophets who were at Bethel came out to Elisha, and said to him, "Do you know that YHWH will take away your master from your head today?"

He said, "Yes, I know it. Hold your peace."

Elijah said to him, "Elisha, please wait here, for YHWH has sent me to Jericho."

He said, "As YHWH lives, and as your soul lives, I will not leave you." So they came to Jericho.

The sons of the prophets who were at Jericho came near to Elisha, and said to him, "Do you know that YHWH will take away your master from your head today?"

He answered, "Yes, I know it. Hold your peace."

Elijah said to him, "Please wait here, for YHWH has sent me to the Jordan."

He said, "As YHWH lives, and as your soul lives, I will not leave you." Then they both went on. Fifty men of the sons of the prophets went, and stood opposite them at a distance; and they both stood by the Jordan. Elijah took his mantle, and rolled it up, and struck the waters, and they were divided here and there, so that they both went over on dry ground. When they had gone over, Elijah said to Elisha, "Ask what I shall do for you, before I am taken from you."

Elisha said, "Please let a double portion of your spirit be on me."

He said, "You have asked a hard thing. If you see me when I am taken from you, it will be so for you; but if not, it will not be so."

As they continued on and talked, behold, a chariot of fire and horses of fire separated them, and Elijah went up by a whirlwind into heaven. Elisha saw it, and he cried, "My father, my father, the chariots of Israel and its horsemen!"

He saw him no more. Then he took hold of his own clothes, and tore them in two pieces. He also took up Elijah's mantle that fell from him, and went back, and stood by the bank of the Jordan. He took Elijah's mantle that fell from him, and struck the waters, and said, "Where is YHWH, the God of Elijah?" When he also had struck the waters, they were divided apart, and Elisha went over. When the sons of the prophets who were at Jericho facing him saw him, they said, "The spirit of Elijah rests on Elisha." They came to meet him, and bowed themselves to the ground before him. They said to him, "See now, there are with your servants fifty strong men. Please let them go and seek your master. Perhaps YHWH's Spirit has taken him up, and put him on some mountain, or into some valley."

He said, "Don't send them."

When they urged him until he was ashamed, he said, "Send them."

Therefore they sent fifty men; and they searched for three days, but didn't find him. They came back to him, while he stayed at Jericho; and he said to them, "Didn't I tell you, 'Don't go?'"

The men of the city said to Elisha, "Behold, please, the situation of this city is pleasant, as my lord sees; but the water is bad, and the land is barren."

He said, "Bring me a new jar, and put salt in it." Then they brought it to him. He went out to the spring of the waters, and threw salt into it, and said, "YHWH says, 'I have healed these waters. There shall not be from there any more death or barren wasteland.'" So the waters were healed to this day, according to Elisha's word which he spoke.

He went up from there to Bethel. As he was going up by the way, some youths came out of the city and mocked him, and said to him, "Go up, you baldy! Go up, you baldy!" He looked behind him and saw them, and cursed them in YHWH's name. Then two female bears came out of the woods, and mauled forty-two of those youths. He went from there to Mount Carmel, and from there he returned to Samaria.

....

Now Jehoram the son of Ahab began to reign over Israel in Samaria in the eighteenth year of Jehoshaphat king of Judah, and reigned twelve years. He did that which was evil in YHWH's sight, but not like his father, and like his mother, for he put away the pillar of Baal that his father had made. Nevertheless he held to the sins of Jeroboam the son of Nebat, with which he made Israel to sin. He didn't depart from them. Now Mesha king of Moab was a sheep breeder; and he supplied the king of Israel with the wool of one hundred thousand lambs, and of one hundred thousand rams. But when Ahab was dead, the king of Moab rebelled against the king of Israel. King Jehoram went out of Samaria at that time, and mustered all Israel. He went and sent to Jehoshaphat the king of Judah, saying, "The king of Moab has rebelled against me. Will you go with me against Moab to battle?"

He said, "I will go up. I am as you are, my people as your people, my horses as your horses." He said, "Which way shall we go up?"

He answered, "The way of the wilderness of Edom." So the king of Israel went with the king of Judah and the king of Edom, and they marched for seven days along a circuitous route. There was no water for the army or for the animals that followed them. The king of Israel said, "Alas! For YHWH has called these three kings together to deliver them into the hand of Moab."

But Jehoshaphat said, "Isn't there a prophet of YHWH here, that we may inquire of YHWH by him?"

One of the king of Israel's servants answered, "Elisha the son of Shaphat, who poured water on the hands of Elijah, is here."

Jehoshaphat said, "YHWH's word is with him." So the king of Israel and Jehoshaphat and the king of Edom went down to him.

Elisha said to the king of Israel, "What have I to do with you? Go to the prophets of your father, and to the prophets of your mother."

The king of Israel said to him, "No, for YHWH has called these three kings together to deliver them into the hand of Moab." Elisha said, "As YHWH of Armies lives, before whom I stand, surely, were it not that I respect the presence of Jehoshaphat the king of Judah, I would not look toward you, nor see you. But now bring me a musician." When the musician played, YHWH's hand came on him. He said, "YHWH says, 'Make this valley full of trenches.' For YHWH says, 'You will not see wind, neither will you see rain, yet that valley will be filled with water, and you will drink, both you and your livestock and your other animals. This is an easy thing in YHWH's sight. He will also deliver the Moabites into your hand. You shall strike every fortified city, and every choice city, and shall fell every good tree, and stop all springs of water, and mar every good piece of land with stones.'"

In the morning, about the time of offering the sacrifice, behold, water came by the way of Edom, and the country was filled with water.

Now when all the Moabites heard that the kings had come up to fight against them, they gathered themselves together, all who were able to put on armor, young and old, and stood on the border. They rose up early in the morning, and the sun shone on the water, and the Moabites saw the water opposite them as red as blood. They said, "This is blood. The kings are surely destroyed, and they have struck each other. Now therefore, Moab, to the plunder!"

When they came to the camp of Israel, the Israelites rose up and struck the Moabites, so that they fled before them; and they went forward into the land attacking the Moabites. They beat down the cities; and on every good piece of land each man cast his stone, and filled it. They also stopped all the springs of water, and cut down all the good trees, until in Kir Hareseth all they left was its stones; however the men armed with slings went around it, and attacked it. When the king of Moab saw that the battle was too severe for him, he took with him seven hundred men who drew a sword, to break through to the king of Edom; but they could not. Then he took his oldest son who would have reigned in his place, and offered him for a burnt offering on the wall. There was great wrath against Israel; and they departed from him, and returned to their own land.

....

Now a certain woman of the wives of the sons of the prophets cried out to Elisha, saying, "Your servant my husband is dead. You know that your servant feared YHWH. Now the creditor has come to take for himself my two children to be slaves."

Elisha said to her, "What should I do for you? Tell me: what do you have in the house?"

She said, "Your servant has nothing in the house, except a pot of oil."

Then he said, "Go, borrow empty containers from all your neighbors. Don't borrow just a few containers. Go in and shut the door on you and on your sons, and pour oil into all those containers; and set aside those which are full."

So she went from him, and shut the door on herself and on her sons. They brought the containers to her, and she poured oil. When the containers were full, she said to her son, "Bring me another container."

He said to her, "There isn't another container." Then the oil stopped flowing.

Then she came and told the man of God. He said, "Go, sell the oil, and pay your debt; and you and your sons live on the rest."

One day Elisha went to Shunem, where there was a prominent woman; and she persuaded him to eat bread. So it was, that as often as he passed by, he turned in there to eat bread. She said to her husband, "See now, I perceive that this is a holy man of God who passes by us continually. Please let's make a little room on the roof. Let's set a bed, a table, a chair, and a lamp stand for him there. When he comes to us, he can stay there."

One day he came there, and he went to the room and lay there. He said to Gehazi his servant, "Call this Shunammite." When he had called her, she stood before him. He said to him, "Say now to her, 'Behold, you have cared for us with all this care. What is to be done for you? Would you like to be spoken for to the king, or to the captain of the army?'"

She answered, "I dwell among my own people."

He said, "What then is to be done for her?"

Gehazi answered, "Most certainly she has no son, and her husband is old."

He said, "Call her." When he had called her, she stood in the door. He said, "At this season, when the time comes around, you will embrace a son."

She said, "No, my lord, you man of God, do not lie to your servant."

The woman conceived, and bore a son at that season, when the time came around, as Elisha had said to her. When the child was grown, one day he went out to his father to the reapers. He said to his father, "My head! My head!"

He said to his servant, "Carry him to his mother."

When he had taken him, and brought him to his mother, he sat on her knees until noon, and then died. She went up and laid him on the man of God's bed, and shut the door on him, and went out. She called to her husband, and said, "Please send me one of the servants, and one of the donkeys, that I may run to the man of God, and come again."

He said, "Why would you want go to him today? It is not a new moon or a Sabbath."

She said, "It's all right."

Then she saddled a donkey, and said to her servant, "Drive, and go forward! Don't slow down for me, unless I ask you to."

So she went, and came to the man of God to Mount Carmel. When the man of God saw her afar off, he said to Gehazi his servant, "Behold, there is the Shunammite. Please run now to meet her, and ask her, 'Is it well with you? Is it well with your husband? Is it well with your child?'"

She answered, "It is well."

When she came to the man of God to the hill, she caught hold of his feet. Gehazi came near to thrust her away; but the man of God said, "Leave her alone; for her soul is troubled within her; and YHWH has hidden it from me, and has not told me."

Then she said, "Did I ask you for a son, my lord? Didn't I say, 'Do not deceive me'?"

Then he said to Gehazi, "Tuck your cloak into your belt, take my staff in your hand, and go your way. If you meet any man, don't greet him; and if anyone greets you, don't answer him again. Then lay my staff on the child's face."

The child's mother said, "As YHWH lives, and as your soul lives, I will not leave you."

So he arose, and followed her.

Gehazi went ahead of them, and laid the staff on the child's face; but there was no voice and no hearing. Therefore he returned to meet him, and told him, "The child has not awakened."

When Elisha had come into the house, behold, the child was dead, and lying on his bed. He went in therefore, and shut the door on them both, and prayed to YHWH. He went up, and lay on the child, and put his mouth on his mouth, and his eyes on his eyes, and his hands on his hands. He stretched himself on him; and the child's flesh grew warm. Then he returned, and walked in the house once back and forth; and went up, and stretched himself out on him. Then the child sneezed seven times, and the child opened his eyes. He called Gehazi, and said, "Call this Shunammite!" So he called her.

When she had come in to him, he said, "Take up your son."

Then she went in, fell at his feet, and bowed herself to the ground; then she picked up her son, and went out.

Elisha came again to Gilgal. There was a famine in the land; and the sons of the prophets were sitting before him; and he said to his servant, "Get the large pot, and boil stew for the sons of the prophets."

One went out into the field to gather herbs, and found a wild vine, and gathered a lap full of wild gourds from it, and came and cut them up into the pot of stew; for they didn't recognize them. So they poured out for the men to eat. As they were eating some of the stew, they cried out, and said, "Man of God, there is death in the pot!" And they could not eat it.

But he said, "Then bring meal." He threw it into the pot; and he said, "Serve it to the people, that they may eat." And there was nothing harmful in the pot.

A man from Baal Shalishah came, and brought the man of God some bread of the first fruits: twenty loaves of barley and fresh ears of grain in his sack. He said, "Give to the people, that they may eat."

His servant said, "What, should I set this before a hundred men?"

But he said, "Give the people, that they may eat; for YHWH says, 'They will eat, and will have some left over.'"

So he set it before them, and they ate, and had some left over, according to YHWH's word.

....

Now Naaman, captain of the army of the king of Syria, was a great man with his master, and honorable, because by him YHWH had given victory to Syria: he was also a mighty man of valor, but he was a leper. The Syrians had gone out in bands, and had brought away captive out of the land of Israel a little maiden; and she waited on Naaman's wife. She said to her mistress, "I wish that my lord were with the prophet who is in Samaria! Then he would heal him of his leprosy."

Someone went in, and told his lord, saying, "The maiden who is from the land of Israel said this."

The king of Syria said, "Go now, and I will send a letter to the king of Israel."

He departed, and took with him ten talents of silver, and six thousand pieces of gold, and ten changes of clothing. He brought the letter to the king of Israel, saying, "Now when this letter has come to you, behold, I have sent Naaman my servant to you, that you may heal him of his leprosy."

When the king of Israel had read the letter, he tore his clothes, and said, "Am I God, to kill and to make alive, that this man sends to me to heal a man of his leprosy? But please consider and see how he seeks a quarrel against me."

It was so, when Elisha the man of God heard that the king of Israel had torn his clothes, that he sent to the king, saying, "Why have you torn your clothes? Let him come now to me, and he shall know that there is a prophet in Israel."

So Naaman came with his horses and with his chariots, and stood at the door of the house of Elisha. Elisha sent a messenger to him, saying, "Go and wash in the Jordan seven times, and your flesh shall come again to you, and you shall be clean."

But Naaman was angry, and went away, and said, "Behold, I thought, 'He will surely come out to me, and stand, and call on the name of YHWH his God, and wave his hand over the place, and heal the leper.' Aren't Abanah and Pharpar, the rivers of Damascus, better than all the waters of Israel? Couldn't I wash in them, and be clean?" So he turned and went away in a rage.

His servants came near, and spoke to him, and said, "My father, if the prophet had asked you do some great thing, wouldn't you have done it? How much rather then, when he says to you, 'Wash, and be clean?'"

Then went he down, and dipped himself seven times in the Jordan, according to the saying of the man of God; and his flesh was restored like the flesh of a little child, and he was clean. He returned to the man of God, he and all his company, and came, and stood before him; and he said, "See now, I know that there is no God in all the earth, but in Israel. Now therefore, please take a gift from your servant."

But he said, "As YHWH lives, before whom I stand, I will receive none."

He urged him to take it; but he refused. Naaman said, "If not, then, please let two mules' burden of earth be given to your servant;

for your servant will from now on offer neither burnt offering nor sacrifice to other gods, but to YHWH. In this thing may YHWH pardon your servant: when my master goes into the house of Rimmon to worship there, and he leans on my hand, and I bow myself in the house of Rimmon. When I bow myself in the house of Rimmon, may YHWH pardon your servant in this thing."

He said to him, "Go in peace."

So he departed from him a little way. But Gehazi the servant of Elisha the man of God, said, "Behold, my master has spared this Naaman the Syrian, in not receiving at his hands that which he brought. As YHWH lives, I will run after him, and take something from him."

So Gehazi followed after Naaman. When Naaman saw one running after him, he came down from the chariot to meet him, and said, "Is all well?"

He said, "All is well. My master has sent me, saying, 'Behold, even now two young men of the sons of the prophets have come to me from the hill country of Ephraim. Please give them a talent of silver and two changes of clothing.'"

Naaman said, "Be pleased to take two talents." He urged him, and bound two talents of silver in two bags, with two changes of clothing, and laid them on two of his servants; and they carried them before him. When he came to the hill, he took them from their hand, and stored them in the house. Then he let the men go, and they departed. But he went in, and stood before his master. Elisha said to him, "Where did you come from, Gehazi?"

He said, "Your servant went nowhere."

He said to him, "Didn't my heart go with you, when the man turned from his chariot to meet you? Is it a time to receive money, and to receive garments, and olive groves and vineyards, and sheep and cattle, and male servants and female servants? Therefore the leprosy of Naaman will cling to you and to your offspring forever."

He went out from his presence a leper, as white as snow.

....

The sons of the prophets said to Elisha, "See now, the place where we live and meet with you is too small for us. Please let us go to the Jordan, and each man take a beam from there, and let's make us a place there, where we may live."

He answered, "Go!"

One said, "Please be pleased to go with your servants."

He answered, "I will go." So he went with them. When they came to the Jordan, they cut down wood. But as one was cutting down a tree, the ax head fell into the water. Then he cried, and said, "Alas, my master! For it was borrowed."

The man of God asked, "Where did it fall?" He showed him the place. He cut down a stick, threw it in there, and made the iron float. He said, "Take it." So he put out his hand and took it.

Now the king of Syria was at war against Israel; and he took counsel with his servants, saying, "My camp will be in such and such a place."

The man of God sent to the king of Israel, saying, "Beware that you not pass this place; for the Syrians are coming down there." The king of Israel sent to the place which the man of God told him and warned him of; and he saved himself there, not once or twice. The king of Syria's heart was very troubled about this. He called his servants, and said to them, "Won't you show me which of us is for the king of Israel?"

One of his servants said, "No, my lord, O king; but Elisha, the prophet who is in Israel, tells the king of Israel the words that you speak in your bedroom."

He said, "Go and see where he is, that I may send and get him."

He was told, "Behold, he is in Dothan."

Therefore he sent horses, chariots, and a great army there. They came by night, and surrounded the city. When the servant of the man of God had risen early, and gone out, behold, an army with horses and chariots was around the city. His servant said to him, "Alas, my master! What shall we do?"

He answered, "Don't be afraid; for those who are with us are more than those who are with them." Elisha prayed, and said, "YHWH, please open his eyes, that he may see." YHWH opened the young man's eyes; and he saw: and behold, the mountain was full of horses and chariots of fire around Elisha. When they came down to him, Elisha prayed to YHWH, and said, "Please strike this people with blindness."

He struck them with blindness according to Elishah's word. Elisha said to them, "This is not the way, neither is this the city. Follow me, and I will bring you to the man whom you seek." He led them to Samaria. When they had come into Samaria, Elisha said, "YHWH, open these men's eyes, that they may see."

YHWH opened their eyes, and they saw; and behold, they were in the middle of Samaria. The king of Israel said to Elisha, when he saw them, "My father, shall I strike them? Shall I strike them?"

He answered, "You shall not strike them. Would you strike those whom you have taken captive with your sword and with your bow? Set bread and water before them, that they may eat and drink, and go to their master."

He prepared a great feast for them. When they had eaten and drunk, he sent them away, and they went to their master. So the bands of Syria stopped raiding the land of Israel.

After this, Benhadad king of Syria gathered all his army, and went up and besieged Samaria. There was a great famine in Samaria. Behold, they besieged it, until a donkey's head was sold for eighty pieces of silver, and the fourth part of a kab of dove's dung for five pieces of silver. As the king of Israel was passing by on the wall, a woman cried to him, saying, "Help, my lord, O king!"

He said, "If YHWH doesn't help you, where could I get help for you? From of the threshing floor, or from the wine press?" The king said to her, "What is your problem?"

She answered, "This woman said to me, 'Give your son, that we may eat him today, and we will eat my son tomorrow.' So we boiled my son, and ate him: and I said to her on the next day, 'Give your son, that we may eat him;' and she has hidden her son."

When the king heard the words of the woman, he tore his clothes. Now he was passing by on the wall, and the people looked, and behold, he had sackcloth underneath on his body. Then he said, "God do so to me, and more also, if the head of Elisha the son of Shaphat stays on him today."

But Elisha was sitting in his house, and the elders were sitting with him. Then the king sent a man from before him; but before the messenger came to him, he said to the elders, "Do you see how this son of a murderer has sent to take away my head? Behold, when the messenger comes, shut the door, and hold the door shut against him. Isn't the sound of his master's feet behind him?"

While he was still talking with them, behold, the messenger came down to him. Then he said, "Behold, this evil is from YHWH. Why should I wait for YHWH any longer?"

Elisha said, "Hear YHWH's word. YHWH says, 'Tomorrow about

this time a seah of fine flour will be sold for a shekel, and two seahs of barley for a shekel, in the gate of Samaria.'"

Then the captain on whose hand the king leaned answered the man of God, and said, "Behold, if YHWH made windows in heaven, could this thing be?"

He said, "Behold, you will see it with your eyes, but will not eat of it."

Now there were four leprous men at the entrance of the gate. They said to one another, "Why do we sit here until we die? If we say, 'We will enter into the city,' then the famine is in the city, and we will die there. If we sit still here, we also die. Now therefore come, and let's surrender to the army of the Syrians. If they save us alive, we will live; and if they kill us, we will only die."

They rose up in the twilight, to go to the camp of the Syrians. When they had come to the outermost part of the camp of the Syrians, behold, no man was there. For the Lord had made the army of the Syrians to hear the sound of chariots, and the sound of horses, even the noise of a great army; and they said to one another, "Behold, the king of Israel has hired against us the kings of the Hittites and the kings of the Egyptians to attack us." Therefore they arose and fled in the twilight, and left their tents, and their horses, and their donkeys, even the camp as it was, and fled for their life. When these lepers came to the outermost part of the camp, they went into one tent, and ate and drank, and carried away silver, gold, and clothing, and went and hid it. Then they came back, and entered into another tent, and carried things from there also, and went and hid them. Then they said to one another, "We aren't doing right. Today is a day of good news, and we keep silent. If we wait until the morning light, punishment will overtake us. Now therefore come, let's go and tell the king's household."

So they came and called to the city gatekeepers; and they told them, "We came to the camp of the Syrians, and, behold, there was no man there, not even a man's voice, but the horses tied, and the donkeys tied, and the tents as they were."

He called the gatekeepers; and they told it to the king's household within. The king arose in the night, and said to his servants, "I will now show you what the Syrians have done to us. They know that we are hungry. Therefore are they gone out of the camp to hide themselves in the field, saying, 'When they come out of the city, we shall take them alive, and get into the city.'"

One of his servants answered, "Please let some people take five of the horses that remain, which are left in the city. Behold, they are like all the multitude of Israel who are left in it. Behold, they are like all the multitude of Israel who are consumed. Let's send and see."

Therefore they took two chariots with horses; and the king sent them out to the Syrian army, saying, "Go and see."

They went after them to the Jordan; and behold, all the path was full of garments and equipment which the Syrians had cast away in their haste. The messengers returned, and told the king. The people went out and plundered the camp of the Syrians. So a seah of fine flour was sold for a shekel, and two measures of barley for a shekel, according to YHWH's word. The king appointed the captain on whose hand he leaned to be in charge of the gate; and the people trampled over him in the gate, and he died as the man of God had said, who spoke when the king came down to him. It happened as the man of God had spoken to the king, saying, "Two seahs of barley for a shekel, and a seah of fine flour for a shekel, shall be tomorrow about this time in the gate of Samaria;" and that captain answered the man of God, and said, "Now, behold, if YHWH made windows in heaven, might such a thing be?" and he said, "Behold, you will see it with your eyes, but will not eat of it." It happened like that to him; for the people trampled over him in the gate, and he died.

....

Now Elisha had spoken to the woman whose son he had restored to life, saying, "Arise, and go, you and your household, and stay for a while wherever you can; for YHWH has called for a famine. It will also come on the land for seven years."

The woman arose, and did according to the man of God's word. She went with her household, and lived in the land of the Philistines for seven years. At the end of seven years, the woman returned from the land of the Philistines. Then she went out to beg the king for her house and for her land. Now the king was talking with Gehazi the servant of the man of God, saying, "Please tell me all the great things that Elisha has done." As he was telling the king how he had restored to life him who was dead, behold, the woman, whose son he had restored to life, begged the king for her house and for her land. Gehazi said, "My lord, O king, this is the woman, and this is her son, whom Elisha restored to life."

When the king asked the woman, she told him. So the king

appointed to her a certain officer, saying, "Restore all that was hers, and all the fruits of the field since the day that she left the land, even until now."

Elisha came to Damascus; and Benhadad the king of Syria was sick. He was told, "The man of God has come here."

The king said to Hazael, "Take a present in your hand, and go, meet the man of God, and inquire of YHWH by him, saying, 'Will I recover from this sickness?'"

So Hazael went to meet him, and took a present with him, even of every good thing of Damascus, forty camels' burden, and came and stood before him, and said, "Your son Benhadad king of Syria has sent me to you, saying, 'Will I recover from this sickness?'"

Elisha said to him, "Go, tell him, 'You will surely recover;' however YHWH has shown me that he will surely die." He settled his gaze steadfastly on him, until he was ashamed. Then the man of God wept.

Hazael said, "Why do you weep, my lord?"

He answered, "Because I know the evil that you will do to the children of Israel. You will set their strongholds on fire, and you will kill their young men with the sword, and will dash their little ones in pieces, and rip up their pregnant women."

Hazael said, "But what is your servant, who is but a dog, that he could do this great thing?"

Elisha answered, "YHWH has shown me that you will be king over Syria."

Then he departed from Elisha, and came to his master, who said to him, "What did Elisha say to you?"

He answered, "He told me that you would surely recover."

On the next day, he took a thick cloth, dipped it in water, and spread it on his face, so that he died. Then Hazael reigned in his place.

In the fifth year of Joram the son of Ahab king of Israel, Jehoshaphat being king of Judah then, Jehoram the son of Jehoshaphat king of Judah began to reign. He was thirty-two years old when he began to reign. He reigned eight years in Jerusalem. He walked in the way of the kings of Israel, as did Ahab's house; for he married Ahab's daughter. He did that which was evil in YHWH's sight. However er YHWH would not destroy Judah, for David his servant's sake, as he promised him to give to him a lamp for his children always.

In his days Edom revolted from under the hand of Judah, and

made a king over themselves. Then Joram passed over to Zair, and all his chariots with him: and he rose up by night, and struck the Edomites who surrounded him, and the captains of the chariots; and the people fled to their tents. So Edom revolted from under the hand of Judah to this day. Then Libnah revolted at the same time. The rest of the acts of Joram, and all that he did, aren't they written in the book of the chronicles of the kings of Judah? Joram slept with his fathers, and was buried with his fathers in David's city; and Ahaziah his son reigned in his place. In the twelfth year of Joram the son of Ahab king of Israel, Ahaziah the son of Jehoram king of Judah began to reign. Ahaziah was twenty-two years old when he began to reign; and he reigned one year in Jerusalem. His mother's name was Athaliah the daughter of Omri king of Israel. He walked in the way of Ahab's house, and did that which was evil in YHWH's sight, as did Ahab's house; for he was the son-in-law of Ahab's house. He went with Joram the son of Ahab to war against Hazael king of Syria at Ramoth Gilead, and the Syrians wounded Joram. King Joram returned to be healed in Jezreel from the wounds which the Syrians had given him at Ramah, when he fought against Hazael king of Syria. Ahaziah the son of Jehoram king of Judah went down to see Joram the son of Ahab in Jezreel, because he was sick.

....

Elisha the prophet called one of the sons of the prophets, and said to him, "Put your belt on your waist, take this vial of oil in your hand, and go to Ramoth Gilead. When you come there, find Jehu the son of Jehoshaphat the son of Nimshi, and go in, and make him rise up from among his brothers, and take him to an inner room. Then take the vial of oil, and pour it on his head, and say, 'YHWH says, "I have anointed you king over Israel."' Then open the door, flee, and don't wait."

So the young man, even the young man, the prophet, went to Ramoth Gilead. When he came, behold, the captains of the army were sitting. Then he said, "I have a message for you, captain."

Jehu said, "To which of us all?"

He said, "To you, O captain." He arose, and went into the house. Then he poured the oil on his head, and said to him, "YHWH, the God of Israel, says, 'I have anointed you king over the people of YHWH, even over Israel. You must strike your master Ahab's house, that I may avenge the blood of my servants the prophets, and the blood of all the servants of YHWH, at the hand of Jezebel. For the whole house of Ahab will perish. I will cut off from Ahab everyone who urinates against a wall, both him who is shut up and him who is left at large in Israel. I will make Ahab's house like the house of Jeroboam the son of Nebat, and like the house of Baasha the son of Ahijah. The dogs will eat Jezebel on the plot of ground of Jezreel, and there shall be no one to bury her.'" Then he opened the door and fled.

When Jehu came out to the servants of his lord, and one said to him, "Is all well? Why did this mad fellow come to you?"

He said to them, "You know the man and how he talks." They said, "That is a lie. Tell us now."

He said, "He said to me, 'YHWH says, I have anointed you king over Israel.'"

Then they hurried, and each man took his cloak, and put it under him on the top of the stairs, and blew the trumpet, saying, "Jehu is king."

So Jehu the son of Jehoshaphat the son of Nimshi conspired against Joram. (Now Joram was keeping Ramoth Gilead, he and all Israel, because of Hazael king of Syria; but king Joram had returned to be healed in Jezreel of the wounds which the Syrians had given him, when he fought with Hazael king of Syria.) Jehu said, "If this is your thinking, then let no one escape and go out of the city, to go to tell it in Jezreel." So Jehu rode in a chariot and went to Jezreel, for Joram lay there. Ahaziah king of Judah had come down to see Joram. Now the watchman was standing on the tower in Jezreel, and he spied the company of Jehu as he came, and said, "I see a company."

Joram said, "Take a horseman, and send to meet them, and let him say, 'Is it peace?'"

So one went on horseback to meet him, and said, "the king says, 'Is it peace?'"

Jehu said, "What do you have to do with peace? Fall in behind me!"

The watchman said, "The messenger came to them, but he isn't coming back."

Then he sent out a second on horseback, who came to them, and said, "The king says, 'Is it peace?'"

Jehu answered, "What do you have to do with peace? Fall in behind me!"

The watchman said, "He came to them, and isn't coming back. The driving is like the driving of Jehu the son of Nimshi, for he drives furiously."

Joram said, "Get ready!"

They got his chariot ready. Then Joram king of Israel and Ahaziah king of Judah went out, each in his chariot, and they went out to meet Jehu, and found him on Naboth the Jezreelite's land. When Joram saw Jehu, he said, "Is it peace, Jehu?"

He answered, "What peace, so long as the prostitution of your mother Jezebel and her witchcraft abound?"

Joram turned his hands, and fled, and said to Ahaziah, "This is treason, Ahaziah!"

Jehu drew his bow with his full strength, and struck Joram between his arms; and the arrow went out at his heart, and he sunk down in his chariot. Then Jehu said to Bidkar his captain, "Pick him up, and throw him in the plot of the field of Naboth the Jezreelite; for remember how, when you and I rode together after Ahab his father, YHWH laid this burden on him: 'Surely I have seen yesterday the blood of Naboth, and the blood of his sons,' says YHWH; 'and I will repay you in this plot of ground,' says YHWH. Now therefore take and cast him onto the plot of ground, according to YHWH's word."

But when Ahaziah the king of Judah saw this, he fled by the way of the garden house. Jehu followed after him, and said, "Strike him also in the chariot!" They struck him at the ascent of Gur, which is by Ibleam. He fled to Megiddo, and died there. His servants carried him in a chariot to Jerusalem, and buried him in his tomb with his fathers in David's city. In the eleventh year of Joram the son of Ahab, Ahaziah began to reign over Judah.

When Jehu had come to Jezreel, Jezebel heard of it; and she painted her eyes, and adorned her head, and looked out at the window. As Jehu entered in at the gate, she said, "Do you come in peace, Zimri, you murderer of your master?"

He lifted up his face to the window, and said, "Who is on my side? Who?"

Two or three eunuchs looked out at him.

He said, "Throw her down!"

So they threw her down; and some of her blood was sprinkled on the wall, and on the horses. Then he trampled her under foot. When he had come in, he ate and drank. Then he said, "See now to this cursed woman, and bury her; for she is a king's daughter."

They went to bury her, but they found no more of her than the skull, the feet, and the palms of her hands. Therefore they came back, and told him.

He said, "This is YHWH's word, which he spoke by his servant Elijah the Tishbite, saying, 'The dogs will eat the flesh of Jezebel on the plot of Jezreel, and the body of Jezebel will be as dung on the face of the field on Jezreel's land, so that they won't say, "This is Jezebel."'"

....

Now Ahab had seventy sons in Samaria. Jehu wrote letters, and sent to Samaria, to the rulers of Jezreel, even the elders, and to those who brought up Ahab's sons, saying, "Now as soon as this letter comes to you, since your master's sons are with you, and you have chariots and horses, a fortified city also, and armor, Select the best and fittest of your master's sons, set him on his father's throne, and fight for your master's house."

But they were exceedingly afraid, and said, "Behold, the two kings didn't stand before him! How then shall we stand?" He who was over the household, and he who was over the city, the elders also, and those who raised the children, sent to Jehu, saying, "We are your servants, and will do all that you ask us. We will not make any man king. You do that which is good in your eyes."

Then he wrote a letter the second time to them, saying, "If you are on my side, and if you will listen to my voice, take the heads of the men who are your master's sons, and come to me to Jezreel by tomorrow this time."

Now the king's sons, being seventy persons, were with the great men of the city, who brought them up. When the letter came to them, they took the king's sons and killed them, even seventy people, and put their heads in baskets, and sent them to him to Jezreel. A messenger came and told him, "They have brought the heads of the king's sons."

He said, "Lay them in two heaps at the entrance of the gate until the morning." In the morning, he went out, and stood, and said to all the people, "You are righteous. Behold, I conspired against my master and killed him, but who killed all these? Know now that nothing will fall to the earth of YHWH's word, which YHWH spoke concerning Ahab's house. For YHWH has done that which he spoke by his servant Elijah."

So Jehu struck all that remained of Ahab's house in Jezreel, with all his great men, his familiar friends, and his priests, until he left him no one remaining.

He arose and departed, and went to Samaria. As he was at the shearing house of the shepherds on the way, Jehu met with the brothers of Ahaziah king of Judah, and said, "Who are you?"

They answered, "We are the brothers of Ahaziah. We are going down to greet the children of the king and the children of the queen."

He said, "Take them alive!"

They took them alive, and killed them at the pit of the shearing house, even forty-two men. He didn't leave any of them.

When he had departed from there, he met Jehonadab the son of Rechab coming to meet him. He greeted him, and said to him, "Is your heart right, as my heart is with your heart?"

Jehonadab answered, "It is."

"If it is, give me your hand." He gave him his hand; and he took him up to him into the chariot. He said, "Come with me, and see my zeal for YHWH." So they made him ride in his chariot. When he came to Samaria, he struck all who remained to Ahab in Samaria, until he had destroyed him, according to YHWH's word, which he spoke to Elijah. Jehu gathered all the people together, and said to them, "Ahab served Baal a little; but Jehu will serve him much. Now therefore call to me all the prophets of Baal, all of his worshipers, and all of his priests. Let no one be absent; for I have a great sacrifice to Baal. Whoever is absent, he shall not live." But Jehu did deceptively, intending to destroy the worshipers of Baal.

Jehu said, "Sanctify a solemn assembly for Baal!"

So they proclaimed it. Jehu sent through all Israel; and all the worshipers of Baal came, so that there was not a man left that didn't come. They came into the house of Baal; and the house of Baal was filled from one end to another. He said to him who kept the wardrobe, "Bring out robes for all the worshipers of Baal!"

So he brought robes out to them. Jehu went with Jehonadab the son of Rechab into the house of Baal. Then he said to the worshipers of Baal, "Search, and see that none of the servants of YHWH are here with you, but only the worshipers of Baal."

So they went in to offer sacrifices and burnt offerings. Now Jehu had appointed for himself eighty men outside, and said, "If any of the men whom I bring into your hands escape, he who lets him go, his life shall be for the life of him."

As soon as he had finished offering the burnt offering, Jehu said to the guard and to the captains, "Go in and kill them! Let no one escape." So they struck them with the edge of the sword. The guard and the captains threw the bodies out, and went to the inner shrine of the house of Baal. They brought out the pillars that were in the house of Baal, and burned them. They broke down the pillar of Baal, and broke down the house of Baal, and made it a latrine, to this day. Thus Jehu destroyed Baal out of Israel.

However, Jehu didn't depart from the sins of Jeroboam the son of Nebat, with which he made Israel to sin, the golden calves that were in Bethel and that were in Dan. YHWH said to Jehu, "Because you have done well in executing that which is right in my eyes, and have done to Ahab's house according to all that was in my heart, your descendants shall sit on the throne of Israel to the fourth generation."

But Jehu took no heed to walk in the law of YHWH, the God of Israel, with all his heart. He didn't depart from the sins of Jeroboam, with which he made Israel to sin. In those days YHWH began to cut away parts of Israel; and Hazael struck them in all the borders of Israel; from the Jordan eastward, all the land of Gilead, the Gadites, and the Reubenites, and the Manassites, from Aroer, which is by the valley of the Arnon, even Gilead and Bashan. Now the rest of the acts of Jehu, and all that he did, and all his might, aren't they written in the book of the chronicles of the kings of Israel? Jehu slept with his fathers; and they buried him in Samaria. Jehoahaz his son reigned in his place. The time that Jehu reigned over Israel in Samaria was twenty-eight years.

....

Now when Athaliah the mother of Ahaziah saw that her son was dead, she arose and destroyed all the royal offspring. But Jehosheba, the daughter of king Joram, sister of Ahaziah, took Joash the son of Ahaziah, and stole him away from among the king's sons who were slain, even him and his nurse, and put them in the bedroom; and they hid him from Athaliah, so that he was not slain. He was with her hidden in YHWH's house six years while Athaliah reigned over the land. In the seventh year Jehoiada sent and fetched the captains over hundreds of the Carites and of the guard, and brought them to him into YHWH's house; and he made a covenant with them, and made a covenant with them in YHWH's house, and showed them the king's son. He commanded them, saying, "This is what you must do: a third of you, who come in on the Sabbath, shall be keepers of the watch of the king's house; a third of you shall be at the gate Sur; and a third of you at the gate behind the guard. So you shall keep the watch of the house, and be a barrier. The two companies of you, even all who go out on the Sabbath, shall keep the watch of YHWH's house around the king. You shall surround the king, every man with his weapons in his hand; and he who comes within the ranks, let him be slain. Be with the king when he goes out, and when he comes in."

The captains over hundreds did according to all that Jehoiada the priest commanded; and they each took his men, those who were to come in on the Sabbath, with those who were to go out on the Sabbath, and came to Jehoiada the priest. The priest delivered to the captains over hundreds the spears and shields that had been king David's, which were in YHWH's house. The guard stood, every man with his weapons in his hand, from the right side of the house to the left side of the house, along by the altar and the house, around the king. Then he brought out the king's son, and put the crown on him, and gave him the covenant; and they made him king, and anointed him; and they clapped their hands, and said, "Long live the king!"

When Athaliah heard the noise of the guard and of the people, she came to the people into YHWH's house: and she looked, and behold, the king stood by the pillar, as the tradition was, with the captains and the trumpets by the king; and all the people of the land rejoiced, and blew trumpets. Then Athaliah tore her clothes, and cried, "Treason! Treason!"

Jehoiada the priest commanded the captains of hundreds who were set over the army, and said to them, "Bring her out between the ranks. Kill anyone who follows her with the sword." For the priest said, "Don't let her be slain in YHWH's house." So they made way for her; and she went by the way of the horses' entry to the king's house, and she was slain there. Jehoiada made a covenant between YHWH and the king and the people, that they should be YHWH's people; also between the king and the people. All the people of the land went to the house of Baal, and broke it down. They broke his altars and his images in pieces thoroughly, and killed Mattan the priest of Baal before the altars. The priest appointed officers over YHWH's house. He took the captains over hundreds, and the Carites, and the guard, and all the people of the land; and they brought down the king from YHWH's house, and came by the way of the gate of the guard to the king's house. He sat on the throne of the kings. So all the people of the land rejoiced, and the city was quiet. They had slain Athaliah with the sword at the king's house.

Jehoash was seven years old when he began to reign.

Jehoash began to reign in the seventh year of Jehu, and he reigned forty years in Jerusalem. His mother's name was Zibiah of Beersheba. Jehoash did that which was right in YHWH's eyes all his days in which Jehoiada the priest instructed him. However the high places were not taken away. The people still sacrificed and burned incense in the high places. Jehoash said to the priests, "All the money of the holy things that is brought into YHWH's house, in current money, the money of the people for whom each man is evaluated, and all the money that it comes into any man's heart to bring into YHWH's house, let the priests take it to them, each man from his donor; and they shall repair the damage to the house, wherever any damage is found."

But it was so, that in the twenty-third year of king Jehoash the priests had not repaired the damage to the house. Then king Jehoash called for Jehoiada the priest, and for the other priests, and said to them, "Why don't you repair the damage to the house? Now therefore take no more money from your treasurers, but deliver it for repair of the damage to the house."

The priests consented that they should take no more money from the people, and not repair the damage to the house. But Jehoiada the priest took a chest, and bored a hole in its lid, and set it beside the altar, on the right side as one comes into YHWH's house; and the priests who kept the threshold put all the money that was brought into YHWH's house into it. When they saw that there was much money in the chest, the king's scribe and the high priest came up, and they put it in bags and counted the money that was found in YHWH's house. They gave the money that was weighed out into the hands of those who did the work, who had the oversight of YHWH's house; and they paid it out to the carpenters and the builders, who worked on YHWH's house, and to the masons and the stone cutters, and for buying timber and cut stone to repair the damage to YHWH's house, and for all that was laid out for the house to repair it. But there were not made for YHWH's house cups of silver, snuffers, basins, trumpets, any vessels of gold, or vessels of silver, of the money that was brought into YHWH's house; for they gave that to those who did the work, and repaired YHWH's house with it. Moreover they didn't demand an accounting from the men into whose hand they delivered the money to give to those who did the work; for they dealt faithfully. The money for the trespass offerings, and the money for the sin offerings was not brought into YHWH's house. It was the priests'.

Then Hazael king of Syria went up, and fought against Gath, and took it; and Hazael set his face to go up to Jerusalem. Jehoash king of Judah took all the holy things that Jehoshaphat and Jehoram and Ahaziah, his fathers, kings of Judah, had dedicated, and his own holy things, and all the gold that was found in the treasures of YHWH's house, and of the king's house, and sent it to Hazael king of Syria; and he went away from Jerusalem. Now the rest of the acts of Joash, and all that he did, aren't they written in the book of the chronicles of the kings of Judah? His servants arose, and made a conspiracy, and struck Joash at the house of Millo, on the way that goes down to Silla. For Jozacar the son of Shimeath, and Jehozabad the son of Shomer, his servants, struck him, and he died; and they buried him with his fathers in David's city; and Amaziah his son reigned in his place.

In the twenty-third year of Joash the son of Ahaziah, king of Judah, Jehoahaz the son of Jehu began to reign over Israel in Samaria for seventeen years. He did that which was evil in YHWH's sight, and followed the sins of Jeroboam the son of Nebat, with which he made Israel to sin. He didn't depart from it. YHWH's anger burned against Israel, and he delivered them into the hand of Hazael king of Syria, and into the hand of Benhadad the son of Hazael, continually. Jehoahaz begged YHWH, and YHWH listened to him; for he saw the oppression of Israel, how the king of Syria oppressed them. (YHWH gave Israel a savior, so that they went out from under the hand of the Syrians; and the children of Israel lived in their tents as before. Nevertheless they didn't depart from the sins of the house of Jeroboam, with which he made Israel to sin, but walked in them; and the Asherah also remained in Samaria.) For he didn't leave to Jehoahaz of the people any more than fifty horsemen, and ten chariots, and ten thousand footmen; for the king of Syria destroyed them, and made them like the dust in threshing. Now the rest of the acts of Jehoahaz, and all that he did, and his might, aren't they written in the book of the chronicles of the kings of Israel? Jehoahaz slept with his fathers; and they buried him in Samaria; and Joash his son reigned in his place.

In the thirty-seventh year of Joash king of Judah, Jehoash the son of Jehoahaz began to reign over Israel in Samaria for sixteen years. He did that which was evil in YHWH's sight. He didn't depart from all the sins of Jeroboam the son of Nebat, with which he made Israel to sin; but he walked in them. Now the rest of the acts of Joash, and all that he did, and his might with which he fought against Amaziah king of Judah, aren't they written in the book of the chronicles of the kings of Israel? Joash slept with his fathers; and Jeroboam sat on his throne. Joash was buried in Samaria with the kings of Israel.

Now Elisha became sick with the illness of which he died; and Joash the king of Israel came down to him, and wept over him, and said, "My father, my father, the chariots of Israel and its horsemen!"

Elisha said to him, "Take bow and arrows;" and he took bow and arrows for himself. He said to the king of Israel, "Put your hand on the bow;" and he put his hand on it. Elisha laid his hands on the king's hands. He said, "Open the window eastward;" and he opened it. Then Elisha said, "Shoot!" and he shot. He said, "YHWH's arrow of victory, even the arrow of victory over Syria; for you will strike the Syrians in Aphek, until you have consumed them."

He said, "Take the arrows;" and he took them. He said to the king of Israel, "Strike the ground;" and he struck three times, and stopped. The man of God was angry with him, and said, "You should have struck five or six times. Then you would have struck Syria until you had consumed it; whereas now you will strike Syria just three times."

Elisha died, and they buried him.

Now the bands of the Moabites invaded the land at the coming in of the year. As they were burying a man, behold, they saw a band of raiders; and they threw the man into Elisha's tomb. As soon as the man touched Elisha's bones, he revived, and stood up on his feet.

Hazael king of Syria oppressed Israel all the days of Jehoahaz. But YHWH was gracious to them, and had compassion on them, and had respect for them, because of his covenant with Abraham, Isaac, and Jacob, and would not destroy them, and he didn't cast them from his presence as yet.

Hazael king of Syria died; and Benhadad his son reigned in his place. Jehoash the son of Jehoahaz took again out of the hand of Benhadad the son of Hazael the cities which he had taken out of the hand of Jehoahaz his father by war. Joash struck him three times, and recovered the cities of Israel.

....

In the second year of Joash son of Joahaz king of Israel Amaziah the son of Joash king of Judah began to reign. He was twenty-five years old when he began to reign; and he reigned twenty-nine years in Jerusalem. His mother's name was Jehoaddin of Jerusalem. He did that which was right in YHWH's eyes, yet not like David his father. He did according to all that Joash his father had done. However the high places were not taken away. The people still sacrificed and burned incense in the high places. As soon as the kingdom was established in his hand, he killed his servants who had slain the king his father, but the children of the murderers he didn't put to death; according to that which is written in the book of the law of Moses, as YHWH commanded, saying, "The fathers shall not be put to death for the children, nor the children be put to death for the fathers; but every man shall die for his own sin."

He killed ten thousand Edomites in the Valley of Salt, and took Sela by war, and called its name Joktheel, to this day. Then Amaziah sent messengers to Jehoash, the son of Jehoahaz son of Jehu, king of Israel, saying, "Come, let's look one another in the face."

Jehoash the king of Israel sent to Amaziah king of Judah, saying, "The thistle that was in Lebanon sent to the cedar that was in Lebanon, saying, 'Give your daughter to my son as wife. Then a wild animal that was in Lebanon passed by, and trampled down the thistle. You have indeed struck Edom, and your heart has lifted you up. Enjoy the glory of it, and stay at home; for why should you meddle to your harm, that you fall, even you, and Judah with you?'" But Amaziah would not listen. So Jehoash king of Israel went up; and he and Amaziah king of Judah looked one another in the face at Beth Shemesh, which belongs to Judah. Judah was defeated by Israel; and each man fled to his tent. Jehoash king of Israel took Amaziah king of Judah, the son of Jehoash the son of Ahaziah, at Beth Shemesh, and came to Jerusalem, and broke down the wall of Jerusalem from the gate of Ephraim to the corner gate, four hundred cubits. He took all the gold and silver, and all the vessels that were found in YHWH's house and in the treasures of the king's house, the hostages also, and returned to Samaria.

Now the rest of the acts of Jehoash which he did, and his might, and how he fought with Amaziah king of Judah, aren't they written in the book of the chronicles of the kings of Israel? Jehoash slept with his fathers, and was buried in Samaria with the kings of Israel; and Jeroboam his son reigned in his place.

Amaziah the son of Joash king of Judah lived after the death of

Jehoash son of Jehoahaz king of Israel fifteen years. Now the rest of the acts of Amaziah, aren't they written in the book of the chronicles of the kings of Judah? They made a conspiracy against him in Jerusalem, and he fled to Lachish; but they sent after him to Lachish, and killed him there. They brought him on horses, and he was buried at Jerusalem with his fathers in David's city.

All the people of Judah took Azariah, who was sixteen years old, and made him king in the place of his father Amaziah. He built Elath, and restored it to Judah. After that the king slept with his fathers.

In the fifteenth year of Amaziah the son of Joash king of Judah, Jeroboam the son of Joash king of Israel began to reign in Samaria for forty-one years. He did that which was evil in YHWH's sight. He didn't depart from all the sins of Jeroboam the son of Nebat, with which he made Israel to sin. He restored the border of Israel from the entrance of Hamath to the sea of the Arabah, according to YHWH, the God of Israel's word, which he spoke by his servant Jonah the son of Amittai, the prophet, who was from Gath Hepher. For YHWH saw the affliction of Israel, that it was very bitter; for all, slave and free, and there was no helper for Israel. YHWH didn't say that he would blot out the name of Israel from under the sky; but he saved them by the hand of Jeroboam the son of Joash. Now the rest of the acts of Jeroboam, and all that he did, and his might, how he fought, and how he recovered Damascus, and Hamath, which had belonged to Judah, for Israel, aren't they written in the book of the chronicles of the kings of Israel? Jeroboam slept with his fathers, even with the kings of Israel; and Zechariah his son reigned in his place.

....

In the twenty-seventh year of Jeroboam king of Israel, Azariah son of Amaziah king of Judah began to reign. He was sixteen years old when he began to reign, and he reigned fifty-two years in Jerusalem. His mother's name was Jecoliah of Jerusalem. He did that which was right in YHWH's eyes, according to all that his father Amaziah had done. However the high places were not taken away. The people still sacrificed and burned incense in the high places. YHWH struck the king, so that he was a leper to the day of his death, and lived in a separate house. Jotham, the king's son was over the household, judging the people of the land. Now the rest of the acts of Azariah, and all that he did, aren't they written in the book of the chronicles of the kings of Judah? Azariah slept with his fathers; and they buried him with his fathers in David's city: and Jotham his son reigned in his place.

In the thirty-eighth year of Azariah king of Judah, Zechariah the son of Jeroboam reigned over Israel in Samaria six months. He did that which was evil in YHWH's sight, as his fathers had done. He didn't depart from the sins of Jeroboam the son of Nebat, with which he made Israel to sin. Shallum the son of Jabesh conspired against him, and struck him before the people, and killed him, and reigned in his place. Now the rest of the acts of Zechariah, behold, they are written in the book of the chronicles of the kings of Israel. This was YHWH's word which he spoke to Jehu, saying, "Your sons to the fourth generation shall sit on the throne of Israel." So it came to pass.

Shallum the son of Jabesh began to reign in the thirty-ninth year of Uzziah king of Judah, and he reigned for a month in Samaria. Menahem the son of Gadi went up from Tirzah, came to Samaria, struck Shallum the son of Jabesh in Samaria, killed him, and reigned in his place. Now the rest of the acts of Shallum, and his conspiracy which he made, behold, they are written in the book of the chronicles of the kings of Israel.

Then Menahem attacked Tiphsah, and all who were in it, and its border areas, from Tirzah. He attacked it because they didn't open their gates to him, and he ripped up all their women who were with child. In the thirty ninth year of Azariah king of Judah, Menahem the son of Gadi began to reign over Israel for ten years in Samaria. He did that which was evil in YHWH's sight. He didn't depart all his days from the sins of Jeroboam the son of Nebat, with which he made Israel to sin. Pul the king of Assyria came against the land, and Menahem gave Pul one thousand talents of silver, that his hand might be with him to confirm the kingdom in his hand. Menahem exacted the money from Israel, even from all the mighty men of wealth, from each man fifty shekels of silver, to give to the king of Assyria. So the king of Assyria turned back, and didn't stay there in the land. Now the rest of the acts of Menahem, and all that he did, aren't they written in the book of the chronicles of the kings of Israel? Menahem slept with his fathers, and Pekahiah his son reigned in his place.

In the fiftieth year of Azariah king of Judah, Pekahiah the son of Menahem began to reign over Israel in Samaria for two years. He did that which was evil in YHWH's sight. He didn't depart from the sins of

Jeroboam the son of Nebat, with which he made Israel to sin. Pekah the son of Remaliah, his captain, conspired against him and attacked him in Samaria, in the fortress of the king's house, with Argob and Arieh; and with him were fifty men of the Gileadites. He killed him, and reigned in his place. Now the rest of the acts of Pekahiah, and all that he did, behold, they are written in the book of the chronicles of the kings of Israel.

In the fifty-second year of Azariah king of Judah, Pekah the son of Remaliah began to reign over Israel in Samaria for twenty years. He did that which was evil in YHWH's sight. He didn't depart from the sins of Jeroboam the son of Nebat, with which he made Israel to sin. In the days of Pekah king of Israel, Tiglath Pileser king of Assyria came and took Ijon, Abel Beth Maacah, Janoah, Kedesh, Hazor, Gilead, and Galilee, all the land of Naphtali; and he carried them captive to Assyria. Hoshea the son of Elah made a conspiracy against Pekah the son of Remaliah, attacked him, killed him, and reigned in his place, in the twentieth year of Jotham the son of Uzziah. Now the rest of the acts of Pekah, and all that he did, behold, they are written in the book of the chronicles of the kings of Israel.

In the second year of Pekah the son of Remaliah king of Israel, Jotham the son of Uzziah king of Judah began to reign. He was twenty-five years old when he began to reign, and he reigned sixteen years in Jerusalem. His mother's name was Jerusha the daughter of Zadok. He did that which was right in YHWH's eyes. He did according to all that his father Uzziah had done. However the high places were not taken away. The people still sacrificed and burned incense in the high places. He built the upper gate of YHWH's house. Now the rest of the acts of Jotham, and all that he did, aren't they written in the book of the chronicles of the kings of Judah? In those days, YHWH began to send Rezin the king of Syria and Pekah the son of Remaliah against Judah. Jotham slept with his fathers, and was buried with his fathers in his father David's city, and Ahaz his son reigned in his place.

....

In the seventeenth year of Pekah the son of Remaliah, Ahaz the son of Jotham king of Judah began to reign. Ahaz was twenty years old when he began to reign, and he reigned sixteen years in Jerusalem. He didn't do that which was right in YHWH his God's eyes, like David his father. But he walked in the way of the kings of Israel, yes, and made his son to pass through the fire, according to the abominations of the nations whom YHWH cast out from before the children of Israel. He sacrificed and burned incense in the high places, on the hills, and under every green tree. Then Rezin king of Syria and Pekah son of Remaliah king of Israel came up to Jerusalem to wage war. They besieged Ahaz, but could not overcome him. At that time Rezin king of Syria recovered Elath to Syria, and drove the Jews from Elath; and the Syrians came to Elath, and lived there, to this day. So Ahaz sent messengers to Tiglath Pileser king of Assyria, saying, "I am your servant and your son. Come up and save me out of the hand of the king of Syria, and out of the hand of the king of Israel, who rise up against me." Ahaz took the silver and gold that was found in YHWH's house, and in the treasures of the king's house, and sent it for a present to the king of Assyria. The king of Assyria listened to him; and the king of Assyria went up against Damascus, and took it, and carried its people captive to Kir, and killed Rezin. King Ahaz went to Damascus to meet Tiglath Pileser king of Assyria, and saw the altar that was at Damascus; and king Ahaz sent to Urijah the priest a drawing of the altar and plans to build it. Urijah the priest built an altar. According to all that king Ahaz had sent from Damascus, so Urijah the priest made it for the coming of king Ahaz from Damascus. When the king had come from Damascus, the king saw the altar; and the king came near to the altar, and offered on it. He burned his burnt offering and his meal offering, poured his drink offering, and sprinkled the blood of his peace offerings on the altar. The bronze altar, which was before YHWH, he brought from the front of the house, from between his altar and YHWH's house, and put it on the north side of his altar. King Ahaz commanded Urijah the priest, saying, "On the great altar burn the morning burnt offering, the evening meal offering, the king's burnt offering, his meal offering, with the burnt offering of all the people of the land, their meal offering, and their drink offerings; and sprinkle on it all the blood of the burnt offering, and all the blood of the sacrifice; but the bronze altar will be for me to inquire by." Urijah the priest did so, according to all that king Ahaz commanded. King Ahaz cut off the panels of the bases, and removed the basin from off them, and took down the sea from off the bronze oxen that were under it, and put it on a pavement of stone. He removed the covered way for the Sabbath that they had built in the house, and the king's entry outside to YHWH's house, because of the king of Assyria. Now the rest of the acts of Ahaz which he did, aren't they written in the book of the chronicles of the kings of Judah? Ahaz slept with his fathers, and was buried with his fathers in David's city, and Hezekiah his son reigned in his place.

....

In the twelfth year of Ahaz king of Judah, Hoshea the son of Elah began to reign in Samaria over Israel for nine years. He did that which was evil in YHWH's sight, yet not as the kings of Israel who were before him. Shalmaneser king of Assyria came up against him, and Hoshea became his servant, and brought him tribute. The king of Assyria found conspiracy in Hoshea; for he had sent messengers to So king of Egypt, and offered no tribute to the king of Assyria, as he had done year by year. Therefore the king of Assyria seized him, and bound him in prison. Then the king of Assyria came up throughout all the land, went up to Samaria, and besieged it three years. In the ninth year of Hoshea the king of Assyria took Samaria, and carried Israel away to Assyria, and placed them in Halah, and on the Habor, the river of Gozan, and in the cities of the Medes. It was so because the children of Israel had sinned against YHWH their God, who brought them up out of the land of Egypt from under the hand of Pharaoh king of Egypt, and had feared other gods, and walked in the statutes of the nations whom YHWH cast out from before the children of Israel, and of the kings of Israel, which they made. The children of Israel secretly did things that were not right against YHWH their God; and they built high places for themselves in all their cities, from the tower of the watchmen to the fortified city; and they set up for themselves pillars and Asherah poles on every high hill, and under every green tree; and there they burned incense in all the high places, as the nations whom YHWH carried away before them did; and they did wicked things to provoke YHWH to anger; and they served idols, of which YHWH had said to them, "You shall not do this thing." Yet YHWH testified to Israel, and to Judah, by every prophet, and every seer, saying, "Turn from your evil ways, and keep my commandments and my statutes, according to all the law which I commanded your fathers, and which I sent to you by my servants the prophets." Notwithstanding, they would not listen, but hardened their neck, like the neck of their fathers, who didn't believe in YHWH their God. They rejected his statutes, and his covenant that he made with their fathers, and his testimonies which he testified to them; and they followed vanity, and became vain, and followed the nations that were around them, concerning whom YHWH had commanded them that they should not do like them. They abandoned all the commandments of YHWH their God, and made molten images for themselves, even two calves, and made an Asherah, and worshiped all the army of the sky, and served Baal. They caused their sons and their daughters to pass through the fire, used divination and enchantments, and sold themselves to do that which was evil in YHWH's sight, to provoke him to anger. Therefore YHWH was very angry with Israel, and removed them out of his sight. There was none left but the tribe of Judah only. Also Judah didn't keep the commandments of YHWH their God, but walked in the statutes of Israel which they made. YHWH rejected all the offspring of Israel, afflicted them, and delivered them into the hands of raiders, until he had cast them out of his sight. For he tore Israel from David's house; and they made Jeroboam the son of Nebat king; and Jeroboam drove Israel from following YHWH, and made them sin a great sin. The children of Israel walked in all the sins of Jeroboam which he did; they didn't depart from them until YHWH removed Israel out of his sight, as he said by all his servants the prophets. So Israel was carried away out of their own land to Assyria to this day.

The king of Assyria brought men from Babylon, from Cuthah, from Avva, and from Hamath and Sepharvaim, and placed them in the cities of Samaria instead of the children of Israel; and they possessed Samaria, and lived in its cities. So it was, at the beginning of their dwelling there, that they didn't fear YHWH. Therefore YHWH sent lions among them, which killed some of them. Therefore they spoke to the king of Assyria, saying, "The nations which you have carried away and placed in the cities of Samaria don't know the law of the god of the land. Therefore he has sent lions among them, and behold, they kill them, because they don't know the law of the god of the land."

Then the king of Assyria commanded, saying, "Carry there one of the priests whom you brought from there; and let them go and dwell there, and let him teach them the law of the god of the land."

So one of the priests whom they had carried away from Samaria came and lived in Bethel, and taught them how they should fear YHWH. However every nation made gods of their own, and put them in the houses of the high places which the Samaritans had made, every nation in their cities in which they lived. The men of Babylon made Succoth Benoth, and the men of Cuth made Nergal, and the men of Hamath made Ashima, and the Avvites made Nibhaz and Tartak; and the Sepharvites burned their children in the fire to Adrammelech and Anammelech, the gods of Sepharvaim. So they feared YHWH, and also made from among themselves priests of the high places for themselves, who sacrificed for them in the houses of the high places. They feared YHWH, and also served their own gods, after the ways of the nations from among whom they had been carried away. To this day they do what they did before. They don't fear YHWH, and they do not follow the statutes, or the ordinances, or the law, or the commandment which YHWH commanded the children of Jacob, whom he named Israel; with whom YHWH had made a covenant, and commanded them, saying, "You shall not fear other gods, nor bow yourselves to them, nor serve them, nor sacrifice to them; but you shall fear YHWH, who brought you up out of the land of Egypt with great power and with an outstretched arm, and you shall bow yourselves to him, and you shall sacrifice to him. The statutes and the ordinances, and the law and the commandment, which he wrote for you, you shall observe to do forever more. You shall not fear other gods. You shall not forget the covenant that I have made with you. You shall not fear other gods. But you shall fear YHWH your God, and he will deliver you out of the hand of all your enemies." However they didn't listen, but they did what they did before. So these nations feared YHWH, and also served their engraved images. Their children did likewise, and so did their children's children. They do as their fathers did to this day.

....

Now in the third year of Hoshea son of Elah king of Israel, Hezekiah the son of Ahaz king of Judah began to reign. He was twenty-five years old when he began to reign, and he reigned twenty-nine years in Jerusalem. His mother's name was Abi the daughter of Zechariah. He did that which was right in YHWH's eyes, according to all that David his father had done. He removed the high places, and broke the pillars, and cut down the Asherah. He also broke in pieces the bronze serpent that Moses had made, because in those days the children of Israel burned incense to it; and he called it Nehushtan. He trusted in YHWH, the God of Israel; so that after him was no one like him among all the kings of Judah, nor among them that were before him. For he joined with YHWH. He didn't depart from following him, but kept his commandments, which YHWH commanded Moses. YHWH was with him. Wherever he went, he prospered. He rebelled against the king of Assyria, and didn't serve him. He struck the Philistines to Gaza and its borders, from the tower of the watchmen to the fortified city.

In the fourth year of king Hezekiah, which was the seventh year of Hoshea son of Elah king of Israel, Shalmaneser king of Assyria came up against Samaria, and besieged it. At the end of three years they took it. In the sixth year of Hezekiah, which was the ninth year of Hoshea king of Israel, Samaria was taken. The king of Assyria carried Israel away to Assyria, and put them in Halah, and on the Habor, the river of Gozan, and in the cities of the Medes, because they didn't obey YHWH their God's voice, but transgressed his covenant, even all that Moses the servant of YHWH commanded, and would not hear it or do it.

Now in the fourteenth year of king Hezekiah, Sennacherib king of Assyria came up against all the fortified cities of Judah, and took them. Hezekiah king of Judah sent to the king of Assyria to Lachish, saying, "I have offended you. Return from me. That which you put on me, I will bear." The king of Assyria appointed to Hezekiah king of Judah three hundred talents of silver and thirty talents of gold. Hezekiah gave him all the silver that was found in YHWH's house, and in the treasures of the king's house. At that time, Hezekiah cut off the gold from the doors of YHWH's temple, and from the pillars which Hezekiah king of Judah had overlaid, and gave it to the king of Assyria.

The king of Assyria sent Tartan and Rabsaris and Rabshakeh from Lachish to king Hezekiah with a great army to Jerusalem. They went up and came to Jerusalem. When they had come up, they came and stood by the conduit of the upper pool, which is in the highway of the fuller's field. When they had called to the king, Eliakim the son of Hilkiah, who was over the household, and Shebnah the scribe, and Joah the son of Asaph the recorder came out to them. Rabshakeh said to them, "Say now to Hezekiah, 'The great king, the king of Assyria, says, "What confidence is this in which you trust? You say (but they are but vain words), 'There is counsel and strength for war.' Now on whom do you trust, that you have rebelled against me? Now, behold, you trust in the staff of this bruised reed, even in Egypt. If a man leans on it, it will go into his hand, and pierce it. So is Pharaoh king of Egypt to all who trust on him. But if you tell me, 'We trust in YHWH our God;' isn't that he whose high places and whose altars Hezekiah has taken away, and has said to Judah and to Jerusalem,

'You shall worship before this altar in Jerusalem?' Now therefore, please give pledges to my master the king of Assyria, and I will give you two thousand horses, if you are able on your part to set riders on them. How then can you turn away the face of one captain of the least of my master's servants, and put your trust on Egypt for chariots and for horsemen? Have I now come up without YHWH against this place to destroy it? YHWH said to me, 'Go up against this land, and destroy it.'"'"

Then Eliakim the son of Hilkiah, Shebnah, and Joah, said to Rabshakeh, "Please speak to your servants in the Syrian language, for we understand it. Don't speak with us in the Jews' language, in the hearing of the people who are on the wall."

But Rabshakeh said to them, "Has my master sent me to your master and to you, to speak these words? Hasn't he sent me to the men who sit on the wall, to eat their own dung, and to drink their own urine with you?" Then Rabshakeh stood, and cried with a loud voice in the Jews' language, and spoke, saying, "Hear the word of the great king, the king of Assyria. The king says, 'Don't let Hezekiah deceive you; for he will not be able to deliver you out of his hand. Don't let Hezekiah make you trust in YHWH, saying, "YHWH will surely deliver us, and this city shall not be given into the hand of the king of Assyria." Don't listen to Hezekiah.' For the king of Assyria says, 'Make your peace with me, and come out to me; and everyone of you eat from his own vine, and everyone from his own fig tree, and everyone drink water from his own cistern; until I come and take you away to a land like your own land, a land of grain and new wine, a land of bread and vineyards, a land of olive trees and of honey, that you may live, and not die. Don't listen to Hezekiah, when he persuades you, saying, "YHWH will deliver us." Has any of the gods of the nations ever delivered his land out of the hand of the king of Assyria? Where are the gods of Hamath, and of Arpad? Where are the gods of Sepharvaim, of Hena, and Ivvah? Have they delivered Samaria out of my hand? Who are they among all the gods of the countries, that have delivered their country out of my hand, that YHWH should deliver Jerusalem out of my hand?'"

But the people stayed quiet, and answered him not a word; for the king's commandment was, "Don't answer him." Then Eliakim the son of Hilkiah, who was over the household, came with Shebna the scribe, and Joah the son of Asaph the recorder, to Hezekiah with their clothes torn, and told him Rabshakeh's words.

....

When king Hezekiah heard it, he tore his clothes, covered himself with sackcloth, and went into YHWH's house. He sent Eliakim, who was over the household, Shebna the scribe, and the elders of the priests, covered with sackcloth, to Isaiah the prophet the son of Amoz. They said to him, "Hezekiah says, 'Today is a day of trouble, of rebuke, and of rejection; for the children have come to the point of birth, and there is no strength to deliver them. It may be YHWH your God will hear all the words of Rabshakeh, whom the king of Assyria his master has sent to defy the living God, and will rebuke the words which YHWH your God has heard. Therefore lift up your prayer for the remnant that is left.'"

So the servants of king Hezekiah came to Isaiah. Isaiah said to them, "Tell your master this: 'YHWH says, "Don't be afraid of the words that you have heard, with which the servants of the king of Assyria have blasphemed me. Behold, I will put a spirit in him, and he will hear news, and will return to his own land. I will cause him to fall by the sword in his own land."'"

So Rabshakeh returned and found the king of Assyria warring against Libnah; for he had heard that he had departed from Lachish. When he heard it said of Tirhakah king of Ethiopia, "Behold, he has come out to fight against you, he sent messengers again to Hezekiah, saying, 'Tell Hezekiah king of Judah this: "Don't let your God in whom you trust deceive you, saying, Jerusalem will not be given into the hand of the king of Assyria. Behold, you have heard what the kings of Assyria have done to all lands, by destroying them utterly. Will you be delivered? Have the gods of the nations delivered them, which my fathers have destroyed, Gozan, Haran, Rezeph, and the children of Eden who were in Telassar? Where is the king of Hamath, the king of Arpad, and the king of the city of Sepharvaim, of Hena, and Ivvah?"'"

Hezekiah received the letter from the hand of the messengers and read it. Then Hezekiah went up to YHWH's house, and spread it before YHWH. Hezekiah prayed before YHWH, and said, "YHWH, the God of Israel, who are enthroned above the cherubim, you are the God, even you alone, of all the kingdoms of the earth. You have made heaven and earth. Incline your ear, YHWH, and hear. Open your eyes, YHWH, and see. Hear the words of Sennacherib, which he has sent to defy the living God. Truly, YHWH, the kings of Assyria have laid waste the nations and their lands, and have cast their gods into the fire; for they were no gods, but the work of men's hands, wood and stone. Therefore they have destroyed them. Now therefore, YHWH our God, save us, I beg you, out of his hand, that all the kingdoms of the earth may know that you, YHWH, are God alone."

Then Isaiah the son of Amoz sent to Hezekiah, saying, "YHWH, the God of Israel, says 'You have prayed to me against Sennacherib king of Assyria, and I have heard you. This is the word that YHWH has spoken concerning him: 'The virgin daughter of Zion has despised you and ridiculed you. The daughter of Jerusalem has shaken her head at you. Whom have you defied and blasphemed? Against whom have you exalted your voice and lifted up your eyes on high? Against the Holy One of Israel! By your messengers, you have defied the Lord, and have said, "With the multitude of my chariots, I have come up to the height of the mountains, to the innermost parts of Lebanon, and I will cut down its tall cedars and its choice cypress trees; and I will enter into his farthest lodging place, the forest of his fruitful field. I have dug and drunk strange waters, and I will dry up all the rivers of Egypt with the sole of my feet." Haven't you heard how I have done it long ago, and formed it of ancient times? Now I have brought it to pass, that it should be yours to lay waste fortified cities into ruinous heaps. Therefore their inhabitants had little power. They were dismayed and confounded. They were like the grass of the field, and like the green herb, like the grass on the housetops, and like grain blasted before it has grown up. But I know your sitting down, your going out, your coming in, and your raging against me. Because of your raging against me, and because your arrogance has come up into my ears, therefore I will put my hook in your nose, and my bridle in your lips, and I will turn you back by the way by which you came.'

"This will be the sign to you: This year, you will eat that which grows of itself, and in the second year that which springs from that; and in the third year sow, and reap, and plant vineyards, and eat its fruit. The remnant that has escaped of the house of Judah will again take root downward, and bear fruit upward. For out of Jerusalem a remnant will go out, and out of Mount Zion those who shall escape. YHWH's zeal will perform this.

"Therefore YHWH says concerning the king of Assyria, 'He will not come to this city, nor shoot an arrow there. He will not come before it with shield, nor cast up a mound against it. He will return the same way that he came, and he will not come to this city,' says YHWH. 'For I will defend this city to save it, for my own sake, and for my servant David's sake.'"

That night, YHWH's angel went out, and struck one hundred eighty-five thousand in the camp of the Assyrians. When men arose early in the morning, behold, these were all dead bodies. So Sennacherib king of Assyria departed, and went and returned, and lived at Nineveh. As he was worshiping in the house of Nisroch his god, Adrammelech and Sharezer struck him with the sword; and they escaped into the land of Ararat. Esar Haddon his son reigned in his place.

....

In those days Hezekiah was sick and dying. Isaiah the prophet the son of Amoz came to him, and said to him, "YHWH says, 'Set your house in order; for you will die, and not live.'"

Then he turned his face to the wall, and prayed to YHWH, saying, "Remember now, YHWH, I beg you, how I have walked before you in truth and with a perfect heart, and have done that which is good in your sight." And Hezekiah wept bitterly.

Before Isaiah had gone out into the middle part of the city, YH-WH's word came to him, saying, "Turn back, and tell Hezekiah the prince of my people, 'YHWH, the God of David your father, says, "I have heard your prayer. I have seen your tears. Behold, I will heal you. On the third day, you will go up to YHWH's house. I will add to your days fifteen years. I will deliver you and this city out of the hand of the king of Assyria. I will defend this city for my own sake, and for my servant David's sake."'"

Isaiah said, "Take a cake of figs."

They took and laid it on the boil, and he recovered. Hezekiah said to Isaiah, "What will be the sign that YHWH will heal me, and that I will go up to YHWH's house the third day?"

Isaiah said, "This will be the sign to you from YHWH, that YHWH will do the thing that he has spoken: should the shadow go forward ten steps, or go back ten steps?"

Hezekiah answered, "It is a light thing for the shadow to go forward ten steps. No, but let the shadow return backward ten steps."

Isaiah the prophet cried to YHWH; and he brought the shadow ten steps backward, by which it had gone down on the sundial of Ahaz.

At that time Berodach Baladan the son of Baladan, king of Babylon, sent letters and a present to Hezekiah; for he had heard that Hezekiah had been sick. Hezekiah listened to them, and showed them all the storehouse of his precious things, the silver, the gold, the spices, and the precious oil, and the house of his armor, and all that was found in his treasures. There was nothing in his house, or in all his dominion, that Hezekiah didn't show them.

Then Isaiah the prophet came to king Hezekiah, and said to him, "What did these men say? From where did they come to you?"

Hezekiah said, "They have come from a far country, even from Babylon."

He said, "What have they seen in your house?"

Hezekiah answered, "They have seen all that is in my house. There is nothing among my treasures that I have not shown them."

Isaiah said to Hezekiah, "Hear YHWH's word. 'Behold, the days come that all that is in your house, and that which your fathers have laid up in store to this day, will be carried to Babylon. Nothing will be left,' says YHWH. 'They will take away some of your sons who will issue from you, whom you will father; and they will be eunuchs in the palace of the king of Babylon.'"

Then Hezekiah said to Isaiah, "YHWH's word which you have spoken is good." He said moreover, "Isn't it so, if peace and truth will be in my days?"

Now the rest of the acts of Hezekiah, and all his might, and how he made the pool, and the conduit, and brought water into the city, aren't they written in the book of the chronicles of the kings of Judah? Hezekiah slept with his fathers, and Manasseh his son reigned in his place.

....

Manasseh was twelve years old when he began to reign, and he reigned fifty-five years in Jerusalem. His mother's name was Hephzibah. He did that which was evil in YHWH's sight, after the abominations of the nations whom YHWH cast out before the children of Israel. For he built again the high places which Hezekiah his father had destroyed; and he raised up altars for Baal, and made an Asherah, as Ahab king of Israel did, and worshiped all the army of the sky, and served them. He built altars in YHWH's house, of which YHWH said, "I will put my name in Jerusalem." He built altars for all the army of the sky in the two courts of YHWH's house. He made his son to pass through the fire, practiced sorcery, used enchantments, and dealt with those who had familiar spirits, and with wizards. He did much evil in YHWH's sight, to provoke him to anger. He set the engraved image of Asherah that he had made in the house of which YHWH said to David and to Solomon his son, "In this house, and in Jerusalem, which I have chosen out of all the tribes of Israel, I will put my name forever; I will not cause the feet of Israel to wander any more out of the land which I gave their fathers, if only they will observe to do according to all that I have commanded them, and according to all the law that my servant Moses commanded them." But they didn't listen, and Manasseh seduced them to do that which is evil more than the nations did whom YHWH destroyed before the children of Israel. YHWH spoke by his servants the prophets, saying, "Because Manasseh king of Judah has done these abominations, and has done wickedly above all that the Amorites did, who were before him, and has also made Judah to sin with his idols; therefore YHWH the God of Israel says, 'Behold, I bring such evil on Jerusalem and Judah that whoever hears of it, both his ears will tingle. I will stretch over Jerusalem the line of Samaria, and the plummet of Ahab's house; and I will wipe Jerusalem as a man wipes a dish, wiping it and turning it upside down. I will cast off the remnant of my inheritance, and deliver them into the hands of their enemies. They will become a prey and a plunder to all their enemies, because they have done that which is evil in my sight, and have provoked me to anger, since the day their fathers came out of Egypt, even to this day.'"

Moreover Manasseh shed innocent blood very much, until he had filled Jerusalem from one end to another; in addition to his sin with which he made Judah to sin, in doing that which was evil in YHWH's sight. Now the rest of the acts of Manasseh, and all that he did, and his sin that he sinned, aren't they written in the book of the chronicles of the kings of Judah? Manasseh slept with his fathers, and was buried in the garden of his own house, in the garden of Uzza; and Amon his son reigned in his place.

Amon was twenty-two years old when he began to reign; and he reigned two years in Jerusalem. His mother's name was Meshullemeth the daughter of Haruz of Jotbah. He did that which was evil in YHWH's sight, as Manasseh his father did. He walked in all the ways that his father walked in, and served the idols that his father served, and worshiped them; and he abandoned YHWH, the God of his fathers, and didn't walk in the way of YHWH. The servants of Amon conspired against him, and put the king to death in his own house. But the people of the land killed all those who had conspired against king Amon; and the people of the land made Josiah his son king in his place. Now the rest of the acts of Amon which he did, aren't they written in the book of the chronicles of the kings of Judah? He was buried in his tomb in the garden of Uzza, and Josiah his son reigned in his place.

··

Josiah was eight years old when he began to reign, and he reigned thirty-one years in Jerusalem. His mother's name was Jedidah the daughter of Adaiah of Bozkath. He did that which was right in YHWH's eyes, and walked in all the way of David his father, and didn't turn away to the right hand or to the left. In the eighteenth year of king Josiah, the king sent Shaphan, the son of Azaliah the son of Meshullam, the scribe, to YHWH's house, saying, "Go up to Hilkiah the high priest, that he may count the money which is brought into YHWH's house, which the keepers of the threshold have gathered of the people. Let them deliver it into the hand of the workmen who have the oversight of YHWH's house; and let them give it to the workmen who are in YHWH's house, to repair the damage to the house, to the carpenters, and to the builders, and to the masons, and for buying timber and cut stone to repair the house. However there was no accounting made with them of the money that was delivered into their hand; for they dealt faithfully."

Hilkiah the high priest said to Shaphan the scribe, "I have found the book of the law in YHWH's house." Hilkiah delivered the book to Shaphan, and he read it. Shaphan the scribe came to the king, and brought the king word again, and said, "Your servants have emptied out the money that was found in the house, and have delivered it into the hands of the workmen who have the oversight of YHWH's house." Shaphan the scribe told the king, saying, "Hilkiah the priest has delivered a book to me." Then Shaphan read it before the king.

When the king had heard the words of the book of the law, he tore his clothes. The king commanded Hilkiah the priest, Ahikam the son of Shaphan, Achbor the son of Micaiah, Shaphan the scribe, and Asaiah the king's servant, saying, "Go inquire of YHWH for me, and for the people, and for all Judah, concerning the words of this book that is found; for great is YHWH's wrath that is kindled against us, because our fathers have not listened to the words of this book, to do according to all that which is written concerning us."

So Hilkiah the priest, Ahikam, Achbor, Shaphan, and Asaiah, went to Huldah the prophetess, the wife of Shallum the son of Tikvah, the son of Harhas, keeper of the wardrobe (now she lived in Jerusalem in the second quarter); and they talked with her. She said to them, "YHWH the God of Israel says, 'Tell the man who sent you to me, "YHWH says, 'Behold, I will bring evil on this place, and on its inhabitants, even all the words of the book which the king of Judah has read. Because they have forsaken me, and have burned incense to other gods, that they might provoke me to anger with all the work of their hands, therefore my wrath shall be kindled against this place, and it will not be quenched.'" But to the king of Judah, who sent you to inquire of YHWH, tell him, "YHWH the God of Israel says, 'Concerning the words which you have heard, because your heart was tender, and you humbled yourself before YHWH, when you heard what I spoke against this place, and against its inhabitants, that they should become a desolation and a curse, and have torn your clothes, and wept before me; I also have heard you,' says YHWH. 'Therefore behold, I will gather you to your fathers, and you will be gathered to your grave in peace. Your eyes will not see all the evil which I will bring on this place.'"'" So they brought this message back to the king.

....

The king sent, and they gathered to him all the elders of Judah and of Jerusalem. The king went up to YHWH's house, and all the men of Judah and all the inhabitants of Jerusalem with him, with the priests, the prophets, and all the people, both small and great; and he read in their hearing all the words of the book of the covenant which was found in YHWH's house. The king stood by the pillar, and made a covenant before YHWH, to walk after YHWH, and to keep his commandments, his testimonies, and his statutes, with all his heart, and all his soul, to confirm the words of this covenant that were written in this book; and all the people agreed to the covenant. The king commanded Hilkiah the high priest, and the priests of the second order, and the keepers of the threshold, to bring out of YHWH's temple all the vessels that were made for Baal, for the Asherah, and for all the army of the sky, and he burned them outside of Jerusalem in the fields of the Kidron, and carried their ashes to Bethel. He got rid of the idolatrous priests, whom the kings of Judah had ordained to burn incense in the high places in the cities of Judah, and in the places around Jerusalem; those also who burned incense to Baal, to the sun, and to the moon, and to the planets, and to all the army of the sky. He brought out the Asherah from YHWH's house, outside of Jerusalem, to the brook Kidron, and burned it at the brook Kidron, and beat it to dust, and cast its dust on the graves of the common people. He broke down the houses of the male shrine prostitutes that were in YHWH's house, where the women wove hangings for the Asherah. He brought all the priests out of the cities of Judah, and defiled the high places where the priests had burned incense, from Geba to Beersheba; and he broke down the high places of the gates that were at the entrance of the gate of Joshua the governor of the city, which were on a man's left hand at the gate of the city. Nevertheless the priests of the high places didn't come up to YHWH's altar in Jerusalem, but they ate unleavened bread among their brothers. He defiled Topheth, which is in the valley of the children of Hinnom, that no man might make his son or his daughter to pass through the fire to Molech. He took away the horses that the kings of Judah had given to the sun, at the entrance of YHWH's house, by the room of Nathan Melech the officer, who was in the court; and he burned the chariots of the sun with fire. The king broke down the altars that were on the roof of the upper room of Ahaz, which the kings of Judah had made, and the altars which Manasseh had made in the two courts of YHWH's house, and beat them down from there, and cast their dust into the brook Kidron. The king defiled the high places that were before Jerusalem, which were on the right hand of the mountain of corruption, which Solomon the king of Israel had built for Ashtoreth the abomination of the Sidonians, and for Chemosh the abomination of Moab, and for Milcom the abomination of the children of Ammon. He broke in pieces the pillars, cut down the Asherah poles, and filled their places with men's bones. Moreover the altar that was at Bethel, and the high place which Jeroboam the son of Nebat, who made Israel to sin, had made, even that altar and the high place he broke down; and he burned the high place and beat it to dust, and burned the Asherah. As Josiah turned himself, he spied the tombs that were there in the mountain; and he sent, and took the bones out of the tombs, and burned them on the altar, and defiled it, according to YHWH's word which the man of God proclaimed, who proclaimed these things. Then he said, "What monument is that which I see?"

The men of the city told him, "It is the tomb of the man of God, who came from Judah, and proclaimed these things that you have done against the altar of Bethel."

He said, "Let him be! Let no one move his bones." So they let his bones alone, with the bones of the prophet who came out of Samaria. All the houses also of the high places that were in the cities of Samaria, which the kings of Israel had made to provoke YHWH to anger, Josiah took away, and did to them according to all the acts that he had done in Bethel. He killed all the priests of the high places that were there, on the altars, and burned men's bones on them; and he returned to Jerusalem.

The king commanded all the people, saying, "Keep the Passover to YHWH your God, as it is written in this book of the covenant." Surely there was not kept such a Passover from the days of the judges who judged Israel, nor in all the days of the kings of Israel, nor of the kings of Judah; but in the eighteenth year of king Josiah, this Passover was kept to YHWH in Jerusalem. Moreover Josiah removed those who had familiar spirits, the wizards, and the teraphim, and the idols, and all the abominations that were seen in the land of Judah and in Jerusalem, that he might confirm the words of the law which were written in the book that Hilkiah the priest found in YH-WH's house. There was no king like him before him, who turned to YHWH with all his heart, and with all his soul, and with all his might, according to all the law of Moses; and there was none like him who arose after him. Notwithstanding, YHWH didn't turn from the fierceness of his great wrath, with which his anger burned against Judah, because of all the provocation with which Manasseh had provoked him. YHWH said, "I will also remove Judah out of my sight, as I have removed Israel, and I will cast off this city which I have chosen, even Jerusalem, and the house of which I said, 'My name shall be there.'"

Now the rest of the acts of Josiah, and all that he did, aren't they written in the book of the chronicles of the kings of Judah? In his days Pharaoh Necoh king of Egypt went up against the king of Assyria to the river Euphrates; and king Josiah went against him; and Pharaoh Necoh killed him at Megiddo, when he had seen him. His servants carried him in a chariot dead from Megiddo, and brought him to Jerusalem, and buried him in his own tomb. The people of the land took Jehoahaz the son of Josiah, and anointed him, and made him king in his father's place.

Jehoahaz was twenty-three years old when he began to reign; and he reigned three months in Jerusalem. His mother's name was

Hamutal the daughter of Jeremiah of Libnah. He did that which was evil in YHWH's sight, according to all that his fathers had done. Pharaoh Necoh put him in bonds at Riblah in the land of Hamath, that he might not reign in Jerusalem; and put the land to a tribute of one hundred talents of silver, and a talent of gold. Pharaoh Necoh made Eliakim the son of Josiah king in the place of Josiah his father, and changed his name to Jehoiakim; but he took Jehoahaz away, and he came to Egypt and died there. Jehoiakim gave the silver and the gold to Pharaoh; but he taxed the land to give the money according to the commandment of Pharaoh. He exacted the silver and the gold of the people of the land, from everyone according to his assessment, to give it to Pharaoh Necoh. Jehoiakim was twenty-five years old when he began to reign, and he reigned eleven years in Jerusalem. His mother's name was Zebidah the daughter of Pedaiah of Rumah. He did that which was evil in YHWH's sight, according to all that his fathers had done.

....

In his days Nebuchadnezzar king of Babylon came up, and Jehoiakim became his servant three years. Then he turned and rebelled against him. YHWH sent against him bands of the Chaldeans, and bands of the Syrians, and bands of the Moabites, and bands of the children of Ammon, and sent them against Judah to destroy it, according to YHWH's word, which he spoke by his servants the prophets. Surely at the commandment of YHWH this came on Judah, to remove them out of his sight, for the sins of Manasseh, according to all that he did, and also for the innocent blood that he shed; for he filled Jerusalem with innocent blood, and YHWH would not pardon. Now the rest of the acts of Jehoiakim, and all that he did, aren't they written in the book of the chronicles of the kings of Judah? So Jehoiakim slept with his fathers, and Jehoiachin his son reigned in his place.

The king of Egypt didn't come out of his land any more; for the king of Babylon had taken, from the brook of Egypt to the river Euphrates, all that belonged to the king of Egypt.

Jehoiachin was eighteen years old when he began to reign, and he reigned in Jerusalem three months. His mother's name was Nehushta the daughter of Elnathan of Jerusalem. He did that which was evil in YHWH's sight, according to all that his father had done. At that time the servants of Nebuchadnezzar king of Babylon came up to Jerusalem, and the city was besieged. Nebuchadnezzar king of Babylon came to the city while his servants were besieging it, and Jehoiachin the king of Judah went out to the king of Babylon, he, and his mother, and his servants, and his princes, and his officers; and the king of Babylon captured him in the eighth year of his reign. He carried out from there all the treasures of YHWH's house, and the treasures of the king's house, and cut in pieces all the vessels of gold, which Solomon king of Israel had made in YHWH's temple, as YHWH had said. He carried away all Jerusalem, and all the princes, and all the mighty men of valor, even ten thousand captives, and all the craftsmen and the smiths. No one remained, except the poorest people of the land. He carried away Jehoiachin to Babylon, with the king's mother, the king's wives, his officers, and the chief men of the land. He carried them into captivity from Jerusalem to Babylon. All the men of might, even seven thousand, and the craftsmen and the smiths one thousand, all of them strong and fit for war, even them the king of Babylon brought captive to Babylon. The king of Babylon made Mattaniah, Jehoiachin's father's brother, king in his place, and changed his name to Zedekiah. Zedekiah was twenty-one years old when he began to reign, and he reigned eleven years in Jerusalem. His mother's name was Hamutal the daughter of Jeremiah of Libnah. He did that which was evil in YHWH's sight, according to all that Jehoiakim had done. For through the anger of YHWH, this happened in Jerusalem and Judah, until he had cast them out from his presence.

Then Zedekiah rebelled against the king of Babylon.

....

In the ninth year of his reign, in the tenth month, in the tenth day of the month, Nebuchadnezzar king of Babylon came, he and all his army, against Jerusalem, and encamped against it; and they built forts against it around it. So the city was besieged until the eleventh year of king Zedekiah. On the ninth day of the fourth month, the famine was severe in the city, so that there was no bread for the people of the land. Then a breach was made in the city, and all the men of war fled by night by the way of the gate between the two walls, which was by the king's garden (now the Chaldeans were against the city around it); and the king went by the way of the Arabah. But the Chaldean army pursued the king, and overtook him in the plains of Jericho; and all his army was scattered from him. Then they captured the king, and carried him up to the king of Babylon to Riblah; and they passed judgment on him. They killed Zedekiah's sons before his eyes, then put out Zedekiah's eyes, bound him in fetters, and carried him to Babylon.

Now in the fifth month, on the seventh day of the month, which was the nineteenth year of king Nebuchadnezzar, king of Babylon, Nebuzaradan the captain of the guard, a servant of the king of Babylon, came to Jerusalem. He burned YHWH's house, the king's house, and all the houses of Jerusalem, even every great house, he burned with fire. All the army of the Chaldeans, who were with the captain of the guard, broke down the walls around Jerusalem. Nebuzaradan the captain of the guard carried away captive the residue of the people who were left in the city, and those who fell away, who fell to the king of Babylon, and the residue of the multitude. But the captain of the guard left some of the poorest of the land to work the vineyards and fields. The Chaldeans broke up the pillars of bronze that were in YHWH's house and the bases and the bronze sea that were in YHWH's house, and carried the bronze pieces to Babylon. They took away the pots, the shovels, the snuffers, the spoons, and all the vessels of bronze with which they ministered. The captain of the guard took away the fire pans, the basins, that which was of gold, in gold, and that which was of silver, in silver. The two pillars, the one sea, and the bases, which Solomon had made for YHWH's house, the bronze of all these vessels was not weighed. The height of the one pillar was eighteen cubits, and a capital of bronze was on it. The height of the capital was three cubits, with network and pomegranates on the capital around it, all of bronze; and the second pillar with its network was like these.

The captain of the guard took Seraiah the chief priest, Zephaniah the second priest, and the three keepers of the threshold; and out of the city he took an officer who was set over the men of war; and five men of those who saw the king's face, who were found in the city; and the scribe, the captain of the army, who mustered the people of the land; and sixty men of the people of the land, who were found in the city. Nebuzaradan the captain of the guard took them, and brought them to the king of Babylon to Riblah. The king of Babylon attacked them, and put them to death at Riblah in the land of Hamath. So Judah was carried away captive out of his land. As for the people who were left in the land of Judah, whom Nebuchadnezzar king of Babylon had left, even over them he made Gedaliah the son of Ahikam, the son of Shaphan, governor. Now when all the captains of the forces, they and their men, heard that the king of Babylon had made Gedaliah governor, they came to Gedaliah to Mizpah, even Ishmael the son of Nethaniah, and Johanan the son of Kareah, and Seraiah the son of Tanhumeth the Netophathite, and Jaazaniah the son of the Maacathite, they and their men. Gedaliah swore to them and to their men, and said to them, "Don't be afraid because of the servants of the Chaldeans. Dwell in the land, and serve the king of Babylon, and it will be well with you."

But in the seventh month, Ishmael the son of Nethaniah, the son of Elishama, of the royal offspring came, and ten men with him, and struck Gedaliah, so that he died, with the Jews and the Chaldeans that were with him at Mizpah. All the people, both small and great, and the captains of the forces, arose, and came to Egypt; for they were afraid of the Chaldeans. In the thirty-seventh year of the captivity of Jehoiachin king of Judah, in the twelfth month, on the twenty-seventh day of the month, Evilmerodach king of Babylon, in the year that he began to reign, lifted up the head of Jehoiachin king of Judah out of prison; and he spoke kindly to him, and set his throne above the throne of the kings who were with him in Babylon, and changed his prison garments. Jehoiachin ate bread before him continually all the days of his life; and for his allowance, there was a continual allowance given him from the king, every day a portion, all the days of his life.

THE BOOK OF

CHRONICLES

PART I

1 HR 47 MIN

Adam, Seth, Enosh, Kenan, Mahalalel, Jared, Enoch, Methuselah, Lamech, Noah, Shem, Ham, and Japheth. The sons of Japheth: Gomer, Magog, Madai, Javan, Tubal, Meshech, and Tiras. The sons of Gomer: Ashkenaz, Diphath, and Togarmah. The sons of Javan: Elishah, Tarshish, Kittim, and Rodanim. The sons of Ham: Cush, Mizraim, Put, and Canaan. The sons of Cush: Seba, Havilah, Sabta, Raama, Sabteca. The sons of Raamah: Sheba and Dedan. Cush became the father of Nimrod. He began to be a mighty one in the earth. Mizraim became the father of Ludim, Anamim, Lehabim, Naphtuhim, Pathrusim, Casluhim (where the Philistines came from), and Caphtorim. Canaan became the father of Sidon his firstborn, Heth, the Jebusite, and the Amorite, the Girgashite, the Hivite, the Arkite, the Sinite, the Arvadite, the Zemarite, and the Hamathite. The sons of Shem: Elam, Asshur, Arpachshad, Lud, Aram, Uz, Hul, Gether, and Meshech. Arpachshad became the father of Shelah, and Shelah became the father of Eber. To Eber were born two sons: the name of the one was Peleg, for in his days the earth was divided; and his brother's name was Joktan. Joktan became the father of Almodad, Sheleph, Hazarmaveth, Jerah, Hadoram, Uzal, Diklah, Ebal, Abimael, Sheba, Ophir, Havilah, and Jobab. All these were the sons of Joktan. Shem, Arpachshad, Shelah, Eber, Peleg, Reu, Serug, Nahor, Terah, Abram (also called Abraham). The sons of Abraham: Isaac and Ishmael. These are their generations: the firstborn of Ishmael, Nebaioth; then Kedar, Adbeel, Mibsam, Mishma, Dumah, Massa, Hadad, Tema, Jetur, Naphish, and Kedemah. These are the sons of Ishmael. The sons of Keturah, Abraham's concubine: she bore Zimran, Jokshan, Medan, Midian, Ishbak, and Shuah. The sons of Jokshan: Sheba and Dedan. The sons of Midian: Ephah, Epher, Hanoch, Abida, and Eldaah. All these were the sons of Keturah. Abraham became the father of Isaac. The sons of Isaac: Esau and Israel. The sons of Esau: Eliphaz, Reuel, Jeush, Jalam, and Korah. The sons of Eliphaz: Teman, Omar, Zephi, Gatam, Kenaz, Timna, and Amalek. The sons of Reuel: Nahath, Zerah, Shammah, and Mizzah. The sons of Seir: Lotan, Shobal, Zibeon, Anah, Dishon, Ezer, and Dishan. The sons of Lotan: Hori and Homam; and Timna was Lotan's sister. The sons of Shobal: Alian, Manahath, Ebal, Shephi, and Onam. The sons of Zibeon: Aiah and Anah. The son of Anah: Dishon. The sons of Dishon: Hamran, Eshban, Ithran, and Cheran. The sons of Ezer: Bilhan, Zaavan, and Jaakan. The sons of Dishan: Uz and Aran.

Now these are the kings who reigned in the land of Edom, before any king reigned over the children of Israel: Bela the son of Beor; and the name of his city was Dinhabah. Bela died, and Jobab the son of Zerah of Bozrah reigned in his place. Jobab died, and Husham of the land of the Temanites reigned in his place. Husham died, and Hadad the son of Bedad, who struck Midian in the field of Moab, reigned in his place; and the name of his city was Avith. Hadad died, and Samlah of Masrekah reigned in his place. Samlah died, and Shaul of Rehoboth by the River reigned in his place. Shaul died, and Baal Hanan the son of Achbor reigned in his place. Baal Hanan died, and Hadad reigned in his place; and the name of his city was Pai: and his wife's name was Mehetabel, the daughter of Matred, the daughter of Mezahab. Then Hadad died. The chiefs of Edom were: chief Timna, chief Aliah, chief Jetheth, chief Oholibamah, chief Elah, chief Pinon, chief Kenaz, chief Teman, chief Mibzar, chief Magdiel, and chief Iram. These are the chiefs of Edom.

....

These are the sons of Israel: Reuben, Simeon, Levi, Judah, Issachar, Zebulun, Dan, Joseph, Benjamin, Naphtali, Gad, and Asher. The sons of Judah: Er, Onan, and Shelah; which three were born to him of Shua's daughter the Canaanitess. Er, Judah's firstborn, was wicked in YHWH's sight; and he killed him. Tamar his daughter-in-law bore him Perez and Zerah. All the sons of Judah were five. The sons of Perez: Hezron and Hamul. The sons of Zerah: Zimri, Ethan, Heman, Calcol, and Dara; five of them in all. The son of Carmi: Achar, the troubler of Israel, who committed a trespass in the devoted thing. The son of Ethan: Azariah. The sons also of Hezron, who were born to him: Jerahmeel, Ram, and Chelubai. Ram became the father of Amminadab, and Amminadab became the father of Nahshon, prince of the children of Judah; and Nahshon became the father of Salma, and Salma became the father of Boaz, and Boaz became the father of Obed, and Obed became the father of Jesse; and Jesse became the father of his firstborn Eliab, and Abinadab the second, and Shimea the third, Nethanel the fourth, Raddai the fifth, Ozem the sixth, David the seventh; and their sisters were Zeruiah and Abigail. The sons of Zeruiah: Abishai, Joab, and Asahel, three. Abigail bore Amasa; and the father of Amasa was Jether the Ishmaelite.

Caleb the son of Hezron became the father of children of Azubah his wife, and of Jerioth; and these were her sons: Jesher, Shobab, and Ardon. Azubah died, and Caleb married Ephrath, who bore him

Hur. Hur became the father of Uri, and Uri became the father of Bezalel.

Afterward Hezron went in to the daughter of Machir the father of Gilead, whom he took as wife when he was sixty years old; and she bore him Segub. Segub became the father of Jair, who had twenty-three cities in the land of Gilead. Geshur and Aram took the towns of Jair from them, with Kenath, and its villages, even sixty cities. All these were the sons of Machir the father of Gilead. After Hezron died in Caleb Ephrathah, Abijah Hezron's wife bore him Ashhur the father of Tekoa. The sons of Jerahmeel the firstborn of Hezron were Ram the firstborn, Bunah, Oren, Ozem, and Ahijah. Jerahmeel had another wife, whose name was Atarah. She was the mother of Onam. The sons of Ram the firstborn of Jerahmeel were Maaz, Jamin, and Eker. The sons of Onam were Shammai and Jada. The sons of Shammai: Nadab and Abishur. The name of the wife of Abishur was Abihail; and she bore him Ahban and Molid. The sons of Nadab: Seled and Appaim; but Seled died without children. The son of Appaim: Ishi. The son of Ishi: Sheshan. The son of Sheshan: Ahlai. The sons of Jada the brother of Shammai: Jether and Jonathan; and Jether died without children. The sons of Jonathan: Peleth and Zaza. These were the sons of Jerahmeel. Now Sheshan had no sons, but daughters. Sheshan had a servant, an Egyptian, whose name was Jarha. Sheshan gave his daughter to Jarha his servant as wife; and she bore him Attai. Attai became the father of Nathan, and Nathan became the father of Zabad, and Zabad became the father of Ephlal, and Ephlal became the father of Obed, and Obed became the father of Jehu, and Jehu became the father of Azariah, and Azariah became the father of Helez, and Helez became the father of Eleasah, and Eleasah became the father of Sismai, and Sismai became the father of Shallum, and Shallum became the father of Jekamiah, and Jekamiah became the father of Elishama. The sons of Caleb the brother of Jerahmeel were Mesha his firstborn, who was the father of Ziph; and the sons of Mareshah the father of Hebron. The sons of Hebron: Korah, Tappuah, Rekem, and Shema. Shema became the father of Raham, the father of Jorkeam; and Rekem became the father of Shammai. The son of Shammai was Maon; and Maon was the father of Beth Zur. Ephah, Caleb's concubine, bore Haran, Moza, and Gazez; and Haran became the father of Gazez. The sons of Jahdai: Regem, Jothan, Geshan, Pelet, Ephah, and Shaaph. Maacah, Caleb's concubine, bore Sheber and Tirhanah. She bore also Shaaph the father of Madmannah, Sheva the father of Machbena, and the father of Gibea; and the daughter of Caleb was Achsah. These were the sons of Caleb, the son of Hur, the firstborn of Ephrathah: Shobal the father of Kiriath Jearim, Salma the father of Bethlehem, and Hareph the father of Beth Gader. Shobal the father of Kiriath Jearim had sons: Haroeh, half of the Menuhoth. The families of Kiriath Jearim: the Ithrites, the Puthites, the Shumathites, and the Mishraites; from them came the Zorathites and the Eshtaolites. The sons of Salma: Bethlehem, the Netophathites, Atroth Beth Joab, and half of the Manahathites, the Zorites. The families of scribes who lived at Jabez: the Tirathites, the Shimeathites, and the Sucathites. These are the Kenites who came from Hammath, the father of the house of Rechab.

....

Now these were the sons of David, who were born to him in Hebron: the firstborn, Amnon, of Ahinoam the Jezreelitess; the second, Daniel, of Abigail the Carmelitess; the third, Absalom the son of Maacah the daughter of Talmai king of Geshur; the fourth, Adonijah the son of Haggith; the fifth, Shephatiah of Abital; the sixth, Ithream by Eglah his wife: six were born to him in Hebron; and he reigned there seven years and six months. He reigned thirty-three years in Jerusalem; and these were born to him in Jerusalem: Shimea, Shobab, Nathan, and Solomon, four, of Bathshua the daughter of Ammiel; and Ibhar, Elishama, Eliphelet, Nogah, Nepheg, Japhia, Elishama, Eliada, and Eliphelet, nine. All these were the sons of David, in addition to the sons of the concubines; and Tamar was their sister.

Solomon's son was Rehoboam, Abijah his son, Asa his son, Jehoshaphat his son, Joram his son, Ahaziah his son, Joash his son, Amaziah his son, Azariah his son, Jotham his son, Ahaz his son, Hezekiah his son, Manasseh his son, Amon his son, and Josiah his son. The sons of Josiah: the firstborn Johanan, the second Jehoiakim, the third Zedekiah, and the fourth Shallum. The sons of Jehoiakim: Jeconiah his son, and Zedekiah his son. The sons of Jeconiah, the captive: Shealtiel his son, Malchiram, Pedaiah, Shenazzar, Jekamiah, Hoshama, and Nedabiah. The sons of Pedaiah: Zerubbabel and Shimei. The sons of Zerubbabel: Meshullam and Hananiah; and Shelomith was their sister; and Hashubah, Ohel, Berechiah, Hasadiah, and Jushab Hesed, five. The sons of Hananiah: Pelatiah and Jeshaiah; the sons of Rephaiah, the sons of Arnan, the sons of Obadiah, the sons of Shecaniah. The son of Shecaniah: Shemaiah. The sons of Shemaiah: Hattush, Igal, Bariah, Neariah, and Shaphat, six. The sons of Neariah: Elioenai, Hizkiah, and Azrikam, three. The sons of Elioenai: Hodaviah, Eliashib, Pelaiah, Akkub, Johanan, Delaiah, and Anani, seven.

....

The sons of Judah: Perez, Hezron, Carmi, Hur, and Shobal. Reaiah the son of Shobal became the father of Jahath; and Jahath became the father of Ahumai and Lahad. These are the families of the Zorathites. These were the sons of the father of Etam: Jezreel, Ishma, and Idbash. The name of their sister was Hazzelelponi. Penuel was the father of Gedor and Ezer the father of Hushah. These are the sons of Hur, the firstborn of Ephrathah, the father of Bethlehem. Ashhur the father of Tekoa had two wives, Helah and Naarah. Naarah bore him Ahuzzam, Hepher, Temeni, and Haahashtari. These were the sons of Naarah. The sons of Helah were Zereth, Izhar, and Ethnan. Hakkoz became the father of Anub, Zobebah, and the families of Aharhel the son of Harum.

Jabez was more honorable than his brothers. His mother named him Jabez, saying, "Because I bore him with sorrow."

Jabez called on the God of Israel, saying, "Oh that you would bless me indeed, and enlarge my border! May your hand be with me, and may you keep me from evil, that I may not cause pain!"

God granted him that which he requested. Chelub the brother of Shuhah became the father of Mehir, who was the father of Eshton. Eshton became the father of Beth Rapha, Paseah, and Tehinnah the father of Ir Nahash. These are the men of Recah. The sons of Kenaz: Othniel and Seraiah. The sons of Othniel: Hathath. Meonothai became the father of Ophrah: and Seraiah became the father of Joab the father of Ge Harashim; for they were craftsmen. The sons of Caleb the son of Jephunneh: Iru, Elah, and Naam. The son of Elah: Kenaz. The sons of Jehallelel: Ziph, Ziphah, Tiria, and Asarel. The sons of Ezrah: Jether, Mered, Epher, and Jalon; and she bore Miriam, Shammai, and Ishbah the father of Eshtemoa. His wife the Jewess bore Jered the father of Gedor, Heber the father of Soco, and Jekuthiel the father of Zanoah. These are the sons of Bithiah the daughter of Pharaoh, whom Mered took. The sons of the wife of Hodiah, the sister of Naham, were the father of Keilah the Garmite, and Eshtemoa the Maacathite. The sons of Shimon: Amnon,

Rinnah, Ben Hanan, and Tilon. The sons of Ishi: Zoheth, and Ben Zoheth. The sons of Shelah the son of Judah: Er the father of Lecah, Laadah the father of Mareshah, and the families of the house of those who worked fine linen, of the house of Ashbea; and Jokim, and the men of Cozeba, and Joash, and Saraph, who had dominion in Moab, and Jashubilehem. These records are ancient. These were the potters, and the inhabitants of Netaim and Gederah: they lived there with the king for his work. The sons of Simeon: Nemuel, Jamin, Jarib, Zerah, Shaul; Shallum his son, Mibsam his son, and Mishma his son. The sons of Mishma: Hammuel his son, Zaccur his son, Shimei his son. Shimei had sixteen sons and six daughters; but his brothers didn't have many children, and all their family didn't multiply like the children of Judah. They lived at Beersheba, Moladah, Hazarshual, at Bilhah, at Ezem, at Tolad, at Bethuel, at Hormah, at Ziklag, at Beth Marcaboth, Hazar Susim, at Beth Biri, and at Shaaraim. These were their cities until David's reign. Their villages were Etam, Ain, Rimmon, Tochen, and Ashan, five cities; and all their villages that were around the same cities, to Baal. These were their settlements, and they have their genealogy. Meshobab, Jamlech, Joshah the son of Amaziah, Joel, Jehu the son of Joshibiah, the son of Seraiah, the son of Asiel, Elioenai, Jaakobah, Jeshohaiah, Asaiah, Adiel, Jesimiel, Benaiah, and Ziza the son of Shiphi, the son of Allon, the son of Jedaiah, the son of Shimri, the son of Shemaiah— these mentioned by name were princes in their families. Their fathers' houses increased greatly.

They went to the entrance of Gedor, even to the east side of the valley, to seek pasture for their flocks. They found fat pasture and good, and the land was wide, and quiet, and peaceful; for those who lived there before were descended from Ham. These written by name came in the days of Hezekiah king of Judah, and struck their tents. The Meunim who were found there, and they destroyed them utterly to this day, and lived in their place; because there was pasture there for their flocks. Some of them, even of the sons of Simeon, five hundred men, went to Mount Seir, having for their captains Pelatiah, Neariah, Rephaiah, and Uzziel, the sons of Ishi. They struck the remnant of the Amalekites who escaped, and have lived there to this day.

The sons of Reuben the firstborn of Israel (for he was the firstborn; but, because he defiled his father's couch, his birthright was given to the sons of Joseph the son of Israel; and the genealogy is not to be listed according to the birthright. For Judah prevailed above his brothers, and from him came the prince; but the birthright was Joseph's)— the sons of Reuben the firstborn of Israel: Hanoch, Pallu, Hezron, and Carmi. The sons of Joel: Shemaiah his son, Gog his son, Shimei his son, Micah his son, Reaiah his son, Baal his son, and Beerah his son, whom Tilgath Pilneser king of Assyria carried away captive. He was prince of the Reubenites. His brothers by their families, when the genealogy of their generations was listed: the chief, Jeiel, and Zechariah, and Bela the son of Azaz, the son of Shema, the son of Joel, who lived in Aroer, even to Nebo and Baal Meon; and he lived eastward even to the entrance of the wilderness from the river Euphrates, because their livestock were multiplied in the land of Gilead.

In the days of Saul, they made war with the Hagrites, who fell by their hand; and they lived in their tents throughout all the land east of Gilead. The sons of Gad lived beside them, in the land of Bashan to Salecah: Joel the chief, Shapham the second, Janai, and Shaphat in Bashan. Their brothers of their fathers' houses: Michael, Meshullam, Sheba, Jorai, Jacan, Zia, and Eber, seven. These were the sons of Abihail, the son of Huri, the son of Jaroah, the son of Gilead, the son of Michael, the son of Jeshishai, the son of Jahdo, the son of Buz; Ahi the son of Abdiel, the son of Guni, chief of their fathers' houses. They lived in Gilead in Bashan, and in its towns, and in all the pasture lands of Sharon, as far as their borders. All these were listed by genealogies in the days of Jotham king of Judah, and in the days of Jeroboam king of Israel.

The sons of Reuben, the Gadites, and the half-tribe of Manasseh, of valiant men, men able to bear buckler and sword, and to shoot with bow, and skillful in war, were forty-four thousand seven hundred sixty, that were able to go out to war. They made war with the Hagrites, with Jetur, and Naphish, and Nodab. They were helped against them, and the Hagrites were delivered into their hand, and all who were with them; for they cried to God in the battle, and he answered them, because they put their trust in him. They took away their livestock; of their camels fifty thousand, and of sheep two hundred fifty thousand, and of donkeys two thousand, and of men one hundred thousand. For many fell slain, because the war was of God. They lived in their place until the captivity. The children of the half-tribe of Manasseh lived in the land: they increased from Bashan to

Baal Hermon, Senir, and Mount Hermon. These were the heads of their fathers' houses: even Epher, Ishi, Eliel, Azriel, Jeremiah, Hodaviah, and Jahdiel, mighty men of valor, famous men, heads of their fathers' houses. They trespassed against the God of their fathers, and played the prostitute after the gods of the peoples of the land, whom God destroyed before them. So the God of Israel stirred up the spirit of Pul king of Assyria, and the spirit of Tilgath Pilneser king of Assyria, and he carried them away, even the Reubenites, and the Gadites, and the half-tribe of Manasseh, and brought them to Halah, Habor, Hara, and to the river of Gozan, to this day.

....

The sons of Levi: Gershon, Kohath, and Merari. The sons of Kohath: Amram, Izhar, and Hebron, and Uzziel. The children of Amram: Aaron, Moses, and Miriam. The sons of Aaron: Nadab, Abihu, Eleazar, and Ithamar. Eleazar became the father of Phinehas, Phinehas became the father of Abishua, Abishua became the father of Bukki. Bukki became the father of Uzzi. Uzzi became the father of Zerahiah. Zerahiah became the father of Meraioth. Meraioth became the father of Amariah. Amariah became the father of Ahitub. Ahitub became the father of Zadok. Zadok became the father of Ahimaaz. Ahimaaz became the father of Azariah. Azariah became the father of Johanan. Johanan became the father of Azariah, who executed the priest's office in the house that Solomon built in Jerusalem. Azariah became the father of Amariah. Amariah became the father of Ahitub. Ahitub became the father of Zadok. Zadok became the father of Shallum. Shallum became the father of Hilkiah. Hilkiah became the father of Azariah. Azariah became the father of Seraiah. Seraiah became the father of Jehozadak. Jehozadak went into captivity, when YHWH carried Judah and Jerusalem away by the hand of Nebuchadnezzar.

The sons of Levi: Gershom, Kohath, and Merari. These are the names of the sons of Gershom: Libni and Shimei. The sons of Kohath were Amram, Izhar, Hebron, and Uzziel. The sons of Merari: Mahli and Mushi. These are the families of the Levites according to their fathers' households. Of Gershom: Libni his son, Jahath his son, Zimmah his son, Joah his son, Iddo his son, Zerah his son, and Jeatherai his son. The sons of Kohath: Amminadab his son, Korah his son, Assir his son, Elkanah his son, and Ebiasaph his son, Assir his son, Tahath his son, Uriel his son, Uzziah his son, and Shaul his son. The sons of Elkanah: Amasai and Ahimoth. As for Elkanah, the sons of Elkanah: Zophai his son, Nahath his son, Eliab his son, Jeroham his son, and Elkanah his son. The sons of Samuel: the first-born, Joel, and the second, Abijah. The sons of Merari: Mahli, Libni his son, Shimei his son, Uzzah his son, Shimea his son, Haggiah his son, Asaiah his son. These are they whom David set over the service of song in YHWH's house, after the ark came to rest there. They ministered with song before the tabernacle of the Tent of Meeting, until Solomon had built YHWH's house in Jerusalem. They performed the duties of their office according to their order. These are those who served, and their sons. Of the sons of the Kohathites: Heman the singer, the son of Joel, the son of Samuel, the son of Elkanah, the son of Jeroham, the son of Eliel, the son of Toah, the son of Zuph, the son of Elkanah, the son of Mahath, the son of Amasai, the son of Elkanah, the son of Joel, the son of Azariah, the son of Zephaniah, the son of Tahath, the son of Assir, the son of Ebiasaph, the son of Korah, the son of Izhar, the son of Kohath, the son of Levi, the son of Israel. His brother Asaph, who stood on his right hand, even Asaph the son of Berechiah, the son of Shimea, the son of Michael, the son of Baaseiah, the son of Malchijah, the son of Ethni, the son of Zerah, the son of Adaiah, the son of Ethan, the son of Zimmah, the son of Shimei, the son of Jahath, the son of Gershom, the son of Levi. On the left hand their brothers the sons of Merari: Ethan the son of Kishi, the son of Abdi, the son of Malluch, the son of Hashabiah, the son of Amaziah, the son of Hilkiah, the son of Amzi, the son of Bani, the son of Shemer, the son of Mahli, the son of Mushi, the son of Merari, the son of Levi. Their brothers the Levites were appointed for all the service of the tabernacle of God's house. But Aaron and his sons offered on the altar of burnt offering, and on the altar of incense, for all the work of the most holy place, and to make atonement for Israel, according to all that Moses the servant of God had commanded.

These are the sons of Aaron: Eleazar his son, Phinehas his son, Abishua his son, Bukki his son, Uzzi his son, Zerahiah his son, Meraioth his son, Amariah his son, Ahitub his son, Zadok his son, and Ahimaaz his son. Now these are their dwelling places according to their encampments in their borders: to the sons of Aaron, of the families of the Kohathites (for theirs was the first lot), to them they gave Hebron in the land of Judah, and its pasture lands around it; but the fields of the city, and its villages, they gave to Caleb the son of Jephunneh. To the sons of Aaron they gave the cities of refuge, Hebron; Libnah also with its pasture lands, Jattir, Eshtemoa with its pasture lands, Hilen with its pasture lands, Debir with its pasture lands, Ashan with its pasture lands, and Beth Shemesh with its pasture lands; and out of the tribe of Benjamin, Geba with its pasture lands, Allemeth with its pasture lands, and Anathoth with its pasture lands. All their cities throughout their families were thirteen cities.

To the rest of the sons of Kohath were given by lot, out of the family of the tribe, out of the half-tribe, the half of Manasseh, ten cities. To the sons of Gershom, according to their families, out of the tribe of Issachar, and out of the tribe of Asher, and out of the tribe of Naphtali, and out of the tribe of Manasseh in Bashan, thirteen cities. To the sons of Merari were given by lot, according to their families, out of the tribe of Reuben, and out of the tribe of Gad, and out of the tribe of Zebulun, twelve cities. The children of Israel gave to the Levites the cities with their pasture lands. They gave by lot out of the tribe of the children of Judah, and out of the tribe of the children of Simeon, and out of the tribe of the children of Benjamin, these cities which are mentioned by name. Some of the families of the sons of Kohath had cities of their borders out of the tribe of Ephraim. They gave to them the cities of refuge, Shechem in the hill country of Ephraim with its pasture lands, and Gezer with its pasture lands, Jokmeam with its pasture lands, Beth Horon with its pasture lands, Aijalon with its pasture lands, Gath Rimmon with its pasture lands; and out of the half-tribe of Manasseh, Aner with its pasture lands, and Bileam with its pasture lands, for the rest of the family of the sons of Kohath.

To the sons of Gershom were given, out of the family of the half-tribe of Manasseh, Golan in Bashan with its pasture lands, and Ashtaroth with its pasture lands; and out of the tribe of Issachar, Kedesh with its pasture lands, Daberath with its pasture lands, Ramoth with its pasture lands, and Anem with its pasture lands; and out of the tribe of Asher, Mashal with its pasture lands, Abdon with its pasture lands, Hukok with its pasture lands, and Rehob with its pasture lands; and out of the tribe of Naphtali, Kedesh in Galilee with its pasture lands, Hammon with its pasture lands, and Kiriathaim with its pasture lands.

To the rest of the Levites, the sons of Merari, were given, out of the tribe of Zebulun, Rimmono with its pasture lands, Tabor with its pasture lands; and beyond the Jordan at Jericho, on the east side of the Jordan, were given them, out of the tribe of Reuben, Bezer in the wilderness with its pasture lands, and Jahzah with its pasture lands, Kedemoth with its pasture lands, and Mephaath with its pasture lands; and out of the tribe of Gad, Ramoth in Gilead with its pasture lands, Mahanaim with its pasture lands, Heshbon with its pasture lands, and Jazer with its pasture lands.

....

Of the sons of Issachar: Tola, and Puah, Jashub, and Shimron, four. The sons of Tola: Uzzi, Rephaiah, Jeriel, Jahmai, Ibsam, and Shemuel, heads of their fathers' houses, of Tola; mighty men of valor in their generations. Their number in the days of David was twenty-two thousand six hundred. The son of Uzzi: Izrahiah. The sons of Izrahiah: Michael, Obadiah, Joel, and Isshiah, five; all of them chief men. With them, by their generations, after their fathers' houses, were bands of the army for war, thirty-six thousand; for they had many wives and sons. Their brothers among all the families of Issachar, mighty men of valor, listed in all by genealogy, were eighty-seven thousand. The sons of Benjamin: Bela, Becher, and Jediael, three. The sons of Bela: Ezbon, Uzzi, Uzziel, Jerimoth, and Iri, five; heads of fathers' houses, mighty men of valor; and they were listed by genealogy twenty-two thousand thirty-four. The sons of Becher: Zemirah, Joash, Eliezer, Elioenai, Omri, Jeremoth, Abijah, Anathoth, and Alemeth. All these were the sons of Becher. They were listed by genealogy, after their generations, heads of their fathers' houses, mighty men of valor, twenty thousand two hundred. The son of Jediael: Bilhan. The sons of Bilhan: Jeush, Benjamin, Ehud, Chenaanah, Zethan, Tarshish, and Ahishahar. All these were sons of Jediael, according to the heads of their fathers' households, mighty men of valor, seventeen thousand two hundred, who were able to go out in the army for war. So were Shuppim, Huppim, the sons of Ir, Hushim, and the sons of Aher.

The sons of Naphtali: Jahziel, Guni, Jezer, Shallum, and the sons of Bilhah. The sons of Manasseh: Asriel, whom his concubine the Aramitess bore. She bore Machir the father of Gilead. Machir took a wife of Huppim and Shuppim, whose sister's name was Maacah. The name of the second was Zelophehad; and Zelophehad had daughters. Maacah the wife of Machir bore a son, and she named him Peresh. The name of his brother was Sheresh; and his sons were Ulam and Rakem. The sons of Ulam: Bedan. These were the sons of Gilead the son of Machir, the son of Manasseh. His sister Hammolecheth bore Ishhod, Abiezer, and Mahlah. The sons of Shemida were Ahian, Shechem, Likhi, and Aniam. The sons of Ephraim: Shuthelah, Bered his son, Tahath his son, Eleadah his son, Tahath his son, Zabad his son, Shuthelah his son, Ezer, and Elead, whom the men of Gath who were born in the land killed, because they came down to take away their livestock. Ephraim their father mourned many days, and his brothers came to comfort him. He went in to his wife, and she conceived, and bore a son, and he named him Beriah, because there was trouble with his house. His daughter was Sheerah, who built Beth Horon the lower and the upper, and Uzzen Sheerah. Rephah was his son, and Resheph, and Telah his son, Tahan his son, Ladan his son, Ammihud his son, Elishama his son, Nun his son, and Joshua his son. Their possessions and settlements were Bethel and its towns, and eastward Naaran, and westward Gezer, with its towns; Shechem also and its towns, to Azzah and its towns; and by the borders of the children of Manasseh, Beth Shean and its towns, Taanach and its towns, Megiddo and its towns, and Dor and its towns. The children of Joseph the son of Israel lived in these. The sons of Asher: Imnah, Ishvah, Ishvi, and Beriah. Serah was their sister. The sons of Beriah: Heber and Malchiel, who was the father of Birzaith. Heber became the father of Japhlet, Shomer, Hotham, and Shua their sister. The sons of Japhlet: Pasach, Bimhal, and Ashvath. These are the children of Japhlet. The sons of Shemer: Ahi, Rohgah, Jehubbah, and Aram. The sons of Helem his brother: Zophah, Imna, Shelesh, and Amal. The sons of Zophah: Suah, Harnepher, Shual, Beri, Imrah, Bezer, Hod, Shamma, Shilshah, Ithran, and Beera. The sons of Jether: Jephunneh, Pispa, and Ara. The sons of Ulla: Arah, Hanniel, and Rizia. All these were the children of Asher, heads of the fathers' houses, choice and mighty men of valor, chief of the princes. The number of them listed by genealogy for service in war was twenty-six thousand men.

....

Benjamin became the father of Bela his firstborn, Ashbel the second, Aharah the third, Nohah the fourth, and Rapha the fifth. Bela had sons: Addar, Gera, Abihud, Abishua, Naaman, Ahoah, Gera, Shephuphan, and Huram. These are the sons of Ehud. These are the heads of fathers' households of the inhabitants of Geba, who were carried captive to Manahath: Naaman, Ahijah, and Gera, who carried them captive; and he became the father of Uzza and Ahihud.

Shaharaim became the father of children in the field of Moab, after he had sent them away. Hushim and Baara were his wives. By Hodesh his wife, he became the father of Jobab, Zibia, Mesha, Malcam, Jeuz, Shachia, and Mirmah. These were his sons, heads of fathers' households. By Hushim, he became the father of Abitub and Elpaal. The sons of Elpaal: Eber, Misham, and Shemed, who built Ono and Lod, with its towns; and Beriah, and Shema, who were heads of fathers' households of the inhabitants of Aijalon, who put to flight the inhabitants of Gath; and Ahio, Shashak, Jeremoth, Zebadiah, Arad, Eder, Michael, Ishpah, Joha, the sons of Beriah, Zebadiah, Meshullam, Hizki, Heber, Ishmerai, Izliah, Jobab, the sons of Elpaal, Jakim, Zichri, Zabdi, Elienai, Zillethai, Eliel, Adaiah, Beraiah, Shimrath, the sons of Shimei, Ishpan, Eber, Eliel, Abdon, Zichri, Hanan, Hananiah, Elam, Anthothijah, Iphdeiah, Penuel, the sons of Shashak, Shamsherai, Shehariah, Athaliah, Jaareshiah, Elijah, Zichri, and the sons of Jeroham. These were heads of fathers' households throughout their generations, chief men. These lived in Jerusalem. The father of Gibeon, whose wife's name was Maacah, lived in Gibeon, with his firstborn son Abdon, Zur, Kish, Baal, Nadab, Gedor, Ahio, and Zecher. Mikloth became the father of Shimeah. They also lived with their brothers in Jerusalem, near their brothers. Ner became the father of Kish. Kish became the father of Saul. Saul became the father of Jonathan, Malchishua, Abinadab, and Eshbaal. The son of Jonathan was Merib Baal. Merib Baal became the father of Micah. The sons of Micah: Pithon, Melech, Tarea, and Ahaz. Ahaz became the father of Jehoaddah. Jehoaddah became the father of Alemeth, Azmaveth, and Zimri. Zimri became the father of Moza. Moza became the father of Binea. Raphah was his son, Eleasah his son, and Azel his son. Azel had six sons, whose names are these: Azrikam, Bocheru, Ishmael, Sheariah, Obadiah, and Hanan. All these were the sons of Azel. The sons of Eshek his brother: Ulam his firstborn, Jeush the second, and Eliphelet the third. The sons of Ulam were mighty men of valor, archers, and had many sons, and sons' sons, one hundred fifty. All these were of the sons of Benjamin.

....

So all Israel were listed by genealogies; and behold, they are written in the book of the kings of Israel. Judah was carried away captive to Babylon for their disobedience. Now the first inhabitants who lived in their possessions in their cities were Israel, the priests, the Levites, and the temple servants. In Jerusalem lived of the children of Judah, of the children of Benjamin, and of the children of Ephraim and Manasseh: Uthai the son of Ammihud, the son of Omri, the son of Imri, the son of Bani, of the children of Perez the son of Judah. Of the Shilonites: Asaiah the firstborn, and his sons. Of the sons of Zerah: Jeuel and their brothers, six hundred ninety. Of the sons of Benjamin: Sallu the son of Meshullam, the son of Hodaviah, the son of Hassenuah, and Ibneiah the son of Jeroham, and Elah the son of Uzzi, the son of Michri, and Meshullam the son of Shephatiah, the son of Reuel, the son of Ibnijah; and their brothers, according to their generations, nine hundred fifty-six. All these men were heads of fathers' households by their fathers' houses.

Of the priests: Jedaiah, Jehoiarib, Jachin, and Azariah the son of Hilkiah, the son of Meshullam, the son of Zadok, the son of Meraioth, the son of Ahitub, the ruler of God's house; and Adaiah the son of Jeroham, the son of Pashhur, the son of Malchijah, and Maasai the son of Adiel, the son of Jahzerah, the son of Meshullam, the son of Meshillemith, the son of Immer; and their brothers, heads of their fathers' houses, one thousand seven hundred sixty; very able men for the work of the service of God's house.

Of the Levites: Shemaiah the son of Hasshub, the son of Azrikam, the son of Hashabiah, of the sons of Merari; and Bakbakkar, Heresh, Galal, and Mattaniah the son of Mica, the son of Zichri, the son of Asaph, and Obadiah the son of Shemaiah, the son of Galal, the son of Jeduthun, and Berechiah the son of Asa, the son of Elkanah, who lived in the villages of the Netophathites.

The gatekeepers: Shallum, Akkub, Talmon, Ahiman, and their brothers (Shallum was the chief), who previously served in the king's gate eastward. They were the gatekeepers for the camp of the children of Levi. Shallum the son of Kore, the son of Ebiasaph, the son of Korah, and his brothers, of his father's house, the Korahites, were over the work of the service, keepers of the thresholds of the tent. Their fathers had been over YHWH's camp, keepers of the entry. Phinehas the son of Eleazar was ruler over them in time past, and YHWH was with him. Zechariah the son of Meshelemiah was gatekeeper of the door of the Tent of Meeting. All these who were chosen to be gatekeepers in the thresholds were two hundred twelve. These were listed by genealogy in their villages, whom David and Samuel the seer ordained in their office of trust. So they and their children had the oversight of the gates of YHWH's house, even the house of the tent, as guards. On the four sides were the gatekeepers, toward the east, west, north, and south. Their brothers, in their villages, were to come in every seven days from time to time to be with them: for the four chief gatekeepers, who were Levites, were in an office of trust, and were over the rooms and over the treasuries in God's house. They stayed around God's house, because that duty was on them; and to their duty was its opening morning by morning. Certain of them were in charge of the vessels of service; for these were brought in by count, and these were taken out by count. Some of them also were appointed over the furniture, and over all the vessels of the sanctuary, over the fine flour, the wine, the oil, the frankincense, and the spices.

Some of the sons of the priests prepared the mixing of the spices. Mattithiah, one of the Levites, who was the firstborn of Shallum the Korahite, had the office of trust over the things that were baked in pans. Some of their brothers, of the sons of the Kohathites, were over the show bread, to prepare it every Sabbath. These are the singers, heads of fathers' households of the Levites, who lived in the rooms and were free from other service; for they were employed in their work day and night. These were heads of fathers' households of the Levites, throughout their generations, chief men. These lived at Jerusalem. Jeiel the father of Gibeon, whose wife's name was Maacah, lived in Gibeon with his firstborn son Abdon, Zur, Kish, Baal, Ner, Nadab, Gedor, Ahio, Zechariah, and Mikloth. Mikloth became the father of Shimeam. They also lived with their brothers in Jerusalem, near their brothers. Ner became the father of Kish. Kish became the father of Saul. Saul became the father of Jonathan, Malchishua, Abinadab, and Eshbaal. The son of Jonathan was Merib Baal. Merib Baal became the father of Micah. The sons of Micah: Pithon, Melech, Tahrea, and Ahaz. Ahaz became the father of Jarah. Jarah became the father of Alemeth, Azmaveth, and Zimri. Zimri became the father of Moza. Moza became the father of Binea; and Rephaiah his son, Eleasah his son, and Azel his son. Azel had six sons, whose names are these: Azrikam, Bocheru, Ishmael, Sheariah, Obadiah, and Hanan. These were the sons of Azel.

....

Now the Philistines fought against Israel, and the men of Israel fled from before the Philistines, and fell down slain on Mount Gilboa. The Philistines followed hard after Saul and after his sons; and the Philistines killed Jonathan, Abinadab, and Malchishua, the sons of Saul. The battle went hard against Saul, and the archers overtook him; and he was distressed by reason of the archers. Then Saul said to his armor bearer, "Draw your sword, and thrust me through with it, lest these uncircumcised come and abuse me."

But his armor bearer would not; for he was terrified. Therefore Saul took his sword, and fell on it. When his armor bearer saw that Saul was dead, he likewise fell on his sword, and died. So Saul died with his three sons; and all his house died together. When all the men of Israel who were in the valley saw that they fled, and that Saul and his sons were dead, they abandoned their cities, and fled; and the Philistines came and lived in them.

On the next day, when the Philistines came to strip the slain, they found Saul and his sons fallen on Mount Gilboa. They stripped him, and took his head and his armor, and sent into the land of the Philistines all around, to carry the news to their idols, and to the people. They put his armor in the house of their gods, and fastened his head in the house of Dagon. When all Jabesh Gilead heard all that the Philistines had done to Saul, all the valiant men arose, and took away the body of Saul, and the bodies of his sons, and brought them to Jabesh, and buried their bones under the oak in Jabesh, and fasted seven days. So Saul died for his trespass which he committed against YHWH, because of YHWH's word, which he didn't keep; and also because he asked counsel of one who had a familiar spirit, to inquire, and didn't inquire of YHWH. Therefore he killed him, and turned the kingdom over to David the son of Jesse.

....

Then all Israel gathered themselves to David to Hebron, saying, "Behold, we are your bone and your flesh. In times past, even when Saul was king, it was you who led out and brought in Israel. YHWH your God said to you, 'You shall be shepherd of my people Israel, and you shall be prince over my people Israel.'"

So all the elders of Israel came to the king to Hebron; and David made a covenant with them in Hebron before YHWH; and they anointed David king over Israel, according to YHWH's word by Samuel. David and all Israel went to Jerusalem (also called Jebus); and the Jebusites, the inhabitants of the land, were there. The inhabitants of Jebus said to David, "You will not come in here." Nevertheless David took the stronghold of Zion. The same is David's city. David said, "Whoever strikes the Jebusites first shall be chief and captain." Joab the son of Zeruiah went up first, and was made chief. David lived in the stronghold; therefore they called it David's city. He built the city all around, from Millo even around; and Joab repaired the rest of the city. David grew greater and greater; for YHWH of Armies was with him. Now these are the chief of the mighty men whom David had, who showed themselves strong with him in his kingdom, together with all Israel, to make him king, according to YHWH's word concerning Israel.

This is the number of the mighty men whom David had: Jashobeam, the son of a Hachmonite, the chief of the thirty; he lifted up his spear against three hundred and killed them at one time. After him was Eleazar the son of Dodo, the Ahohite, who was one of the three mighty men. He was with David at Pasdammim, and there the Philistines were gathered together to battle, where there was a plot of ground full of barley; and the people fled from before the Philistines. They stood in the middle of the plot, defended it, and killed the Philistines; and YHWH saved them by a great victory. Three of the thirty chief men went down to the rock to David, into the cave of Adullam; and the army of the Philistines were encamped in the valley of Rephaim. David was then in the stronghold, and the garrison of the Philistines was in Bethlehem at that time. David longed, and said, "Oh that one would give me water to drink from the well of Bethlehem, which is by the gate!"

The three broke through the army of the Philistines, and drew water out of the well of Bethlehem, that was by the gate, and took it, and brought it to David; but David would not drink any of it, but poured it out to YHWH, and said, "My God forbid me, that I should do this! Shall I drink the blood of these men who have put their lives in jeopardy?" For they risked their lives to bring it. Therefore he would not drink it. The three mighty men did these things.

Abishai, the brother of Joab, he was chief of the three; for he lifted up his spear against three hundred and killed them, and had a name among the three. Of the three, he was more honorable than the two, and was made their captain; however he wasn't included in the three. Benaiah the son of Jehoiada, the son of a valiant man of Kabzeel, who had done mighty deeds, killed the two sons of Ariel of Moab. He also went down and killed a lion in the middle of a pit on a snowy day. He killed an Egyptian, a man of great stature, five cubits high. In the Egyptian's hand was a spear like a weaver's beam; and he went down to him with a staff, plucked the spear out of the Egyptian's hand, and killed him with his own spear. Benaiah the son of Jehoiada did these things, and had a name among the three mighty men. Behold, he was more honorable than the thirty, but he didn't attain to the three; and David set him over his guard.

The mighty men of the armies also include Asahel the brother of Joab, Elhanan the son of Dodo of Bethlehem, Shammoth the Harorite, Helez the Pelonite, Ira the son of Ikkesh the Tekoite, Abiezer the Anathothite, Sibbecai the Hushathite, Ilai the Ahohite, Maharai the Netophathite, Heled the son of Baanah the Netophathite, Ithai the son of Ribai of Gibeah of the children of Benjamin, Benaiah the Pirathonite, Hurai of the brooks of Gaash, Abiel the Arbathite, Azmaveth the Baharumite, Eliahba the Shaalbonite, the sons of Hashem the Gizonite, Jonathan the son of Shagee the Hararite, Ahiam the son of Sacar the Hararite, Eliphal the son of Ur, Hepher the Mecherathite, Ahijah the Pelonite, Hezro the Carmelite, Naarai the son of Ezbai, Joel the brother of Nathan, Mibhar the son of Hagri, Zelek the Ammonite, Naharai the Berothite, the armor bearer of Joab the son of Zeruiah, Ira the Ithrite, Gareb the Ithrite, Uriah the Hittite, Zabad the son of Ahlai, Adina the son of Shiza the Reubenite, a chief of the Reubenites, and thirty with him, Hanan the son of Maacah, and Joshaphat the Mithnite, Uzzia the Ashterathite, Shama and Jeiel the sons of Hotham the Aroerite, Jediael the son of Shimri, and Joha his brother, the Tizite, Eliel the Mahavite, and Jeribai, and Joshaviah, the sons of Elnaam, and Ithmah the Moabite, Eliel, and Obed, and Jaasiel the Mezobaite.

....

Now these are those who came to David to Ziklag, while he was a fugitive from Saul the son of Kish. They were among the mighty men, his helpers in war. They were armed with bows, and could use both the right hand and the left in slinging stones and in shooting arrows from the bow. They were of Saul's relatives of the tribe of Benjamin. The chief was Ahiezer, then Joash, the sons of Shemaah the Gibeathite; Jeziel and Pelet, the sons of Azmaveth; Beracah; Jehu the Anathothite; Ishmaiah the Gibeonite, a mighty man among the thirty and a leader of the thirty; Jeremiah; Jahaziel; Johanan; Jozabad the Gederathite; Eluzai; Jerimoth; Bealiah; Shemariah; Shephatiah the Haruphite; Elkanah, Isshiah Azarel, Joezer, and Jashobeam, the Korahites; and Joelah and Zebadiah, the sons of Jeroham of Gedor.

Some Gadites joined David in the stronghold in the wilderness, mighty men of valor, men trained for war, who could handle shield and spear; whose faces were like the faces of lions, and they were as swift as the gazelles on the mountains: Ezer the chief, Obadiah the second, Eliab the third, Mishmannah the fourth, Jeremiah the fifth, Attai the sixth, Eliel the seventh, Johanan the eighth, Elzabad the ninth, Jeremiah the tenth, and Machbannai the eleventh. These of the sons of Gad were captains of the army: he who was least was equal to one hundred, and the greatest to one thousand. These are those who went over the Jordan in the first month, when it had overflowed all its banks; and they put to flight all who lived in the valleys, both toward the east and toward the west. Some of the children of Benjamin and Judah came to the stronghold to David. David went out to meet them, and answered them, "If you have come peaceably to me to help me, my heart will be united with you; but if you have come to betray me to my adversaries, since there is no wrong in my hands, may the God of our fathers see this and rebuke it." Then the Spirit came on Amasai, who was chief of the thirty, and he said, "We are yours, David, and on your side, you son of Jesse. Peace, peace be to you, and peace be to your helpers; for your God helps you." Then David received them, and made them captains of the band. Some of Manasseh also joined David, when he came with the Philistines against Saul to battle; but they didn't help them; for the lords of the Philistines sent him away after consultation, saying, "He will desert to his master Saul to the jeopardy of our heads."

As he went to Ziklag, some from Manasseh joined him: Adnah, Jozabad, Jediael, Michael, Jozabad, Elihu, and Zillethai, captains of thousands who were of Manasseh. They helped David against the band of rovers; for they were all mighty men of valor, and were captains in the army. For from day to day men came to David to help him, until there was a great army, like God's army.

These are the numbers of the heads of those who were armed for war, who came to David to Hebron, to turn the kingdom of Saul to him, according to YHWH's word. The children of Judah who bore shield and spear were six thousand eight hundred, armed for war. Of the children of Simeon, mighty men of valor for the war: seven thousand one hundred. Of the children of Levi: four thousand six hundred. Jehoiada was the leader of the household of Aaron; and with him were three thousand seven hundred, and Zadok, a young man mighty of valor, and of his father's house twenty-two captains.

Of the children of Benjamin, Saul's relatives: three thousand, for until then, the greatest part of them had kept their allegiance to Saul's house. Of the children of Ephraim: twenty thousand eight hundred, mighty men of valor, famous men in their fathers' houses. Of the half-tribe of Manasseh: eighteen thousand, who were mentioned by name, to come and make David king. Of the children of Issachar, men who had understanding of the times, to know what Israel ought to do, their heads were two hundred; and all their brothers were at their command. Of Zebulun, such as were able to go out in the army, who could set the battle in array, with all kinds of instruments of war: fifty thousand who could command and were not of double heart. Of Naphtali: one thousand captains, and with them with shield and spear thirty-seven thousand. Of the Danites who could set the battle in array: twenty-eight thousand six hundred. Of Asher, such as were able to go out in the army, who could set the battle in array: forty thousand. On the other side of the Jordan, of the Reubenites, the Gadites, and of the half-tribe of Manasseh, with all kinds of instruments of war for the battle: one hundred twenty thousand. All these were men of war, who could order the battle array, and came with a perfect heart to Hebron, to make David king over all Israel; and all the rest also of Israel were of one heart to make David king. They were there with David three days, eating and drinking; for their brothers had supplied provisions for them. Moreover those who were near to them, as far as Issachar, Zebulun, and Naphtali, brought bread on donkeys, on camels, on mules, and on oxen: supplies of flour, cakes of figs, clusters of raisins, wine, oil, cattle, and sheep in abundance; for there was joy in Israel.

....

David consulted with the captains of thousands and of hundreds, even with every leader. David said to all the assembly of Israel, "If it seems good to you, and if it is of YHWH our God, let's send word everywhere to our brothers who are left in all the land of Israel, with whom the priests and Levites are in their cities that have pasture lands, that they may gather themselves to us. Also, let's bring the ark of our God back to us again; for we didn't seek it in the days of Saul."

All the assembly said that they would do so; for the thing was right in the eyes of all the people. So David assembled all Israel together, from the Shihor the brook of Egypt even to the entrance of Hamath, to bring God's ark from Kiriath Jearim.

David went up with all Israel to Baalah, that is, to Kiriath Jearim, which belonged to Judah, to bring up from there God YHWH's ark that sits above the cherubim, that is called by the Name. They carried God's ark on a new cart, and brought it out of Abinadab's house; and Uzza and Ahio drove the cart. David and all Israel played before God with all their might, even with songs, with harps, with stringed instruments, with tambourines, with cymbals, and with trumpets. When they came to Chidon's threshing floor, Uzza put out his hand to hold the ark; for the oxen stumbled. YHWH's anger burned against Uzza, and he struck him, because he put his hand on the ark; and he died there before God. David was displeased, because YHWH had broken out against Uzza. He called that place Perez Uzza, to this day. David was afraid of God that day, saying, "How can I bring God's ark home to me?" So David didn't move the ark with him into David's city, but carried it aside into Obed-Edom the Gittite's house. God's ark remained with the family of Obed-Edom in his house three months; and YHWH blessed Obed-Edom's house and all that he had.

....

Hiram king of Tyre sent messengers to David with cedar trees, masons, and carpenters, to build him a house. David perceived that YHWH had established him king over Israel; for his kingdom was exalted on high, for his people Israel's sake. David took more wives at Jerusalem, and David became the father of more sons and daughters. These are the names of the children whom he had in Jerusalem: Shammua, Shobab, Nathan, Solomon, Ibhar, Elishua, Elpelet, Nogah, Nepheg, Japhia, Elishama, Beeliada, and Eliphelet.

When the Philistines heard that David was anointed king over all Israel, all the Philistines went up to seek David; and David heard of it, and went out against them. Now the Philistines had come and made a raid in the valley of Rephaim. David inquired of God, saying, "Shall I go up against the Philistines? Will you deliver them into my hand?"

YHWH said to him, "Go up; for I will deliver them into your hand."

So they came up to Baal Perazim, and David defeated them there. David said, God has broken my enemies by my hand, like waters breaking out. Therefore they called the name of that place Baal Perazim. They left their gods there; and David gave a command, and they were burned with fire.

The Philistines made a another raid in the valley. David inquired again of God; and God said to him, "You shall not go up after them. Turn away from them, and come on them opposite the mulberry trees. When you hear the sound of marching in the tops of the mulberry trees, then go out to battle; for God has gone out before you to strike the army of the Philistines."

David did as God commanded him; and they attacked the army of the Philistines from Gibeon even to Gezer. The fame of David went out into all lands; and YHWH brought the fear of him on all nations.

....

David made himself houses in David's city; and he prepared a place for God's ark, and pitched a tent for it. Then David said, "No one ought to carry God's ark but the Levites. For YHWH has chosen them to carry God's ark, and to minister to him forever."

David assembled all Israel at Jerusalem, to bring up YHWH's ark to its place, which he had prepared for it. David gathered together the sons of Aaron and the Levites: of the sons of Kohath, Uriel the chief, and his brothers one hundred twenty; of the sons of Merari, Asaiah the chief, and his brothers two hundred twenty; of the sons of Gershom, Joel the chief, and his brothers one hundred thirty; of the sons of Elizaphan, Shemaiah the chief, and his brothers two hundred; of the sons of Hebron, Eliel the chief, and his brothers eighty; of the sons of Uzziel, Amminadab the chief, and his brothers one hundred twelve. David called for Zadok and Abiathar the priests, and for the Levites, for Uriel, Asaiah, Joel, Shemaiah, Eliel, and Amminadab, and said to them, "You are the heads of the fathers' households of the Levites. Sanctify yourselves, both you and your brothers, that you may bring the ark of YHWH, the God of Israel, up to the place that I have prepared for it. For because you didn't carry it at first, YHWH our God broke out in anger against us, because we didn't seek him according to the ordinance."

So the priests and the Levites sanctified themselves to bring up the ark of YHWH, the God of Israel. The children of the Levites bore God's ark on their shoulders with its poles, as Moses commanded according to YHWH's word. David spoke to the chief of the Levites to appoint their brothers as singers with instruments of music, stringed instruments, harps, and cymbals, sounding aloud and lifting up their voices with joy. So the Levites appointed Heman the son of Joel; and of his brothers, Asaph the son of Berechiah; and of the sons of Merari their brothers, Ethan the son of Kushaiah; and with them their brothers of the second rank, Zechariah, Ben, Jaaziel, Shemiramoth, Jehiel, Unni, Eliab, Benaiah, Maaseiah, Mattithiah, Eliphelehu, Mikneiah, Obed-Edom, and Jeiel, the doorkeepers. So the singers, Heman, Asaph, and Ethan, were given cymbals of bronze to sound aloud; and Zechariah, Aziel, Shemiramoth, Jehiel, Unni, Eliab, Maaseiah, and Benaiah, with stringed instruments set to Alamoth; and Mattithiah, Eliphelehu, Mikneiah, Obed-Edom, Jeiel, and Azaziah, with harps tuned to the eight-stringed lyre, to lead. Chenaniah, chief of the Levites, was over the singing. He taught the singers, because he was skillful. Berechiah and Elkanah were doorkeepers for the ark. Shebaniah, Joshaphat, Nethanel, Amasai, Zechariah, Benaiah, and Eliezer, the priests, blew the trumpets before God's ark; and Obed-Edom and Jehiah were doorkeepers for the ark.

So David, the elders of Israel, and the captains over thousands, went to bring the ark of YHWH's covenant up out of the house of Obed-Edom with joy. When God helped the Levites who bore the ark of YHWH's covenant, they sacrificed seven bulls and seven rams. David was clothed with a robe of fine linen, as were all the Levites who bore the ark, the singers, and Chenaniah the choir master with the singers; and David had an ephod of linen on him. Thus all Israel brought the ark of YHWH's covenant up with shouting, with sound of the cornet, with trumpets, and with cymbals, sounding aloud with stringed instruments and harps. As the ark of YHWH's covenant came to David's city, Michal the daughter of Saul looked out at the window, and saw king David dancing and playing; and she despised him in her heart.

....

They brought in God's ark, and set it in the middle of the tent that David had pitched for it; and they offered burnt offerings and peace offerings before God. When David had finished offering the burnt offering and the peace offerings, he blessed the people in YHWH's name. He gave to everyone of Israel, both man and woman, to everyone a loaf of bread, a portion of meat, and a cake of raisins. He appointed some of the Levites to minister before YHWH's ark, and to commemorate, to thank, and to praise YHWH, the God of Israel: Asaph the chief, and second to him Zechariah, then Jeiel, Shemiramoth, Jehiel, Mattithiah, Eliab, Benaiah, Obed-Edom, and Jeiel, with stringed instruments and with harps; and Asaph with cymbals, sounding aloud; with Benaiah and Jahaziel the priests with trumpets continually, before the ark of the covenant of God.

Then on that day David first ordained to give thanks to YHWH, by the hand of Asaph and his brothers.

> *Oh give thanks to YHWH.*
> *Call on his name.*
> *Make what he has done known among the peoples.*
> *Sing to him.*
> *Sing praises to him.*
> *Tell of all his marvelous works.*
> *Glory in his holy name.*
> *Let the heart of those who seek YHWH rejoice.*
> *Seek YHWH and his strength.*
> *Seek his face forever more.*
> *Remember his marvelous works that he has done,*
> *his wonders, and the judgments of his mouth,*
> *you offspring of Israel his servant,*
> *you children of Jacob, his chosen ones.*
> *He is YHWH our God.*
> *His judgments are in all the earth.*
> *Remember his covenant forever,*
> *the word which he commanded to a thousand generations,*
> *the covenant which he made with Abraham,*
> *his oath to Isaac.*
> *He confirmed it to Jacob for a statute,*
> *and to Israel for an everlasting covenant,*
> *saying, "I will give you the land of Canaan,*
> *The lot of your inheritance,"*
> *when you were but a few men in number,*
> *yes, very few, and foreigners were in it.*
> *They went about from nation to nation,*
> *from one kingdom to another people.*
> *He allowed no man to do them wrong.*
> *Yes, he reproved kings for their sakes,*
> *"Don't touch my anointed ones!*
> *Do my prophets no harm!"*
> *Sing to YHWH, all the earth!*
> *Display his salvation from day to day.*

Declare his glory among the nations,
  and his marvelous works among all the peoples.
For great is YHWH, *and greatly to be praised.*
  He also is to be feared above all gods.
For all the gods of the peoples are idols,
  but YHWH *made the heavens.*
Honor and majesty are before him.
  Strength and gladness are in his place.
Ascribe to YHWH, *you relatives of the peoples,*
  ascribe to YHWH *glory and strength!*
Ascribe to YHWH *the glory due to his name.*
  Bring an offering, and come before him.
  Worship YHWH *in holy array.*
Tremble before him, all the earth.
  The world also is established that it can't be moved.
Let the heavens be glad,
  and let the earth rejoice!
  *Let them say among the nations, "*YHWH *reigns!"*
Let the sea roar, and its fullness!
  Let the field exult, and all that is in it!
Then the trees of the forest will sing for joy before YHWH,
  for he comes to judge the earth.
Oh give thanks to YHWH, *for he is good,*
  for his loving kindness endures forever.
Say, "Save us, God of our salvation!
  Gather us together and deliver us from the nations,
  to give thanks to your holy name,
  to triumph in your praise."
Blessed be YHWH, *the God of Israel,*
  from everlasting even to everlasting.

All the people said, "Amen," and praised YHWH.

So he left Asaph and his brothers there before the ark of YHWH's covenant, to minister before the ark continually, as every day's work required; and Obed-Edom with their brothers, sixty-eight; Obed-Edom also the son of Jeduthun and Hosah to be doorkeepers; and Zadok the priest, and his brothers the priests, before YHWH's tabernacle in the high place that was at Gibeon, to offer burnt offerings to YHWH on the altar of burnt offering continually morning and evening, even according to all that is written in YHWH's law, which he commanded to Israel; and with them Heman and Jeduthun, and the rest who were chosen, who were mentioned by name, to give thanks to YHWH, because his loving kindness endures forever; and with them Heman and Jeduthun with trumpets and cymbals for those that should sound aloud, and with instruments for the songs of God; and the sons of Jeduthun to be at the gate. All the people departed, each man to his house; and David returned to bless his house.

....

When David lived in his house, David said to Nathan the prophet, "Behold, I dwell in a house of cedar, but the ark of YHWH's covenant is in a tent."

Nathan said to David, "Do all that is in your heart; for God is with you."

That same night, the word of God came to Nathan, saying, "Go and tell David my servant, 'YHWH says, "You shall not build me a house to dwell in; for I have not lived in a house since the day that I brought up Israel to this day, but have gone from tent to tent, and from one tent to another. In all places in which I have walked with all Israel, did I speak a word with any of the judges of Israel, whom I commanded to be shepherd of my people, saying, 'Why have you not built me a house of cedar?'"'

"Now therefore, you shall tell my servant David, 'YHWH of Armies says, "I took you from the sheep pen, from following the sheep, to be prince over my people Israel. I have been with you wherever you have gone, and have cut off all your enemies from before you. I will make you a name like the name of the great ones who are in the earth. I will appoint a place for my people Israel, and will plant them, that they may dwell in their own place, and be moved no more. The children of wickedness will not waste them any more, as at the first, and from the day that I commanded judges to be over my people Israel. I will subdue all your enemies. Moreover I tell you that YHWH will build you a house. It will happen, when your days are fulfilled that you must go to be with your fathers, that I will set up your offspring after you, who will be of your sons; and I will establish his kingdom. He will build me a house, and I will establish his throne forever. I will be his father, and he will be my son. I will not take my loving kindness away from him, as I took it from him that was before you; but I will settle him in my house and in my kingdom forever. His throne will be established forever."'" According to all these words, and according to all this vision, so Nathan spoke to David.

Then David the king went in, and sat before YHWH; and he said, "Who am I, YHWH God, and what is my house, that you have brought me this far? This was a small thing in your eyes, God; but you have spoken of your servant's house for a great while to come, and have respected me according to the standard of a man of high degree, YHWH God. What can David say yet more to you concerning the honor which is done to your servant? For you know your servant. YHWH, for your servant's sake, and according to your own heart, you have done all this greatness, to make known all these great things. YHWH, there is no one like you, neither is there any God besides you, according to all that we have heard with our ears. What one nation in the earth is like your people Israel, whom God went to redeem to himself for a people, to make you a name by great and awesome things, in driving out nations from before your people, whom you redeem out of Egypt? For you made your people Israel your own people forever; and you, YHWH, became their God. Now, YHWH, let the word that you have spoken concerning your servant, and concerning his house, be established forever, and do as you have spoken. Let your name be established and magnified forever, saying, 'YHWH of Armies is the God of Israel, even a God to Israel. The house of David your servant is established before you.' For you, my God, have revealed to your servant that you will build him a house. Therefore your servant has found courage to pray before you. Now, YHWH, you are God, and have promised this good thing to your servant. Now it has pleased you to bless the house of your servant, that it may continue forever before you; for you, YHWH, have blessed, and it is blessed forever."

....

After this, David defeated the Philistines and subdued them, and took Gath and its towns out of the hand of the Philistines. He defeated Moab; and the Moabites became servants to David, and brought tribute. David defeated Hadadezer king of Zobah to Hamath, as he went to establish his dominion by the river Euphrates. David took from him one thousand chariots, seven thousand horsemen, and twenty thousand footmen; and David hamstrung all the chariot horses, but reserved of them enough for one hundred chariots. When the Syrians of Damascus came to help Hadadezer king of Zobah, David struck twenty-two thousand men of the Syrians. Then David put garrisons in Syria of Damascus; and the Syrians became servants to David, and brought tribute. YHWH gave victory to David wherever he went. David took the shields of gold that were on the servants of Hadadezer, and brought them to Jerusalem. From Tibhath and from Cun, cities of Hadadezer, David took very much bronze, with which Solomon made the bronze sea, the pillars, and the vessels of bronze.

When Tou king of Hamath heard that David had struck all the army of Hadadezer king of Zobah, he sent Hadoram his son to king David, to Greet him, and to bless him, because he had fought against Hadadezer and struck him (for Hadadezer had wars with Tou); and he had with him all kinds of vessels of gold and silver and bronze. King David also dedicated these to YHWH, with the silver and the gold that he carried away from all the nations; from Edom, from Moab, from the children of Ammon, from the Philistines, and from Amalek. Moreover Abishai the son of Zeruiah struck eighteen thousand of the Edomites in the Valley of Salt. He put garrisons in Edom; and all the Edomites became servants to David. YHWH gave victory to David wherever he went.

David reigned over all Israel; and he executed justice and righteousness for all his people. Joab the son of Zeruiah was over the army; Jehoshaphat the son of Ahilud was recorder; Zadok the son of Ahitub, and Abimelech the son of Abiathar, were priests; Shavsha was scribe; and Benaiah the son of Jehoiada was over the Cherethites and the Pelethites; and the sons of David were chief officials serving the king.

....

After this, Nahash the king of the children of Ammon died, and his son reigned in his place. David said, "I will show kindness to Hanun the son of Nahash, because his father showed kindness to me."

So David sent messengers to comfort him concerning his father. David's servants came into the land of the children of Ammon to Hanun, to comfort him. But the princes of the children of Ammon said to Hanun, "Do you think that David honors your father, in that he has sent comforters to you? Haven't his servants come to you to search, to overthrow, and to spy out the land?" So Hanun took David's servants, shaved them, and cut off their garments in the middle at their buttocks, and sent them away. Then some people went and told David how the men were treated. He sent to meet them; for the men were greatly humiliated. The king said, "Stay at Jericho until your beards have grown, and then return."

When the children of Ammon saw that they had made themselves odious to David, Hanun and the children of Ammon sent one thousand talents of silver to hire chariots and horsemen out of Mesopotamia, out of Aram-maacah, and out of Zobah. So they hired for themselves thirty-two thousand chariots, and the king of Maacah with his people, who came and encamped near Medeba. The children of Ammon gathered themselves together from their cities, and came to battle. When David heard of it, he sent Joab with all the army of the mighty men. The children of Ammon came out, and put the battle in array at the gate of the city; and the kings who had come were by themselves in the field. Now when Joab saw that the battle was set against him before and behind, he chose some of all the choice men of Israel, and put them in array against the Syrians. The rest of the people he committed into the hand of Abishai his brother; and they put themselves in array against the children of Ammon. He said, "If the Syrians are too strong for me, then you are to help me; but if the children of Ammon are too strong for you, then I will help you. Be courageous, and let's be strong for our people and for the cities of our God. May YHWH do that which seems good to him."

So Joab and the people who were with him came near to the front of the Syrians to the battle; and they fled before him. When the children of Ammon saw that the Syrians had fled, they likewise fled before Abishai his brother, and entered into the city. Then Joab came to Jerusalem.

When the Syrians saw that they were defeated by Israel, they sent messengers, and called out the Syrians who were beyond the River, with Shophach the captain of the army of Hadadezer leading them. David was told that; so he gathered all Israel together, passed over the Jordan, came to them, and set the battle in array against them. So when David had put the battle in array against the Syrians, they fought with him. The Syrians fled before Israel; and David killed of the Syrian men seven thousand chariots, and forty thousand footmen, and also killed Shophach the captain of the army. When the servants of Hadadezer saw that they were defeated by Israel, they made peace with David, and served him. The Syrians would not help the children of Ammon any more.

....

At the time of the return of the year, at the time when kings go out, Joab led out the army, and wasted the country of the children of Ammon, and came and besieged Rabbah. But David stayed at Jerusalem. Joab struck Rabbah, and overthrew it. David took the crown of their king from off his head, and found it to weigh a talent of gold, and there were precious stones in it. It was set on David's head, and he brought very much plunder out of the city. He brought out the people who were in it, and had them cut with saws, with iron picks, and with axes. David did so to all the cities of the children of Ammon. Then David and all the people returned to Jerusalem.

After this, war arose at Gezer with the Philistines. Then Sibbecai the Hushathite killed Sippai, of the sons of the giant; and they were subdued.

Again there was war with the Philistines; and Elhanan the son of Jair killed Lahmi the brother of Goliath the Gittite, the staff of whose spear was like a weaver's beam. There was again war at Gath, where there was a man of great stature, who had twenty-four fingers and toes, six on each hand, and six on each foot; and he also was born to the giant. When he defied Israel, Jonathan the son of Shimea David's brother killed him. These were born to the giant in Gath; and they fell by the hand of David, and by the hand of his servants.

....

Satan stood up against Israel, and moved David to take a census of Israel. David said to Joab and to the princes of the people, "Go, count Israel from Beersheba even to Dan; and bring me word, that I may know how many there are."

Joab said, "May YHWH make his people a hundred times as many as they are. But, my lord the king, aren't they all my lord's servants? Why does my lord require this thing? Why will he be a cause of guilt to Israel?"

Nevertheless the king's word prevailed against Joab. Therefore Joab departed, and went throughout all Israel, then came to Jerusalem. Joab gave up the sum of the census of the people to David. All those of Israel were one million one hundred thousand men who drew a sword; and in Judah were four hundred seventy thousand men who drew a sword. But he didn't count Levi and Benjamin among them; for the king's word was abominable to Joab.

God was displeased with this thing; therefore he struck Israel. David said to God, "I have sinned greatly, in that I have done this thing. But now put away, I beg you, the iniquity of your servant; for

I have done very foolishly."

YHWH spoke to Gad, David's seer, saying, "Go and speak to David, saying, 'YHWH says, "I offer you three things. Choose one of them, that I may do it to you."'"

So Gad came to David, and said to him, "YHWH says, 'Take your choice: either three years of famine; or three months to be consumed before your foes, while the sword of your enemies overtakes you; or else three days the sword of YHWH, even pestilence in the land, and YHWH's angel destroying throughout all the borders of Israel. Now therefore consider what answer I shall return to him who sent me.'"

David said to Gad, "I am in distress. Let me fall, I pray, into YHWH's hand; for his mercies are very great. Don't let me fall into man's hand."

So YHWH sent a pestilence on Israel, and seventy thousand men of Israel fell. God sent an angel to Jerusalem to destroy it. As he was about to destroy, YHWH saw, and he relented of the disaster, and said to the destroying angel, "It is enough. Now withdraw your hand." YHWH's angel was standing by the threshing floor of Ornan the Jebusite. David lifted up his eyes, and saw YHWH's angel standing between earth and the sky, having a drawn sword in his hand stretched out over Jerusalem.

Then David and the elders, clothed in sackcloth, fell on their faces. David said to God, "Isn't it I who commanded the people to be counted? It is even I who have sinned and done very wickedly; but these sheep, what have they done? Please let your hand, O YHWH my God, be against me, and against my father's house; but not against your people, that they should be plagued."

Then YHWH's angel commanded Gad to tell David that David should go up and raise an altar to YHWH on the threshing floor of Ornan the Jebusite. David went up at the saying of Gad, which he spoke in YHWH's name.

Ornan turned back, and saw the angel; and his four sons who were with him hid themselves. Now Ornan was threshing wheat. As David came to Ornan, Ornan looked and saw David, and went out of the threshing floor, and bowed himself to David with his face to the ground.

Then David said to Ornan, "Give me the place of this threshing floor, that I may build an altar to YHWH on it. You shall sell it to me for the full price, that the plague may be stopped from afflicting the people."

Ornan said to David, "Take it for yourself, and let my lord the king do that which is good in his eyes. Behold, I give the oxen for burnt offerings, and the threshing instruments for wood, and the wheat for the meal offering. I give it all."

King David said to Ornan, "No; but I will most certainly buy it for the full price. For I will not take that which is yours for YHWH, nor offer a burnt offering that costs me nothing."

So David gave to Ornan six hundred shekels of gold by weight for the place. David built an altar to YHWH there, and offered burnt offerings and peace offerings, and called on YHWH; and he answered him from the sky by fire on the altar of burnt offering.

Then YHWH commanded the angel, and he put his sword back into its sheath. At that time, when David saw that YHWH had answered him in the threshing floor of Ornan the Jebusite, then he sacrificed there. For YHWH's tabernacle, which Moses made in the wilderness, and the altar of burnt offering, were at that time in the high place at Gibeon. But David couldn't go before it to inquire of God; for he was afraid because of the sword of YHWH's angel.

....

Then David said, "This is the house of YHWH God, and this is the altar of burnt offering for Israel."

David gave orders to gather together the foreigners who were in the land of Israel; and he set masons to cut dressed stones to build God's house. David prepared iron in abundance for the nails for the doors of the gates, and for the couplings; and bronze in abundance without weight; and cedar trees without number, for the Sidonians and the people of Tyre brought cedar trees in abundance to David. David said, "Solomon my son is young and tender, and the house that is to be built for YHWH must be exceedingly magnificent, of fame and of glory throughout all countries. I will therefore make preparation for it." So David prepared abundantly before his death. Then he called for Solomon his son, and commanded him to build a house for YHWH, the God of Israel. David said to Solomon his son, "As for me, it was in my heart to build a house to the name of YHWH my God. But YHWH's word came to me, saying, 'You have shed blood abundantly, and have made great wars. You shall not build a house to my name, because you have shed much blood on the earth in my sight. Behold, a son shall be born to you, who shall be a man of peace. I will give him rest from all his enemies all around; for his name shall be Solomon, and I will give peace and quietness to Israel in his days. He shall build a house for my name; and he will be my son, and I will be his father; and I will establish the throne of his kingdom over Israel forever.' Now, my son, may YHWH be with you and prosper you, and build the house of YHWH your God, as he has spoken concerning you. May YHWH give you discretion and understanding, and put you in charge of Israel; that so you may keep the law of YHWH your God. Then you will prosper, if you observe to do the statutes and the ordinances which YHWH gave Moses concerning Israel. Be strong and courageous. Don't be afraid, and don't be dismayed. Now, behold, in my affliction I have prepared for YHWH's house one hundred thousand talents of gold, one million talents of silver, and bronze and iron without weight; for it is in abundance. I have also prepared timber and stone; and you may add to them. There are also workmen with you in abundance, cutters and workers of stone and timber, and all kinds of men who are skillful in every kind of work; of the gold, the silver, the bronze, and the iron, there is no number. Arise and be doing, and may YHWH be with you."

David also commanded all the princes of Israel to help Solomon his son, saying, "Isn't YHWH your God with you? Hasn't he given you rest on every side? For he has delivered the inhabitants of the land into my hand; and the land is subdued before YHWH, and before his people. Now set your heart and your soul to follow YHWH your God. Arise therefore, and build the sanctuary of YHWH God, to bring the ark of YHWH's covenant and the holy vessels of God into the house that is to be built for YHWH's name."

....

Now David was old and full of days; and he made Solomon his son king over Israel. He gathered together all the princes of Israel, with the priests and the Levites. The Levites were counted from thirty years old and upward; and their number by their polls, man by man, was thirty-eight thousand. David said, "Of these, twenty-four thousand were to oversee the work of YHWH's house, six thousand were officers and judges, four thousand were doorkeepers, and four thousand praised YHWH with the instruments which I made for giving praise."

David divided them into divisions according to the sons of Levi: Gershon, Kohath, and Merari.

Of the Gershonites: Ladan and Shimei. The sons of Ladan: Jehiel the chief, Zetham, and Joel, three. The sons of Shimei: Shelomoth, Haziel, and Haran, three. These were the heads of the fathers' households of Ladan. The sons of Shimei: Jahath, Zina, Jeush, and Beriah. These four were the sons of Shimei. Jahath was the chief, and Zizah the second; but Jeush and Beriah didn't have many sons; therefore they became a fathers' house in one reckoning.

The sons of Kohath: Amram, Izhar, Hebron, and Uzziel, four. The sons of Amram: Aaron and Moses; and Aaron was separated, that he should sanctify the most holy things, he and his sons, forever, to burn incense before YHWH, to minister to him, and to bless in his name, forever. But as for Moses the man of God, his sons were named among the tribe of Levi. The sons of Moses: Gershom and Eliezer. The sons of Gershom: Shebuel the chief. The sons of Eliezer were: Rehabiah the chief; and Eliezer had no other sons; but the sons of Rehabiah were very many. The sons of Izhar: Shelomith the chief. The sons of Hebron: Jeriah the chief, Amariah the second, Jahaziel the third, and Jekameam the fourth. The sons of Uzziel: Micah the chief, and Isshiah the second. The sons of Merari: Mahli and Mushi. The sons of Mahli: Eleazar and Kish. Eleazar died, and had no sons, but daughters only: and their brothers the sons of Kish took them as wives. The sons of Mushi: Mahli, Eder, and Jeremoth, three.

These were the sons of Levi after their fathers' houses, even the heads of the fathers' houses of those who were counted individually, in the number of names by their polls, who did the work for the service of YHWH's house, from twenty years old and upward. For David said, "YHWH, the God of Israel, has given rest to his people; and he dwells in Jerusalem forever. Also the Levites will no longer need to carry the tabernacle and all its vessels for its service." For by the last words of David the sons of Levi were counted, from twenty years old and upward. For their office was to wait on the sons of Aaron for the service of YHWH's house, in the courts, and in the rooms, and in the purifying of all holy things, even the work of the service of God's house; for the show bread also, and for the fine flour for a meal offering, whether of unleavened wafers, or of that which is baked in the pan, or of that which is soaked, and for all measurements of quantity and size; and to stand every morning to thank and praise YHWH, and likewise in the evening; and to offer all burnt offerings to YHWH, on the Sabbaths, on the new moons, and on the set feasts, in number according to the ordinance concerning them, continually before YHWH; and that they should keep the duty of the Tent of Meeting, the duty of the holy place, and the duty of the sons of Aaron their brothers, for the service of YHWH's house.

....

These were the divisions of the sons of Aaron. The sons of Aaron: Nadab, Abihu, Eleazar, and Ithamar. But Nadab and Abihu died before their father, and had no children: therefore Eleazar and Ithamar executed the priest's office. David with Zadok of the sons of Eleazar and Ahimelech of the sons of Ithamar, divided them according to their ordering in their service. There were more chief men found of the sons of Eleazar than of the sons of Ithamar; and they were divided like this: of the sons of Eleazar there were sixteen, heads of fathers' houses; and of the sons of Ithamar, according to their fathers' houses, eight. Thus they were divided impartially by drawing lots; for there were princes of the sanctuary, and princes of God, both of the sons of Eleazar, and of the sons of Ithamar. Shemaiah the son of Nethanel the scribe, who was of the Levites, wrote them in the presence of the king, the princes, Zadok the priest, Ahimelech the son of Abiathar, and the heads of the fathers' households of the priests and of the Levites; one fathers' house being taken for Eleazar, and one taken for Ithamar. Now the first lot came out to Jehoiarib, the second to Jedaiah, the third to Harim, the fourth to Seorim, the fifth to Malchijah, the sixth to Mijamin, the seventh to Hakkoz, the eighth to Abijah, the ninth to Jeshua, the tenth to Shecaniah, the eleventh to Eliashib, the twelfth to Jakim, the thirteenth to Huppah, the fourteenth to Jeshebeab, the fifteenth to Bilgah, the sixteenth to Immer, the seventeenth to Hezir, the eighteenth to Happizzez, the nineteenth to Pethahiah, the twentieth to Jehezkel, the twenty-first to Jachin, the twenty-second to Gamul, the twenty-third to Delaiah, and the twenty-fourth to Maaziah. This was their ordering in their service, to come into YHWH's house according to the ordinance given to them by Aaron their father, as YHWH, the God of Israel, had commanded him.

Of the rest of the sons of Levi: of the sons of Amram, Shubael; of the sons of Shubael, Jehdeiah. Of Rehabiah: of the sons of Rehabiah, Isshiah the chief. Of the Izharites, Shelomoth; of the sons of Shelomoth, Jahath. The sons of Hebron: Jeriah, Amariah the second, Jahaziel the third, and Jekameam the fourth. The sons of Uzziel: Micah; of the sons of Micah, Shamir. The brother of Micah: Isshiah; of the sons of Isshiah, Zechariah. The sons of Merari: Mahli and Mushi.

The son of Jaaziah: Beno. The sons of Merari: of Jaaziah, Beno, Sho-ham, Zaccur, and Ibri. Of Mahli: Eleazar, who had no sons. Of Kish, the son of Kish: Jerahmeel. The sons of Mushi: Mahli, Eder, and Jer-imoth. These were the sons of the Levites after their fathers' houses. These likewise cast lots even as their brothers the sons of Aaron in the presence of David the king, Zadok, Ahimelech, and the heads of the fathers' households of the priests and of the Levites; the fathers' households of the chief even as those of his younger brother.

....

Moreover, David and the captains of the army set apart for the service certain of the sons of Asaph, and of Heman, and of Jeduthun, who were to prophesy with harps, with stringed instruments, and with cymbals. The number of those who did the work according to their service was: of the sons of Asaph: Zaccur, Joseph, Nethaniah, and Asharelah. The sons of Asaph were under the hand of Asaph, who prophesied at the order of the king. Of Jeduthun, the sons of Jeduthun: Gedaliah, Zeri, Jeshaiah, Shimei, Hashabiah, and Mat-tithiah, six, under the hands of their father Jeduthun, who prophe-sied in giving thanks and praising YHWH with the harp. Of Heman, the sons of Heman: Bukkiah, Mattaniah, Uzziel, Shebuel, Jerim-oth, Hananiah, Hanani, Eliathah, Giddalti, Romamti-Ezer, Josh-bekashah, Mallothi, Hothir, and Mahazioth. All these were the sons of Heman the king's seer in the words of God, to lift up the horn. God gave to Heman fourteen sons and three daughters. All these were under the hands of their father for song in YHWH's house, with cymbals, stringed instruments, and harps, for the service of God's house: Asaph, Jeduthun, and Heman being under the order of the king. The number of them, with their brothers who were instructed in singing to YHWH, even all who were skillful, was two hundred eighty-eight. They cast lots for their offices, all alike, the small as well as the great, the teacher as well as the student.

Now the first lot came out for Asaph to Joseph; the second to Gedaliah, he and his brothers and sons were twelve; the third to Zac-cur, his sons and his brothers, twelve; the fourth to Izri, his sons and his brothers, twelve; the fifth to Nethaniah, his sons and his brothers, twelve; the sixth to Bukkiah, his sons and his brothers, twelve; the seventh to Jesharelah, his sons and his brothers, twelve; the eighth to Jeshaiah, his sons and his brothers, twelve; the ninth to Mattaniah, his sons and his brothers, twelve; the tenth to Shimei, his sons and his brothers, twelve; the eleventh to Azarel, his sons and his brothers, twelve; the twelfth to Hashabiah, his sons and his brothers, twelve; for the thirteenth, Shubael, his sons and his brothers, twelve; for the fourteenth, Mattithiah, his sons and his brothers, twelve; for the fifteenth to Jeremoth, his sons and his brothers, twelve; for the sixteenth to Hananiah, his sons and his brothers, twelve; for the seventeenth to Joshbekashah, his sons and his brothers, twelve; for the eighteenth to Hanani, his sons and his brothers, twelve; for the nineteenth to Mallothi, his sons and his brothers, twelve; for the twentieth to Eliathah, his sons and his brothers, twelve; for the twenty-first to Hothir, his sons and his brothers, twelve; for the twenty-second to Giddalti, his sons and his brothers, twelve; for the twenty-third to Mahazioth, his sons and his brothers, twelve; for the twenty-fourth to Romamti-Ezer, his sons and his brothers, twelve.

....

For the divisions of the doorkeepers: of the Korahites, Meshelemiah the son of Kore, of the sons of Asaph. Meshelemiah had sons: Zechariah the firstborn, Jediael the second, Zebadiah the third, Jathniel the fourth, Elam the fifth, Jehohanan the sixth, and Eliehoenai the seventh. Obed-Edom had sons: Shemaiah the firstborn, Jehozabad the second, Joah the third, Sacar the fourth, Nethanel the fifth, Ammiel the sixth, Issachar the seventh, and Peullethai the eighth; for God blessed him. Sons were also born to Shemaiah his son, who ruled over the house of their father; for they were mighty men of valor. The sons of Shemaiah: Othni, Rephael, Obed, and Elzabad, whose brothers were valiant men, Elihu, and Semachiah. All these were of the sons of Obed-Edom: they and their sons and their brothers, able men in strength for the service: sixty-two of Obed-Edom. Meshelemiah had sons and brothers, valiant men, eighteen. Also Hosah, of the children of Merari, had sons: Shimri the chief (for though he was not the firstborn, yet his father made him chief), Hilkiah the second, Tebaliah the third, and Zechariah the fourth. All the sons and brothers of Hosah were thirteen. Of these were the divisions of the doorkeepers, even of the chief men, having offices like their brothers, to minister in YHWH's house. They cast lots, the small as well as the great, according to their fathers' houses, for every gate. The lot eastward fell to Shelemiah. Then for Zechariah his son, a wise counselor, they cast lots; and his lot came out northward. To Obed-Edom southward; and to his sons the storehouse. To Shuppim and Hosah westward, by the gate of Shallecheth, at the causeway that goes up, watchman opposite watchman. Eastward were six Levites, northward four a day, southward four a day, and for the storehouse two and two. For Parbar westward, four at the causeway, and two at Parbar. These were the divisions of the doorkeepers; of the sons of the Korahites, and of the sons of Merari.

Of the Levites, Ahijah was over the treasures of God's house and over the treasures of the dedicated things. The sons of Ladan, the sons of the Gershonites belonging to Ladan, the heads of the fathers' households belonging to Ladan the Gershonite: Jehieli. The sons of Jehieli: Zetham, and Joel his brother, over the treasures of YHWH's house. Of the Amramites, of the Izharites, of the Hebronites, of the Uzzielites: and Shebuel the son of Gershom, the son of Moses, was ruler over the treasures. His brothers: of Eliezer, Rehabiah his son, and Jeshaiah his son, and Joram his son, and Zichri his son, and Shelomoth his son. This Shelomoth and his brothers were over all the treasures of the dedicated things, which David the king, and the heads of the fathers' households, the captains over thousands and hundreds, and the captains of the army, had dedicated. They dedicated some of the plunder won in battles to repair YHWH's house. All that Samuel the seer, and Saul the son of Kish, and Abner the son of Ner, and Joab the son of Zeruiah, had dedicated, whoever had dedicated anything, it was under the hand of Shelomoth, and of his brothers. Of the Izharites, Chenaniah and his sons were for the outward business over Israel, for officers and judges. Of the Hebronites, Hashabiah and his brothers, men of valor, one thousand seven hundred, had the oversight of Israel beyond the Jordan westward, for all the business of YHWH, and for the service of the king. Of the Hebronites, Jerijah was the chief, even of the Hebronites, according to their generations by fathers' households. They were sought for in the fortieth year of the reign of David, and mighty men of valor were found among them at Jazer of Gilead. His brothers, men of valor, were two thousand seven hundred, heads of fathers' households, whom king David made overseers over the Reubenites, the Gadites, and the half-tribe of the Manassites, for every matter pertaining to God, and for the affairs of the king.

....

Now the children of Israel after their number, the heads of fathers' households and the captains of thousands and of hundreds, and their officers who served the king, in any matter of the divisions which came in and went out month by month throughout all the months of the year—of every division were twenty-four thousand. Over the first division for the first month was Jashobeam the son of Zabdiel: and in his division were twenty-four thousand. He was of the children of Perez, the chief of all the captains of the army for the first month. Over the division of the second month was Dodai the Ahohite, and his division; and Mikloth the ruler: and in his division were twenty-four thousand. The third captain of the army for the third month was Benaiah, the son of Jehoiada the chief priest. In his division were twenty-four thousand. This is that Benaiah who was the mighty man of the thirty, and over the thirty: and of his division was Ammizabad his son. The fourth captain for the fourth month was Asahel the brother of Joab, and Zebadiah his son after him: and in his division were twenty-four thousand. The fifth captain for the fifth month was Shamhuth the Izrahite: and in his division were twenty-four thousand. The sixth captain for the sixth month was Ira the son of Ikkesh the Tekoite: and in his division were twenty-four thousand. The seventh captain for the seventh month was Helez the Pelonite, of the children of Ephraim. In his division were twenty-four thousand. The eighth captain for the eighth month was Sibbecai the Hushathite, of the Zerahites. In his division were twenty-four thousand. The ninth captain for the ninth month was Abiezer the Anathothite, of the Benjamites. In his division were twenty-four thousand. The tenth captain for the tenth month was Maharai the Netophathite, of the Zerahites. In his division were twenty-four thousand. The eleventh captain for the eleventh month was Benaiah the Pirathonite, of the children of Ephraim. In his division were twenty-four thousand. The twelfth captain for the twelfth month was Heldai the Netophathite, of Othniel. In his division were twenty-four thousand. Furthermore over the tribes of Israel: of the Reubenites, Eliezer the son of Zichri was the ruler; of the Simeonites, Shephatiah the son of Maacah; of Levi, Hashabiah the son of Kemuel; of Aaron, Zadok; of Judah, Elihu, one of the brothers of David; of Issachar, Omri the son of Michael; of Zebulun, Ishmaiah the son of Obadiah; of Naphtali, Jeremoth the son of Azriel; of the children of Ephraim, Hoshea the son of Azaziah; of the half-tribe of Manasseh, Joel the son of Pedaiah; of the half-tribe of Manasseh in Gilead, Iddo the son of Zechariah; of Benjamin, Jaasiel the son of Abner; of Dan, Azarel the son of Jeroham. These were the captains of the tribes of Israel. But David didn't take the number of them from twenty years old and under, because YHWH had said he would increase Israel like the stars of the sky. Joab the son of Zeruiah began to take a census, but didn't finish; and wrath came on Israel for this. The number wasn't put into the account in the chronicles of king David.

Over the king's treasures was Azmaveth the son of Adiel: and over the treasures in the fields, in the cities, and in the villages, and in the towers, was Jonathan the son of Uzziah; Over those who did the work of the field for tillage of the ground was Ezri the son of Chelub; and over the vineyards was Shimei the Ramathite; and over the increase of the vineyards for the wine cellars was Zabdi the Shiphmite; and over the olive trees and the sycamore trees that were in the lowland was Baal Hanan the Gederite; and over the cellars of oil was Joash; and over the herds that fed in Sharon was Shitrai the Sharonite; and over the herds that were in the valleys was Shaphat the son of Adlai; and over the camels was Obil the Ishmaelite; and over the donkeys was Jehdeiah the Meronothite; and over the flocks was Jaziz the Hagrite. All these were the rulers of the property which was king David's.

Also Jonathan, David's uncle, was a counselor, a man of understanding, and a scribe. Jehiel the son of Hachmoni was with the king's sons. Ahithophel was the king's counselor. Hushai the Archite was the king's friend. After Ahithophel was Jehoiada the son of Benaiah, and Abiathar. Joab was the captain of the king's army.

....

David assembled all the princes of Israel, the princes of the tribes, the captains of the companies who served the king by division, the captains of thousands, the captains of hundreds, and the rulers over all the substance and possessions of the king and of his sons, with the officers and the mighty men, even all the mighty men of valor, to Jerusalem. Then David the king stood up on his feet, and said, "Hear me, my brothers, and my people! As for me, it was in my heart to build a house of rest for the ark of YHWH's covenant, and for the footstool of our God; and I had prepared for the building. But God said to me, 'You shall not build a house for my name, because you are a man of war, and have shed blood.' However YHWH, the God of Israel, chose me out of all the house of my father to be king over Israel forever. For he has chosen Judah to be prince; and in the house of Judah, the house of my father; and among the sons of my father he took pleasure in me to make me king over all Israel. Of all my sons (for YHWH has given me many sons), he has chosen Solomon my son to sit on the throne of YHWH's kingdom over Israel. He said to me, 'Solomon, your son, shall build my house and my courts; for I have chosen him to be my son, and I will be his father. I will establish his kingdom forever if he continues to do my commandments and my ordinances, as it is today.'

Now therefore, in the sight of all Israel, YHWH's assembly, and in the audience of our God, observe and seek out all the commandments of YHWH your God; that you may possess this good land, and leave it for an inheritance to your children after you forever. You, Solomon my son, know the God of your father, and serve him with a perfect heart and with a willing mind; for YHWH searches all hearts, and understands all the imaginations of the thoughts. If you seek him, he will be found by you; but if you forsake him, he will cast you off forever. Take heed now; for YHWH has chosen you to build a house for the sanctuary. Be strong, and do it."

Then David gave to Solomon his son the plans for the porch of the temple, for its houses, for its treasuries, for its upper rooms, for its inner rooms, for the place of the mercy seat; and the plans of all that he had by the Spirit, for the courts of YHWH's house, for all the surrounding rooms, for the treasuries of God's house, and for the treasuries of the dedicated things; also for the divisions of the priests and the Levites, for all the work of the service of YHWH's house, and for all the vessels of service in YHWH's house; of gold by weight for the gold, for all vessels of every kind of service; for all the vessels of silver by weight, for all vessels of every kind of service; by weight also for the lamp stands of gold, and for its lamps, of gold, by weight for every lamp stand and for its lamps; and for the lamp stands of silver, by weight for every lamp stand and for its lamps, according to the use of every lamp stand; and the gold by weight for the tables of show bread, for every table; and silver for the tables of silver; and the forks, the basins, and the cups, of pure gold; and for the golden bowls by weight for every bowl; and for the silver bowls by weight for every bowl; and for the altar of incense refined gold by weight; and gold for the plans for the chariot, and the cherubim that spread out and cover the ark of YHWH's covenant. "All this", David said, "I have been made to understand in writing from YHWH's hand, even all the works of this pattern."

David said to Solomon his son, "Be strong and courageous, and do it. Don't be afraid, nor be dismayed; for YHWH God, even my God, is with you. He will not fail you, nor forsake you, until all the work for the service of YHWH's house is finished. Behold, there are the divisions of the priests and the Levites, for all the service of God's house. Every willing man who has skill, for any kind of service, shall be with you in all kinds of work. Also the captains and all the people will be entirely at your command."

....

David the king said to all the assembly, "Solomon my son, whom alone God has chosen, is yet young and tender, and the work is great; for the palace is not for man, but for YHWH God. Now I have prepared with all my might for the house of my God the gold for the things of gold, the silver for the things of silver, the bronze for the things of bronze, iron for the things of iron, and wood for the things of wood; also onyx stones, stones to be set, stones for inlaid work, of various colors, all kinds of precious stones, and marble stones in abundance. In addition, because I have set my affection on the house of my God, since I have a treasure of my own of gold and silver, I give it to the house of my God, over and above all that I have prepared for the holy house, even three thousand talents of gold, of the gold of Ophir, and seven thousand talents of refined silver, with which to overlay the walls of the houses; of gold for the things of gold, and of silver for the things of silver, and for all kinds of work to be made by the hands of artisans. Who then offers willingly to consecrate himself today to YHWH?"

Then the princes of the fathers' households, and the princes of the tribes of Israel, and the captains of thousands and of hundreds, with the rulers over the king's work, offered willingly; and they gave for the service of God's house of gold five thousand talents and ten thousand darics, of silver ten thousand talents, of bronze eighteen thousand talents, and of iron one hundred thousand talents. People with whom precious stones were found gave them to the treasure of YHWH's house, under the hand of Jehiel the Gershonite. Then the people rejoiced, because they offered willingly, because with a perfect heart they offered willingly to YHWH; and David the king also rejoiced with great joy. Therefore David blessed YHWH before all the assembly; and David said, "You are blessed, YHWH, the God of Israel our father, forever and ever. Yours, YHWH, is the greatness, the power, the glory, the victory, and the majesty! For all that is in the heavens and in the earth is yours. Yours is the kingdom, YHWH, and you are exalted as head above all. Both riches and honor come from you, and you rule over all! In your hand is power and might! It is in your hand to make great, and to give strength to all! Now therefore, our God, we thank you, and praise your glorious name. But who am I, and what is my people, that we should be able to offer so willingly as this? For all things come from you, and we have given you of your own. For we are strangers before you, and foreigners, as all our fathers were. Our days on the earth are as a shadow, and there is no remaining. YHWH our God, all this store that we have prepared to build you a house for your holy name comes from your hand, and is all your own. I know also, my God, that you try the heart, and have pleasure in uprightness. As for me, in the uprightness of my heart I have willingly offered all these things. Now I have seen with joy your people, who are present here, offer willingly to you. YHWH, the God of Abraham, of Isaac, and of Israel, our fathers, keep this desire forever in the thoughts of the heart of your people, and prepare their heart for you; and give to Solomon my son a perfect heart, to keep your commandments, your testimonies, and your statutes, and to do all these things, and to build the palace, for which I have made provision."

Then David said to all the assembly, "Now bless YHWH your God!"

All the assembly blessed YHWH, the God of their fathers, and bowed down their heads and prostrated themselves before YHWH and the king. They sacrificed sacrifices to YHWH, and offered burnt offerings to YHWH, on the next day after that day, even one thousand bulls, one thousand rams, and one thousand lambs, with their drink offerings and sacrifices in abundance for all Israel, and ate and drank before YHWH on that day with great gladness. They made Solomon the son of David king the second time, and anointed him before YHWH to be prince, and Zadok to be priest.

Then Solomon sat on the throne of YHWH as king instead of David his father, and prospered; and all Israel obeyed him. All the princes, the mighty men, and also all of the sons of king David submitted themselves to Solomon the king. YHWH magnified Solomon exceedingly in the sight of all Israel, and gave to him such royal majesty as had not been on any king before him in Israel. Now David the son of Jesse reigned over all Israel. The time that he reigned over Israel was forty years; he reigned seven years in Hebron, and he reigned thirty-three years in Jerusalem. He died at a good old age, full of days, riches, and honor; and Solomon his son reigned in his place. Now the acts of David the king, first and last, behold, they are written in the history of Samuel the seer, and in the history of Nathan the prophet, and in the history of Gad the seer, with all his reign and his might, and the times that went over him, and over Israel, and over all the kingdoms of the countries.

THE BOOK OF

CHRONICLES

PART II

2 HR 16 MIN

Solomon the son of David was firmly established in his kingdom, and YHWH his God was with him, and made him exceedingly great. Solomon spoke to all Israel, to the captains of thousands and of hundreds, to the judges, and to every prince in all Israel, the heads of the fathers' households. So Solomon, and all the assembly with him, went to the high place that was at Gibeon; for God's Tent of Meeting was there, which YHWH's servant Moses had made in the wilderness. But David had brought God's ark up from Kiriath Jearim to the place that David had prepared for it; for he had pitched a tent for it at Jerusalem. Moreover the bronze altar that Bezalel the son of Uri, the son of Hur, had made was there before YHWH's tabernacle; and Solomon and the assembly were seeking counsel there. Solomon went up there to the bronze altar before YHWH, which was at the Tent of Meeting, and offered one thousand burnt offerings on it.

That night, God appeared to Solomon and said to him, "Ask for what you want me to give you."

Solomon said to God, "You have shown great loving kindness to David my father, and have made me king in his place. Now, YHWH God, let your promise to David my father be established; for you have made me king over a people like the dust of the earth in multitude. Now give me wisdom and knowledge, that I may go out and come in before this people; for who can judge this great people of yours?"

God said to Solomon, "Because this was in your heart, and you have not asked riches, wealth, honor, or the life of those who hate you, nor yet have you asked for long life; but have asked for wisdom and knowledge for yourself, that you may judge my people, over whom I have made you king, therefore wisdom and knowledge is granted to you. I will give you riches, wealth, and honor, such as none of the kings have had who have been before you had, and none after you will have."

So Solomon came from the high place that was at Gibeon, from before the Tent of Meeting, to Jerusalem; and he reigned over Israel.

Solomon gathered chariots and horsemen. He had one thousand four hundred chariots and twelve thousand horsemen that he placed in the chariot cities, and with the king at Jerusalem. The king made silver and gold to be as common as stones in Jerusalem, and he made cedars to be as common as the sycamore trees that are in the lowland. The horses which Solomon had were brought out of Egypt and from Kue. The king's merchants purchased them from Kue. They brought up and brought out of Egypt a chariot for six hundred pieces of silver, and a horse for one hundred fifty. They also exported them to the Hittite kings and the Syrian kings.

....

Now Solomon decided to build a house for YHWH's name, and a house for his kingdom. Solomon counted out seventy thousand men to bear burdens, eighty thousand men who were stone cutters in the mountains, and three thousand six hundred to oversee them. Solomon sent to Huram the king of Tyre, saying, "As you dealt with David my father, and sent him cedars to build him a house in which to dwell, so deal with me. Behold, I am about to build a house for the name of YHWH my God, to dedicate it to him, to burn before him incense of sweet spices, for the continual show bread, and for the burnt offerings morning and evening, on the Sabbaths, on the new moons, and on the set feasts of YHWH our God. This is an ordinance forever to Israel.

"The house which I am building will be great; for our God is greater than all gods. But who is able to build him a house, since heaven and the heaven of heavens can't contain him? Who am I then, that I should build him a house, except just to burn incense before him?

"Now therefore send me a man skillful to work in gold, in silver, in bronze, in iron, and in purple, crimson, and blue, and who knows how to engrave engravings, to be with the skillful men who are with me in Judah and in Jerusalem, whom David my father provided.

"Send me also cedar trees, cypress trees, and algum trees out of Lebanon; for I know that your servants know how to cut timber in Lebanon. Behold, my servants will be with your servants, even to prepare me timber in abundance; for the house which I am about to build will be great and wonderful. Behold, I will give to your servants, the cutters who cut timber, twenty thousand cors of beaten wheat, twenty thousand baths of barley, twenty thousand baths of wine, and twenty thousand baths of oil."

Then Huram the king of Tyre answered in writing, which he sent to Solomon, "Because YHWH loves his people, he has made you king over them." Huram continued, "Blessed be YHWH, the God of Israel, who made heaven and earth, who has given to David the king a wise son, endowed with discretion and understanding, who would build a house for YHWH, and a house for his kingdom. Now I have sent a skillful man, endowed with understanding, of Huram my father's, the son of a woman of the daughters of Dan; and his father was a man of Tyre, skillful to work in gold, in silver, in bronze, in iron, in stone, in timber, and in purple, in blue, in fine linen, and in crimson, also to engrave any kind of engraving and to devise any device; that there may be a place appointed to him with your skillful men, and with the skillful men of my lord David your father.

"Now therefore the wheat, the barley, the oil, and the wine, which my lord has spoken of, let him send to his servants; and we will cut wood out of Lebanon, as much as you need. We will bring it to you in rafts by sea to Joppa; then you shall carry it up to Jerusalem."

Solomon counted all the foreigners who were in the land of Israel, after the census with which David his father had counted them; and they found one hundred fifty-three thousand six hundred. He set seventy thousand of them to bear burdens, eighty thousand who were stone cutters in the mountains, and three thousand six hundred overseers to assign the people their work.

....

Then Solomon began to build YHWH's house at Jerusalem on Mount Moriah, where YHWH appeared to David his father, which he prepared in the place that David had appointed, on the threshing floor of Ornan the Jebusite. He began to build in the second day of the second month, in the fourth year of his reign. Now these are the foundations which Solomon laid for the building of God's house. The length by cubits after the first measure was sixty cubits, and the width twenty cubits. The porch that was in front, its length, according to the width of the house, was twenty cubits, and the height one hundred twenty; and he overlaid it within with pure gold. He made the larger room with a ceiling of cypress wood, which he overlaid with fine gold, and ornamented it with palm trees and chains. He decorated the house with precious stones for beauty. The gold was gold from Parvaim. He also overlaid the house, the beams, the thresholds, its walls, and its doors with gold; and engraved cherubim on the walls.

He made the most holy place. Its length, according to the width of the house, was twenty cubits, and its width twenty cubits; and he overlaid it with fine gold, amounting to six hundred talents. The weight of the nails was fifty shekels of gold. He overlaid the upper rooms with gold.

In the most holy place he made two cherubim by carving; and they overlaid them with gold. The wings of the cherubim were twenty cubits long: the wing of the one was five cubits, reaching to the wall of the house; and the other wing was five cubits, reaching to the wing of the other cherub. The wing of the other cherub was five cubits, reaching to the wall of the house; and the other wing was five cubits, joining to the wing of the other cherub. The wings of these cherubim spread themselves out twenty cubits. They stood on their feet, and their faces were toward the house. He made the veil of blue, purple, crimson, and fine linen, and ornamented it with cherubim.

Also he made before the house two pillars of thirty-five cubits height, and the capital that was on the top of each of them was five cubits. He made chains in the inner sanctuary, and put them on the tops of the pillars; and he made one hundred pomegranates, and put them on the chains. He set up the pillars before the temple, one on the right hand, and the other on the left; and called the name of that on the right hand Jachin, and the name of that on the left Boaz.

....

Then he made an altar of bronze, twenty cubits long, twenty cubits wide, and ten cubits high. Also he made the molten sea of ten cubits from brim to brim. It was round, five cubits high, and thirty cubits in circumference. Under it was the likeness of oxen, which encircled it, for ten cubits, encircling the sea. The oxen were in two rows, cast when it was cast. It stood on twelve oxen, three looking toward the north, and three looking toward the west, and three looking toward the south, and three looking toward the east; and the sea was set on them above, and all their hindquarters were inward. It was a handbreadth thick; and its brim was made like the brim of a cup, like the flower of a lily. It received and held three thousand baths. He also made ten basins, and put five on the right hand, and five on the left, to wash in them. The things that belonged to the burnt offering were washed in them; but the sea was for the priests to wash in.

He made the ten lamp stands of gold according to the ordinance concerning them; and he set them in the temple, five on the right hand, and five on the left. He made also ten tables, and placed them in the temple, five on the right side, and five on the left. He made one hundred basins of gold. Furthermore he made the court of the priests, the great court, and doors for the court, and overlaid their doors with bronze. He set the sea on the right side of the house eastward, toward the south.

Huram made the pots, the shovels, and the basins.

So Huram finished doing the work that he did for king Solomon in God's house: the two pillars, the bowls, the two capitals which were on the top of the pillars, the two networks to cover the two bowls of the capitals that were on the top of the pillars, and the four hundred pomegranates for the two networks; two rows of pomegranates for each network, to cover the two bowls of the capitals that were on the pillars. He also made the bases, and he made the basins on the bases; one sea, and the twelve oxen under it. Huram his father also made the pots, the shovels, the forks, and all its vessels for king Solomon, for YHWH's house, of bright bronze. The king cast them in the plain of the Jordan, in the clay ground between Succoth and Zeredah. Thus Solomon made all these vessels in great abundance; for the weight of the bronze could not be determined.

Solomon made all the vessels that were in God's house, the golden altar also, and the tables with the show bread on them; and the lamp stands with their lamps, to burn according to the ordinance before the inner sanctuary, of pure gold; and the flowers, the lamps, and the tongs of gold that was perfect gold; and the snuffers, the basins, the spoons, and the fire pans of pure gold. As for the entry of the house, its inner doors for the most holy place and the doors of the main hall of the temple were of gold.

....

Thus all the work that Solomon did for YHWH's house was finished. Solomon brought in the things that David his father had dedicated, even the silver, the gold, and all the vessels, and put them in the treasuries of God's house.

Then Solomon assembled the elders of Israel, and all the heads of the tribes, the princes of the fathers' households of the children of Israel, to Jerusalem, to bring up the ark of YHWH's covenant out of David's city, which is Zion. So all the men of Israel assembled themselves to the king at the feast, which was in the seventh month. All the elders of Israel came. The Levites took up the ark; and they brought up the ark, the Tent of Meeting, and all the holy vessels that were in the Tent; these the Levitical priests brought up. King Solomon and all the congregation of Israel, who were assembled to him, were before the ark, sacrificing sheep and cattle that could not be counted or numbered for multitude. The priests brought in the ark of YHWH's covenant to its place, into the inner sanctuary of the house, to the most holy place, even under the wings of the cherubim. For the cherubim spread out their wings over the place of the ark, and the cherubim covered the ark and its poles above. The poles were so long that the ends of the poles were seen from the ark in front of the inner sanctuary; but they were not seen outside; and it is there to this day. There was nothing in the ark except the two tablets which Moses put at Horeb, when YHWH made a covenant with the children of Israel, when they came out of Egypt.

When the priests had come out of the holy place (for all the priests who were present had sanctified themselves, and didn't keep their divisions; also the Levites who were the singers, all of them, even Asaph, Heman, Jeduthun, and their sons and their brothers, arrayed in fine linen, with cymbals and stringed instruments and harps, stood at the east end of the altar, and with them one hundred twenty priests sounding with trumpets); when the trumpeters and singers were as one, to make one sound to be heard in praising and thanking YHWH; and when they lifted up their voice with the trumpets and cymbals and instruments of music, and praised YHWH, saying,

> "For he is good;
>   for his loving kindness endures forever!"

then the house was filled with a cloud, even YHWH's house, so that the priests could not stand to minister by reason of the cloud; for YHWH's glory filled God's house.

....

Then Solomon said, "YHWH has said that he would dwell in the thick darkness. But I have built you a house and home, a place for you to dwell in forever."

The king turned his face, and blessed all the assembly of Israel: and all the assembly of Israel stood.

He said, "Blessed be YHWH, the God of Israel, who spoke with his mouth to David my father, and has with his hands fulfilled it, saying, 'Since the day that I brought my people out of the land of Egypt, I chose no city out of all the tribes of Israel to build a house in, that my name might be there and I chose no man to be prince over my people Israel; but now I have chosen Jerusalem, that my name might be there; and I have chosen David to be over my people

Israel.' Now it was in the heart of David my father to build a house for the name of YHWH, the God of Israel. But YHWH said to David my father, 'Whereas it was in your heart to build a house for my name, you did well that it was in your heart; nevertheless you shall not build the house; but your son who will come out of your body, he shall build the house for my name.'

"YHWH has performed his word that he spoke; for I have risen up in the place of David my father, and sit on the throne of Israel, as YHWH promised, and have built the house for the name of YHWH, the God of Israel. There I have set the ark, in which is YHWH's covenant, which he made with the children of Israel."

He stood before YHWH's altar in the presence of all the assembly of Israel, and spread out his hands (for Solomon had made a bronze platform, five cubits long, and five cubits wide, and three cubits high, and had set it in the middle of the court; and he stood on it, and knelt down on his knees before all the assembly of Israel, and spread out his hands toward heaven) and he said, "YHWH, the God of Israel, there is no God like you in heaven or on earth; you who keep covenant and loving kindness with your servants who walk before you with all their heart; who have kept with your servant David my father that which you promised him. Yes, you spoke with your mouth, and have fulfilled it with your hand, as it is today.

"Now therefore, YHWH, the God of Israel, keep with your servant David my father that which you have promised him, saying, 'There shall not fail you a man in my sight to sit on the throne of Israel, if only your children take heed to their way, to walk in my law as you have walked before me.' Now therefore, YHWH, the God of Israel, let your word be verified, which you spoke to your servant David.

"But will God indeed dwell with men on the earth? Behold, heaven and the heaven of heavens can't contain you; how much less this house which I have built! Yet have respect for the prayer of your servant, and to his supplication, YHWH my God, to listen to the cry and to the prayer which your servant prays before you; that your eyes may be open toward this house day and night, even toward the place where you have said that you would put your name; to listen to the prayer which your servant will pray toward this place. Listen to the petitions of your servant, and of your people Israel, when they pray toward this place. Yes, hear from your dwelling place, even from heaven; and when you hear, forgive.

"If a man sins against his neighbor, and an oath is laid on him to cause him to swear, and he comes and swears before your altar in this house; then hear from heaven, act, and judge your servants, bringing retribution to the wicked, to bring his way on his own head; and justifying the righteous, to give him according to his righteousness.

"If your people Israel are struck down before the enemy because they have sinned against you, and they turn again and confess your name, and pray and make supplication before you in this house; then hear from heaven, and forgive the sin of your people Israel, and bring them again to the land which you gave to them and to their fathers.

"When the sky is shut up, and there is no rain, because they have sinned against you; if they pray toward this place, and confess your name, and turn from their sin, when you afflict them; then hear in heaven, and forgive the sin of your servants of your people Israel, when you teach them the good way in which they should walk; and send rain on your land, which you have given to your people for an inheritance.

"If there is famine in the land, if there is pestilence, if there is blight or mildew, locust or caterpillar; if their enemies besiege them in the land of their cities; whatever plague or whatever sickness there is; whatever prayer and supplication is made by any man, or by all your people Israel, who will each know his own plague and his own sorrow, and shall spread out his hands toward this house; then hear from heaven your dwelling place and forgive, and render to every man according to all his ways, whose heart you know (for you, even you only, know the hearts of the children of men) that they may fear you, to walk in your ways, so long as they live in the land which you gave to our fathers.

"Moreover concerning the foreigner, who is not of your people Israel, when he comes from a far country for your great name's sake, and your mighty hand, and your outstretched arm; when they come and pray toward this house; then hear from heaven, even from your dwelling place, and do according to all that the foreigner calls to you for; that all the peoples of the earth may know your name and fear you, as do your people Israel, and that they may know that this house which I have built is called by your name.

"If your people go out to battle against their enemies, by whatever way you send them, and they pray to you toward this city which you have chosen, and the house which I have built for your name; then hear from heaven their prayer and their supplication, and maintain their cause.

"If they sin against you (for there is no man who doesn't sin), and you are angry with them, and deliver them to the enemy, so that they carry them away captive to a land far off or near; yet if they come to their senses in the land where they are carried captive, and turn again, and make supplication to you in the land of their captivity, saying, 'We have sinned, we have done perversely, and have dealt wickedly;' if they return to you with all their heart and with all their soul in the land of their captivity, where they have carried them captive, and pray toward their land, which you gave to their fathers, and the city which you have chosen, and toward the house which I have built for your name; then hear from heaven, even from your dwelling place, their prayer and their petitions, and maintain their cause, and forgive your people who have sinned against you.

"Now, my God, let, I beg you, your eyes be open, and let your ears be attentive, to the prayer that is made in this place.

"Now therefore arise, YHWH God, into your resting place, you, and the ark of your strength. Let your priests, YHWH God, be clothed with salvation, and let your saints rejoice in goodness.

"YHWH God, don't turn away the face of your anointed. Remember your loving kindnesses to David your servant."

....

Now when Solomon had finished praying, fire came down from heaven and consumed the burnt offering and the sacrifices; and YHWH's glory filled the house. The priests could not enter into YHWH's house, because YHWH's glory filled YHWH's house. All the children of Israel looked on, when the fire came down, and YHWH's glory was on the house. They bowed themselves with their faces to the ground on the pavement, worshiped, and gave thanks to YHWH, saying,

"For he is good;
for his loving kindness endures forever."

Then the king and all the people offered sacrifices before YHWH. King Solomon offered a sacrifice of twenty-two thousand head of cattle and a hundred twenty thousand sheep. So the king and all the people dedicated God's house. The priests stood, according to their positions; the Levites also with instruments of music of YHWH, which David the king had made to give thanks to YHWH, when David praised by their ministry, saying "For his loving kindness endures forever." The priests sounded trumpets before them; and all Israel stood.

Moreover Solomon made the middle of the court that was before YHWH's house holy; for there he offered the burnt offerings, and the fat of the peace offerings, because the bronze altar which Solomon had made was not able to receive the burnt offering, the meal offering, and the fat.

So Solomon held the feast at that time for seven days, and all Israel with him, a very great assembly, from the entrance of Hamath to the brook of Egypt.

On the eighth day, they held a solemn assembly; for they kept the dedication of the altar seven days, and the feast seven days. On the twenty-third day of the seventh month, he sent the people away to their tents, joyful and glad of heart for the goodness that YHWH had shown to David, and to Solomon, and to Israel his people.

Thus Solomon finished YHWH's house and the king's house; and he successfully completed all that came into Solomon's heart to make in YHWH's house and in his own house.

YHWH appeared to Solomon by night, and said to him, "I have heard your prayer, and have chosen this place for myself for a house of sacrifice.

"If I shut up the sky so that there is no rain, or if I command the locust to devour the land, or if I send pestilence among my people; if my people, who are called by my name, will humble themselves, pray, seek my face, and turn from their wicked ways; then I will hear from heaven, will forgive their sin, and will heal their land. Now my eyes will be open and my ears attentive to prayer that is made in this place. For now I have chosen and made this house holy, that my name may be there forever; and my eyes and my heart will be there perpetually.

"As for you, if you will walk before me as David your father walked, and do according to all that I have commanded you, and will keep my statutes and my ordinances; then I will establish the throne of your kingdom, according as I covenanted with David your father, saying, 'There shall not fail you a man to be ruler in Israel.'

But if you turn away, and forsake my statutes and my commandments which I have set before you, and shall go and serve other gods, and worship them; then I will pluck them up by the roots out of my land which I have given them; and this house, which I have made holy for my name, I will cast out of my sight, and I will make it a proverb and a byword among all peoples. This house, which is so high, everyone who passes by it shall be astonished, and shall say,

'Why has YHWH done this to this land and to this house?' They shall answer, 'Because they abandoned YHWH, the God of their fathers, who brought them out of the land of Egypt, and took other gods, worshiped them, and served them. Therefore he has brought all this evil on them.'"

....

At the end of twenty years, in which Solomon had built YHWH's house and his own house, Solomon built the cities which Huram had given to Solomon, and caused the children of Israel to dwell there.

Solomon went to Hamath Zobah, and prevailed against it. He built Tadmor in the wilderness, and all the storage cities, which he built in Hamath. Also he built Beth Horon the upper and Beth Horon the lower, fortified cities, with walls, gates, and bars; and Baalath, and all the storage cities that Solomon had, and all the cities for his chariots, the cities for his horsemen, and all that Solomon desired to build for his pleasure in Jerusalem, in Lebanon, and in all the land of his dominion.

As for all the people who were left of the Hittites, the Amorites, the Perizzites, the Hivites, and the Jebusites, who were not of Israel; of their children who were left after them in the land, whom the children of Israel didn't consume, of them Solomon conscripted forced labor to this day. But of the children of Israel, Solomon made no servants for his work; but they were men of war, and chief of his captains, and rulers of his chariots and of his horsemen. These were the chief officers of king Solomon, even two-hundred fifty, who ruled over the people.

Solomon brought up Pharaoh's daughter out of David's city to the house that he had built for her; for he said, "My wife shall not dwell in the house of David king of Israel, because the places where YHWH's ark has come are holy."

Then Solomon offered burnt offerings to YHWH on YHWH's altar, which he had built before the porch, even as the duty of every day required, offering according to the commandment of Moses, on the Sabbaths, on the new moons, and on the set feasts, three times per year, during the feast of unleavened bread, during the feast of weeks, and during the feast of booths.

He appointed, according to the ordinance of David his father, the divisions of the priests to their service, and the Levites to their offices, to praise and to minister before the priests, as the duty of every day required; the doorkeepers also by their divisions at every gate, for David the man of God had so commanded. They didn't depart from the commandment of the king to the priests and Levites concerning any matter, or concerning the treasures.

Now all the work of Solomon was prepared from the day of the foundation of YHWH's house until it was finished. So YHWH's house was completed.

Then Solomon went to Ezion Geber and to Eloth, on the seashore in the land of Edom. Huram sent him ships and servants who had knowledge of the sea by the hands of his servants; and they came with the servants of Solomon to Ophir, and brought from there four hundred fifty talents of gold, and brought them to king Solomon.

When the queen of Sheba heard of the fame of Solomon, she came to test Solomon with hard questions at Jerusalem, with a very great caravan, including camels that bore spices, gold in abundance, and precious stones. When she had come to Solomon, she talked with him about all that was in her heart. Solomon answered all her questions. There wasn't anything hidden from Solomon which he didn't tell her. When the queen of Sheba had seen the wisdom of Solomon, the house that he had built, the food of his table, the seating of his servants, the attendance of his ministers, their clothing, his cup bearers also, their clothing, and his ascent by which he went up to YHWH's house; there was no more spirit in her.

She said to the king, "It was a true report that I heard in my own land of your acts and of your wisdom. However I didn't believe their words until I came, and my eyes had seen it; and behold half of the greatness of your wisdom wasn't told me. You exceed the fame that I heard! Happy are your men, and happy are these your servants, who stand continually before you, and hear your wisdom. Blessed be YHWH your God, who delighted in you, to set you on his throne, to be king for YHWH your God; because your God loved Israel, to establish them forever. Therefore he made you king over them, to do justice and righteousness."

She gave the king one hundred and twenty talents of gold, spices in great abundance, and precious stones. There was never before such spice as the queen of Sheba gave to king Solomon. The servants of Huram and the servants of Solomon, who brought gold from Ophir, also brought algum trees and precious stones. The king used algum tree wood to make terraces for YHWH's house and for the king's house, and harps and stringed instruments for the singers. There were none like these seen before in the land of Judah. King Solomon gave to the queen of Sheba all her desire, whatever she asked, in addition to that which she had brought to the king. So she turned, and went to her own land, she and her servants.

Now the weight of gold that came to Solomon in one year was six hundred sixty-six talents of gold, in addition to that which the traders and merchants brought. All the kings of Arabia and the governors of the country brought gold and silver to Solomon. King Solomon made two hundred bucklers of beaten gold. Six hundred shekels of beaten gold went to one buckler. He made three hundred shields of beaten gold. Three hundred shekels of gold went to one shield. The king put them in the House of the Forest of Lebanon. Moreover the king made a great throne of ivory, and overlaid it with pure gold. There were six steps to the throne, with a footstool of gold, which were fastened to the throne, and armrests on either side by the place of the seat, and two lions standing beside the armrests. Twelve lions stood there on the one side and on the other on the six steps. There was nothing like it made in any other kingdom. All king Solomon's drinking vessels were of gold, and all the vessels of the House of the Forest of Lebanon were of pure gold. Silver was not considered valuable in the days of Solomon. For the king had ships that went to Tarshish with Huram's servants. Once every three years, the ships of Tarshish came bringing gold, silver, ivory, apes, and peacocks.

So king Solomon exceeded all the kings of the earth in riches and wisdom. All the kings of the earth sought the presence of Solomon, to hear his wisdom, which God had put in his heart. They each brought tribute, vessels of silver, vessels of gold, clothing, armor, spices, horses, and mules every year. Solomon had four thousand stalls for horses and chariots, and twelve thousand horsemen, that he stationed in the chariot cities, and with the king at Jerusalem. He ruled over all the kings from the River even to the land of the Philistines, and to the border of Egypt. The king made silver as common in Jerusalem as stones, and he made cedars to be as abundant as the sycamore trees that are in the lowland. They brought horses for Solomon out of Egypt and out of all lands.

Now the rest of the acts of Solomon, first and last, aren't they written in the history of Nathan the prophet, and in the prophecy of Ahijah the Shilonite, and in the visions of Iddo the seer concerning

Jeroboam the son of Nebat? Solomon reigned in Jerusalem over all Israel forty years. Solomon slept with his fathers, and he was buried in his father David's city: and Rehoboam his son reigned in his place.

....

Rehoboam went to Shechem; for all Israel had come to Shechem to make him king. When Jeroboam the son of Nebat heard of it (for he was in Egypt, where he had fled from the presence of king Solomon), Jeroboam returned out of Egypt. They sent and called him; and Jeroboam and all Israel came, and they spoke to Rehoboam, saying, "Your father made our yoke grievous: now therefore make the grievous service of your father, and his heavy yoke which he put on us, lighter, and we will serve you."

He said to them, "Come again to me after three days."

So the people departed. King Rehoboam took counsel with the old men, who had stood before Solomon his father while he yet lived, saying, "What counsel do you give me about how to answer these people?"

They spoke to him, saying, "If you are kind to these people, please them, and speak good words to them, then they will be your servants forever."

But he abandoned the counsel of the old men which they had given him, and took counsel with the young men who had grown up with him, who stood before him. He said to them, "What counsel do you give, that we may give an answer to these people, who have spoken to me, saying, 'Make the yoke that your father put on us lighter?'"

The young men who had grown up with him spoke to him, saying, "Thus you shall tell the people who spoke to you, saying, 'Your father made our yoke heavy, but make it lighter on us;' thus you shall say to them, 'My little finger is thicker than my father's waist. Now whereas my father burdened you with a heavy yoke, I will add to your yoke. My father chastised you with whips, but I will chastise you with scorpions.'"

So Jeroboam and all the people came to Rehoboam the third day, as the king asked, saying, "Come to me again the third day." The king answered them roughly; and king Rehoboam abandoned the counsel of the old men, and spoke to them after the counsel of the young men, saying, "My father made your yoke heavy, but I will add to it. My father chastised you with whips, but I will chastise you with scorpions."

So the king didn't listen to the people; for it was brought about by God, that YHWH might establish his word, which he spoke by Ahijah the Shilonite to Jeroboam the son of Nebat. When all Israel saw that the king didn't listen to them, the people answered the king, saying, "What portion do we have in David? We don't have an inheritance in the son of Jesse! Every man to your tents, Israel! Now see to your own house, David." So all Israel departed to their tents.

But as for the children of Israel who lived in the cities of Judah, Rehoboam reigned over them. Then king Rehoboam sent Hadoram, who was over the men subject to forced labor; and the children of Israel stoned him to death with stones. King Rehoboam hurried to get himself up to his chariot, to flee to Jerusalem. So Israel rebelled against David's house to this day.

....

When Rehoboam had come to Jerusalem, he assembled the house of Judah and Benjamin, one hundred eighty thousand chosen men who were warriors, to fight against Israel, to bring the kingdom again to Rehoboam. But YHWH's word came to Shemaiah the man of God, saying, "Speak to Rehoboam the son of Solomon, king of Judah, and to all Israel in Judah and Benjamin, saying, 'YHWH says, "You shall not go up, nor fight against your brothers! Every man return to his house; for this thing is of me."'" So they listened to YHWH's words, and returned from going against Jeroboam.

Rehoboam lived in Jerusalem, and built cities for defense in Judah. He built Bethlehem, Etam, Tekoa, Beth Zur, Soco, Adullam, Gath, Mareshah, Ziph, Adoraim, Lachish, Azekah, Zorah, Aijalon, and Hebron, which are fortified cities in Judah and in Benjamin. He fortified the strongholds, and put captains in them, and stores of food, oil and wine. He put shields and spears in every city, and made them exceedingly strong. Judah and Benjamin belonged to him.

The priests and the Levites who were in all Israel stood with him out of all their territory. For the Levites left their pasture lands and their possession, and came to Judah and Jerusalem; for Jeroboam and his sons cast them off, that they should not execute the priest's office to YHWH. He himself appointed priests for the high places, for the male goats, and for the calves which he had made. After them, out of all the tribes of Israel, those who set their hearts to seek YHWH, the God of Israel, came to Jerusalem to sacrifice to YHWH, the God of their fathers. So they strengthened the kingdom of Judah, and made Rehoboam the son of Solomon strong for three years; for they walked three years in the way of David and Solomon.

Rehoboam took a wife for himself, Mahalath the daughter of Jerimoth the son of David and of Abihail the daughter of Eliab the son of Jesse. She bore him sons: Jeush, Shemariah, and Zaham. After her, he took Maacah the daughter of Absalom; and she bore him Abijah, Attai, Ziza, and Shelomith. Rehoboam loved Maacah the daughter of Absalom above all his wives and his concubines; for he took eighteen wives and sixty concubines, and became the father of twenty-eight sons and sixty daughters. Rehoboam appointed Abijah the son of Maacah to be chief, the prince among his brothers; for he intended to make him king. He dealt wisely, and dispersed of all his sons throughout all the lands of Judah and Benjamin, to every fortified city. He gave them food in abundance and he sought many wives for them.

....

When the kingdom of Rehoboam was established and he was strong, he abandoned YHWH's law, and all Israel with him. In the fifth year of king Rehoboam, Shishak king of Egypt came up against Jerusalem, because they had trespassed against YHWH, with twelve hundred chariots, and sixty thousand horsemen. The people were without number who came with him out of Egypt: the Lubim, the Sukkiim, and the Ethiopians. He took the fortified cities which belonged to Judah, and came to Jerusalem. Now Shemaiah the prophet came to Rehoboam, and to the princes of Judah, who were gathered together to Jerusalem because of Shishak, and said to them, "YHWH says, 'You have forsaken me, therefore I have also left you in the hand of Shishak.'"

Then the princes of Israel and the king humbled themselves; and they said, "YHWH is righteous."

When YHWH saw that they humbled themselves, YHWH's word came to Shemaiah, saying, "They have humbled themselves. I will not destroy them; but I will grant them some deliverance, and my wrath won't be poured out on Jerusalem by the hand of Shishak. Nevertheless they will be his servants, that they may know my service, and the service of the kingdoms of the countries."

So Shishak king of Egypt came up against Jerusalem and took away the treasures of YHWH's house and the treasures of the king's house. He took it all away. He also took away the shields of gold which Solomon had made. King Rehoboam made shields of bronze in their place, and committed them to the hands of the captains of the guard, who kept the door of the king's house. As often as the king entered into YHWH's house, the guard came and bore them, then brought them back into the guard room. When he humbled himself, YHWH's wrath turned from him, so as not to destroy him altogether. Moreover, there were good things found in Judah.

So king Rehoboam strengthened himself in Jerusalem and reigned; for Rehoboam was forty-one years old when he began to reign, and he reigned seventeen years in Jerusalem, the city which YHWH had chosen out of all the tribes of Israel to put his name there. His mother's name was Naamah the Ammonitess. He did that which was evil, because he didn't set his heart to seek YHWH.

Now the acts of Rehoboam, first and last, aren't they written in the histories of Shemaiah the prophet and of Iddo the seer, in the genealogies? There were wars between Rehoboam and Jeroboam continually. Rehoboam slept with his fathers, and was buried in David's city; and Abijah his son reigned in his place.

....

In the eighteenth year of king Jeroboam, Abijah began to reign over Judah. He reigned three years in Jerusalem. His mother's name was Micaiah the daughter of Uriel of Gibeah. There was war between Abijah and Jeroboam. Abijah joined battle with an army of valiant men of war, even four hundred thousand chosen men; and Jeroboam set the battle in array against him with eight hundred thousand chosen men, who were mighty men of valor. Abijah stood up on Mount Zemaraim, which is in the hill country of Ephraim, and said, "Hear me, Jeroboam and all Israel: Ought you not to know that YHWH, the God of Israel, gave the kingdom over Israel to David forever, even to him and to his sons by a covenant of salt? Yet Jeroboam the son of Nebat, the servant of Solomon the son of David, rose up, and rebelled against his lord. Worthless men were gathered to him, wicked fellows who strengthened themselves against Rehoboam the son of Solomon, when Rehoboam was young and tender hearted, and could not withstand them.

"Now you intend to withstand the kingdom of YHWH in the hand of the sons of David. You are a great multitude, and the golden calves which Jeroboam made you for gods are with you. Haven't you driven out the priests of YHWH, the sons of Aaron, and the Levites, and made priests for yourselves according to the ways of the peoples of other lands? Whoever comes to consecrate himself with a young bull and seven rams may be a priest of those who are no gods.

"But as for us, YHWH is our God, and we have not forsaken him. We have priests serving YHWH, the sons of Aaron, and the Levites in their work; and they burn to YHWH every morning and every evening burnt offerings and sweet incense. They also set the show bread in order on the pure table; and the lamp stand of gold with its lamps, to burn every evening; for we keep the instruction of YHWH our God, but you have forsaken him. Behold, God is with us at our head, and his priests with the trumpets of alarm to sound an alarm against you. Children of Israel, don't fight against YHWH, the God of your fathers; for you will not prosper."

But Jeroboam caused an ambush to come about behind them; so they were before Judah, and the ambush was behind them. When Judah looked back, behold, the battle was before and behind them; and they cried to YHWH, and the priests sounded with the trumpets. Then the men of Judah gave a shout. As the men of Judah shouted, God struck Jeroboam and all Israel before Abijah and Judah. The children of Israel fled before Judah, and God delivered them into their hand. Abijah and his people killed them with a great slaughter, so five hundred thousand chosen men of Israel fell down slain. Thus the children of Israel were brought under at that time, and the children of Judah prevailed, because they relied on YHWH, the God of their fathers. Abijah pursued Jeroboam, and took cities from him, Bethel with its villages, Jeshanah with its villages, and Ephron with its villages.

Jeroboam didn't recover strength again in the days of Abijah. YHWH struck him, and he died. But Abijah grew mighty, and took for himself fourteen wives, and became the father of twenty-two sons, and sixteen daughters. The rest of the acts of Abijah, his ways, and his sayings are written in the commentary of the prophet Iddo.

So Abijah slept with his fathers, and they buried him in David's city; and Asa his son reigned in his place. In his days, the land was quiet ten years. Asa did that which was good and right in YHWH his God's eyes; for he took away the foreign altars and the high places, broke down the pillars, cut down the Asherah poles, and commanded Judah to seek YHWH, the God of their fathers, and to obey his law and command. Also he took away out of all the cities of Judah the high places and the sun images; and the kingdom was quiet before him. He built fortified cities in Judah; for the land was quiet, and he had no war in those years, because YHWH had given him rest. For he said to Judah, "Let's build these cities, and make walls around them, with towers, gates, and bars. The land is yet before us, because we have sought YHWH our God. We have sought him, and he has given us rest on every side." So they built and prospered.

Asa had an army of three hundred thousand out of Judah who bore bucklers and spears, and two hundred eighty thousand out of Benjamin who bore shields and drew bows. All these were mighty men of valor.

Zerah the Ethiopian came out against them with an army of a million troops and three hundred chariots, and he came to Mareshah. Then Asa went out to meet him, and they set the battle in array in the valley of Zephathah at Mareshah. Asa cried to YHWH his God, and said, "YHWH, there is no one besides you to help, between the mighty and him who has no strength. Help us, YHWH our God; for we rely on you, and in your name are we come against this multitude. YHWH, you are our God. Don't let man prevail against you."

So YHWH struck the Ethiopians before Asa and before Judah; and the Ethiopians fled. Asa and the people who were with him pursued them to Gerar: and so many of the Ethiopians fell that they could not recover themselves; for they were destroyed before YHWH and before his army; and they carried away very much booty. They struck all the cities around Gerar; for the fear of YHWH came on them, and they plundered all the cities; for there was much plunder in them. They also struck the tents of livestock, and carried away sheep in abundance, and camels, and returned to Jerusalem.

....

The Spirit of God came on Azariah the son of Oded: and he went out to meet Asa, and said to him, "Hear me, Asa, and all Judah and Benjamin! YHWH is with you, while you are with him; and if you seek him, he will be found by you; but if you forsake him, he will forsake you. Now for a long time Israel was without the true God, without a teaching priest, and without law. But when in their distress they turned to YHWH, the God of Israel, and sought him, he was found by them. In those times there was no peace to him who went out, nor to him who came in; but great troubles were on all the inhabitants of the lands. They were broken in pieces, nation against nation, and city against city; for God troubled them with all adversity. But you be strong, and don't let your hands be slack; for your work will be rewarded."

When Asa heard these words, and the prophecy of Oded the prophet, he took courage, and put away the abominations out of all the land of Judah and Benjamin, and out of the cities which he had taken from the hill country of Ephraim; and he renewed YHWH's altar that was before YHWH's porch. He gathered all Judah and Benjamin, and those who lived with them out of Ephraim, Manasseh, and Simeon; for they came to him out of Israel in abundance when they saw that YHWH his God was with him. So they gathered themselves together at Jerusalem in the third month, in the fifteenth year of Asa's reign. They sacrificed to YHWH in that day, of the plunder which they had brought, seven hundred head of cattle and seven thousand sheep. They entered into the covenant to seek YHWH, the God of their fathers, with all their heart and with all their soul; and that whoever would not seek YHWH, the God of Israel, should be put to death, whether small or great, whether man or woman. They swore to YHWH with a loud voice, with shouting, with trumpets, and with cornets. All Judah rejoiced at the oath, for they had sworn with all their heart, and sought him with their whole desire; and he was found by them. Then YHWH gave them rest all around.

Also Maacah, the mother of Asa the king, he removed from being queen, because she had made an abominable image for an Asherah; so Asa cut down her image, ground it into dust, and burned it at the brook Kidron. But the high places were not taken away out of Israel; nevertheless the heart of Asa was perfect all his days. He brought the things that his father had dedicated, and that he himself had dedicated, silver, gold, and vessels into God's house. There was no more war to the thirty-fifth year of Asa's reign.

In the thirty-sixth year of Asa's reign, Baasha king of Israel went up against Judah, and built Ramah, that he might not allow anyone to go out or come in to Asa king of Judah. Then Asa brought out silver and gold out of the treasures of YHWH's house and of the king's house, and sent to Ben Hadad king of Syria, who lived at Damascus, saying, "Let there be a treaty between me and you, as there was between my father and your father. Behold, I have sent you silver and gold. Go, break your treaty with Baasha king of Israel, that he may depart from me."

Ben Hadad listened to king Asa, and sent the captains of his armies against the cities of Israel; and they struck Ijon, Dan, Abel Maim, and all the storage cities of Naphtali. When Baasha heard of it, he stopped building Ramah, and let his work cease. Then Asa the king took all Judah, and they carried away the stones of Rama, and its timber, with which Baasha had built; and he built Geba and Mizpah with them.

At that time Hanani the seer came to Asa king of Judah, and said to him, "Because you have relied on the king of Syria, and have not relied on YHWH your God, therefore the army of the king of Syria has escaped out of your hand. Weren't the Ethiopians and the Lubim a huge army, with chariots and exceedingly many horsemen? Yet, because you relied on YHWH, he delivered them into your hand. For YHWH's eyes run back and forth throughout the whole earth, to show himself strong in the behalf of them whose heart is perfect toward him. You have done foolishly in this; for from now on you will have wars."

Then Asa was angry with the seer, and put him in the prison; for he was in a rage with him because of this thing. Asa oppressed some of the people at the same time.

Behold, the acts of Asa, first and last, behold, they are written in the book of the kings of Judah and Israel. In the thirty-ninth year of his reign, Asa was diseased in his feet. His disease was exceedingly great: yet in his disease he didn't seek YHWH, but just the physicians. Asa slept with his fathers, and died in the forty-first year of his reign. They buried him in his own tomb, which he had dug out for himself in David's city, and laid him in the bed which was filled with sweet odors and various kinds of spices prepared by the perfumers' art; and they made a very great fire for him.

....

Jehoshaphat his son reigned in his place, and strengthened himself against Israel. He placed forces in all the fortified cities of Judah, and set garrisons in the land of Judah, and in the cities of Ephraim, which Asa his father had taken. YHWH was with Jehoshaphat, because he walked in the first ways of his father David, and didn't seek the Baals, but sought to the God of his father, and walked in his commandments, and not in the ways of Israel. Therefore YHWH established the kingdom in his hand. All Judah brought tribute to Jehoshaphat, and he had riches and honor in abundance. His heart was lifted up in the ways of YHWH. Furthermore, he took away the high places and the Asherah poles out of Judah. Also in the third year of his reign he sent his princes, even Ben Hail, Obadiah, Zechariah, Nethanel, and Micaiah, to teach in the cities of Judah; and with them the Levites, even Shemaiah, Nethaniah, Zebadiah, Asahel, Shemiramoth, Jehonathan, Adonijah, Tobijah, and Tobadonijah, the Levites; and with them Elishama and Jehoram, the priests. They taught in Judah, having the book of YHWH's law with them. They went about throughout all the cities of Judah and taught among the people. The fear of YHWH fell on all the kingdoms of the lands that were around Judah, so that they made no war against Jehoshaphat. Some of the Philistines brought Jehoshaphat presents and silver for tribute. The Arabians also brought him flocks, seven thousand seven hundred rams, and seven thousand seven hundred male goats. Jehoshaphat grew great exceedingly; and he built fortresses and store cities in Judah. He had many works in the cities of Judah; and men of war, mighty men of valor, in Jerusalem. This was the numbering of them according to their fathers' houses: From Judah, the captains of thousands: Adnah the captain, and with him three hundred thousand mighty men of valor; and next to him Jehohanan the captain, and with him two hundred eighty thousand; and next to him Amasiah the son of Zichri, who willingly offered himself to YHWH, and with him two hundred thousand mighty men of valor. From Benjamin: Eliada, a mighty man of valor, and with him two hundred thousand armed with bow and shield; and next to him Jehozabad, and with him one hundred eighty thousand ready and prepared for war. These were those who waited on the king, in addition to those whom the king put in the fortified cities throughout all Judah.

....

Now Jehoshaphat had riches and honor in abundance; and he allied himself with Ahab. After some years, he went down to Ahab to Samaria. Ahab killed sheep and cattle for him in abundance, and for the people who were with him, and moved him to go up with him to Ramoth Gilead. Ahab king of Israel said to Jehoshaphat king of Judah, "Will you go with me to Ramoth Gilead?"

He answered him, "I am as you are, and my people as your people. We will be with you in the war." Jehoshaphat said to the king of Israel, "Please inquire first for YHWH's word."

Then the king of Israel gathered the prophets together, four hundred men, and said to them, "Shall we go to Ramoth Gilead to battle, or shall I forbear?"

They said, "Go up; for God will deliver it into the hand of the king."

But Jehoshaphat said, "Isn't there here a prophet of YHWH besides, that we may inquire of him?"

The king of Israel said to Jehoshaphat, "There is yet one man by whom we may inquire of YHWH; but I hate him, for he never prophesies good concerning me, but always evil. He is Micaiah the son of Imla."

Jehoshaphat said, "Don't let the king say so."

Then the king of Israel called an officer, and said, "Get Micaiah the son of Imla quickly."

Now the king of Israel and Jehoshaphat the king of Judah each sat on his throne, arrayed in their robes, and they were sitting in an open place at the entrance of the gate of Samaria; and all the prophets were prophesying before them. Zedekiah the son of Chenaanah made himself horns of iron and said, "YHWH says, 'With these you shall push the Syrians, until they are consumed.'"

All the prophets prophesied so, saying, "Go up to Ramoth Gilead, and prosper; for YHWH will deliver it into the hand of the king."

The messenger who went to call Micaiah spoke to him, saying, "Behold, the words of the prophets declare good to the king with one mouth. Let your word therefore, please be like one of theirs, and speak good."

Micaiah said, "As YHWH lives, I will say what my God says."

When he had come to the king, the king said to him, "Micaiah, shall we go to Ramoth Gilead to battle, or shall I forbear?"

He said, "Go up, and prosper. They shall be delivered into your hand."

The king said to him, "How many times shall I adjure you that you speak to me nothing but the truth in YHWH's name?"

He said, "I saw all Israel scattered on the mountains, as sheep that have no shepherd. YHWH said, 'These have no master. Let them each return to his house in peace.'"

The king of Israel said to Jehoshaphat, "Didn't I tell you that he would not prophesy good concerning me, but evil?"

Micaiah said, "Therefore hear YHWH's word: I saw YHWH sitting on his throne, and all the army of heaven standing on his right hand and on his left. YHWH said, 'Who will entice Ahab king of Israel, that he may go up and fall at Ramoth Gilead?' One spoke saying in this way, and another saying in that way. A spirit came out, stood before YHWH, and said, 'I will entice him.'

"YHWH said to him, 'How?'

"He said, 'I will go, and will be a lying spirit in the mouth of all his prophets.'

"He said, 'You will entice him, and will prevail also. Go and do so.'

"Now therefore, behold, YHWH has put a lying spirit in the mouth of these your prophets; and YHWH has spoken evil concerning you."

Then Zedekiah the son of Chenaanah came near, and struck Micaiah on the cheek, and said, "Which way did YHWH's Spirit go from me to speak to you?"

Micaiah said, "Behold, you shall see on that day, when you go into an inner room to hide yourself."

The king of Israel said, "Take Micaiah, and carry him back to Amon the governor of the city, and to Joash the king's son; and say, 'The king says, "Put this fellow in the prison, and feed him with bread of affliction and with water of affliction, until I return in peace."'"

Micaiah said, "If you return at all in peace, YHWH has not spoken by me." He said, "Listen, you people, all of you!"

So the king of Israel and Jehoshaphat the king of Judah went up to Ramoth Gilead. The king of Israel said to Jehoshaphat, "I will disguise myself, and go into the battle; but you put on your robes." So the king of Israel disguised himself; and they went into the battle. Now the king of Syria had commanded the captains of his chariots, saying, "Don't fight with small nor great, except only with the king of Israel."

When the captains of the chariots saw Jehoshaphat, they said, "It is the king of Israel!" Therefore they turned around to fight against him. But Jehoshaphat cried out, and YHWH helped him; and God moved them to depart from him. When the captains of the chariots saw that it was not the king of Israel, they turned back from pursuing him. A certain man drew his bow at random, and struck the king of Israel between the joints of the armor. Therefore he said to the driver of the chariot, "Turn your hand, and carry me out of the army; for

I am severely wounded." The battle increased that day. However the king of Israel propped himself up in his chariot against the Syrians until the evening; and at about sunset, he died.

....

Jehoshaphat the king of Judah returned to his house in peace to Jerusalem. Jehu the son of Hanani the seer went out to meet him, and said to king Jehoshaphat, "Should you help the wicked, and love those who hate YHWH? Because of this, wrath is on you from before YHWH. Nevertheless there are good things found in you, in that you have put away the Asheroth out of the land, and have set your heart to seek God."

Jehoshaphat lived at Jerusalem; and he went out again among the people from Beersheba to the hill country of Ephraim, and brought them back to YHWH, the God of their fathers. He set judges in the land throughout all the fortified cities of Judah, city by city, and said to the judges, "Consider what you do, for you don't judge for man, but for YHWH; and he is with you in the judgment. Now therefore let the fear of YHWH be on you. Take heed and do it; for there is no iniquity with YHWH our God, nor respect of persons, nor taking of bribes."

Moreover in Jerusalem Jehoshaphat appointed Levites and priests, and of the heads of the fathers' households of Israel, for the judgment of YHWH, and for controversies. They returned to Jerusalem. He commanded them, saying, "You shall do this in the fear of YHWH, faithfully, and with a perfect heart. Whenever any controversy comes to you from your brothers who dwell in their cities, between blood and blood, between law and commandment, statutes and ordinances, you must warn them, that they not be guilty toward YHWH, and so wrath come on you and on your brothers. Do this, and you will not be guilty. Behold, Amariah the chief priest is over you in all matters of YHWH; and Zebadiah the son of Ishmael, the ruler of the house of Judah, in all the king's matters. Also the Levites shall be officers before you. Deal courageously, and may YHWH be with the good."

....

After this, the children of Moab, the children of Ammon, and with them some of the Ammonites, came against Jehoshaphat to battle. Then some came who told Jehoshaphat, saying, "A great multitude is coming against you from beyond the sea from Syria. Behold, they are in Hazazon Tamar" (that is, En Gedi). Jehoshaphat was alarmed, and set himself to seek to YHWH. He proclaimed a fast throughout all Judah. Judah gathered themselves together to seek help from YHWH. They came out of all the cities of Judah to seek YHWH.

Jehoshaphat stood in the assembly of Judah and Jerusalem, in YHWH's house, before the new court; and he said, "YHWH, the God of our fathers, aren't you God in heaven? Aren't you ruler over all the kingdoms of the nations? Power and might are in your hand, so that no one is able to withstand you. Didn't you, our God, drive out the inhabitants of this land before your people Israel, and give it to the offspring of Abraham your friend forever? They lived in it, and have built you a sanctuary in it for your name, saying, 'If evil comes on us—the sword, judgment, pestilence, or famine—we will stand before this house, and before you (for your name is in this house), and cry to you in our affliction, and you will hear and save.' Now, behold, the children of Ammon and Moab and Mount Seir, whom you would not let Israel invade when they came out of the land of Egypt, but they turned away from them, and didn't destroy them; behold, how they reward us, to come to cast us out of your possession, which you have given us to inherit. Our God, will you not judge them? For we have no might against this great company that comes against us. We don't know what to do, but our eyes are on you."

All Judah stood before YHWH, with their little ones, their wives, and their children.

Then YHWH's Spirit came on Jahaziel the son of Zechariah, the son of Benaiah, the son of Jeiel, the son of Mattaniah, the Levite, of the sons of Asaph, in the middle of the assembly; and he said, "Listen, all Judah, and you inhabitants of Jerusalem, and you, king Jehoshaphat. YHWH says to you, 'Don't be afraid, and don't be dismayed because of this great multitude; for the battle is not yours, but God's. Tomorrow, go down against them. Behold, they are coming up by the ascent of Ziz. You will find them at the end of the valley, before the wilderness of Jeruel. You will not need to fight this battle. Set yourselves, stand still, and see the salvation of YHWH with you, O Judah and Jerusalem. Don't be afraid, nor be dismayed. Go out against them tomorrow, for YHWH is with you.'"

Jehoshaphat bowed his head with his face to the ground; and all Judah and the inhabitants of Jerusalem fell down before YHWH, worshiping YHWH. The Levites, of the children of the Kohathites and of the children of the Korahites, stood up to praise YHWH, the God of Israel, with an exceedingly loud voice.

They rose early in the morning, and went out into the wilderness of Tekoa. As they went out, Jehoshaphat stood and said, "Listen to me, Judah, and you inhabitants of Jerusalem! Believe in YHWH your God, so you will be established! Believe his prophets, so you will prosper."

When he had taken counsel with the people, he appointed those who were to sing to YHWH, and give praise in holy array, as they go out before the army, and say, "Give thanks to YHWH; for his loving kindness endures forever." When they began to sing and to praise, YHWH set ambushers against the children of Ammon, Moab, and Mount Seir, who had come against Judah; and they were struck. For the children of Ammon and Moab stood up against the inhabitants of Mount Seir to utterly kill and destroy them. When they had finished the inhabitants of Seir, everyone helped to destroy each other.

When Judah came to the place overlooking the wilderness, they looked at the multitude; and behold, they were dead bodies fallen to the earth, and there were none who escaped. When Jehoshaphat and his people came to take their plunder, they found among them in abundance both riches and dead bodies, and precious jewels, which they stripped off for themselves, more than they could carry away. They took plunder for three days, it was so much. On the fourth day, they assembled themselves in Beracah Valley, for there they blessed YHWH. Therefore the name of that place was called "Beracah Valley" to this day. Then they returned, every man of Judah and Jerusalem, with Jehoshaphat in front of them, to go again to Jerusalem with joy; for YHWH had made them to rejoice over their enemies. They came to Jerusalem with stringed instruments, harps, and trumpets to YHWH's house. The fear of God was on all the kingdoms of the countries, when they heard that YHWH fought against the enemies of Israel. So the realm of Jehoshaphat was quiet, for his God gave him rest all around.

Jehoshaphat reigned over Judah. He was thirty-five years old when he began to reign; and he reigned twenty-five years in Jerusalem. His mother's name was Azubah the daughter of Shilhi. He walked in the way of Asa his father, and didn't turn away from it, doing that which was right in YHWH's eyes. However the high places were not taken away, and the people had still not set their hearts on the God of their fathers. Now the rest of the acts of Jehoshaphat, first and last, behold, they are written in the history of Jehu the son of Hanani, which is included in the book of the kings of Israel. After this, Jehoshaphat king of Judah joined himself with Ahaziah king of Israel. The same did very wickedly. He joined himself with him to make ships to go to Tarshish. They made the ships in Ezion Geber. Then Eliezer the son of Dodavahu of Mareshah prophesied against Jehoshaphat, saying, "Because you have joined yourself with Ahaziah, YHWH has destroyed your works." The ships were wrecked, so that they were not able to go to Tarshish.

....

Jehoshaphat slept with his fathers, and was buried with his fathers in David's city, and Jehoram his son reigned in his place. He had brothers, the sons of Jehoshaphat: Azariah, Jehiel, Zechariah, Azariah, Michael, and Shephatiah. All these were the sons of Jehoshaphat king of Israel. Their father gave them great gifts of silver, of gold, and of precious things, with fortified cities in Judah; but he gave the kingdom to Jehoram, because he was the firstborn. Now when Jehoram had risen up over the kingdom of his father, and had strengthened himself, he killed all his brothers with the sword, and also some of the princes of Israel. Jehoram was thirty-two years old when he began to reign, and he reigned eight years in Jerusalem. He walked in the way of the kings of Israel, as did Ahab's house; for he had Ahab's daughter as his wife. He did that which was evil in YHWH's sight. However YHWH would not destroy David's house, because of the covenant that he had made with David, and as he promised to give a lamp to him and to his children always.

In his days Edom revolted from under the hand of Judah, and made a king over themselves. Then Jehoram went there with his captains and all his chariots with him. He rose up by night and struck the Edomites who surrounded him, along with the captains of the chariots. So Edom revolted from under the hand of Judah to this day. Then Libnah revolted at the same time from under his hand, because he had forsaken YHWH, the God of his fathers.

Moreover he made high places in the mountains of Judah, and made the inhabitants of Jerusalem play the prostitute, and led Judah astray. A letter came to him from Elijah the prophet, saying, "YHWH, the God of David your father, says, 'Because you have not walked in the ways of Jehoshaphat your father, nor in the ways of

Asa king of Judah, but have walked in the way of the kings of Israel, and have made Judah and the inhabitants of Jerusalem to play the prostitute like Ahab's house did, and also have slain your brothers of your father's house, who were better than yourself, behold, YHWH will strike your people with a great plague, including your children, your wives, and all your possessions; and you will have great sickness with a disease of your bowels, until your bowels fall out by reason of the sickness, day by day.'"

YHWH stirred up against Jehoram the spirit of the Philistines, and of the Arabians who are beside the Ethiopians; and they came up against Judah, broke into it, and carried away all the possessions that were found in the king's house, including his sons and his wives; so that there was no son left him, except Jehoahaz, the youngest of his sons.

After all this YHWH struck him in his bowels with an incurable disease. In process of time, at the end of two years, his bowels fell out by reason of his sickness, and he died of severe diseases. His people made no burning for him, like the burning of his fathers. He was thirty-two years old when he began to reign, and he reigned in Jerusalem eight years. He departed without being missed; and they buried him in David's city, but not in the tombs of the kings.

....

The inhabitants of Jerusalem made Ahaziah his youngest son king in his place, because the band of men who came with the Arabians to the camp had slain all the oldest. So Ahaziah the son of Jehoram king of Judah reigned. Ahaziah was forty-two years old when he began to reign, and he reigned one year in Jerusalem. His mother's name was Athaliah the daughter of Omri. He also walked in the ways of Ahab's house, because his mother was his counselor in acting wickedly. He did that which was evil in YHWH's sight, as did Ahab's house, for they were his counselors after the death of his father, to his destruction. He also followed their counsel, and went with Jehoram the son of Ahab king of Israel to war against Hazael king of Syria at Ramoth Gilead, and the Syrians wounded Joram. He returned to be healed in Jezreel of the wounds which they had given him at Ramah, when he fought against Hazael king of Syria. Azariah the son of Jehoram king of Judah went down to see Jehoram the son of Ahab in Jezreel, because he was sick.

Now the destruction of Ahaziah was of God, in that he went

to Joram; for when he had come, he went out with Jehoram against Jehu the son of Nimshi, whom YHWH had anointed to cut off Ahab's house. When Jehu was executing judgment on Ahab's house, he found the princes of Judah and the sons of the brothers of Ahaziah, serving Ahaziah, and killed them. He sought Ahaziah, and they caught him (now he was hiding in Samaria), and they brought him to Jehu, and killed him; and they buried him, for they said, "He is the son of Jehoshaphat, who sought YHWH with all his heart." The house of Ahaziah had no power to hold the kingdom.

Now when Athaliah the mother of Ahaziah saw that her son was dead, she arose and destroyed all the royal offspring of the house of Judah. But Jehoshabeath, the king's daughter, took Joash the son of Ahaziah, and stealthily rescued him from among the king's sons who were slain, and put him and his nurse in the bedroom. So Jehoshabeath, the daughter of king Jehoram, the wife of Jehoiada the priest (for she was the sister of Ahaziah), hid him from Athaliah, so that she didn't kill him. He was with them hidden in God's house six years while Athaliah reigned over the land.

....

In the seventh year, Jehoiada strengthened himself, and took the captains of hundreds, Azariah the son of Jeroham, Ishmael the son of Jehohanan, Azariah the son of Obed, Maaseiah the son of Adaiah, and Elishaphat the son of Zichri, into a covenant with him. They went around in Judah, and gathered the Levites out of all the cities of Judah, and the heads of fathers' households of Israel, and they came to Jerusalem. All the assembly made a covenant with the king in God's house. He said to them, "Behold, the king's son must reign, as YHWH has spoken concerning the sons of David. This is the thing that you must do. A third part of you, who come in on the Sabbath, of the priests and of the Levites, shall be gatekeepers of the thresholds. A third part shall be at the king's house; and a third part at the gate of the foundation. All the people will be in the courts of YHWH's house. But let no one come into YHWH's house, except the priests and those who minister of the Levites. They shall come in, for they are holy, but all the people shall follow YHWH's instructions. The Levites shall surround the king, every man with his weapons in his hand. Whoever comes into the house, let him be slain. Be with the king when he comes in, and when he goes out."

So the Levites and all Judah did according to all that Jehoiada the priest commanded: and they each took his men, those who were to come in on the Sabbath; with those who were to go out on the Sabbath; for Jehoiada the priest didn't dismiss the shift. Jehoiada the priest delivered to the captains of hundreds the spears, and bucklers, and shields, that had been king David's, which were in God's house. He set all the people, every man with his weapon in his hand, from the right side of the house to the left side of the house, near the altar and the house, around the king. Then they brought out the king's son, and put the crown on him, and gave him the covenant, and made him king. Jehoiada and his sons anointed him, and they said, "Long live the king!"

When Athaliah heard the noise of the people running and praising the king, she came to the people into YHWH's house. Then she looked, and, behold, the king stood by his pillar at the entrance, and the captains and the trumpets by the king. All the people of the land rejoiced, and blew trumpets. The singers also played musical instruments, and led the singing of praise. Then Athaliah tore her clothes, and said, "Treason! treason!"

Jehoiada the priest brought out the captains of hundreds who were set over the army, and said to them, "Bring her out between the ranks; and whoever follows her, let him be slain with the sword." For the priest said, "Don't kill her in YHWH's house." So they made way for her. She went to the entrance of the horse gate to the king's house; and they killed her there.

Jehoiada made a covenant between himself, all the people, and the king, that they should be YHWH's people. All the people went to the house of Baal, broke it down, broke his altars and his images in pieces, and killed Mattan the priest of Baal before the altars. Jehoiada appointed the officers of YHWH's house under the hand of the Levitical priests, whom David had distributed in YHWH's house, to offer the burnt offerings of YHWH, as it is written in the law of Moses, with rejoicing and with singing, as David had ordered. He set the gatekeepers at the gates of YHWH's house, that no one who was unclean in anything should enter in. He took the captains of hundreds, the nobles, the governors of the people, and all the people of the land, and brought the king down from YHWH's house. They came through the upper gate to the king's house, and set the king on the throne of the kingdom. So all the people of the land rejoiced, and the city was quiet. They had slain Athaliah with the sword.

Joash was seven years old when he began to reign, and he reigned forty years in Jerusalem. His mother's name was Zibiah, of Beersheba. Joash did that which was right in Yhwh's eyes all the days of Jehoiada the priest. Jehoiada took for him two wives, and he became the father of sons and daughters.

After this, Joash intended to restore Yhwh's house. He gathered together the priests and the Levites, and said to them, "Go out to the cities of Judah, and gather money to repair the house of your God from all Israel from year to year. See that you expedite this matter." However the Levites didn't do it right away. The king called for Jehoiada the chief, and said to him, "Why haven't you required of the Levites to bring in the tax of Moses the servant of Yhwh, and of the assembly of Israel, out of Judah and out of Jerusalem, for the Tent of the Testimony?" For the sons of Athaliah, that wicked woman, had broken up God's house; and they also gave all the dedicated things of Yhwh's house to the Baals.

So the king commanded, and they made a chest, and set it outside at the gate of Yhwh's house. They made a proclamation through Judah and Jerusalem, to bring in for Yhwh the tax that Moses the servant of God laid on Israel in the wilderness. All the princes and all the people rejoiced, and brought in, and cast into the chest, until they had filled it. Whenever the chest was brought to the king's officers by the hand of the Levites, and when they saw that there was much money, the king's scribe and the chief priest's officer came and emptied the chest, and took it, and carried it to its place again. Thus they did day by day, and gathered money in abundance. The king and Jehoiada gave it to those who did the work of the service of Yhwh's house. They hired masons and carpenters to restore Yhwh's house, and also those who worked iron and bronze to repair Yhwh's house. So the workmen worked, and the work of repairing went forward in their hands. They set up God's house as it was designed, and strengthened it. When they had finished, they brought the rest of the money before the king and Jehoiada, from which were made vessels for Yhwh's house, even vessels with which to minister and to offer, including spoons and vessels of gold and silver. They offered burnt offerings in Yhwh's house continually all the days of Jehoiada.

But Jehoiada grew old and was full of days, and he died. He was one hundred thirty years old when he died. They buried him in David's city among the kings, because he had done good in Israel, and toward God and his house.

Now after the death of Jehoiada, the princes of Judah came, and bowed down to the king. Then the king listened to them. They abandoned the house of YHWH, the God of their fathers, and served the Asherah poles and the idols, so wrath came on Judah and Jerusalem for this their guiltiness. Yet he sent prophets to them, to bring them again to YHWH, and they testified against them; but they would not listen.

The Spirit of God came on Zechariah the son of Jehoiada the priest; and he stood above the people, and said to them, "God says, 'Why do you disobey YHWH's commandments, so that you can't prosper? Because you have forsaken YHWH, he has also forsaken you.'"

They conspired against him, and stoned him with stones at the commandment of the king in the court of YHWH's house. Thus Joash the king didn't remember the kindness which Jehoiada his father had done to him, but killed his son. When he died, he said, "May YHWH look at it, and repay it."

At the end of the year, the army of the Syrians came up against him: and they came to Judah and Jerusalem, and destroyed all the princes of the people from among the people, and sent all their plunder to the king of Damascus. For the army of the Syrians came with a small company of men; and YHWH delivered a very great army into their hand, because they had forsaken YHWH, the God of their fathers. So they executed judgment on Joash.

When they had departed from him (for they left him very sick), his own servants conspired against him for the blood of the sons of Jehoiada the priest, and killed him on his bed, and he died. They buried him in David's city, but they didn't bury him in the tombs of the kings. These are those who conspired against him: Zabad the son of Shimeath the Ammonitess and Jehozabad the son of Shimrith the Moabitess. Now concerning his sons, the greatness of the burdens laid on him, and the rebuilding of God's house, behold, they are written in the commentary of the book of the kings. Amaziah his son reigned in his place.

Amaziah was twenty-five years old when he began to reign, and he reigned twenty-nine years in Jerusalem. His mother's name was Jehoaddan, of Jerusalem. He did that which was right in YHWH's eyes, but not with a perfect heart. Now when the kingdom was established to him, he killed his servants who had killed his father the king. But he didn't put their children to death, but did according to that which is written in the law in the book of Moses, as YHWH commanded, saying, "The fathers shall not die for the children, neither shall the children die for the fathers; but every man shall die for his own sin."

Moreover Amaziah gathered Judah together, and ordered them according to their fathers' houses, under captains of thousands and captains of hundreds, even all Judah and Benjamin. He counted them from twenty years old and upward, and found that there were three hundred thousand chosen men, able to go out to war, who could handle spear and shield. He also hired one hundred thousand mighty men of valor out of Israel for one hundred talents of silver. A man of God came to him, saying, "O king, don't let the army of Israel go with you, for YHWH is not with Israel, with all the children of Ephraim. But if you will go, take action, and be strong for the battle. God will overthrow you before the enemy; for God has power to help, and to overthrow."

Amaziah said to the man of God, "But what shall we do for the hundred talents which I have given to the army of Israel?"

The man of God answered, "YHWH is able to give you much more than this."

Then Amaziah separated them, the army that had come to him out of Ephraim, to go home again. Therefore their anger was greatly kindled against Judah, and they returned home in fierce anger. Amaziah took courage, and led his people out, and went to the Valley of Salt, and struck ten thousand of the children of Seir. The children of Judah carried away ten thousand alive, and brought them to the top of the rock, and threw them down from the top of the rock, so that they all were broken in pieces. But the men of the army whom Amaziah sent back, that they should not go with him to battle, fell on the cities of Judah, from Samaria even to Beth Horon, and struck of them three thousand, and took much plunder.

Now after Amaziah had come from the slaughter of the Edomites, he brought the gods of the children of Seir, and set them up to be his gods, and bowed down himself before them, and burned incense to them. Therefore YHWH's anger burned against Amaziah, and he sent to him a prophet, who said to him, "Why have you sought after the gods of the people, which have not delivered their own people out of your hand?"

As he talked with him, the king said to him, "Have we made you one of the king's counselors? Stop! Why should you be struck down?"

Then the prophet stopped, and said, "I know that God has determined to destroy you, because you have done this, and have not listened to my counsel."

Then Amaziah king of Judah consulted his advisers, and sent to Joash, the son of Jehoahaz the son of Jehu, king of Israel, saying, "Come! Let's look one another in the face."

Joash king of Israel sent to Amaziah king of Judah, saying, "The thistle that was in Lebanon sent to the cedar that was in Lebanon, saying, 'Give your daughter to my son as his wife. Then a wild animal that was in Lebanon passed by, and trampled down the thistle. You say to yourself that you have struck Edom; and your heart lifts you up to boast. Now stay at home. Why should you meddle with trouble, that you should fall, even you, and Judah with you?'"

But Amaziah would not listen; for it was of God, that he might deliver them into the hand of their enemies, because they had sought after the gods of Edom. So Joash king of Israel went up, and he and Amaziah king of Judah looked one another in the face at Beth Shemesh, which belongs to Judah. Judah was defeated by Israel; so every man fled to his tent.

Joash king of Israel took Amaziah king of Judah, the son of Joash the son of Jehoahaz, at Beth Shemesh, and brought him to Jerusalem, and broke down the wall of Jerusalem from the gate of Ephraim to the corner gate, four hundred cubits. He took all the gold and silver, and all the vessels that were found in God's house with Obed-Edom, and the treasures of the king's house, the hostages also, and returned to Samaria.

Amaziah the son of Joash king of Judah lived for fifteen years after the death of Joash son of Jehoahaz king of Israel. Now the rest of the acts of Amaziah, first and last, behold, aren't they written in the book of the kings of Judah and Israel? Now from the time that Amaziah turned away from following YHWH, they made a conspiracy against him in Jerusalem. He fled to Lachish, but they sent after him to Lachish, and killed him there. They brought him on horses, and buried him with his fathers in the City of Judah.

....

All the people of Judah took Uzziah, who was sixteen years old, and made him king in the place of his father Amaziah. He built Eloth, and restored it to Judah, after that the king slept with his fathers. Uzziah was sixteen years old when he began to reign; and he reigned fifty-two years in Jerusalem. His mother's name was Jechiliah, of Jerusalem. He did that which was right in YHWH's eyes, according to all that his father Amaziah had done. He set himself to seek God in the days of Zechariah, who had understanding in the vision of God; and as long as he sought YHWH, God made him prosper.

He went out and fought against the Philistines, and broke down the wall of Gath, the wall of Jabneh, and the wall of Ashdod; and he built cities in the country of Ashdod, and among the Philistines. God helped him against the Philistines, and against the Arabians who lived in Gur Baal, and the Meunim. The Ammonites gave tribute to Uzziah. His name spread abroad even to the entrance of Egypt; for he grew exceedingly strong. Moreover Uzziah built towers in Jerusalem at the corner gate, at the valley gate, and at the turning of the wall, and fortified them. He built towers in the wilderness, and dug out many cisterns, for he had much livestock; in the lowland also, and in the plain. He had farmers and vineyard keepers in the mountains and in the fruitful fields, for he loved farming. Moreover Uzziah had an army of fighting men, who went out to war by bands, according to the number of their reckoning made by Jeiel the scribe and Maaseiah the officer, under the hand of Hananiah, one of the king's captains. The whole number of the heads of fathers' households, even the mighty men of valor, was two thousand six hundred. Under their hand was an army, three hundred seven thousand five hundred, who made war with mighty power, to help the king against the enemy. Uzziah prepared for them, even for all the army, shields, spears, helmets, coats of mail, bows, and stones for slinging. In Jerusalem, he made devices, invented by skillful men, to be on the towers and on the battlements, with which to shoot arrows and great stones. His name spread far abroad, because he was marvelously helped until he was strong.

But when he was strong, his heart was lifted up, so that he did corruptly, and he trespassed against YHWH his God; for he went into YHWH's temple to burn incense on the altar of incense. Azariah the priest went in after him, and with him eighty priests of YHWH, who were valiant men. They resisted Uzziah the king, and said to him, "It isn't for you, Uzziah, to burn incense to YHWH, but for the priests the sons of Aaron, who are consecrated to burn incense. Go out of the sanctuary, for you have trespassed. It will not be for your honor from YHWH God."

Then Uzziah was angry. He had a censer in his hand to burn incense, and while he was angry with the priests, the leprosy broke out on his forehead before the priests in YHWH's house, beside the altar of incense. Azariah the chief priest, and all the priests, looked at him, and behold, he was leprous in his forehead, and they thrust him out quickly from there. Yes, he himself also hurried to go out, because YHWH had struck him. Uzziah the king was a leper to the day of his death, and lived in a separate house, being a leper; for he was cut off from YHWH's house. Jotham his son was over the king's house, judging the people of the land. Now the rest of the acts of Uzziah, first and last, Isaiah the prophet, the son of Amoz, wrote. So Uzziah slept with his fathers; and they buried him with his fathers in the field of burial which belonged to the kings, for they said, "He is a leper." Jotham his son reigned in his place.

....

Jotham was twenty-five years old when he began to reign, and he reigned sixteen years in Jerusalem. His mother's name was Jerushah the daughter of Zadok. He did that which was right in YHWH's eyes, according to all that his father Uzziah had done. However he didn't enter into YHWH's temple. The people still acted corruptly. He built the upper gate of YHWH's house, and he built much on the wall of Ophel. Moreover he built cities in the hill country of Judah, and in the forests he built fortresses and towers. He also fought with the king of the children of Ammon, and prevailed against them. The children of Ammon gave him the same year one hundred talents of silver, ten thousand cors of wheat, and ten thousand cors of barley. The children of Ammon also gave that much to him in the second year, and in the third. So Jotham became mighty, because he ordered his ways before YHWH his God. Now the rest of the acts of Jotham, and all his wars, and his ways, behold, they are written in the book of the kings of Israel and Judah. He was five and twenty years old when he began to reign, and reigned sixteen years in Jerusalem. Jotham slept with his fathers, and they buried him in David's city; and Ahaz his son reigned in his place.

....

Ahaz was twenty years old when he began to reign, and he reigned sixteen years in Jerusalem. He didn't do that which was right in YHWH's eyes, like David his father, but he walked in the ways of the kings of Israel, and also made molten images for the Baals. Moreover he burned incense in the valley of the son of Hinnom, and burned his children in the fire, according to the abominations of the nations whom YHWH cast out before the children of Israel. He sacrificed and burned incense in the high places, and on the hills, and under every green tree.

Therefore YHWH his God delivered him into the hand of the king of Syria. They struck him, and carried away from him a great multitude of captives, and brought them to Damascus. He was also delivered into the hand of the king of Israel, who struck him with a great slaughter. For Pekah the son of Remaliah killed in Judah one hundred twenty thousand in one day, all of them valiant men, because they had forsaken YHWH, the God of their fathers. Zichri, a mighty man of Ephraim, killed Maaseiah the king's son, Azrikam the ruler of the house, and Elkanah who was next to the king. The children of Israel carried away captive of their brothers two hundred thousand women, sons, and daughters, and also took away much plunder from them, and brought the plunder to Samaria. But a prophet of YHWH was there, whose name was Oded; and he went out to meet the army that came to Samaria, and said to them, "Behold, because YHWH, the God of your fathers, was angry with Judah, he has delivered them into your hand, and you have slain them in a rage which has reached up to heaven. Now you intend to degrade the children of Judah and Jerusalem as male and female slaves for yourselves. Aren't there even with you trespasses of your own against YHWH your God? Now hear me therefore, and send back the captives that you have taken captive from your brothers, for the fierce wrath of YHWH is on you." Then some of the heads of the children of Ephraim, Azariah the son of Johanan, Berechiah the son of Meshillemoth, Jehizkiah the son of Shallum, and Amasa the son of Hadlai, stood up against those who came from the war, and said to them, "You must not bring in the captives here, for you intend that which will bring on us a trespass against YHWH, to add to our sins and to our guilt; for our guilt is great, and there is fierce wrath against Israel."

So the armed men left the captives and the plunder before the princes and all the assembly. The men who have been mentioned by name rose up and took the captives, and with the plunder clothed all who were naked among them, dressed them, gave them sandals, and gave them something to eat and to drink, anointed them, carried all the feeble of them on donkeys, and brought them to Jericho, the city of palm trees, to their brothers. Then they returned to Samaria.

At that time king Ahaz sent to the kings of Assyria to help him. For again the Edomites had come and struck Judah, and carried away captives. The Philistines also had invaded the cities of the lowland, and of the South of Judah, and had taken Beth Shemesh, Aijalon, Gederoth, Soco with its villages, Timnah with its villages, and also Gimzo and its villages; and they lived there. For YHWH brought Judah low because of Ahaz king of Israel, because he acted without restraint in Judah and trespassed severely against YHWH. Tilgath Pilneser king of Assyria came to him, and gave him trouble, but didn't strengthen him. For Ahaz took away a portion out of YHWH's house, and out of the house of the king and of the princes, and gave it to the king of Assyria; but it didn't help him.

In the time of his distress, he trespassed yet more against YHWH, this same king Ahaz. For he sacrificed to the gods of Damascus, which struck him. He said, "Because the gods of the kings of Syria helped them, so I will sacrifice to them, that they may help me." But they were the ruin of him, and of all Israel. Ahaz gathered together the vessels of God's house, and cut the vessels of God's house in pieces, and shut up the doors of YHWH's house; and he made himself altars in every corner of Jerusalem. In every city of Judah he made high places to burn incense to other gods, and provoked YHWH, the God of his fathers, to anger.

Now the rest of his acts, and all his ways, first and last, behold, they are written in the book of the kings of Judah and Israel. Ahaz slept with his fathers, and they buried him in the city, even in Jerusalem, because they didn't bring him into the tombs of the kings of Israel; and Hezekiah his son reigned in his place.

....

Hezekiah began to reign when he was twenty-five years old, and he reigned twenty-nine years in Jerusalem. His mother's name was Abijah, the daughter of Zechariah. He did that which was right in YHWH's eyes, according to all that David his father had done. In the first year of his reign, in the first month, he opened the doors of YHWH's house, and repaired them. He brought in the priests and the Levites, and gathered them together into the wide place on the east, and said to them, "Listen to me, you Levites! Now sanctify yourselves, and sanctify YHWH, the God of your fathers' house, and carry the filthiness out of the holy place. For our fathers were unfaithful, and have done that which was evil in YHWH our God's sight, and have forsaken him, and have turned away their faces from the habitation of YHWH, and turned their backs. Also they have shut up the doors of the porch, and put out the lamps, and have not burned incense nor offered burnt offerings in the holy place to the God of Israel. Therefore YHWH's wrath was on Judah and Jerusalem, and he has delivered them to be tossed back and forth, to be an astonishment, and a hissing, as you see with your eyes. For, behold, our fathers have fallen by the sword, and our sons and our daughters and our wives are in captivity for this. Now it is in my heart to make a covenant with YHWH, the God of Israel, that his fierce anger may turn away from us. My sons, don't be negligent now; for YHWH has chosen you to stand before him, to minister to him, and that you should be his ministers, and burn incense."

Then the Levites arose, Mahath, the son of Amasai, and Joel the son of Azariah, of the sons of the Kohathites; and of the sons of Merari, Kish the son of Abdi, and Azariah the son of Jehallelel; and of the Gershonites, Joah the son of Zimmah, and Eden the son of Joah; and of the sons of Elizaphan, Shimri and Jeuel; and of the sons of Asaph, Zechariah and Mattaniah; and of the sons of Heman, Jehuel and Shimei; and of the sons of Jeduthun, Shemaiah and Uzziel. They gathered their brothers, sanctified themselves, and went in, according to the commandment of the king by YHWH's words, to cleanse YHWH's house. The priests went into the inner part of YHWH's house to cleanse it, and brought out all the uncleanness that they found in YHWH's temple into the court of YHWH's house. The Levites took it from there to carry it out to the brook Kidron. Now they began on the first day of the first month to sanctify, and on the eighth day of the month they came to YHWH's porch. They sanctified YHWH's house in eight days, and on the sixteenth day of the first month they finished. Then they went in to Hezekiah the king within the palace, and said, "We have cleansed all YHWH's house, including the altar of burnt offering with all its vessels, and the table of show bread with all its vessels. Moreover have we prepared and sanctified all the vessels which king Ahaz threw away in his reign, when he was unfaithful. Behold, they are before YHWH's altar."

Then Hezekiah the king arose early, gathered the princes of the city, and went up to YHWH's house. They brought seven bulls, seven rams, seven lambs, and seven male goats, for a sin offering for the kingdom, for the sanctuary, and for Judah. He commanded the priests the sons of Aaron to offer them on YHWH's altar. So they killed the bulls, and the priests received the blood, and sprinkled it on the altar. They killed the rams, and sprinkled the blood on the altar. They also killed the lambs, and sprinkled the blood on the altar. They brought near the male goats for the sin offering before the king and the assembly; and they laid their hands on them. Then the priests killed them, and they made a sin offering with their blood on the altar, to make atonement for all Israel; for the king commanded that the burnt offering and the sin offering should be made for all Israel.

He set the Levites in YHWH's house with cymbals, with stringed instruments, and with harps, according to the commandment of David, of Gad the king's seer, and Nathan the prophet; for the commandment was from YHWH by his prophets. The Levites stood with David's instruments, and the priests with the trumpets. Hezekiah commanded them to offer the burnt offering on the altar. When the burnt offering began, YHWH's song also began, along with the trumpets and David king of Israel's instruments. All the assembly worshiped, the singers sang, and the trumpeters sounded. All this continued until the burnt offering was finished.

When they had finished offering, the king and all who were present with him bowed themselves and worshiped. Moreover Hezekiah the king and the princes commanded the Levites to sing praises to YHWH with the words of David, and of Asaph the seer. They sang praises with gladness, and they bowed their heads and worshiped.

Then Hezekiah answered, "Now you have consecrated yourselves to YHWH. Come near and bring sacrifices and thank offerings into YHWH's house." The assembly brought in sacrifices and thank offerings, and as many as were of a willing heart brought burnt offerings. The number of the burnt offerings which the assembly brought was seventy bulls, one hundred rams, and two hundred lambs. All these were for a burnt offering to YHWH. The consecrated things were six hundred head of cattle and three thousand sheep. But the priests were too few, so that they could not skin all the burnt offerings. Therefore their brothers the Levites helped them, until the work was ended, and until the priests had sanctified themselves; for the Levites were more upright in heart to sanctify themselves than the priests. Also the burnt offerings were in abundance, with the fat of the peace offerings, and with the drink offerings for every burnt offering. So the service of YHWH's house was set in order. Hezekiah and all the people rejoiced, because of that which God had prepared for the people; for the thing was done suddenly.

....

Hezekiah sent to all Israel and Judah, and wrote letters also to Ephraim and Manasseh, that they should come to YHWH's house at Jerusalem, to keep the Passover to YHWH, the God of Israel. For the king had taken counsel with his princes and all the assembly in Jerusalem to keep the Passover in the second month. For they could not keep it at that time, because the priests had not sanctified themselves in sufficient number, and the people had not gathered themselves together to Jerusalem. The thing was right in the eyes of the king and of all the assembly. So they established a decree to make proclamation throughout all Israel, from Beersheba even to Dan, that they should come to keep the Passover to YHWH, the God of Israel, at Jerusalem, for they had not kept it in great numbers in the way it is written.

So the couriers went with the letters from the king and his princes throughout all Israel and Judah, and according to the commandment of the king, saying, "You children of Israel, turn again to YHWH, the God of Abraham, Isaac, and Israel, that he may return to the remnant of you that have escaped out of the hand of the kings of Assyria. Don't be like your fathers and like your brothers, who trespassed against YHWH, the God of their fathers, so that he gave them up to desolation, as you see. Now don't be stiff-necked, as your fathers were, but yield yourselves to YHWH, and enter into his sanctuary, which he has sanctified forever, and serve YHWH your God, that his fierce anger may turn away from you. For if you turn again to YHWH, your brothers and your children will find compassion before those who led them captive, and will come again into this land, because YHWH your God is gracious and merciful, and will not turn away his face from you, if you return to him."

So the couriers passed from city to city through the country of Ephraim and Manasseh, even to Zebulun, but people ridiculed them and mocked them. Nevertheless some men of Asher, Manasseh, and Zebulun humbled themselves, and came to Jerusalem. Also the hand of God came on Judah to give them one heart, to do the commandment of the king and of the princes by YHWH's word.

Many people assembled at Jerusalem to keep the feast of unleavened bread in the second month, a very great assembly. They arose and took away the altars that were in Jerusalem, and they took away all the altars for incense and threw them into the brook Kidron. Then they killed the Passover on the fourteenth day of the second month. The priests and the Levites were ashamed, and sanctified themselves, and brought burnt offerings into YHWH's house. They stood in their place after their order, according to the law of Moses the man of God. The priests sprinkled the blood which they received of the hand of the Levites. For there were many in the assembly who had not sanctified themselves: therefore the Levites were in charge of killing the Passovers for everyone who was not clean, to sanctify them to YHWH. For a multitude of the people, even many of Ephraim, Manasseh, Issachar, and Zebulun, had not cleansed themselves, yet they ate the Passover other than the way it is written. For Hezekiah had prayed for them, saying, "May the good YHWH pardon everyone who sets his heart to seek God, YHWH, the God of his fathers, even if they aren't clean according to the purification of the sanctuary."

YHWH listened to Hezekiah, and healed the people. The children of Israel who were present at Jerusalem kept the feast of unleavened bread seven days with great gladness. The Levites and the priests praised YHWH day by day, singing with loud instruments to YHWH. Hezekiah spoke encouragingly to all the Levites who had good understanding in the service of YHWH. So they ate throughout the feast for the seven days, offering sacrifices of peace offerings, and making confession to YHWH, the God of their fathers.

The whole assembly took counsel to keep another seven days, and they kept another seven days with gladness. For Hezekiah king of Judah gave to the assembly for offerings one thousand bulls and seven thousand sheep; and the princes gave to the assembly a thousand bulls and ten thousand sheep: and a great number of priests sanctified themselves. All the assembly of Judah, with the priests and the Levites, and all the assembly who came out of Israel, and the foreigners who came out of the land of Israel, and who lived in Judah, rejoiced. So there was great joy in Jerusalem; for since the time of Solomon the son of David king of Israel there was nothing like this in Jerusalem. Then the Levitical priests arose and blessed the people. Their voice was heard, and their prayer came up to his holy habitation, even to heaven.

....

Now when all this was finished, all Israel who were present went out to the cities of Judah, and broke the pillars in pieces, cut down the Asherah poles, and broke down the high places and the altars out of all Judah and Benjamin, also in Ephraim and Manasseh, until they had destroyed them all. Then all the children of Israel returned, every man to his possession, into their own cities.

Hezekiah appointed the divisions of the priests and the Levites after their divisions, every man according to his service, both the priests and the Levites, for burnt offerings and for peace offerings, to minister, to give thanks, and to praise in the gates of YHWH's camp. He also appointed the king's portion of his possessions for the burnt offerings, for the morning and evening burnt offerings, and the burnt offerings for the Sabbaths, for the new moons, and for the set feasts, as it is written in YHWH's law. Moreover he commanded the people who lived in Jerusalem to give the portion of the priests and the Levites, that they might give themselves to YHWH's law. As soon as the commandment went out, the children of Israel gave in abundance the first fruits of grain, new wine, oil, honey, and of all the increase of the field; and they brought in the tithe of all things abundantly. The children of Israel and Judah, who lived in the cities of Judah, also brought in the tithe of cattle and sheep, and the tithe of dedicated things which were consecrated to YHWH their God, and laid them in heaps.

In the third month they began to lay the foundation of the heaps, and finished them in the seventh month. When Hezekiah and the princes came and saw the heaps, they blessed YHWH and his people Israel. Then Hezekiah questioned the priests and the Levites about the heaps. Azariah the chief priest, of the house of Zadok, answered him and said, "Since people began to bring the offerings into YHWH's house, we have eaten and had enough, and have plenty left over, for YHWH has blessed his people; and that which is left is this great store."

Then Hezekiah commanded them to prepare rooms in YHWH's house, and they prepared them. They brought in the offerings, the tithes, and the dedicated things faithfully. Conaniah the Levite was ruler over them, and Shimei his brother was second. Jehiel, Azaziah, Nahath, Asahel, Jerimoth, Jozabad, Eliel, Ismachiah, Mahath, and Benaiah were overseers under the hand of Conaniah and Shimei his brother, by the appointment of Hezekiah the king and Azariah the ruler of God's house. Kore the son of Imnah the Levite, the gate-keeper at the east gate, was over the free will offerings of God, to distribute YHWH's offerings and the most holy things. Under him were Eden, Miniamin, Jeshua, Shemaiah, Amariah, and Shecaniah, in the cities of the priests, in their office of trust, to give to their brothers by divisions, to the great as well as to the small; in addition to those who were listed by genealogy of males, from three years old and upward, even everyone who entered into YHWH's house, as the duty of every day required, for their service in their offices according to their divisions; and those who were listed by genealogy of the priests by their fathers' houses, and the Levites from twenty years old and upward, in their offices by their divisions; and those who were listed by genealogy of all their little ones, their wives, their sons, and their daughters, through all the congregation; for in their office of trust they sanctified themselves in holiness. Also for the sons of Aaron the priests, who were in the fields of the pasture lands of their cities, in every city, there were men who were mentioned by name, to give portions to all the males among the priests, and to all who were listed by genealogy among the Levites.

Hezekiah did so throughout all Judah; and he did that which was good, right, and faithful before YHWH his God. In every work that he began in the service of God's house, in the law, and in the commandments, to seek his God, he did it with all his heart, and prospered.

After these things and this faithfulness, Sennacherib king of Assyria came, entered into Judah, and encamped against the fortified cities, and intended to win them for himself. When Hezekiah saw that Sennacherib had come, and that he was planning to fight against Jerusalem, he took counsel with his princes and his mighty men to stop the waters of the springs which were outside of the city, and they helped him. So, many people gathered together and they stopped all the springs and the brook that flowed through the middle of the land, saying, "Why should the kings of Assyria come, and find abundant water?"

He took courage, built up all the wall that was broken down, and raised it up to the towers, with the other wall outside, and strengthened Millo in David's city, and made weapons and shields in abundance. He set captains of war over the people, and gathered them together to him in the wide place at the gate of the city, and spoke encouragingly to them, saying, "Be strong and courageous. Don't be afraid or dismayed because of the king of Assyria, nor for all the multitude who is with him; for there is a greater one with us than with him. An arm of flesh is with him, but YHWH our God is with us to help us and to fight our battles." The people rested themselves on the words of Hezekiah king of Judah.

After this, Sennacherib king of Assyria sent his servants to Jerusalem, (now he was before Lachish, and all his power with him), to Hezekiah king of Judah, and to all Judah who were at Jerusalem, saying, Sennacherib king of Assyria says, "In whom do you trust, that you remain under siege in Jerusalem? Doesn't Hezekiah persuade you, to give you over to die by famine and by thirst, saying, 'YHWH our God will deliver us out of the hand of the king of Assyria?' Hasn't the same Hezekiah taken away his high places and his altars, and commanded Judah and Jerusalem, saying, 'You shall worship before one altar, and you shall burn incense on it?' Don't you know what I and my fathers have done to all the peoples of the lands? Were the gods of the nations of the lands in any way able to deliver their land out of my hand? Who was there among all the gods of those nations which my fathers utterly destroyed, that could deliver his people out of my hand, that your God should be able to deliver you out of my hand? Now therefore don't let Hezekiah deceive you, nor persuade you in this way. Don't believe him, for no god of any nation or kingdom was able to deliver his people out of my hand, and out of the hand of my fathers. How much less will your God deliver you out of my hand?"

His servants spoke yet more against YHWH God, and against his servant Hezekiah. He also wrote letters insulting YHWH, the God of Israel, and speaking against him, saying, "As the gods of the nations of the lands, which have not delivered their people out of my hand, so shall the God of Hezekiah not deliver his people out of my hand." They called out with a loud voice in the Jews' language to the people of Jerusalem who were on the wall, to frighten them, and to trouble them; that they might take the city. They spoke of the God of Jerusalem as of the gods of the peoples of the earth, which are the work of men's hands.

Hezekiah the king and Isaiah the prophet the son of Amoz, prayed because of this, and cried to heaven.

YHWH sent an angel, who cut off all the mighty men of valor, and the leaders and captains, in the camp of the king of Assyria. So he returned with shame of face to his own land. When he had come into the house of his god, those who came out of his own body killed him there with the sword. Thus YHWH saved Hezekiah and the inhabitants of Jerusalem from the hand of Sennacherib the king of Assyria and from the hand of all others, and guided them on every side. Many brought gifts to YHWH to Jerusalem, and precious things to Hezekiah king of Judah; so that he was exalted in the sight of all nations from then on.

In those days Hezekiah was terminally ill, and he prayed to YHWH; and he spoke to him, and gave him a sign. But Hezekiah didn't reciprocate appropriate to the benefit done for him, because his heart was lifted up. Therefore there was wrath on him, and on Judah and Jerusalem. Notwithstanding Hezekiah humbled himself for the pride of his heart, both he and the inhabitants of Jerusalem, so that YHWH's wrath didn't come on them in the days of Hezekiah.

Hezekiah had exceedingly much riches and honor. He provided himself with treasuries for silver, for gold, for precious stones, for spices, for shields, and for all kinds of valuable vessels; also storehouses for the increase of grain, new wine, and oil; and stalls for all kinds of animals, and flocks in folds. Moreover he provided for himself cities, and possessions of flocks and herds in abundance; for God had given him abundant possessions. This same Hezekiah also stopped the upper spring of the waters of Gihon, and brought them straight down on the west side of David's city. Hezekiah prospered in all his works.

However concerning the ambassadors of the princes of Babylon, who sent to him to inquire of the wonder that was done in the land, God left him, to try him, that he might know all that was in his heart.

Now the rest of the acts of Hezekiah, and his good deeds, behold, they are written in the vision of Isaiah the prophet the son of Amoz, in the book of the kings of Judah and Israel. Hezekiah slept with his fathers, and they buried him in the ascent of the tombs of the sons of David. All Judah and the inhabitants of Jerusalem honored him at his death. Manasseh his son reigned in his place.

....

Manasseh was twelve years old when he began to reign, and he reigned fifty-five years in Jerusalem. He did that which was evil in YHWH's sight, after the abominations of the nations whom YHWH cast out before the children of Israel. For he built again the high places which Hezekiah his father had broken down; and he raised up altars for the Baals, made Asheroth, and worshiped all the army of the sky, and served them. He built altars in YHWH's house, of which YHWH said, "My name shall be in Jerusalem forever." He built altars for all the army of the sky in the two courts of YHWH's house. He also made his children to pass through the fire in the valley of the son of Hinnom. He practiced sorcery, divination, and witchcraft, and dealt with those who had familiar spirits and with wizards. He did much evil in YHWH's sight, to provoke him to anger. He set the engraved image of the idol, which he had made, in God's house, of which God said to David and to Solomon his son, "In this house, and in Jerusalem, which I have chosen out of all the tribes of Israel, I will put my name forever. I will not any more remove the foot of Israel from off the land which I have appointed for your fathers, if only they will observe to do all that I have commanded them, even all the law, the statutes, and the ordinances given by Moses." Manasseh seduced Judah and the inhabitants of Jerusalem, so that they did more evil than did the nations whom YHWH destroyed before the children of Israel.

YHWH spoke to Manasseh, and to his people; but they didn't listen. Therefore YHWH brought on them the captains of the army of the king of Assyria, who took Manasseh in chains, bound him with fetters, and carried him to Babylon.

When he was in distress, he begged YHWH his God, and humbled himself greatly before the God of his fathers. He prayed to him; and he was entreated by him, and heard his supplication, and brought him again to Jerusalem into his kingdom. Then Manasseh knew that YHWH was God.

Now after this, he built an outer wall to David's city, on the west side of Gihon, in the valley, even to the entrance at the fish gate. He encircled Ophel with it, and raised it up to a very great height; and he put valiant captains in all the fortified cities of Judah. He took away the foreign gods, and the idol out of YHWH's house, and all the altars that he had built in the mountain of YHWH's house, and in Jerusalem, and cast them out of the city. He built up YHWH's altar, and offered sacrifices of peace offerings and of thanksgiving on it, and commanded Judah to serve YHWH, the God of Israel. Nevertheless the people sacrificed still in the high places, but only to YHWH their God.

Now the rest of the acts of Manasseh, and his prayer to his God, and the words of the seers who spoke to him in the name of YHWH, the God of Israel, behold, they are written among the acts of the kings of Israel. His prayer also, and how God was entreated of him, and all his sin and his trespass, and the places in which he built high places, and set up the Asherah poles and the engraved images, before he humbled himself: behold, they are written in the history of Hozai. So Manasseh slept with his fathers, and they buried him in his own house; and Amon his son reigned in his place.

Amon was twenty-two years old when he began to reign; and he reigned two years in Jerusalem. He did that which was evil in YHWH's sight, as did Manasseh his father; and Amon sacrificed to all the engraved images which Manasseh his father had made, and served them. He didn't humble himself before YHWH, as Manasseh his father had humbled himself; but this same Amon trespassed more and more. His servants conspired against him, and put him to death in his own house. But the people of the land killed all those who had conspired against king Amon; and the people of the land made Josiah his son king in his place.

....

Josiah was eight years old when he began to reign, and he reigned thirty-one years in Jerusalem. He did that which was right in YHWH's eyes, and walked in the ways of David his father, and didn't turn away to the right hand or to the left. For in the eighth year of his reign, while he was yet young, he began to seek after the God of David his father; and in the twelfth year he began to purge Judah and Jerusalem from the high places, the Asherah poles, the engraved images, and the molten images. They broke down the altars of the Baals in his presence; and he cut down the incense altars that were on high above them. He broke the Asherah poles, the engraved images, and the molten images in pieces, made dust of them, and scattered it on the graves of those who had sacrificed to them. He burned the bones of the priests on their altars, and purged Judah and Jerusalem. He did this in the cities of Manasseh, Ephraim, and Simeon, even to Naphtali, around in their ruins. He broke down the altars, and beat the Asherah poles and the engraved images into powder, and cut down all the incense altars throughout all the land of Israel, then returned to Jerusalem.

Now in the eighteenth year of his reign, when he had purged the land and the house, he sent Shaphan the son of Azaliah, and Maaseiah the governor of the city, and Joah the son of Joahaz the recorder, to repair YHWH his God's house. They came to Hilkiah the high priest, and delivered the money that was brought into God's house, which the Levites, the keepers of the threshold, had gathered from the hands of Manasseh, Ephraim, of all the remnant of Israel, of all Judah and Benjamin, and of the inhabitants of Jerusalem. They delivered it into the hands of the workmen who had the oversight of YHWH's house; and the workmen who labored in YHWH's house gave it to mend and repair the house. They gave it to the carpenters and to the builders, to buy cut stone and timber for couplings, and to make beams for the houses which the kings of Judah had destroyed. The men did the work faithfully. Their overseers were Jahath and Obadiah, the Levites, of the sons of Merari; and Zechariah and Meshullam, of the sons of the Kohathites, to give direction; and others of the Levites, who were all skillful with musical instruments. Also they were over the bearers of burdens, and directed all who did the work in every kind of service. Of the Levites, there were scribes, officials, and gatekeepers.

When they brought out the money that was brought into YHWH's house, Hilkiah the priest found the book of YHWH's law given by Moses. Hilkiah answered Shaphan the scribe, "I have found the book of the law in YHWH's house." So Hilkiah delivered the book to Shaphan.

Shaphan carried the book to the king, and moreover brought back word to the king, saying, "All that was committed to your servants, they are doing. They have emptied out the money that was found in YHWH's house, and have delivered it into the hand of the overseers, and into the hand of the workmen." Shaphan the scribe told the king, saying, "Hilkiah the priest has delivered me a book." Shaphan read from it to the king.

When the king had heard the words of the law, he tore his clothes. The king commanded Hilkiah, Ahikam the son of Shaphan, Abdon the son of Micah, Shaphan the scribe, and Asaiah the king's servant, saying, "Go inquire of YHWH for me, and for those who are left in Israel and in Judah, concerning the words of the book that is found; for great is YHWH's wrath that is poured out on us, because our fathers have not kept YHWH's word, to do according to all that is written in this book."

So Hilkiah, and they whom the king had commanded, went to Huldah the prophetess, the wife of Shallum the son of Tokhath, the son of Hasrah, keeper of the wardrobe (now she lived in Jerusalem in the second quarter), and they spoke to her to that effect.

She said to them, "YHWH, the God of Israel says: 'Tell the man who sent you to me, "yhwh says, 'Behold, I will bring evil on this place, and on its inhabitants, even all the curses that are written in the book which they have read before the king of Judah. Because they have forsaken me, and have burned incense to other gods, that they might provoke me to anger with all the works of their hands; therefore my wrath is poured out on this place, and it will not be quenched.'" But to the king of Judah, who sent you to inquire of yhwh, you shall tell him this, 'yhwh, the God of Israel says: "About the words which you have heard, because your heart was tender, and you humbled yourself before God, when you heard his words against this place, and against its inhabitants, and have humbled yourself before me, and have torn your clothes, and wept before me, I also have heard you," says yhwh. "Behold, I will gather you to your fathers, and you will be gathered to your grave in peace. Your eyes won't see all the evil that I will bring on this place and on its inhabitants."'"

They brought back word to the king.

Then the king sent and gathered together all the elders of Judah and Jerusalem. The king went up to yhwh's house, with all the men of Judah and the inhabitants of Jerusalem, the priests, the Levites, and all the people, both great and small; and he read in their hearing all the words of the book of the covenant that was found in yh-wh's house. The king stood in his place, and made a covenant before yhwh, to walk after yhwh, and to keep his commandments, and his testimonies, and his statutes, with all his heart, and with all his soul, to perform the words of the covenant that were written in this book. He caused all who were found in Jerusalem and Benjamin to stand. The inhabitants of Jerusalem did according to the covenant of God, the God of their fathers. Josiah took away all the abominations out of all the countries that belonged to the children of Israel, and made all who were found in Israel to serve, even to serve yhwh their God. All his days they didn't depart from following yhwh, the God of their fathers.

....

Josiah kept a Passover to yhwh in Jerusalem. They killed the Passover on the fourteenth day of the first month. He set the priests in their offices, and encouraged them in the service of yhwh's house. He said to the Levites who taught all Israel, who were holy to yhwh, "Put the holy ark in the house which Solomon the son of David king of Israel built. It will no longer be a burden on your shoulders. Now serve YHWH your God, and his people Israel. Prepare yourselves after your fathers' houses by your divisions, according to the writing of David king of Israel, and according to the writing of Solomon his son. Stand in the holy place according to the divisions of the fathers' houses of your brothers the children of the people, and let there be for each a portion of a fathers' house of the Levites. Kill the Passover, sanctify yourselves, and prepare for your brothers, to do according to YHWH's word by Moses."

Josiah gave to the children of the people, of the flock, lambs and young goats, all of them for the Passover offerings, to all who were present, to the number of thirty thousand, and three thousand bulls. These were of the king's substance. His princes gave for a free will offering to the people, to the priests, and to the Levites. Hilkiah, Zechariah, and Jehiel, the rulers of God's house, gave to the priests for the Passover offerings two thousand six hundred small livestock, and three hundred head of cattle. Conaniah also, and Shemaiah and Nethanel, his brothers, and Hashabiah, Jeiel, and Jozabad, the chiefs of the Levites, gave to the Levites for the Passover offerings five thousand small livestock and five hundred head of cattle.

So the service was prepared, and the priests stood in their place, and the Levites by their divisions, according to the king's commandment. They killed the Passover, and the priests sprinkled the blood which they received of their hand, and the Levites skinned them. They removed the burnt offerings, that they might give them according to the divisions of the fathers' houses of the children of the people, to offer to YHWH, as it is written in the book of Moses. They did the same with the cattle. They roasted the Passover with fire according to the ordinance. They boiled the holy offerings in pots, in cauldrons, and in pans, and carried them quickly to all the children of the people. Afterward they prepared for themselves and for the priests, because the priests the sons of Aaron were busy with offering the burnt offerings and the fat until night. Therefore the Levites prepared for themselves and for the priests the sons of Aaron. The singers the sons of Asaph were in their place, according to the commandment of David, Asaph, Heman, and Jeduthun the king's seer; and the gatekeepers were at every gate. They didn't need to depart from their service, because their brothers the Levites prepared for them.

So all the service of YHWH was prepared the same day, to keep the Passover, and to offer burnt offerings on YHWH's altar, according to the commandment of king Josiah. The children of Israel who were present kept the Passover at that time, and the feast of unleavened bread seven days. There was no Passover like that kept in Israel from the days of Samuel the prophet, nor did any of the kings of Israel keep such a Passover as Josiah kept, with the priests, the Levites, and all Judah and Israel who were present, and the inhabitants of Jerusalem. This Passover was kept in the eighteenth year of the reign of Josiah.

After all this, when Josiah had prepared the temple, Neco king of Egypt went up to fight against Carchemish by the Euphrates, and Josiah went out against him. But he sent ambassadors to him, saying, "What have I to do with you, you king of Judah? I come not against you today, but against the house with which I have war. God has commanded me to make haste. Beware that it is God who is with me, that he not destroy you."

Nevertheless Josiah would not turn his face from him, but disguised himself, that he might fight with him, and didn't listen to the words of Neco from the mouth of God, and came to fight in the valley of Megiddo. The archers shot at king Josiah; and the king said to his servants, "Take me away, because I am seriously wounded!"

So his servants took him out of the chariot, and put him in the second chariot that he had, and brought him to Jerusalem; and he died, and was buried in the tombs of his fathers. All Judah and Jerusalem mourned for Josiah. Jeremiah lamented for Josiah, and all the singing men and singing women spoke of Josiah in their lamentations to this day; and they made them an ordinance in Israel. Behold, they are written in the lamentations. Now the rest of the acts of Josiah, and his good deeds, according to that which is written in YHWH's law, and his acts, first and last, behold, they are written in the book of the kings of Israel and Judah.

....

Then the people of the land took Jehoahaz the son of Josiah, and made him king in his father's place in Jerusalem. Joahaz was twenty-three years old when he began to reign; and he reigned three months in Jerusalem. The king of Egypt removed him from office at Jerusalem, and fined the land one hundred talents of silver and a talent of gold. The king of Egypt made Eliakim his brother king over Judah and Jerusalem, and changed his name to Jehoiakim. Neco took Joahaz his brother, and carried him to Egypt.

Jehoiakim was twenty-five years old when he began to reign,

and he reigned eleven years in Jerusalem. He did that which was evil in YHWH his God's sight. Nebuchadnezzar king of Babylon came up against him, and bound him in fetters to carry him to Babylon. Nebuchadnezzar also carried some of the vessels of YHWH's house to Babylon, and put them in his temple at Babylon. Now the rest of the acts of Jehoiakim, and his abominations which he did, and that which was found in him, behold, they are written in the book of the kings of Israel and Judah; and Jehoiachin his son reigned in his place.

Jehoiachin was eight years old when he began to reign, and he reigned three months and ten days in Jerusalem. He did that which was evil in YHWH's sight. At the return of the year, king Nebuchadnezzar sent and brought him to Babylon, with the valuable vessels of YHWH's house, and made Zedekiah his brother king over Judah and Jerusalem.

Zedekiah was twenty-one years old when he began to reign, and he reigned eleven years in Jerusalem. He did that which was evil in YHWH his God's sight. He didn't humble himself before Jeremiah the prophet speaking from YHWH's mouth. He also rebelled against king Nebuchadnezzar, who had made him swear by God; but he stiffened his neck, and hardened his heart against turning to YHWH, the God of Israel. Moreover all the chiefs of the priests, and the people, trespassed very greatly after all the abominations of the nations; and they polluted YHWH's house which he had made holy in Jerusalem. YHWH, the God of their fathers, sent to them by his messengers, rising up early and sending, because he had compassion on his people, and on his dwelling place; but they mocked the messengers of God, and despised his words, and scoffed at his prophets, until YHWH's wrath arose against his people, until there was no remedy.

Therefore he brought on them the king of the Chaldeans, who killed their young men with the sword in the house of their sanctuary, and had no compassion on young man or virgin, old man or gray-headed. He gave them all into his hand. All the vessels of God's house, great and small, and the treasures of YHWH's house, and the treasures of the king, and of his princes, all these he brought to Babylon. They burned God's house, and broke down the wall of Jerusalem, and burned all its palaces with fire, and destroyed all of its valuable vessels. He carried those who had escaped from the sword away to Babylon, and they were servants to him and his sons until the reign of the kingdom of Persia, to fulfill YHWH's word by Jeremiah's mouth, until the land had enjoyed its Sabbaths. As long as it lay desolate, it kept Sabbath, to fulfill seventy years.

Now in the first year of Cyrus king of Persia, that YHWH's word by the mouth of Jeremiah might be accomplished, YHWH stirred up the spirit of Cyrus king of Persia, so that he made a proclamation throughout all his kingdom, and put it also in writing, saying, "Cyrus king of Persia says, 'YHWH, the God of heaven, has given all the kingdoms of the earth to me; and he has commanded me to build him a house in Jerusalem, which is in Judah. Whoever there is among you of all his people, YHWH his God be with him, and let him go up.'"

THE BOOK OF

EZRA

37 MIN

Now in the first year of Cyrus king of Persia, that YHWH's word by Jeremiah's mouth might be accomplished, YHWH stirred up the spirit of Cyrus king of Persia, so that he made a proclamation throughout all his kingdom, and put it also in writing, saying, "Cyrus king of Persia says, 'YHWH, the God of heaven, has given me all the kingdoms of the earth; and he has commanded me to build him a house in Jerusalem, which is in Judah. Whoever there is among you of all his people, may his God be with him, and let him go up to Jerusalem, which is in Judah, and build the house of YHWH, the God of Israel (he is God), which is in Jerusalem. Whoever is left, in any place where he lives, let the men of his place help him with silver, with gold, with goods, and with animals, in addition to the free will offering for God's house which is in Jerusalem.'"

Then the heads of fathers' households of Judah and Benjamin, the priests, and the Levites, all whose spirit God had stirred to go up rose up to build YHWH's house which is in Jerusalem. All those who were around them strengthened their hands with vessels of silver, with gold, with goods, with animals, and with precious things, in addition to all that was willingly offered. Also Cyrus the king brought out the vessels of YHWH's house, which Nebuchadnezzar had brought out of Jerusalem, and had put in the house of his gods; even those, Cyrus king of Persia brought out by the hand of Mithredath the treasurer, and counted them out to Sheshbazzar, the prince of Judah. This is the number of them: thirty platters of gold, one thousand platters of silver, twenty-nine knives, thirty bowls of gold, four hundred ten silver bowls of a second sort, and one thousand other vessels. All the vessels of gold and of silver were five thousand four hundred. Sheshbazzar brought all these up when the captives were brought up from Babylon to Jerusalem.

....

Now these are the children of the province, who went up out of the captivity of those who had been carried away, whom Nebuchadnezzar the king of Babylon had carried away to Babylon, and who returned to Jerusalem and Judah, everyone to his city; who came with Zerubbabel, Jeshua, Nehemiah, Seraiah, Reelaiah, Mordecai, Bilshan, Mispar, Bigvai, Rehum, and Baanah.

The number of the men of the people of Israel: The children of Parosh, two thousand one hundred seventy-two. The children of Shephatiah, three hundred seventy-two. The children of Arah, seven hundred seventy-five. The children of Pahathmoab, of the children of Jeshua and Joab, two thousand eight hundred twelve. The children of Elam, one thousand two hundred fifty-four. The children of Zattu, nine hundred forty-five. The children of Zaccai, seven hundred sixty. The children of Bani, six hundred forty-two. The children of Bebai, six hundred twenty-three. The children of Azgad, one thousand two hundred twenty-two. The children of Adonikam, six hundred sixty-six. The children of Bigvai, two thousand fifty-six. The children of Adin, four hundred fifty-four. The children of Ater, of Hezekiah, ninety-eight. The children of Bezai, three hundred twenty-three. The children of Jorah, one hundred twelve. The children of Hashum, two hundred twenty-three. The children of Gibbar, ninety-five. The children of Bethlehem, one hundred twenty-three. The men of Netophah, fifty-six. The men of Anathoth, one hundred twenty-eight. The children of Azmaveth, forty-two. The children of Kiriath Arim, Chephirah, and Beeroth, seven hundred forty-three. The children of Ramah and Geba, six hundred twenty-one. The men of Michmas, one hundred twenty-two. The men of Bethel and Ai, two hundred twenty-three. The children of Nebo, fifty-two. The children of Magbish, one hundred fifty-six. The children of the other Elam, one thousand two hundred fifty-four. The children of Harim, three hundred twenty. The children of Lod, Hadid, and Ono, seven hundred twenty-five. The children of Jericho, three hundred forty-five. The children of Senaah, three thousand six hundred thirty.

The priests: the children of Jedaiah, of the house of Jeshua, nine hundred seventy-three. The children of Immer, one thousand fifty-two. The children of Pashhur, one thousand two hundred forty-seven. The children of Harim, one thousand seventeen.

The Levites: the children of Jeshua and Kadmiel, of the children of Hodaviah, seventy-four. The singers: the children of Asaph, one hundred twenty-eight. The children of the gatekeepers: the children of Shallum, the children of Ater, the children of Talmon, the children of Akkub, the children of Hatita, the children of Shobai, in all one hundred thirty-nine.

The temple servants: the children of Ziha, the children of Hasupha, the children of Tabbaoth, the children of Keros, the children of Siaha, the children of Padon, the children of Lebanah, the children of Hagabah, the children of Akkub, the children of Hagab, the children of Shamlai, the children of Hanan, the children of Giddel, the children of Gahar, the children of Reaiah, the children of Rezin, the children of Nekoda, the children of Gazzam, the children of Uzza, the children of Paseah, the children of Besai, the children of Asnah, the children of Meunim, the children of Nephisim, the children of Bakbuk, the children of Hakupha, the children of Harhur, the children of Bazluth, the children of Mehida, the children of Harsha, the children of Barkos, the children of Sisera, the children of Temah, the children of Neziah, the children of Hatipha.

The children of Solomon's servants: the children of Sotai, the children of Hassophereth, the children of Peruda, the children of Jaalah, the children of Darkon, the children of Giddel, the children of Shephatiah, the children of Hattil, the children of Pochereth Hazzebaim, the children of Ami. All the temple servants, and the children of Solomon's servants, were three hundred ninety-two.

These were those who went up from Tel Melah, Tel Harsha, Cherub, Addan, and Immer; but they could not show their fathers' houses, and their offspring, whether they were of Israel: the children of Delaiah, the children of Tobiah, the children of Nekoda, six hundred fifty-two. Of the children of the priests: the children of Habaiah, the children of Hakkoz, and the children of Barzillai, who took a wife of the daughters of Barzillai the Gileadite, and was called after their name. These sought their place among those who were registered by genealogy, but they were not found: therefore were they deemed disqualified and removed from the priesthood. The governor told them that they should not eat of the most holy things until a priest stood up to serve with Urim and with Thummim.

The whole assembly together was forty-two thousand three hundred sixty, in addition to their male servants and their female servants, of whom there were seven thousand three hundred thirty-seven; and they had two hundred singing men and singing women. Their horses were seven hundred thirty-six; their mules, two hundred forty-five; their camels, four hundred thirty-five; their donkeys, six thousand seven hundred twenty.

Some of the heads of fathers' households, when they came to YHWH's house which is in Jerusalem, offered willingly for God's house to set it up in its place. They gave according to their ability into the treasury of the work sixty-one thousand darics of gold, and five thousand minas of silver, and one hundred priests' garments.

So the priests and the Levites, with some of the people, the singers, the gatekeepers, and the temple servants, lived in their cities, and all Israel in their cities.

....

When the seventh month had come, and the children of Israel were in the cities, the people gathered themselves together as one man to Jerusalem. Then Jeshua the son of Jozadak stood up with his brothers the priests, and Zerubbabel the son of Shealtiel and his brothers, and built the altar of the God of Israel, to offer burnt offerings on it, as it is written in the law of Moses the man of God. In spite of their fear because of the peoples of the surrounding lands, they set the altar on its base; and they offered burnt offerings on it to YHWH, even burnt offerings morning and evening. They kept the feast of booths, as it is written, and offered the daily burnt offerings by number, according to the ordinance, as the duty of every day required; and afterward the continual burnt offering, the offerings of the new moons, of all the set feasts of YHWH that were consecrated, and of everyone who willingly offered a free will offering to YHWH. From the first day of the seventh month, they began to offer burnt offerings to YHWH; but the foundation of YHWH's temple was not yet laid. They also gave money to the masons, and to the carpenters. They also gave food, drink, and oil to the people of Sidon and Tyre, to bring cedar trees from Lebanon to the sea, to Joppa, according to the grant that they had from Cyrus King of Persia.

Now in the second year of their coming to God's house at Jerusalem, in the second month, Zerubbabel the son of Shealtiel, and Jeshua the son of Jozadak, and the rest of their brothers the priests and the Levites, and all those who had come out of the captivity to Jerusalem, began the work and appointed the Levites, from twenty years old and upward, to have the oversight of the work of YHWH's house. Then Jeshua stood with his sons and his brothers, Kadmiel and his sons, the sons of Judah, together, to have the oversight of the workmen in God's house: the sons of Henadad, with their sons and their brothers the Levites. When the builders laid the foundation of YHWH's temple, they set the priests in their clothing with trumpets, with the Levites the sons of Asaph with cymbals, to praise YHWH, according to the directions of David king of Israel. They sang to one another in praising and giving thanks to YHWH, "For he is good, for his loving kindness endures forever toward Israel." All the people shouted with a great shout, when they praised YHWH, because the foundation of YHWH's house had been laid.

But many of the priests and Levites and heads of fathers' households, the old men who had seen the first house, when the foundation of this house was laid before their eyes, wept with a loud voice. Many also shouted aloud for joy, so that the people could not discern the noise of the shout of joy from the noise of the weeping of the people; for the people shouted with a loud shout, and the noise was heard far away.

....

Now when the adversaries of Judah and Benjamin heard that the children of the captivity were building a temple to YHWH, the God of Israel; they came near to Zerubbabel, and to the heads of fathers' households, and said to them, "Let us build with you; for we seek your God, as you do; and we have been sacrificing to him since the days of Esar Haddon king of Assyria, who brought us up here."

But Zerubbabel, and Jeshua, and the rest of the heads of fathers' households of Israel, said to them, "You have nothing to do with us in building a house to our God; but we ourselves together will build to YHWH, the God of Israel, as king Cyrus the king of Persia has commanded us."

Then the people of the land weakened the hands of the people of Judah, and troubled them in building. They hired counselors against them, to frustrate their purpose, all the days of Cyrus king of Persia, even until the reign of Darius king of Persia. In the reign of Ahasuerus, in the beginning of his reign, they wrote an accusation against the inhabitants of Judah and Jerusalem.

In the days of Artaxerxes, Bishlam, Mithredath, Tabeel, and the rest of his companions, wrote to Artaxerxes king of Persia; and the writing of the letter was written in Syrian, and delivered in the Syrian language. Rehum the chancellor and Shimshai the scribe wrote a letter against Jerusalem to Artaxerxes the king as follows, then Rehum the chancellor, Shimshai the scribe, and the rest of their companions, the Dinaites, and the Apharsathchites, the Tarpelites, the Apharsites, the Archevites, the Babylonians, the Shushanchites, the Dehaites, the Elamites, and the rest of the nations whom the great and noble Osnappar brought over, and set in the city of Samaria, and in the rest of the country beyond the River, and so forth, wrote.

This is the copy of the letter that they sent:

To King Artaxerxes,
From your servants the men beyond the River.

Be it known to the king that the Jews who came up from you have come to us to Jerusalem. They are building the rebellious and bad city, and have finished the walls, and repaired the foundations. Be it known now to the king that if this city is built and the walls finished, they will not pay tribute, custom, or toll, and in the end it will be hurtful to the kings. Now because we eat the salt of the palace, and it is not appropriate for us to see the king's dishonor, therefore we have sent and informed the king, that search may be made in the book of the records of your fathers. You will see in the book of the records, and know that this city is a rebellious city, and hurtful to kings and provinces, and that they have started rebellions within it in the past. That is why this city was destroyed. We inform the king that, if this city is built and the walls finished, then you will have no possession beyond the River.

Then the king sent an answer to Rehum the chancellor, and to Shimshai the scribe, and to the rest of their companions who live in Samaria, and in the rest of the country beyond the River:

Peace.

The letter which you sent to us has been plainly read before me. I decreed, and search has been made, and it was found that this city has made insurrection against kings in the past, and that rebellion and revolts have been made in it. There have also been mighty kings over Jerusalem, who have ruled over all the country beyond the River; and tribute, custom, and toll, was paid to them. Make a decree now to cause these men to cease, and that this city not be built, until a decree is made by me. Be careful that you not be slack doing so. Why should damage grow to the hurt of the kings?

Then when the copy of king Artaxerxes' letter was read before Rehum, Shimshai the scribe, and their companions, they went in haste to Jerusalem to the Jews, and made them to cease by force of arms. Then work stopped on God's house which is at Jerusalem. It stopped until the second year of the reign of Darius king of Persia.

....

Now the prophets, Haggai the prophet and Zechariah the son of

Iddo, prophesied to the Jews who were in Judah and Jerusalem. They prophesied to them in the name of the God of Israel. Then Zerubbabel the son of Shealtiel, and Jeshua the son of Jozadak rose up and began to build God's house which is at Jerusalem; and with them were the prophets of God, helping them. At the same time Tattenai, the governor beyond the River came to them, with Shetharbozenai, and their companions, and asked them, "Who gave you a decree to build this house, and to finish this wall?" They also asked for the names of the men were who were making this building. But the eye of their God was on the elders of the Jews, and they didn't make them cease, until the matter should come to Darius, and an answer should be returned by letter concerning it.

The copy of the letter that Tattenai, the governor beyond the River, and Shetharbozenai, and his companions the Apharsachites, who were beyond the River, sent to Darius the king follows. They sent a letter to him, in which was written:

To Darius the king, all peace.

Be it known to the king that we went into the province of Judah, to the house of the great God, which is built with great stones, and timber is laid in the walls. This work goes on with diligence and prospers in their hands. Then we asked those elders, and said to them thus, "Who gave you a decree to build this house, and to finish this wall?" We asked them their names also, to inform you that we might write the names of the men who were at their head. Thus they returned us answer, saying, "We are the servants of the God of heaven and earth, and are building the house that was built these many years ago, which a great king of Israel built and finished. But after our fathers had provoked the God of heaven to wrath, he gave them into the hand of Nebuchadnezzar king of Babylon, the Chaldean, who destroyed this house, and carried the people away into Babylon. But in the first year of Cyrus king of Babylon, Cyrus the king made a decree to build this house of God. The gold and silver vessels of God's house, which Nebuchadnezzar took out of the temple that was in Jerusalem, and brought into the temple of Babylon, those Cyrus the king also took out of the temple of Babylon, and they were delivered to one whose name was Sheshbazzar, whom he had made governor. He said to him, 'Take these vessels, go, put them in the temple that is in Jerusalem, and let God's house be built in its place.' Then the same Sheshbazzar came and laid the foundations of God's house which is in Jerusalem. Since that time even until now it has been being built, and yet it is not completed.

Now therefore, if it seems good to the king, let a search be made in the king's treasure house, which is there at Babylon, whether it is so, that a decree was made of Cyrus the king to build this house of God at Jerusalem; and let the king send his pleasure to us concerning this matter."

....

Then Darius the king made a decree, and the house of the archives, where the treasures were laid up in Babylon, was searched. A scroll was found at Achmetha, in the palace that is in the province of Media, and in it this was written for a record:

In the first year of Cyrus the king, Cyrus the king made a decree: Concerning God's house at Jerusalem, let the house be built, the place where they offer sacrifices, and let its foundations be strongly laid; with its height sixty cubits, and its width sixty cubits; with three courses of great stones and a course of new timber. Let the expenses be given out of the king's house. Also let the gold and silver vessels of God's house, which Nebuchadnezzar took out of the temple which is at Jerusalem, and brought to Babylon, be restored and brought again to the temple which is at Jerusalem, everything to its place. You shall put them in God's house.

Now therefore, Tattenai, governor beyond the River, Shethar-bozenai, and your companions the Apharsachites, who are beyond the River, you must stay far from there. Leave the work of this house of God alone; let the governor of the Jews and the elders of the Jews build this house of God in its place. Moreover I make a decree what you shall do for these elders of the Jews for the building of this house of God: that of the king's goods, even of the tribute beyond the River, expenses must be given with all diligence to these men, that they not be hindered. That which they have need of, including young bulls, rams, and lambs, for burnt offerings to the God of heaven; also wheat, salt, wine, and oil, according to the word of the priests who are at Jerusalem, let it be given them day by day without fail; that they may offer sacrifices of pleasant aroma to the God of heaven, and pray for the life of the king, and of his sons. I have also made a decree that whoever alters this message, let a beam be pulled out from his house, and let him be lifted up and fastened on it; and let his house be made a dunghill for this. May the God who has caused his name to dwell there overthrow all kings and peoples who stretch out their hand to alter this, to destroy this house of God which is at Jerusalem. I Darius have made a decree. Let it be done with all diligence.

Then Tattenai, the governor beyond the River, Shetharbozenai, and their companions did accordingly with all diligence, because Darius the king had sent a decree.

The elders of the Jews built and prospered, through the prophesying of Haggai the prophet and Zechariah the son of Iddo. They built and finished it, according to the commandment of the God of Israel, and according to the decree of Cyrus, Darius, and Artaxerxes king of Persia. This house was finished on the third day of the month Adar, which was in the sixth year of the reign of Darius the king.

The children of Israel, the priests, the Levites, and the rest of the children of the captivity, kept the dedication of this house of God with joy. They offered at the dedication of this house of God one hundred bulls, two hundred rams, four hundred lambs; and for a sin offering for all Israel, twelve male goats, according to the number of the tribes of Israel. They set the priests in their divisions, and the Levites in their courses, for the service of God, which is at Jerusalem, as it is written in the book of Moses.

The children of the captivity kept the Passover on the fourteenth day of the first month. Because the priests and the Levites had purified themselves together, all of them were pure. They killed the Passover for all the children of the captivity, for their brothers the priests, and for themselves. The children of Israel who had returned out of the captivity, and all who had separated themselves to them from the filthiness of the nations of the land, to seek YHWH, the God of Israel, ate, and kept the feast of unleavened bread seven days with joy; because YHWH had made them joyful, and had turned the heart of the king of Assyria to them, to strengthen their hands in the work of God, the God of Israel's house.

Now after these things, in the reign of Artaxerxes king of Persia, Ezra the son of Seraiah, the son of Azariah, the son of Hilkiah, the son of Shallum, the son of Zadok, the son of Ahitub, the son of Amariah, the son of Azariah, the son of Meraioth, the son of Zerahiah, the son of Uzzi, the son of Bukki, the son of Abishua, the son of Phinehas, the son of Eleazar, the son of Aaron the chief priest—this Ezra went up from Babylon. He was a skilled scribe in the law of Moses, which YHWH, the God of Israel, had given; and the king granted him all his request, according to YHWH his God's hand on him. Some of the children of Israel, including some of the priests, the Levites, the singers, the gatekeepers, and the temple servants went up to Jerusalem in the seventh year of Artaxerxes the king. He came to Jerusalem in the fifth month, which was in the seventh year of the king. For on the first day of the first month he began to go up from Babylon; and on the first day of the fifth month he came to Jerusalem, according to the good hand of his God on him. For Ezra had set his heart to seek YHWH's law, and to do it, and to teach statutes and ordinances in Israel.

Now this is the copy of the letter that the king Artaxerxes gave to Ezra the priest, the scribe, even the scribe of the words of YHWH's commandments, and of his statutes to Israel:

Artaxerxes, king of kings,

To Ezra the priest, the scribe of the law of the perfect God of heaven.

Now I make a decree, that all those of the people of Israel, and their priests and the Levites, in my realm, who intend of their own free will to go to Jerusalem, go with you. Because you are sent by the king and his seven counselors, to inquire concerning Judah and Jerusalem, according to the law of your God which is in your hand, and to carry the silver and gold, which the king and his counselors have freely offered to the God of Israel, whose habitation is in Jerusalem, and all the silver and gold that you will find in all the province of Babylon, with the free will offering of the people, and of the priests, offering willingly for the house of their God which is in Jerusalem; therefore you shall with all diligence buy with this money bulls, rams, lambs, with their meal offerings and their drink offerings, and shall offer them on the altar of the house of your God which is in Jerusalem. Whatever seems good to you and to your brothers to do with the rest of the silver and the gold, do that according to the will of your God. The vessels that are given to you for the service of the house of your God, deliver before the God of Jerusalem. Whatever more will be needed for the house of your God, which you may have occasion to give, give it out of the king's treasure house.

I, even I Artaxerxes the king, make a decree to all the treasurers who are beyond the River, that whatever Ezra the priest, the scribe of the law of the God of heaven, requires of you, it shall be done with all diligence, up to one hundred talents of silver, and to one hundred cors of wheat, and to one hundred baths of wine, and to one hundred baths of oil, and salt without prescribing how much. Whatever is commanded by the God of heaven, let it be done exactly for the house of the God of heaven; for why should there be wrath against the realm of the king and his sons?

Also we inform you that it shall not be lawful to impose tribute, custom, or toll, on any of the priests, Levites, singers, gatekeepers, temple servants, or laborers of this house of God.

You, Ezra, according to the wisdom of your God that is in your hand, appoint magistrates and judges, who may judge all the people who are beyond the River, who all know the laws of your God; and teach him who doesn't know them. Whoever will not do the law of your God and the law of the king, let judgment be executed on him with all diligence, whether it is to death, or to banishment, or to confiscation of goods, or to imprisonment.

Blessed be YHWH, the God of our fathers, who has put such a thing as this in the king's heart, to beautify YHWH's house which is in Jerusalem; and has extended loving kindness to me before the king and his counselors, and before all the king's mighty princes. I was strengthened according to YHWH my God's hand on me, and I gathered together chief men out of Israel to go up with me.

....

Now these are the heads of their fathers' households, and this is the genealogy of those who went up with me from Babylon, in the reign of Artaxerxes the king:

Of the sons of Phinehas, Gershom.

Of the sons of Ithamar, Daniel.

Of the sons of David, Hattush.

Of the sons of Shecaniah, of the sons of Parosh, Zechariah; and with him were listed by genealogy of the males one hundred fifty.

Of the sons of Pahathmoab, Eliehoenai the son of Zerahiah; and with him two hundred males.

Of the sons of Shecaniah, the son of Jahaziel; and with him three hundred males.

Of the sons of Adin, Ebed the son of Jonathan; and with him

fifty males.

Of the sons of Elam, Jeshaiah the son of Athaliah; and with him seventy males.

Of the sons of Shephatiah, Zebadiah the son of Michael; and with him eighty males.

Of the sons of Joab, Obadiah the son of Jehiel; and with him two hundred eighteen males.

Of the sons of Shelomith, the son of Josiphiah; and with him one hundred sixty males.

Of the sons of Bebai, Zechariah the son of Bebai; and with him twenty-eight males.

Of the sons of Azgad, Johanan the son of Hakkatan; and with him one hundred ten males.

Of the sons of Adonikam, who were the last; and these are their names: Eliphelet, Jeuel, and Shemaiah; and with them sixty males.

Of the sons of Bigvai, Uthai and Zabbud; and with them seventy males.

I gathered them together to the river that runs to Ahava; and there we encamped three days: and I looked around at the people and the priests, and found there were none of the sons of Levi. Then sent I for Eliezer, for Ariel, for Shemaiah, for Elnathan, for Jarib, for Elnathan, for Nathan, for Zechariah, and for Meshullam, chief men; also for Joiarib and for Elnathan, who were teachers. I sent them out to Iddo the chief at the place Casiphia; and I told them what they should tell Iddo, and his brothers the temple servants, at the place Casiphia, that they should bring to us ministers for the house of our God. According to the good hand of our God on us they brought us a man of discretion, of the sons of Mahli, the son of Levi, the son of Israel; and Sherebiah, with his sons and his brothers, eighteen; and Hashabiah, and with him Jeshaiah of the sons of Merari, his brothers and their sons, twenty; and of the temple servants, whom David and the princes had given for the service of the Levites, two hundred twenty temple servants. All of them were mentioned by name.

Then I proclaimed a fast there, at the river Ahava, that we might humble ourselves before our God, to seek from him a straight way for us, and for our little ones, and for all our possessions. For I was ashamed to ask of the king a band of soldiers and horsemen to help us against the enemy on the way, because we had spoken to the king, saying, "The hand of our God is on all those who seek him, for good; but his power and his wrath is against all those who forsake him." So we fasted and begged our God for this: and he granted our request.

Then I set apart twelve of the chiefs of the priests, even Shere-biah, Hashabiah, and ten of their brothers with them, and weighed to them the silver, the gold, and the vessels, even the offering for the house of our God, which the king, his counselors, his princes, and all Israel there present, had offered. I weighed into their hand six hundred fifty talents of silver, one hundred talents of silver vessels; one hundred talents of gold, twenty bowls of gold weighing one thousand darics; and two vessels of fine bright bronze, precious as gold. I said to them, "You are holy to YHWH, and the vessels are holy. The silver and the gold are a free will offering to YHWH, the God of your fathers. Watch and keep them, until you weigh them before the chiefs of the priests and the Levites, and the princes of the fathers' households of Israel, at Jerusalem, in the rooms of YHWH's house."

So the priests and the Levites received the weight of the silver and the gold, and the vessels, to bring them to Jerusalem to the house of our God. Then we departed from the river Ahava on the twelfth day of the first month, to go to Jerusalem. The hand of our God was on us, and he delivered us from the hand of the enemy and the bandit by the way. We came to Jerusalem, and stayed there three days. On the fourth day the silver and the gold and the vessels were weighed in the house of our God into the hand of Meremoth the son of Uriah the priest; and with him was Eleazar the son of Phinehas; and with them was Jozabad the son of Jeshua, and Noadiah the son of Binnui, the Levite; everything by number and by weight; and all the weight was written at that time.

The children of the captivity, who had come out of exile, of-fered burnt offerings to the God of Israel, twelve bulls for all Israel, ninety-six rams, seventy-seven lambs, and twelve male goats for a sin offering. All this was a burnt offering to YHWH. They delivered the king's commissions to the king's local governors, and to the gov-ernors beyond the River. So they supported the people and God's house.

....

Now when these things were done, the princes came near to me, saying, "The people of Israel, the priests, and the Levites, have not separated themselves from the peoples of the lands, following their abominations, even those of the Canaanites, the Hittites, the Perizz-ites, the Jebusites, the Ammonites, the Moabites, the Egyptians, and the Amorites. For they have taken of their daughters for themselves and for their sons, so that the holy offspring have mixed themselves with the peoples of the lands. Yes, the hand of the princes and rulers has been chief in this trespass."

When I heard this thing, I tore my garment and my robe, and pulled the hair out of my head and of my beard, and sat down confounded. Then everyone who trembled at the words of the God of Israel were assembled to me, because of their trespass of the captivity; and I sat confounded until the evening offering.

At the evening offering I arose up from my humiliation, even with my garment and my robe torn; and I fell on my knees, and spread out my hands to YHWH my God; and I said, "My God, I am ashamed and blush to lift up my face to you, my God; for our iniquities have increased over our head, and our guiltiness has grown up to the heavens. Since the days of our fathers we have been exceedingly guilty to this day; and for our iniquities we, our kings, and our priests, have been delivered into the hand of the kings of the lands, to the sword, to captivity, to plunder, and to confusion of face, as it is this day. Now for a little moment grace has been shown from YHWH our God, to leave us a remnant to escape, and to give us a nail in his holy place, that our God may lighten our eyes, and revived us a little in our bondage. For we are bondservants; yet our God has not forsaken us in our bondage, but has extended loving kindness to us in the sight of the kings of Persia, to revive us, to set up the house of our God, and to repair its ruins, and to give us a wall in Judah and in Jerusalem.

"Now, our God, what shall we say after this? For we have forsaken your commandments, which you have commanded by your servants the prophets, saying, 'The land, to which you go to possess it, is an unclean land through the uncleanness of the peoples of the lands, through their abominations, which have filled it from one end to another with their filthiness. Now therefore don't give your daughters to their sons. Don't take their daughters to your sons, nor seek their peace or their prosperity forever; that you may be strong, and eat the good of the land, and leave it for an inheritance to your children forever.'

"After all that has come on us for our evil deeds, and for our great guilt, since you, our God, have punished us less than our iniquities deserve, and have given us such a remnant, shall we again break your commandments, and join ourselves with the peoples that do these abominations? Wouldn't you be angry with us until you had consumed us, so that there would be no remnant, nor any to escape? YHWH, the God of Israel, you are righteous; for we are left a remnant that has escaped, as it is today. Behold, we are before you in our guiltiness; for no one can stand before you because of this."

....

Now while Ezra prayed and made confession, weeping and casting himself down before God's house, there was gathered together to him out of Israel a very great assembly of men and women and children; for the people wept very bitterly. Shecaniah the son of Jehiel, one of the sons of Elam, answered Ezra, "We have trespassed against our God, and have married foreign women of the peoples of the land. Yet now there is hope for Israel concerning this thing. Now therefore let's make a covenant with our God to put away all the wives, and those who are born of them, according to the counsel of my lord, and of those who tremble at the commandment of our God. Let it be done according to the law. Arise; for the matter belongs to you, and we are with you. Be courageous, and do it."

Then Ezra arose, and made the chiefs of the priests, the Levites, and all Israel, to swear that they would do according to this word. So they swore. Then Ezra rose up from before God's house, and went into the room of Jehohanan the son of Eliashib. When he came there, he ate no bread, nor drank water; for he mourned because of their trespass of the captivity. They made a proclamation throughout Judah and Jerusalem to all the children of the captivity, that they should gather themselves together to Jerusalem; and that whoever didn't come within three days, according to the counsel of the princes and the elders, all his possessions should be forfeited, and himself separated from the assembly of the captivity.

Then all the men of Judah and Benjamin gathered themselves together to Jerusalem within the three days. It was the ninth month, on the twentieth day of the month; and all the people sat in the wide place in front of God's house, trembling because of this matter, and because of the great rain.

Ezra the priest stood up and said to them, "You have trespassed, and have married foreign women, to increase the guilt of Israel. Now therefore make confession to YHWH, the God of your fathers, and do his pleasure; and separate yourselves from the peoples of the land, and from the foreign women."

Then all the assembly answered with a loud voice, "We must do as you have said concerning us. But the people are many, and it is a time of much rain, and we are not able to stand outside. This is not a work of one day or two, for we have greatly transgressed in this matter. Now let our princes be appointed for all the assembly, and let all those who are in our cities who have married foreign women come at appointed times, and with them the elders of every city, and its judges, until the fierce wrath of our God is turned from us, until this matter is resolved."

Only Jonathan the son of Asahel and Jahzeiah the son of Tikvah stood up against this; and Meshullam and Shabbethai the Levite helped them.

The children of the captivity did so. Ezra the priest, with certain heads of fathers' households, after their fathers' houses, and all of them by their names, were set apart; and they sat down in the first day of the tenth month to examine the matter. They finished with all the men who had married foreign women by the first day of the first month.

Among the sons of the priests there were found who had married foreign women:

of the sons of Jeshua, the son of Jozadak, and his brothers, Maaseiah, and Eliezer, and Jarib, and Gedaliah. They gave their hand that they would put away their wives; and being guilty, they offered a ram of the flock for their guilt.

Of the sons of Immer: Hanani and Zebadiah.

Of the sons of Harim: Maaseiah, and Elijah, and Shemaiah, and Jehiel, and Uzziah.

Of the sons of Pashhur: Elioenai, Maaseiah, Ishmael, Nethanel, Jozabad, and Elasah.

Of the Levites: Jozabad, and Shimei, and Kelaiah (also called Kelita), Pethahiah, Judah, and Eliezer.

Of the singers: Eliashib. Of the gatekeepers: Shallum, and Telem, and Uri.

Of Israel: Of the sons of Parosh: Ramiah, and Izziah, and Malchijah, and Mijamin, and Eleazar, and Malchijah, and Benaiah.

Of the sons of Elam: Mattaniah, Zechariah, and Jehiel, and Abdi, and Jeremoth, and Elijah.

Of the sons of Zattu: Elioenai, Eliashib, Mattaniah, and Jeremoth, and Zabad, and Aziza.

Of the sons of Bebai: Jehohanan, Hananiah, Zabbai, Athlai.

Of the sons of Bani: Meshullam, Malluch, and Adaiah, Jashub, and Sheal, Jeremoth.

Of the sons of Pahathmoab: Adna, and Chelal, Benaiah, Maaseiah, Mattaniah, Bezalel, and Binnui, and Manasseh.

Of the sons of Harim: Eliezer, Isshijah, Malchijah, Shemaiah, Shimeon, Benjamin, Malluch, Shemariah.

Of the sons of Hashum: Mattenai, Mattattah, Zabad, Eliphelet, Jeremai, Manasseh, Shimei.

Of the sons of Bani: Maadai, Amram, and Uel, Benaiah, Bedeiah, Cheluhi, Vaniah, Meremoth, Eliashib, Mattaniah, Mattenai, and Jaasu, and Bani, and Binnui, Shimei, and Shelemiah, and Nathan, and Adaiah, Machnadebai, Shashai, Sharai, Azarel, and Shelemiah, Shemariah, Shallum, Amariah, Joseph.

Of the sons of Nebo: Jeiel, Mattithiah, Zabad, Zebina, Iddo, and Joel, Benaiah.

All these had taken foreign wives; and some of them had wives by whom they had children.

THE BOOK OF

NEHEMIAH

56 MIN

The words of Nehemiah the son of Hacaliah.

Now in the month Chislev, in the twentieth year, as I was in Susa the palace, Hanani, one of my brothers, came, he and certain men out of Judah; and I asked them about the Jews who had escaped, who were left of the captivity, and concerning Jerusalem. They said to me, "The remnant who are left of the captivity there in the province are in great affliction and reproach. The wall of Jerusalem is also broken down, and its gates are burned with fire."

When I heard these words, I sat down and wept, and mourned several days; and I fasted and prayed before the God of heaven, and said, "I beg you, YHWH, the God of heaven, the great and awesome God, who keeps covenant and loving kindness with those who love him and keep his commandments: Let your ear now be attentive, and your eyes open, that you may listen to the prayer of your servant, which I pray before you at this time, day and night, for the children of Israel your servants, while I confess the sins of the children of Israel, which we have sinned against you. Yes, I and my father's house have sinned. We have dealt very corruptly against you, and have not kept the commandments, nor the statutes, nor the ordinances, which you commanded your servant Moses.

"Remember, I beg you, the word that you commanded your servant Moses, saying, 'If you trespass, I will scatter you among the peoples; but if you return to me, and keep my commandments and do them, though your outcasts were in the uttermost part of the heavens, yet I will gather them from there, and will bring them to the place that I have chosen, to cause my name to dwell there.'

"Now these are your servants and your people, whom you have redeemed by your great power, and by your strong hand. Lord, I beg you, let your ear be attentive now to the prayer of your servant, and to the prayer of your servants, who delight to fear your name; and please prosper your servant today, and grant him mercy in the sight of this man."

Now I was cup bearer to the king.

....

In the month Nisan, in the twentieth year of Artaxerxes the king, when wine was before him, I picked up the wine, and gave it to the king. Now I had not been sad before in his presence. The king said to me, "Why is your face sad, since you are not sick? This is nothing else but sorrow of heart."

Then I was very much afraid. I said to the king, "Let the king live forever! Why shouldn't my face be sad, when the city, the place of my fathers' tombs, lies waste, and its gates have been consumed with fire?"

Then the king said to me, "What is your request?"

So I prayed to the God of heaven. I said to the king, "If it pleases the king, and if your servant has found favor in your sight, that you would send me to Judah, to the city of my fathers' tombs, that I may build it."

The king said to me (the queen was also sitting by him), "How long will your journey be? When will you return?"

So it pleased the king to send me, and I set a time for him. Moreover I said to the king, "If it pleases the king, let letters be given me to the governors beyond the River, that they may let me pass through until I come to Judah; and a letter to Asaph the keeper of the king's forest, that he may give me timber to make beams for the gates of the citadel by the temple, for the wall of the city, and for the house that I will occupy."

The king granted my requests, because of the good hand of my God on me. Then I came to the governors beyond the River, and gave them the king's letters. Now the king had sent captains of the army and horsemen with me. When Sanballat the Horonite, and Tobiah the servant, the Ammonite, heard of it, it grieved them exceedingly, because a man had come to seek the welfare of the children of Israel. So I came to Jerusalem, and was there three days. I arose in the night, I and a few men with me. I didn't tell anyone what my God put into my heart to do for Jerusalem. There wasn't any animal with me, except the animal that I rode on. I went out by night by the valley gate, even toward the jackal's well, then to the dung gate, and inspected the walls of Jerusalem, which were broken down, and its gates were consumed with fire. Then I went on to the spring gate and to the king's pool, but there was no place for the animal that was under me to pass. Then I went up in the night by the brook, and inspected the wall; and I turned back, and entered by the valley gate, and so returned. The rulers didn't know where I went, or what I did. I had not as yet told it to the Jews, nor to the priests, nor to the nobles, nor to the rulers, nor to the rest who did the work.

Then I said to them, "You see the bad situation that we are in, how Jerusalem lies waste, and its gates are burned with fire. Come, let's build up the wall of Jerusalem, that we won't be disgraced." I told them of the hand of my God which was good on me, as also of the king's words that he had spoken to me.

They said, "Let's rise up and build." So they strengthened their hands for the good work.

But when Sanballat the Horonite, Tobiah the Ammonite servant, and Geshem the Arabian, heard it, they ridiculed us, and despised us, and said, "What is this thing that you are doing? Will you rebel against the king?"

Then I answered them, and said to them, "The God of heaven will prosper us. Therefore we, his servants, will arise and build; but you have no portion, nor right, nor memorial, in Jerusalem."

....

Then Eliashib the high priest rose up with his brothers the priests, and they built the sheep gate. They sanctified it, and set up its doors. They sanctified it even to the tower of Hammeah, to the tower of Hananel. Next to him the men of Jericho built. Next to them Zaccur the son of Imri built.

The sons of Hassenaah built the fish gate. They laid its beams, and set up its doors, its bolts, and its bars. Next to them, Meremoth the son of Uriah, the son of Hakkoz made repairs. Next to them, Meshullam the son of Berechiah, the son of Meshezabel made repairs. Next to them, Zadok the son of Baana made repairs. Next to them, the Tekoites made repairs; but their nobles didn't put their necks to the Lord's work.

Joiada the son of Paseah and Meshullam the son of Besodeiah repaired the old gate. They laid its beams, and set up its doors, and its bolts, and its bars. Next to them, Melatiah the Gibeonite, and Jadon the Meronothite, the men of Gibeon and of Mizpah, repaired the residence of the governor beyond the River. Next to him, Uzziel the son of Harhaiah, goldsmiths, made repairs. Next to him, Hananiah, one of the perfumers, made repairs, and they fortified Jerusalem even to the wide wall. Next to them, Rephaiah the son of Hur, the ruler of half the district of Jerusalem, made repairs. Next to them, Jedaiah the son of Harumaph made repairs across from his house. Next to him, Hattush the son of Hashabneiah made repairs. Malchijah the son of Harim, and Hasshub the son of Pahathmoab, repaired another portion, and the tower of the furnaces. Next to him, Shallum the son of Hallohesh, the ruler of half the district of Jerusalem, he and his daughters, made repairs.

Hanun and the inhabitants of Zanoah repaired the valley gate. They built it, and set up its doors, its bolts, and its bars, and one thousand cubits of the wall to the dung gate.

Malchijah the son of Rechab, the ruler of the district of Beth Haccherem repaired the dung gate. He built it, and set up its doors, its bolts, and its bars.

Shallun the son of Colhozeh, the ruler of the district of Mizpah repaired the spring gate. He built it, and covered it, and set up its doors, its bolts, and its bars, and the wall of the pool of Shelah by the king's garden, even to the stairs that go down from David's city. After him, Nehemiah the son of Azbuk, the ruler of half the district of Beth Zur, made repairs to the place opposite the tombs of David, and to the pool that was made, and to the house of the mighty men. After him, the Levites, Rehum the son of Bani made repairs. Next to him, Hashabiah, the ruler of half the district of Keilah, made repairs for his district. After him, their brothers, Bavvai the son of Henadad, the ruler of half the district of Keilah made repairs. Next to him, Ezer the son of Jeshua, the ruler of Mizpah, repaired another portion, across from the ascent to the armory at the turning of the wall. After him, Baruch the son of Zabbai earnestly repaired another portion, from the turning of the wall to the door of the house of Eliashib the high priest. After him, Meremoth the son of Uriah the son of Hakkoz repaired another portion, from the door of the house of Eliashib even to the end of the house of Eliashib. After him, the priests, the men of the Plain made repairs. After them, Benjamin and Hasshub made repairs across from their house. After them, Azariah the son of Maaseiah the son of Ananiah made repairs beside his own house. After him, Binnui the son of Henadad repaired another portion, from the house of Azariah to the turning of the wall, and to the corner. Palal the son of Uzai made repairs opposite the turning of the wall, and the tower that stands out from the upper house of the king, which is by the court of the guard. After him Pedaiah the son of Parosh made repairs. (Now the temple servants lived in Ophel, to the place opposite the water gate toward the east, and the tower that stands out.) After him the Tekoites repaired another portion, opposite the great tower that stands out, and to the wall of Ophel.

Above the horse gate, the priests made repairs, everyone across from his own house. After them, Zadok the son of Immer made repairs across from his own house. After him, Shemaiah the son of Shecaniah, the keeper of the east gate made repairs. After him, Hananiah the son of Shelemiah, and Hanun the sixth son of Zalaph, repaired another portion. After him, Meshullam the son of Berechiah made repairs across from his room. After him, Malchijah, one of the goldsmiths to the house of the temple servants, and of the merchants, made repairs opposite the gate of Hammiphkad, and to the ascent of the corner. Between the ascent of the corner and the sheep gate, the goldsmiths and the merchants made repairs.

....

But when Sanballat heard that we were building the wall, he was angry, and was very indignant, and mocked the Jews. He spoke before his brothers and the army of Samaria, and said, "What are these feeble Jews doing? Will they fortify themselves? Will they sacrifice? Will they finish in a day? Will they revive the stones out of the heaps of rubbish, since they are burned?"

Now Tobiah the Ammonite was by him, and he said, "What they are building, if a fox climbed up it, he would break down their stone wall."

"Hear, our God; for we are despised. Turn back their reproach on their own head. Give them up for a plunder in a land of captivity. Don't cover their iniquity. Don't let their sin be blotted out from before you; for they have insulted the builders."

So we built the wall; and all the wall was joined together to half its height: for the people had a mind to work.

But when Sanballat, Tobiah, the Arabians, the Ammonites, and the Ashdodites heard that the repairing of the walls of Jerusalem went forward, and that the breaches began to be filled, they were very angry; and they all conspired together to come and fight against Jerusalem, and to cause confusion among us. But we made our prayer to our God, and set a watch against them day and night because of them. Judah said, "The strength of the bearers of burdens is fading, and there is much rubble; so that we are not able to build the wall." Our adversaries said, "They will not know or see, until we come in among them and kill them, and cause the work to cease."

When the Jews who lived by them came, they said to us ten times from all places, "Wherever you turn, they will attack us."

Therefore I set guards in the lowest parts of the space behind the wall, in the open places. I set the people by family groups with their swords, their spears, and their bows. I looked, and rose up, and said to the nobles, to the rulers, and to the rest of the people, "Don't be afraid of them! Remember the Lord, who is great and awesome, and fight for your brothers, your sons, your daughters, your wives, and your houses."

When our enemies heard that it was known to us, and God had brought their counsel to nothing, all of us returned to the wall, everyone to his work. From that time forth, half of my servants did the work, and half of them held the spears, the shields, the bows, and the coats of mail; and the rulers were behind all the house of Judah. Those who built the wall, and those who bore burdens loaded themselves; everyone with one of his hands did the work, and with the other held his weapon. Among the builders, everyone wore his sword at his side, and so built. He who sounded the trumpet was by me. I said to the nobles, and to the rulers and to the rest of the people, "The work is great and large, and we are separated on the wall, far from one another. Wherever you hear the sound of the trumpet, rally there to us. Our God will fight for us."

So we did the work. Half of the people held the spears from the rising of the morning until the stars appeared. Likewise at the same time I said to the people, "Let everyone with his servant lodge within Jerusalem, that in the night they may be a guard to us, and may labor in the day." So neither I, nor my brothers, nor my servants, nor the men of the guard who followed me, none of us took off our clothes. Everyone took his weapon to the water.

....

Then there arose a great cry of the people and of their wives against their brothers the Jews. For there were some who said, "We, our sons and our daughters, are many. Let us get grain, that we may eat and live." There were also some who said, "We are mortgaging our fields, our vineyards, and our houses. Let us get grain, because of the famine." There were also some who said, "We have borrowed money for the king's tribute using our fields and our vineyards as collateral. Yet now our flesh is as the flesh of our brothers, our children as their children. Behold, we bring our sons and our daughters into bondage to be servants, and some of our daughters have been brought into bondage. It is also not in our power to help it, because other men have our fields and our vineyards."

I was very angry when I heard their cry and these words. Then I consulted with myself, and contended with the nobles and the rulers, and said to them, "You exact usury, everyone of his brother." I held a great assembly against them. I said to them, "We, after our ability, have redeemed our brothers the Jews that were sold to the nations; and would you even sell your brothers, and should they be sold to us?" Then they held their peace, and found not a word to say. Also I said, "The thing that you do is not good. Shouldn't you walk in the fear of our God, because of the reproach of the nations our enemies? I likewise, my brothers and my servants, lend them money and grain. Please let us stop this usury. Please restore to them, even today, their fields, their vineyards, their olive groves, and their houses, also the hundredth part of the money, and of the grain, the new wine, and the oil, that you are charging them."

Then they said, "We will restore them, and will require nothing of them. We will do so, even as you say."

Then I called the priests, and took an oath of them, that they would do according to this promise. Also I shook out my lap, and said, "So may God shake out every man from his house, and from his labor, that doesn't perform this promise; even may he be shaken out and emptied like this."

All the assembly said, "Amen," and praised YHWH. The people did according to this promise.

Moreover from the time that I was appointed to be their governor in the land of Judah, from the twentieth year even to the thirty-second year of Artaxerxes the king, that is, twelve years, I and my brothers have not eaten the bread of the governor. But the former governors who were before me were supported by the people, and took bread and wine from them, plus forty shekels of silver; yes, even their servants ruled over the people; but I didn't do so, because of the fear of God. Yes, I also continued in the work of this wall. We didn't buy any land. All my servants were gathered there to the work. Moreover there were at my table, of the Jews and the rulers, one hundred fifty men, in addition to those who came to us from among the nations that were around us. Now that which was prepared for one day was one ox and six choice sheep. Also fowls were prepared for me, and once in ten days a store of all sorts of wine. Yet for all this, I didn't demand the governor's pay, because the bondage was heavy on this people. Remember me, my God, for good, all that I have done for this people.

....

Now when it was reported to Sanballat, Tobiah, and to Geshem the Arabian, and to the rest of our enemies, that I had built the wall, and that there was no breach left in it (though even to that time I had not set up the doors in the gates) Sanballat and Geshem sent to me, saying, "Come! Let's meet together in the villages in the plain of Ono." But they intended to harm me.

I sent messengers to them, saying, "I am doing a great work, so that I can't come down. Why should the work cease, while I leave it, and come down to you?" They sent to me four times like this; and I answered them the same way. Then Sanballat sent his servant to me the same way the fifth time with an open letter in his hand, in which was written, "It is reported among the nations, and Gashmu says it, that you and the Jews intend to rebel. Because of that, you are building the wall. You would be their king, according to these words. You have also appointed prophets to proclaim of you at Jerusalem, saying, 'There is a king in Judah!' Now it will be reported to the king according to these words. Come now therefore, and let's take counsel together."

Then I sent to him, saying, "There are no such things done as you say, but you imagine them out of your own heart." For they all would have made us afraid, saying, "Their hands will be weakened from the work, that it not be done." But now, strengthen my hands.

I went to the house of Shemaiah the son of Delaiah the son of Mehetabel, who was shut in at his home; and he said, "Let us meet together in God's house, within the temple, and let's shut the doors of the temple; for they will come to kill you. Yes, in the night they will come to kill you."

I said, "Should a man like me flee? Who is there that, being such as I, would go into the temple to save his life? I will not go in." I discerned, and behold, God had not sent him; but he pronounced this prophecy against me. Tobiah and Sanballat had hired him. He hired so that I would be afraid, do so, and sin, and that they might have material for an evil report, that they might reproach me. "Remember, my God, Tobiah and Sanballat according to these their works, and also the prophetess Noadiah, and the rest of the prophets, that would have put me in fear."

So the wall was finished in the twenty-fifth day of Elul, in fifty-two days. When all our enemies heard of it, all the nations that were around us were afraid, and they lost their confidence; for they perceived that this work was done by our God. Moreover in those days the nobles of Judah sent many letters to Tobiah, and Tobiah's letters came to them. For there were many in Judah sworn to him, because he was the son-in-law of Shecaniah the son of Arah; and his son Jehohanan had taken the daughter of Meshullam the son of Berechiah as wife. Also they spoke of his good deeds before me, and reported my words to him. Tobiah sent letters to put me in fear.

....

Now when the wall was built, and I had set up the doors, and the gatekeepers and the singers and the Levites were appointed, I put my brother Hanani, and Hananiah the governor of the fortress, in charge of Jerusalem; for he was a faithful man, and feared God above many. I said to them, "Don't let the gates of Jerusalem be opened until the sun is hot; and while they stand guard, let them shut the doors, and you bar them: and appoint watches of the inhabitants of Jerusalem, everyone in his watch, with everyone near his house."

Now the city was wide and large; but the people were few therein, and the houses were not built.

My God put into my heart to gather together the nobles, and the rulers, and the people, that they might be listed by genealogy. I found the book of the genealogy of those who came up at the first, and I found this written in it:

These are the children of the province who went up out of the captivity of those who had been carried away, whom Nebuchadnezzar the king of Babylon had carried away, and who returned to Jerusalem and to Judah, everyone to his city, who came with Zerubbabel, Jeshua, Nehemiah, Azariah, Raamiah, Nahamani, Mordecai, Bilshan, Mispereth, Bigvai, Nehum, Baanah.

The number of the men of the people of Israel:

The children of Parosh: two thousand one hundred seventy-two.

The children of Shephatiah: three hundred seventy-two.

The children of Arah: six hundred fifty-two.

The children of Pahathmoab, of the children of Jeshua and Joab: two thousand eight hundred eighteen.

The children of Elam: one thousand two hundred fifty-four.

The children of Zattu: eight hundred forty-five.

The children of Zaccai: seven hundred sixty.

The children of Binnui: six hundred forty-eight.

The children of Bebai: six hundred twenty-eight.

The children of Azgad: two thousand three hundred twenty-two.

The children of Adonikam: six hundred sixty-seven.

The children of Bigvai: two thousand sixty-seven.

The children of Adin: six hundred fifty-five.

The children of Ater: of Hezekiah, ninety-eight.

The children of Hashum: three hundred twenty-eight.

The children of Bezai: three hundred twenty-four.

The children of Hariph: one hundred twelve.

The children of Gibeon: ninety-five.

The men of Bethlehem and Netophah: one hundred eighty-eight.

The men of Anathoth: one hundred twenty-eight.

The men of Beth Azmaveth: forty-two.

The men of Kiriath Jearim, Chephirah, and Beeroth: seven hundred forty-three.

The men of Ramah and Geba: six hundred twenty-one.

The men of Michmas: one hundred twenty-two.

The men of Bethel and Ai: one hundred twenty-three.

The men of the other Nebo: fifty-two.

The children of the other Elam: one thousand two hundred fifty-four.

The children of Harim: three hundred twenty.

The children of Jericho: three hundred forty-five.

The children of Lod, Hadid, and Ono: seven hundred twenty-one.

The children of Senaah: three thousand nine hundred thirty.

The priests: The children of Jedaiah, of the house of Jeshua: nine hundred seventy-three.

The children of Immer: one thousand fifty-two.

The children of Pashhur: one thousand two hundred forty-seven.

The children of Harim: one thousand seventeen.

The Levites: the children of Jeshua, of Kadmiel, of the children of Hodevah: seventy-four.

The singers: the children of Asaph: one hundred forty-eight.

The gatekeepers: the children of Shallum, the children of Ater, the children of Talmon, the children of Akkub, the children of Hatita, the children of Shobai: one hundred thirty-eight.

The temple servants: the children of Ziha, the children of Hasupha, the children of Tabbaoth, the children of Keros, the children of Sia, the children of Padon, the children of Lebana, the children of Hagaba, the children of Salmai, the children of Hanan, the children of Giddel, the children of Gahar, the children of Reaiah, the children of Rezin, the children of Nekoda, the children of Gazzam, the children of Uzza, the children of Paseah. The children of Besai, the children of Meunim, the children of Nephushesim, the children of Bakbuk, the children of Hakupha, the children of Harhur, the children of Bazlith, the children of Mehida, the children of Harsha, the children of Barkos, the children of Sisera, the children of Temah, the children of Neziah, and the children of Hatipha.

The children of Solomon's servants: the children of Sotai, the children of Sophereth, the children of Perida, the children of Jaala, the children of Darkon, the children of Giddel, the children of Shephatiah, the children of Hattil, the children of Pochereth Hazzebaim, and the children of Amon. All the temple servants and the children of Solomon's servants were three hundred ninety-two.

These were those who went up from Tel Melah, Tel Harsha, Cherub, Addon, and Immer; but they could not show their fathers' houses, nor their offspring, whether they were of Israel:

The children of Delaiah, the children of Tobiah, the children of Nekoda: six hundred forty-two.

Of the priests: the children of Hobaiah, the children of Hakkoz, the children of Barzillai, who took a wife of the daughters of Barzillai the Gileadite, and was called after their name.

These searched for their genealogical records, but couldn't find them. Therefore they were deemed disqualified and removed from the priesthood. The governor told that they should not eat of the most holy things until a priest stood up to minister with Urim and Thummim.

The whole assembly together was forty-two thousand three hundred sixty, in addition to their male servants and their female servants, of whom there were seven thousand three hundred thirty-seven. They had two hundred forty-five singing men and singing women. Their horses were seven hundred thirty-six; their mules, two hundred forty-five; their camels, four hundred thirty-five; their donkeys, six thousand seven hundred twenty.

Some from among the heads of fathers' households gave to the work. The governor gave to the treasury one thousand darics of gold, fifty basins, and five hundred thirty priests' garments. Some of the heads of fathers' households gave into the treasury of the work twenty thousand darics of gold, and two thousand two hundred minas of silver. That which the rest of the people gave was twenty thousand darics of gold, plus two thousand minas of silver, and sixty-seven priests' garments.

So the priests, the Levites, the gatekeepers, the singers, some of the people, the temple servants, and all Israel, lived in their cities.

When the seventh month had come, the children of Israel were in their cities.

....

All the people gathered themselves together as one man into the wide place that was in front of the water gate; and they spoke to Ezra the scribe to bring the book of the law of Moses, which YHWH had commanded to Israel. Ezra the priest brought the law before the assembly, both men and women, and all who could hear with understanding, on the first day of the seventh month. He read from it before the wide place that was in front of the water gate from early morning until midday, in the presence of the men and the women, and of those who could understand. The ears of all the people were attentive to the book of the law. Ezra the scribe stood on a pulpit of wood, which they had made for the purpose; and beside him stood Mattithiah, Shema, Anaiah, Uriah, Hilkiah, and Maaseiah, on his right hand; and on his left hand, Pedaiah, Mishael, Malchijah, Hashum, Hashbaddanah, Zechariah, and Meshullam. Ezra opened the book in the sight of all the people (for he was above all the people), and when he opened it, all the people stood up. Then Ezra blessed YHWH, the great God.

All the people answered, "Amen, Amen," with the lifting up of their hands. They bowed their heads, and worshiped YHWH with their faces to the ground. Also Jeshua, Bani, Sherebiah, Jamin, Akkub, Shabbethai, Hodiah, Maaseiah, Kelita, Azariah, Jozabad, Hanan, Pelaiah, and the Levites, caused the people to understand the law; and the people stayed in their place. They read in the book, in the law of God, distinctly; and they gave the sense, so that they understood the reading.

Nehemiah, who was the governor, and Ezra the priest and scribe, and the Levites who taught the people, said to all the people, "Today is holy to YHWH your God. Don't mourn, nor weep." For all the people wept when they heard the words of the law. Then he said to them, "Go your way. Eat the fat, drink the sweet, and send portions to him for whom nothing is prepared, for today is holy to our Lord. Don't be grieved, for the joy of YHWH is your strength."

So the Levites calmed all the people, saying, "Hold your peace, for the day is holy. Don't be grieved."

All the people went their way to eat, to drink, to send portions, and to celebrate, because they had understood the words that were declared to them.

On the second day, the heads of fathers' households of all the people, the priests, and the Levites were gathered together to Ezra the scribe, to study the words of the law. They found written in the law how YHWH had commanded by Moses that the children of Israel should dwell in booths in the feast of the seventh month; and that they should publish and proclaim in all their cities, and in Jerusalem, saying, "Go out to the mountain, and get olive branches, branches of wild olive, myrtle branches, palm branches, and branches of thick trees, to make temporary shelters, as it is written."

So the people went out, and brought them, and made themselves temporary shelters, everyone on the roof of his house, in their courts, in the courts of God's house, in the wide place of the water gate, and in the wide place of Ephraim's gate. All the assembly of those who had come back out of the captivity made temporary shelters, and lived in the temporary shelters; for since the days of Jeshua the son of Nun to that day the children of Israel had not done so. There was very great gladness. Also day by day, from the first day to the last day, he read in the book of the law of God. They kept the feast seven days; and on the eighth day was a solemn assembly, according to the ordinance.

....

Now in the twenty-fourth day of this month the children of Israel were assembled with fasting, with sackcloth, and dirt on them. The offspring of Israel separated themselves from all foreigners and stood and confessed their sins and the iniquities of their fathers. They stood up in their place, and read in the book of the law of YHWH their God a fourth part of the day; and a fourth part they confessed, and worshiped YHWH their God. Then Jeshua, Bani, Kadmiel, Shebaniah, Bunni, Sherebiah, Bani, and Chenani of the Levites stood up on the stairs, and cried with a loud voice to YHWH their God.

Then the Levites, Jeshua, and Kadmiel, Bani, Hashabneiah, Sherebiah, Hodiah, Shebaniah, and Pethahiah, said, "Stand up and bless YHWH your God from everlasting to everlasting! Blessed be your glorious name, which is exalted above all blessing and praise! You are YHWH, even you alone. You have made heaven, the heaven of heavens, with all their army, the earth and all things that are on it, the seas and all that is in them, and you preserve them all. The army of heaven worships you. You are YHWH, the God who chose Abram, brought him out of Ur of the Chaldees, gave him the name of Abraham, found his heart faithful before you, and made a covenant with him to give the land of the Canaanite, the Hittite, the Amorite, the Perizzite, the Jebusite, and the Girgashite, to give it to his offspring, and have performed your words; for you are righteous.

"You saw the affliction of our fathers in Egypt, and heard their cry by the Red Sea, and showed signs and wonders against Pharaoh, and against all his servants, and against all the people of his land; for you knew that they dealt proudly against them, and made a name for yourself, as it is today. You divided the sea before them, so that they went through the middle of the sea on the dry land; and you cast their pursuers into the depths, as a stone into the mighty waters. Moreover, in a pillar of cloud you led them by day; and in a pillar of fire by night, to give them light in the way in which they should go.

"You also came down on Mount Sinai, and spoke with them from heaven, and gave them right ordinances and true laws, good statutes and commandments, and made known to them your holy Sabbath, and commanded them commandments, statutes, and a law, by Moses your servant, and gave them bread from the sky for their hunger, and brought water out of the rock for them for their thirst, and commanded them that they should go in to possess the land which you had sworn to give them.

"But they and our fathers behaved proudly, hardened their neck, didn't listen to your commandments, and refused to obey. They weren't mindful of your wonders that you did among them, but hardened their neck, and in their rebellion appointed a captain to return to their bondage. But you are a God ready to pardon, gracious and merciful, slow to anger, and abundant in loving kindness, and didn't forsake them. Yes, when they had made themselves a molded calf, and said, 'This is your God who brought you up out of Egypt,' and had committed awful blasphemies; yet you in your manifold mercies didn't forsake them in the wilderness. The pillar of cloud didn't depart from over them by day, to lead them in the way; neither did the pillar of fire by night, to show them light, and the way in which they should go. You gave also your good Spirit to instruct them, and didn't withhold your manna from their mouth, and gave them water for their thirst.

"Yes, forty years you sustained them in the wilderness. They lacked nothing. Their clothes didn't grow old, and their feet didn't swell. Moreover you gave them kingdoms and peoples, which you allotted according to their portions. So they possessed the land of Sihon, even the land of the king of Heshbon, and the land of Og king of Bashan. You also multiplied their children as the stars of the sky, and brought them into the land concerning which you said to their fathers, that they should go in to possess it.

"So the children went in and possessed the land, and you subdued before them the inhabitants of the land, the Canaanites, and gave them into their hands, with their kings and the peoples of the land, that they might do with them as they pleased. They took fortified cities and a rich land, and possessed houses full of all good things, cisterns dug out, vineyards, olive groves, and fruit trees in abundance. So they ate, were filled, became fat, and delighted themselves in your great goodness.

"Nevertheless they were disobedient, and rebelled against you, cast your law behind their back, killed your prophets that testified against them to turn them again to you, and they committed awful blasphemies. Therefore you delivered them into the hand of their adversaries, who distressed them. In the time of their trouble, when they cried to you, you heard from heaven; and according to your manifold mercies you gave them saviors who saved them out of the hands of their adversaries. But after they had rest, they did evil again before you; therefore you left them in the hands of their enemies, so that they had the dominion over them; yet when they returned, and cried to you, you heard from heaven; and many times you delivered them according to your mercies, and testified against them, that you might bring them again to your law. Yet they were arrogant, and didn't listen to your commandments, but sinned against your ordinances (which if a man does, he shall live in them), turned their backs, stiffened their neck, and would not hear. Yet many years you put up with them, and testified against them by your Spirit through your prophets. Yet they would not listen. Therefore you gave them into the hand of the peoples of the lands.

"Nevertheless in your manifold mercies you didn't make a full end of them, nor forsake them; for you are a gracious and merciful

God.

Now therefore, our God, the great, the mighty, and the awesome God, who keeps covenant and loving kindness, don't let all the travail seem little before you, that has come on us, on our kings, on our princes, on our priests, on our prophets, on our fathers, and on all your people, since the time of the kings of Assyria to this day. However you are just in all that has come on us; for you have dealt truly, but we have done wickedly. Also our kings, our princes, our priests, and our fathers have not kept your law, nor listened to your commandments and your testimonies with which you testified against them. For they have not served you in their kingdom, and in your great goodness that you gave them, and in the large and rich land which you gave before them. They didn't turn from their wicked works.

"Behold, we are servants today, and as for the land that you gave to our fathers to eat its fruit and its good, behold, we are servants in it. It yields much increase to the kings whom you have set over us because of our sins. Also they have power over our bodies and over our livestock, at their pleasure, and we are in great distress. Yet for all this, we make a sure covenant, and write it; and our princes, our Levites, and our priests, seal it."

....

Now those who sealed were: Nehemiah the governor, the son of Hacaliah, and Zedekiah, Seraiah, Azariah, Jeremiah, Pashhur, Amariah, Malchijah, Hattush, Shebaniah, Malluch, Harim, Meremoth, Obadiah, Daniel, Ginnethon, Baruch, Meshullam, Abijah, Mijamin, Maaziah, Bilgai, and Shemaiah. These were the priests. The Levites: namely, Jeshua the son of Azaniah, Binnui of the sons of Henadad, Kadmiel; and their brothers, Shebaniah, Hodiah, Kelita, Pelaiah, Hanan, Mica, Rehob, Hashabiah, Zaccur, Sherebiah, Shebaniah, Hodiah, Bani, and Beninu. The chiefs of the people: Parosh, Pahathmoab, Elam, Zattu, Bani, Bunni, Azgad, Bebai, Adonijah, Bigvai, Adin, Ater, Hezekiah, Azzur, Hodiah, Hashum, Bezai, Hariph, Anathoth, Nobai, Magpiash, Meshullam, Hezir, Meshezabel, Zadok, Jaddua, Pelatiah, Hanan, Anaiah, Hoshea, Hananiah, Hasshub, Hallohesh, Pilha, Shobek, Rehum, Hashabnah, Maaseiah, Ahiah, Hanan, Anan, Malluch, Harim, and Baanah.

The rest of the people, the priests, the Levites, the gatekeepers, the singers, the temple servants, and all those who had separated themselves from the peoples of the lands to the law of God, their wives, their sons, and their daughters—everyone who had knowledge, and understanding— joined with their brothers, their nobles, and entered into a curse, and into an oath, to walk in God's law, which was given by Moses the servant of God, and to observe and do all the commandments of YHWH our Lord, and his ordinances and his statutes; and that we would not give our daughters to the peoples of the land, nor take their daughters for our sons; and if the peoples of the land bring wares or any grain on the Sabbath day to sell, that we would not buy from them on the Sabbath, or on a holy day; and that we would forego the seventh year, and the exaction of every debt.

Also we made ordinances for ourselves, to charge ourselves yearly with the third part of a shekel for the service of the house of our God; for the show bread, for the continual meal offering, for the continual burnt offering, for the Sabbaths, for the new moons, for the set feasts, and for the holy things, and for the sin offerings to make atonement for Israel, and for all the work of the house of our God. We, the priests, the Levites, and the people, cast lots for the wood offering, to bring it into the house of our God, according to our fathers' houses, at times appointed, year by year, to burn on YHWH our God's altar, as it is written in the law; and to bring the first fruits of our ground, and the first fruits of all fruit of all kinds of trees, year by year, to YHWH's house; also the firstborn of our sons, and of our livestock, as it is written in the law, and the firstborn of our herds and of our flocks, to bring to the house of our God, to the priests who minister in the house of our God; and that we should bring the first fruits of our dough, our wave offerings, the fruit of all kinds of trees, and the new wine and the oil, to the priests, to the rooms of the house of our God; and the tithes of our ground to the Levites; for they, the Levites, take the tithes in all the cities of our tillage. The priest the son of Aaron shall be with the Levites, when the Levites take tithes. The Levites shall bring up the tithe of the tithes to the house of our God, to the rooms, into the treasure house. For the children of Israel and the children of Levi shall bring the wave offering of the grain, of the new wine, and of the oil, to the rooms, where the vessels of the sanctuary are, and the priests who minister, with the gatekeepers and the singers. We will not forsake the house of our God.

....

The princes of the people lived in Jerusalem. The rest of the people also cast lots, to bring one of ten to dwell in Jerusalem the holy city, and nine parts in the other cities. The people blessed all the men who willingly offered themselves to dwell in Jerusalem.

Now these are the chiefs of the province who lived in Jerusalem; but in the cities of Judah everyone lived in his possession in their cities: Israel, the priests, the Levites, the temple servants, and the children of Solomon's servants. Some of the children of Judah and of the children of Benjamin lived in Jerusalem. Of the children of Judah: Athaiah the son of Uzziah, the son of Zechariah, the son of Amariah, the son of Shephatiah, the son of Mahalalel, of the children of Perez; and Maaseiah the son of Baruch, the son of Colhozeh, the son of Hazaiah, the son of Adaiah, the son of Joiarib, the son of Zechariah, the son of the Shilonite. All the sons of Perez who lived in Jerusalem were four hundred sixty-eight valiant men.

These are the sons of Benjamin: Sallu the son of Meshullam, the son of Joed, the son of Pedaiah, the son of Kolaiah, the son of Maaseiah, the son of Ithiel, the son of Jeshaiah. After him Gabbai, Sallai, nine hundred twenty-eight. Joel the son of Zichri was their overseer; and Judah the son of Hassenuah was second over the city.

Of the priests: Jedaiah the son of Joiarib, Jachin, Seraiah the son of Hilkiah, the son of Meshullam, the son of Zadok, the son of Meraioth, the son of Ahitub, the ruler of God's house, and their brothers who did the work of the house, eight hundred twenty-two; and Adaiah the son of Jeroham, the son of Pelaliah, the son of Amzi, the son of Zechariah, the son of Pashhur, the son of Malchijah, and his brothers, chiefs of fathers' households, two hundred forty-two; and Amashsai the son of Azarel, the son of Ahzai, the son of Meshillemoth, the son of Immer, and their brothers, mighty men of valor, one hundred twenty-eight; and their overseer was Zabdiel, the son of Haggedolim.

Of the Levites: Shemaiah the son of Hasshub, the son of Azrikam, the son of Hashabiah, the son of Bunni; and Shabbethai and Jozabad, of the chiefs of the Levites, who had the oversight of the outward business of God's house; and Mattaniah the son of Mica, the son of Zabdi, the son of Asaph, who was the chief to begin the thanksgiving in prayer, and Bakbukiah, the second among his brothers; and Abda the son of Shammua, the son of Galal, the son of Jeduthun. All the Levites in the holy city were two hundred eighty-four.

Moreover the gatekeepers, Akkub, Talmon, and their brothers, who kept watch at the gates, were one hundred seventy-two. The residue of Israel, of the priests, the Levites, were in all the cities of Judah, everyone in his inheritance. But the temple servants lived in Ophel: and Ziha and Gishpa were over the temple servants.

The overseer also of the Levites at Jerusalem was Uzzi the son of Bani, the son of Hashabiah, the son of Mattaniah, the son of Mica, of the sons of Asaph, the singers, over the business of God's house. For there was a commandment from the king concerning them, and a settled provision for the singers, as every day required. Pethahiah the son of Meshezabel, of the children of Zerah the son of Judah, was at the king's hand in all matters concerning the people.

As for the villages, with their fields, some of the children of Judah lived in Kiriath Arba and its towns, in Dibon and its towns, in Jekabzeel and its villages, in Jeshua, in Moladah, Beth Pelet, in Hazar Shual, in Beersheba and its towns, in Ziklag, in Meconah and in its towns, in En Rimmon, in Zorah, in Jarmuth, Zanoah, Adullam, and their villages, Lachish and its fields, and Azekah and its towns. So they encamped from Beersheba to the valley of Hinnom. The children of Benjamin also lived from Geba onward, at Michmash and Aija, and at Bethel and its towns, at Anathoth, Nob, Ananiah, Hazor, Ramah, Gittaim, Hadid, Zeboim, Neballat, Lod, and Ono, the valley of craftsmen. Of the Levites, certain divisions in Judah settled in Benjamin's territory.

··

Now these are the priests and the Levites who went up with Zerubbabel the son of Shealtiel, and Jeshua: Seraiah, Jeremiah, Ezra, Amariah, Malluch, Hattush, Shecaniah, Rehum, Meremoth, Iddo, Ginnethoi, Abijah, Mijamin, Maadiah, Bilgah, Shemaiah, and Joiarib, Jedaiah. Sallu, Amok, Hilkiah, and Jedaiah. These were the chiefs of the priests and of their brothers in the days of Jeshua.

Moreover the Levites: Jeshua, Binnui, Kadmiel, Sherebiah, Judah, and Mattaniah, who was over the thanksgiving, he and his brothers. Also Bakbukiah and Unno, their brothers, were close to them according to their offices. Jeshua became the father of Joiakim, and Joiakim became the father of Eliashib, and Eliashib became the father of Joiada, and Joiada became the father of Jonathan, and Jonathan became the father of Jaddua.

In the days of Joiakim were priests, heads of fathers' households:

of Seraiah, Meraiah; of Jeremiah, Hananiah; of Ezra, Meshullam; of Amariah, Jehohanan; of Malluchi, Jonathan; of Shebaniah, Joseph; of Harim, Adna; of Meraioth, Helkai; of Iddo, Zechariah; of Ginnethon, Meshullam; of Abijah, Zichri; of Miniamin, of Moadiah, Piltai; of Bilgah, Shammua; of Shemaiah, Jehonathan; and of Joiarib, Mattenai; of Jedaiah, Uzzi; of Sallai, Kallai; of Amok, Eber; of Hilkiah, Hashabiah; of Jedaiah, Nethanel.

As for the Levites, in the days of Eliashib, Joiada, and Johanan, and Jaddua, there were recorded the heads of fathers' households; also the priests, in the reign of Darius the Persian. The sons of Levi, heads of fathers' households, were written in the book of the chronicles, even until the days of Johanan the son of Eliashib. The chiefs of the Levites: Hashabiah, Sherebiah, and Jeshua the son of Kadmiel, with their brothers close to them, to praise and give thanks, according to the commandment of David the man of God, watch next to watch. Mattaniah, and Bakbukiah, Obadiah, Meshullam, Talmon, Akkub, were gatekeepers keeping the watch at the storehouses of the gates. These were in the days of Joiakim the son of Jeshua, the son of Jozadak, and in the days of Nehemiah the governor, and of Ezra the priest and scribe.

At the dedication of the wall of Jerusalem, they sought the Levites out of all their places, to bring them to Jerusalem, to keep the dedication with gladness, both with giving thanks, and with singing, with cymbals, stringed instruments, and with harps. The sons of the singers gathered themselves together, both out of the plain around Jerusalem and from the villages of the Netophathites; also from Beth Gilgal, and out of the fields of Geba and Azmaveth: for the singers had built themselves villages around Jerusalem. The priests and the Levites purified themselves; and they purified the people, and the gates, and the wall.

Then I brought up the princes of Judah on the wall, and appointed two great companies who gave thanks and went in procession. One went on the right hand on the wall toward the dung gate; and after them went Hoshaiah, with half of the princes of Judah, and Azariah, Ezra, and Meshullam, Judah, Benjamin, Shemaiah, Jeremiah, and some of the priests' sons with trumpets: Zechariah the son of Jonathan, the son of Shemaiah, the son of Mattaniah, the son of Micaiah, the son of Zaccur, the son of Asaph; and his brothers, Shemaiah, Azarel, Milalai, Gilalai, Maai, Nethanel, Judah, and Hanani, with the musical instruments of David the man of God; and Ezra the scribe was before them. By the spring gate, and straight before them, they went up by the stairs of David's city, at the ascent of the wall, above David's house, even to the water gate eastward.

The other company of those who gave thanks went to meet them, and I after them, with the half of the people, on the wall, above the tower of the furnaces, even to the wide wall, and above the gate of Ephraim, and by the old gate, and by the fish gate, and the tower of Hananel, and the tower of Hammeah, even to the sheep gate: and they stood still in the gate of the guard. So the two companies of those who gave thanks in God's house stood, and I, and the half of the rulers with me; and the priests, Eliakim, Maaseiah, Miniamin, Micaiah, Elioenai, Zechariah, and Hananiah, with trumpets; and Maaseiah, Shemaiah, Eleazar, Uzzi, Jehohanan, Malchijah, Elam, and Ezer. The singers sang loud, with Jezrahiah their overseer. They offered great sacrifices that day, and rejoiced; for God had made them rejoice with great joy; and the women and the children also rejoiced; so that the joy of Jerusalem was heard even far away.

On that day, men were appointed over the rooms for the treasures, for the wave offerings, for the first fruits, and for the tithes, to gather into them, according to the fields of the cities, the portions appointed by the law for the priests and Levites; for Judah rejoiced for the priests and for the Levites who waited. They performed the duty of their God, and the duty of the purification, and so did the singers and the gatekeepers, according to the commandment of David, and of Solomon his son. For in the days of David and Asaph of old there was a chief of the singers, and songs of praise and thanksgiving to God. All Israel in the days of Zerubbabel, and in the days of Nehemiah, gave the portions of the singers and the gatekeepers, as every day required; and they set apart that which was for the Levites; and the Levites set apart that which was for the sons of Aaron.

....

On that day they read in the book of Moses in the hearing of the people; and it was found written in it that an Ammonite and a Moabite should not enter into the assembly of God forever, because they didn't meet the children of Israel with bread and with water, but hired Balaam against them, to curse them; however our God turned the curse into a blessing. It came to pass, when they had heard the law, that they separated all the mixed multitude from Israel.

Now before this, Eliashib the priest, who was appointed over the rooms of the house of our God, being allied to Tobiah, had prepared for him a great room, where before they laid the meal offerings, the frankincense, the vessels, and the tithes of the grain, the new wine, and the oil, which were given by commandment to the Levites, the singers, and the gatekeepers; and the wave offerings for the priests. But in all this, I was not at Jerusalem; for in the thirty-second year of Artaxerxes king of Babylon I went to the king; and after some days I asked leave of the king, and I came to Jerusalem, and understood the evil that Eliashib had done for Tobiah, in preparing him a room in the courts of God's house. It grieved me severely. Therefore I threw all Tobiah's household stuff out of the room. Then I commanded, and they cleansed the rooms. I brought into them the vessels of God's house, with the meal offerings and the frankincense again.

I perceived that the portions of the Levites had not been given them; so that the Levites and the singers, who did the work, had each fled to his field. Then I contended with the rulers, and said, "Why is God's house forsaken?" I gathered them together, and set them in their place. Then all Judah brought the tithe of the grain, the new wine, and the oil to the treasuries. I made treasurers over the treasuries, Shelemiah the priest, and Zadok the scribe, and of the Levites, Pedaiah: and next to them was Hanan the son of Zaccur, the son of Mattaniah; for they were counted faithful, and their business was to distribute to their brothers.

Remember me, my God, concerning this, and don't wipe out my good deeds that I have done for the house of my God, and for its observances.

In those days I saw some men treading wine presses on the Sabbath in Judah, bringing in sheaves, and loading donkeys; also with wine, grapes, figs, and all kinds of burdens, which they brought into Jerusalem on the Sabbath day; and I testified against them in the day in which they sold food. Some men of Tyre also lived there, who brought in fish and all kinds of wares, and sold on the Sabbath to the children of Judah, and in Jerusalem. Then I contended with the nobles of Judah, and said to them, "What evil thing is this that you do, and profane the Sabbath day? Didn't your fathers do this, and didn't our God bring all this evil on us, and on this city? Yet you bring more wrath on Israel by profaning the Sabbath."

It came to pass that when the gates of Jerusalem began to be dark before the Sabbath, I commanded that the doors should be shut, and commanded that they should not be opened until after the Sabbath.

I set some of my servants over the gates, so that no burden should be brought in on the Sabbath day. So the merchants and sellers of all kinds of wares camped outside of Jerusalem once or twice. Then I testified against them, and said to them, "Why do you stay around the wall? If you do so again, I will lay hands on you." From that time on, they didn't come on the Sabbath. I commanded the Levites that they should purify themselves, and that they should come and keep the gates, to sanctify the Sabbath day. Remember to me, my God, this also, and spare me according to the greatness of your loving kindness.

In those days I also saw the Jews who had married women of Ashdod, of Ammon, and of Moab; and their children spoke half in the speech of Ashdod, and could not speak in the Jews' language, but according to the language of each people. I contended with them, and cursed them, and struck certain of them, and plucked off their hair, and made them swear by God, "You shall not give your daughters to their sons, nor take their daughters for your sons, or for yourselves. Didn't Solomon king of Israel sin by these things? Yet among many nations there was no king like him, and he was loved by his God, and God made him king over all Israel. Nevertheless foreign women caused even him to sin. Shall we then listen to you to do all this great evil, to trespass against our God in marrying foreign women?"

One of the sons of Joiada, the son of Eliashib the high priest, was son-in-law to Sanballat the Horonite; therefore I chased him from me. Remember them, my God, because they have defiled the priesthood, and the covenant of the priesthood and of the Levites.

Thus I cleansed them from all foreigners, and appointed duties for the priests and for the Levites, everyone in his work; and for the wood offering, at times appointed, and for the first fruits. Remember me, my God, for good.

THE BOOK OF

ESTHER

30 MIN

Now in the days of Ahasuerus (this is Ahasuerus who reigned from India even to Ethiopia, over one hundred twenty-seven provinces), in those days, when the King Ahasuerus sat on the throne of his kingdom, which was in Susa the palace, in the third year of his reign, he made a feast for all his princes and his servants; the power of Persia and Media, the nobles and princes of the provinces, being before him. He displayed the riches of his glorious kingdom and the honor of his excellent majesty many days, even one hundred eighty days. When these days were fulfilled, the king made a seven day feast for all the people who were present in Susa the palace, both great and small, in the court of the garden of the king's palace. There were hangings of white and blue material, fastened with cords of fine linen and purple to silver rings and marble pillars. The couches were of gold and silver, on a pavement of red, white, yellow, and black marble. They gave them drinks in golden vessels of various kinds, including royal wine in abundance, according to the bounty of the king. In accordance with the law, the drinking was not compulsory; for so the king had instructed all the officials of his house, that they should do according to every man's pleasure.

Also Vashti the queen made a feast for the women in the royal house which belonged to King Ahasuerus.

On the seventh day, when the heart of the king was merry with wine, he commanded Mehuman, Biztha, Harbona, Bigtha, and Abagtha, Zethar, and Carcass, the seven eunuchs who served in the presence of Ahasuerus the king, to bring Vashti the queen before the king with the royal crown, to show the people and the princes her beauty; for she was beautiful. But the queen Vashti refused to come at the king's commandment by the eunuchs. Therefore the king was very angry, and his anger burned in him.

Then the king said to the wise men, who knew the times (for it was the king's custom to consult those who knew law and judgment; and the next to him were Carshena, Shethar, Admatha, Tarshish, Meres, Marsena, and Memucan, the seven princes of Persia and Media, who saw the king's face, and sat first in the kingdom), "What shall we do to the queen Vashti according to law, because she has not done the bidding of the King Ahasuerus by the eunuchs?"

Memucan answered before the king and the princes, "Vashti the queen has not done wrong to just the king, but also to all the princes, and to all the people who are in all the provinces of the King Ahasuerus. For this deed of the queen will become known to all women, causing them to show contempt for their husbands, when it is reported, 'King Ahasuerus commanded Vashti the queen to be brought in before him, but she didn't come.' Today, the princesses of Persia and Media who have heard of the queen's deed will tell all the king's princes. This will cause much contempt and wrath.

"If it pleases the king, let a royal commandment go from him, and let it be written among the laws of the Persians and the Medes, so that it cannot be altered, that Vashti may never again come before King Ahasuerus; and let the king give her royal estate to another who is better than she. When the king's decree which he shall make is published throughout all his kingdom (for it is great), all the wives will give their husbands honor, both great and small."

This advice pleased the king and the princes, and the king did according to the word of Memucan: for he sent letters into all the king's provinces, into every province according to its writing, and to every people in their language, that every man should rule his own house, speaking in the language of his own people.

....

After these things, when the wrath of King Ahasuerus was pacified, he remembered Vashti, and what she had done, and what was decreed against her. Then the king's servants who served him said, "Let beautiful young virgins be sought for the king. Let the king appoint officers in all the provinces of his kingdom, that they may gather together all the beautiful young virgins to the citadel of Susa, to the women's house, to the custody of Hegai the king's eunuch, keeper of the women. Let cosmetics be given them; and let the maiden who pleases the king be queen instead of Vashti." The thing pleased the king, and he did so.

There was a certain Jew in the citadel of Susa, whose name was Mordecai, the son of Jair, the son of Shimei, the son of Kish, a Benjamite, who had been carried away from Jerusalem with the captives who had been carried away with Jeconiah king of Judah, whom Nebuchadnezzar the king of Babylon had carried away. He brought up Hadassah, that is, Esther, his uncle's daughter; for she had neither father nor mother. The maiden was fair and beautiful; and when her father and mother were dead, Mordecai took her for his own daughter.

So, when the king's commandment and his decree was heard, and when many maidens were gathered together to the citadel of

Susa, to the custody of Hegai, Esther was taken into the king's house, to the custody of Hegai, keeper of the women. The maiden pleased him, and she obtained kindness from him. He quickly gave her cosmetics and her portions of food, and the seven choice maidens who were to be given her out of the king's house. He moved her and her maidens to the best place in the women's house. Esther had not made known her people nor her relatives, because Mordecai had instructed her that she should not make it known. Mordecai walked every day in front of the court of the women's house, to find out how Esther was doing, and what would become of her.

Each young woman's turn came to go in to King Ahasuerus after her purification for twelve months (for so were the days of their purification accomplished, six months with oil of myrrh, and six months with sweet fragrances and with preparations for beautifying women). The young woman then came to the king like this: whatever she desired was given her to go with her out of the women's house to the king's house. In the evening she went, and on the next day she returned into the second women's house, to the custody of Shaashgaz, the king's eunuch, who kept the concubines. She came in to the king no more, unless the king delighted in her, and she was called by name. Now when the turn of Esther, the daughter of Abihail the uncle of Mordecai, who had taken her for his daughter, came to go in to the king, she required nothing but what Hegai the king's eunuch, the keeper of the women, advised. Esther obtained favor in the sight of all those who looked at her.

So Esther was taken to King Ahasuerus into his royal house in the tenth month, which is the month Tebeth, in the seventh year of his reign. The king loved Esther more than all the women, and she obtained favor and kindness in his sight more than all the virgins; so that he set the royal crown on her head, and made her queen instead of Vashti.

Then the king made a great feast for all his princes and his servants, even Esther's feast; and he proclaimed a holiday in the provinces, and gave gifts according to the king's bounty.

When the virgins were gathered together the second time, Mordecai was sitting in the king's gate. Esther had not yet made known her relatives nor her people, as Mordecai had commanded her; for Esther obeyed Mordecai, like she did when she was brought up by him. In those days, while Mordecai was sitting in the king's gate, two of the king's eunuchs, Bigthan and Teresh, who were doorkeepers, were angry, and sought to lay hands on the King Ahasuerus. This thing became known to Mordecai, who informed Esther the queen; and Esther informed the king in Mordecai's name. When this matter was investigated, and it was found to be so, they were both hanged on a gallows; and it was written in the book of the chronicles in the king's presence.

....

After these things King Ahasuerus promoted Haman the son of Hammedatha the Agagite, and advanced him, and set his seat above all the princes who were with him. All the king's servants who were in the king's gate bowed down, and paid homage to Haman; for the king had so commanded concerning him. But Mordecai didn't bow down or pay him homage. Then the king's servants, who were in the king's gate, said to Mordecai, "Why do you disobey the king's commandment?" Now it came to pass, when they spoke daily to him, and he didn't listen to them, that they told Haman, to see whether Mordecai's reason would stand; for he had told them that he was a Jew. When Haman saw that Mordecai didn't bow down, nor pay him homage, Haman was full of wrath. But he scorned the thought of laying hands on Mordecai alone, for they had made known to him Mordecai's people. Therefore Haman sought to destroy all the Jews who were throughout the whole kingdom of Ahasuerus, even Mordecai's people.

In the first month, which is the month Nisan, in the twelfth year of King Ahasuerus, they cast Pur, that is, the lot, before Haman from day to day, and from month to month, and chose the twelfth month, which is the month Adar. Haman said to King Ahasuerus, "There is a certain people scattered abroad and dispersed among the peoples in all the provinces of your kingdom, and their laws are different from other people's. They don't keep the king's laws. Therefore it is not for the king's profit to allow them to remain. If it pleases the king, let it be written that they be destroyed; and I will pay ten thousand talents of silver into the hands of those who are in charge of the king's business, to bring it into the king's treasuries."

The king took his ring from his hand, and gave it to Haman the son of Hammedatha the Agagite, the Jews' enemy. The king said to Haman, "The silver is given to you, the people also, to do with them as it seems good to you."

Then the king's scribes were called in on the first month, on the thirteenth day of the month; and all that Haman commanded was written to the king's local governors, and to the governors who were over every province, and to the princes of every people, to every province according to its writing, and to every people in their language. It was written in the name of King Ahasuerus, and it was sealed with the king's ring. Letters were sent by couriers into all the king's provinces, to destroy, to kill, and to cause to perish, all Jews, both young and old, little children and women, in one day, even on the thirteenth day of the twelfth month, which is the month Adar, and to plunder their possessions. A copy of the letter, that the decree should be given out in every province, was published to all the peoples, that they should be ready against that day. The couriers went out in haste by the king's commandment, and the decree was given out in the citadel of Susa. The king and Haman sat down to drink; but the city of Susa was perplexed.

....

Now when Mordecai found out all that was done, Mordecai tore his clothes, and put on sackcloth with ashes, and went out into the middle of the city, and wailed loudly and bitterly. He came even before the king's gate, for no one is allowed inside the king's gate clothed with sackcloth. In every province, wherever the king's commandment and his decree came, there was great mourning among the Jews, and fasting, and weeping, and wailing; and many lay in sackcloth and ashes.

Esther's maidens and her eunuchs came and told her this, and the queen was exceedingly grieved. She sent clothing to Mordecai, to replace his sackcloth; but he didn't receive it. Then Esther called for Hathach, one of the king's eunuchs, whom he had appointed to attend her, and commanded him to go to Mordecai, to find out what this was, and why it was. So Hathach went out to Mordecai, to city square which was before the king's gate. Mordecai told him of all that had happened to him, and the exact sum of the money that Haman had promised to pay to the king's treasuries for the destruction of the Jews. He also gave him the copy of the writing of the decree that was given out in Susa to destroy them, to show it to Esther, and to declare it to her, and to urge her to go in to the king, to make supplication to him, and to make request before him, for her people.

Hathach came and told Esther the words of Mordecai. Then Esther spoke to Hathach, and gave him a message to Mordecai: "All the king's servants, and the people of the king's provinces, know, that whoever, whether man or woman, comes to the king into the inner court without being called, there is one law for him, that he be put to death, except those to whom the king might hold out the golden scepter, that he may live. I have not been called to come in to the king these thirty days."

They told Esther's words to Mordecai. Then Mordecai asked them to return this answer to Esther: "Don't think to yourself that you will escape in the king's house any more than all the Jews. For if you remain silent now, then relief and deliverance will come to the Jews from another place, but you and your father's house will perish. Who knows if you haven't come to the kingdom for such a time as this?"

Then Esther asked them to answer Mordecai, "Go, gather together all the Jews who are present in Susa, and fast for me, and neither eat nor drink three days, night or day. I and my maidens will also fast the same way. Then I will go in to the king, which is against the law; and if I perish, I perish." So Mordecai went his way, and did according to all that Esther had commanded him.

....

Now on the third day, Esther put on her royal clothing, and stood in the inner court of the king's house, next to the king's house. The king sat on his royal throne in the royal house, next to the entrance of the house. When the king saw Esther the queen standing in the court, she obtained favor in his sight; and the king held out to Esther the golden scepter that was in his hand. So Esther came near, and touched the top of the scepter. Then the king asked her, "What would you like, queen Esther? What is your request? It shall be given you even to the half of the kingdom."

Esther said, "If it seems good to the king, let the king and Haman come today to the banquet that I have prepared for him."

Then the king said, "Bring Haman quickly, so that it may be done as Esther has said." So the king and Haman came to the banquet that Esther had prepared.

The king said to Esther at the banquet of wine, "What is your petition? It shall be granted you. What is your request? Even to the half of the kingdom it shall be performed."

Then Esther answered and said, "My petition and my request is this. If I have found favor in the sight of the king, and if it pleases the king to grant my petition and to perform my request, let the king and Haman come to the banquet that I will prepare for them, and I will do tomorrow as the king has said."

Then Haman went out that day joyful and glad of heart, but when Haman saw Mordecai in the king's gate, that he didn't stand up nor move for him, he was filled with wrath against Mordecai. Nevertheless Haman restrained himself, and went home. There, he sent and called for his friends and Zeresh his wife. Haman recounted to them the glory of his riches, the multitude of his children, all the things in which the king had promoted him, and how he had advanced him above the princes and servants of the king. Haman also said, "Yes, Esther the queen let no man come in with the king to the banquet that she had prepared but myself; and tomorrow I am also invited by her together with the king. Yet all this avails me nothing, so long as I see Mordecai the Jew sitting at the king's gate."

Then Zeresh his wife and all his friends said to him, "Let a gallows be made fifty cubits high, and in the morning speak to the king about hanging Mordecai on it. Then go in merrily with the king to the banquet." This pleased Haman, so he had the gallows made.

....

On that night, the king couldn't sleep. He commanded the book of records of the chronicles to be brought, and they were read to the king. It was found written that Mordecai had told of Bigthana and Teresh, two of the king's eunuchs, who were doorkeepers, who had tried to lay hands on the King Ahasuerus. The king said, "What honor and dignity has been given to Mordecai for this?"

Then the king's servants who attended him said, "Nothing has been done for him."

The king said, "Who is in the court?" Now Haman had come into the outer court of the king's house, to speak to the king about hanging Mordecai on the gallows that he had prepared for him.

The king's servants said to him, "Behold, Haman stands in the court."

The king said, "Let him come in." So Haman came in. The king said to him, "What shall be done to the man whom the king delights to honor?"

Now Haman said in his heart, "Who would the king delight to honor more than myself?" Haman said to the king, "For the man whom the king delights to honor, let royal clothing be brought which the king uses to wear, and the horse that the king rides on, and on the head of which a royal crown is set. Let the clothing and the horse be delivered to the hand of one of the king's most noble princes, that they may array the man whom the king delights to honor with them, and have him ride on horseback through the city square, and proclaim before him, 'Thus it shall be done to the man whom the king delights to honor!'"

Then the king said to Haman, "Hurry and take the clothing and the horse, as you have said, and do this for Mordecai the Jew, who sits at the king's gate. Let nothing fail of all that you have spoken."

Then Haman took the clothing and the horse, and arrayed Mordecai, and had him ride through the city square, and proclaimed before him, "Thus it shall be done to the man whom the king delights to honor!"

Mordecai came back to the king's gate, but Haman hurried to his house, mourning and having his head covered. Haman recounted to Zeresh his wife and all his friends everything that had happened to him. Then his wise men and Zeresh his wife said to him, "If Mordecai, before whom you have begun to fall, is of Jewish descent, you will not prevail against him, but you will surely fall before him." While they were yet talking with him, the king's eunuchs came, and hurried to bring Haman to the banquet that Esther had prepared.

....

So the king and Haman came to banquet with Esther the queen. The king said again to Esther on the second day at the banquet of wine, "What is your petition, queen Esther? It shall be granted you. What is your request? Even to the half of the kingdom it shall be performed."

Then Esther the queen answered, "If I have found favor in your sight, O king, and if it pleases the king, let my life be given me at my petition, and my people at my request. For we are sold, I and my people, to be destroyed, to be slain, and to perish. But if we had been sold for male and female slaves, I would have held my peace, although the adversary could not have compensated for the king's loss."

Then King Ahasuerus said to Esther the queen, "Who is he, and where is he who dared presume in his heart to do so?"

Esther said, "An adversary and an enemy, even this wicked Haman!"

Then Haman was afraid before the king and the queen. The king arose in his wrath from the banquet of wine and went into the palace garden. Haman stood up to make request for his life to Esther the queen; for he saw that there was evil determined against him by the king. Then the king returned out of the palace garden into the place of the banquet of wine; and Haman had fallen on the couch where Esther was. Then the king said, "Will he even assault the queen in front of me in the house?" As the word went out of the king's mouth, they covered Haman's face.

Then Harbonah, one of the eunuchs who were with the king said, "Behold, the gallows fifty cubits high, which Haman has made for Mordecai, who spoke good for the king, is standing at Haman's house."

The king said, "Hang him on it!"

So they hanged Haman on the gallows that he had prepared for Mordecai. Then the king's wrath was pacified.

....

On that day, King Ahasuerus gave the house of Haman, the Jews' enemy, to Esther the queen. Mordecai came before the king; for Esther had told what he was to her. The king took off his ring, which he had taken from Haman, and gave it to Mordecai. Esther set Mordecai over the house of Haman.

Esther spoke yet again before the king, and fell down at his feet, and begged him with tears to put away the mischief of Haman the Agagite, and his plan that he had planned against the Jews. Then the king held out to Esther the golden scepter. So Esther arose, and stood before the king. She said, "If it pleases the king, and if I have found favor in his sight, and the thing seem right to the king, and I am pleasing in his eyes, let it be written to reverse the letters devised by Haman, the son of Hammedatha the Agagite, which he wrote to destroy the Jews who are in all the king's provinces. For how can I endure to see the evil that would come to my people? How can I endure to see the destruction of my relatives?"

Then King Ahasuerus said to Esther the queen and to Mordecai the Jew, "See, I have given Esther the house of Haman, and they have hanged him on the gallows, because he laid his hand on the Jews. Write also to the Jews, as it pleases you, in the king's name, and seal it with the king's ring; for the writing which is written in the king's name, and sealed with the king's ring, may not be reversed by any man."

Then the king's scribes were called at that time, in the third month, which is the month Sivan, on the twenty-third day of the month; and it was written according to all that Mordecai commanded to the Jews, and to the local governors, and the governors and princes of the provinces which are from India to Ethiopia, one hundred twenty-seven provinces, to every province according to its writing, and to every people in their language, and to the Jews in their writing, and in their language. He wrote in the name of King Ahasuerus, and sealed it with the king's ring, and sent letters by courier on horseback, riding on royal horses that were bred from swift steeds. In those letters, the king granted the Jews who were in every city to gather themselves together, and to defend their life, to destroy, to kill, and to cause to perish, all the power of the people and province that would assault them, their little ones and women, and to plunder their possessions, on one day in all the provinces of King Ahasuerus, on the thirteenth day of the twelfth month, which is the month Adar. A copy of the letter, that the decree should be given out in every province, was published to all the peoples, that the Jews should be ready for that day to avenge themselves on their enemies. So the couriers who rode on royal horses went out, hastened and pressed on by the king's commandment. The decree was given out in the citadel of Susa.

Mordecai went out of the presence of the king in royal clothing of blue and white, and with a great crown of gold, and with a robe of fine linen and purple; and the city of Susa shouted and was glad. The Jews had light, gladness, joy, and honor. In every province, and in every city, wherever the king's commandment and his decree came, the Jews had gladness, joy, a feast, and a good day. Many from among the peoples of the land became Jews; for the fear of the Jews was fallen on them.

....

Now in the twelfth month, which is the month Adar, on the thirteenth day of the month, when the king's commandment and his decree came near to be put in execution, on the day that the enemies of the Jews hoped to conquer them, (but it was turned out the opposite happened, that the Jews conquered those who hated them), the Jews gathered themselves together in their cities throughout all the provinces of the King Ahasuerus, to lay hands on those who wanted to harm them. No one could withstand them, because the fear of them had fallen on all the people. All the princes of the provinces, the local governors, the governors, and those who did the king's business helped the Jews, because the fear of Mordecai had fallen on them. For Mordecai was great in the king's house, and his fame went out throughout all the provinces; for the man Mordecai grew greater and greater. The Jews struck all their enemies with the stroke of the sword, and with slaughter and destruction, and did what they wanted to those who hated them. In the citadel of Susa, the Jews killed and destroyed five hundred men. They killed Parshandatha, Dalphon, Aspatha, Poratha, Adalia, Aridatha, Parmashta, Arisai, Aridai, and Vaizatha, the ten sons of Haman the son of Hammedatha, the Jews' enemy, but they didn't lay their hand on the plunder.

On that day, the number of those who were slain in the citadel of Susa was brought before the king. The king said to Esther the queen, "The Jews have slain and destroyed five hundred men in the citadel of Susa, including the ten sons of Haman; what then have they done in the rest of the king's provinces! Now what is your petition? It shall be granted you. What is your further request? It shall be done."

Then Esther said, "If it pleases the king, let it be granted to the Jews who are in Susa to do tomorrow also according to today's decree, and let Haman's ten sons be hanged on the gallows."

The king commanded this to be done. A decree was given out in Susa; and they hanged Haman's ten sons. The Jews who were in Susa gathered themselves together on the fourteenth day also of the month Adar, and killed three hundred men in Susa; but they didn't lay their hand on the plunder. The other Jews who were in the king's provinces gathered themselves together, defended their lives, had rest from their enemies, and killed seventy-five thousand of those who hated them; but they didn't lay their hand on the plunder.

This was done on the thirteenth day of the month Adar; and on the fourteenth day of that month they rested and made it a day of feasting and gladness. But the Jews who were in Susa assembled together on the thirteenth and on the fourteenth days of the month; and on the fifteenth day of that month, they rested, and made it a day of feasting and gladness. Therefore the Jews of the villages, who live in the unwalled towns, make the fourteenth day of the month Adar a day of gladness and feasting, a good day, and a day of sending presents of food to one another.

Mordecai wrote these things, and sent letters to all the Jews who were in all the provinces of the king Ahasuerus, both near and far, to enjoin them that they should keep the fourteenth and fifteenth days of the month Adar yearly, as the days in which the Jews had rest from their enemies, and the month which was turned to them from sorrow to gladness, and from mourning into a good day; that they should make them days of feasting and gladness, and of sending presents of food to one another, and gifts to the needy. The Jews accepted the custom that they had begun, as Mordecai had written to them; because Haman the son of Hammedatha, the Agagite, the enemy of all the Jews, had plotted against the Jews to destroy them, and had cast "Pur", that is the lot, to consume them, and to destroy them; but when this became known to the king, he commanded by letters that his wicked plan, which he had planned against the Jews, should return on his own head, and that he and his sons should be hanged on the gallows.

Therefore they called these days "Purim", from the word "Pur." Therefore because of all the words of this letter, and of that which they had seen concerning this matter, and that which had come to them, the Jews established and imposed on themselves, and on their descendants, and on all those who joined themselves to them, so that it should not fail that they would keep these two days according to what was written, and according to its appointed time, every year; and that these days should be remembered and kept throughout every generation, every family, every province, and every city; and that these days of Purim should not fail from among the Jews, nor their memory perish from their offspring,

Then Esther the queen, the daughter of Abihail, and Mordecai the Jew, wrote with all authority to confirm this second letter of Purim. He sent letters to all the Jews, to the hundred twenty-seven provinces of the kingdom of Ahasuerus, with words of peace and truth, to confirm these days of Purim in their appointed times, as Mordecai the Jew and Esther the queen had decreed, and as they had imposed upon themselves and their descendants, in the matter of the fastings and their cry. The commandment of Esther confirmed these matters of Purim; and it was written in the book.

....

King Ahasuerus laid a tribute on the land, and on the islands of the sea. All the acts of his power and of his might, and the full account of the greatness of Mordecai, to which the king advanced him, aren't they written in the book of the chronicles of the kings of Media and Persia? For Mordecai the Jew was next to King Ahasuerus, and great among the Jews, and accepted by the multitude of his brothers, seeking the good of his people, and speaking peace to all his descendants.

APPENDICES

GLOSSARY

The following words used in the World English Bible are not very common, either because they refer to ancient weights, measures, or money, or because they are in some way unique to the Bible.

Abaddon *Abaddon is Hebrew for destruction.*

Abba *Abba is a Chaldee word for father, used in a respectful, affectionate, and familiar way, like papa, dad, or daddy. Often used in prayer to refer to our Father in Heaven.*

adultery *Adultery is having sexual intercourse with someone besides your own husband or wife. In the Bible, the only legitimate sexual intercourse is between a man and a woman who are married to each other.*

alpha *Alpha is the first letter of the Greek alphabet. It is sometimes used to mean the beginning or the first.*

amen *Amen means "so be it" or "it is certainly so."*

angel *"Angel" literally means "messenger" or "envoy," and is usually used to refer to spiritual beings who normally are invisible to us, but can also appear as exceedingly strong creatures or as humans.*

Apollyon *Apollyon is Greek for destroyer.*

apostle *"Apostle" means a delegate, messenger, or one sent forth with orders. This term is applied in the New Testament in both a general sense connected with a* *ministry of establishing and strengthening church fellowships, as well as in a specific sense to "The 12 Apostles of the Lamb" (Revelation 21:14). The former category applies to a specific ministry that continues in the Church (Ephesians 4:11-13) and which includes many more than 12 people, while the latter refers to the apostles named in Matthew 10:2-4, except with Judas Iscariot replaced by Matthias (Acts 1:26).*

Armageddon   *See Har-magedon.*

assarion   *An assarion is a small Roman copper coin worth one tenth of a drachma, or about an hour's wages for an agricultural laborer.*

aureus   *An aureus is a Roman gold coin, worth 25 silver denarii. An aureus weighed from 115 to 126.3 grains (7.45 to 8.18 grams).*

baptize   *Baptize means to immerse in, or wash with something, usually water. Baptism in the Holy Spirit, fire, the Body of Christ, and suffering are also mentioned in the New Testament, along with baptism in water. Baptism is not just to cleanse the body, but as an outward sign of an inward spiritual cleansing and commitment. Baptism is a sign of repentance, as practiced by John the Baptizer, and of faith in Jesus Christ, as practiced by Jesus' disciples.*

bath   *A bath is a liquid measure of about 22 liters, 5.8 U. S. gallons, or 4.8 imperial gallons.*

batos   *A batos is a liquid measure of about 39.5 liters, 10.4 U. S. gallons, or 8.7 imperial gallons.*

Beelzebul   *literally, lord of the flies. A name used for the devil.*

Beersheba *Beersheba is Hebrew for "well of the oath" or "well of the seven." A city in Israel.*

behold *Look! See! Wow! Notice this! Lo!*

cherub *A cherub is a kind of angel with wings and hands that is associated with the throne room of God and guardian duty. See Ezekiel 10.*

cherubim *Cherubim means more than one cherub or a mighty cherub.*

choenix *A choenix is a dry volume measure that is a little more than a liter (which is a little more than a quart). A choenix was the daily ration of grain for a soldier in some armies.*

concubine *a woman who is united to a man for the purpose of providing him with sexual pleasure and children, but not being honored as a full partner in marriage; a second-class wife. In Old Testament times (and in some places now), it was the custom of middle-eastern kings, chiefs, and wealthy men to marry multiple wives and concubines, but God commanded the Kings of Israel not to do so (Deuteronomy 17:17) and Jesus encouraged people to either remain single or marry as God originally intended: one man married to one woman (Matthew 19:3-12; 1 Corinthians 7:1-13).*

cor *A cor is a dry measure of about 391 liters, 103 U. S. gallons, or 86 imperial gallons.*

corban *Corban is a Hebrew word for an offering devoted to God.*

crucify *Crucify means to execute someone by nailing them to a cross with metal spikes. Their hands are stretched out on the crossbeam with spikes driven through their wrists or hands. Their feet or ankles are attached to a cross with a metal spike. The weight of the victim's body tends to force the air out of his lungs. To rise up to breathe, the victim has to put weight on the wounds, and use a lot of strength. The victim is nailed to the cross while the cross is on the ground, then the cross is raised up and dropped into a hole, thus jarring the wounds. Before crucifixion, the victim was usually whipped with a Roman cat of nine tails, which had bits of glass and metal tied to its ends. This caused chunks of flesh to be removed and open wounds to be placed against the raw wood of the cross. The victim was made to carry the heavy crossbeam of his cross from the place of judgment to the place of crucifixion, but often was physically unable after the scourging, so another person would be pressed into involuntary service to carry the cross for him. Roman crucifixion was generally done totally naked to maximize both shame and discomfort. Eventually, the pain, weakness, dehydration, and exhaustion of the muscles needed to breathe make breathing impossible, and the victim suffocates.*

cubit *A cubit is a unit of linear measure, from the elbow to the tip of the longest finger of a man. This unit is commonly converted to 0.46 meters or 18 inches, although that varies with height of the man doing the measurement. There is also a "long" cubit that is longer than a regular cubit by a handbreadth. (Ezekiel 43:13)*

cummin *Cummin is an aromatic seed from Cuminum cyminum, resembling caraway in flavor and appearance. It is used as a spice.*

darnel   *Darnel is a weed grass (probably bearded darnel or Lolium temulentum) that looks very much like wheat until it is mature, when the seeds reveal a great difference. Darnel seeds aren't good for much except as chicken feed or to burn to prevent the spread of this weed.*

denarii   *denarii: plural form of denarius, a silver Roman coin worth about a day's wages for a laborer.*

denarius   *A denarius is a silver Roman coin worth about a day's wages for an agricultural laborer. A denarius was worth 1/25th of a Roman aureus.*

devil   *The word "devil" comes from the Greek "diabolos," which means "one prone to slander; a liar." "Devil" is used to refer to a fallen angel, also called "Satan," who works to steal, kill, destroy, and do evil. The devil's doom is certain, and it is only a matter of time before he is thrown into the Lake of Fire, never to escape.*

didrachma   *A didrachma is a Greek silver coin worth 2 drachmas, about as much as 2 Roman denarii, or about 2 days wages. It was commonly used to pay the half-shekel temple tax.*

distaff   *part of a spinning wheel used for twisting threads.*

drachma   *A drachma is a Greek silver coin worth about one Roman denarius, or about a day's wages for an agricultural laborer.*

El-Elohe-Israel   *El-Elohe-Israel means "God, the God of Israel" or "The God of Israel is mighty."*

ephah An ephah is a measure of volume of about 22 liters, 5.8 U. S. gallons, 4.8 imperial gallons, or a bit more than half a bushel.

Gehenna Gehenna is one word used for Hell. It comes from the Hebrew Gey-Hinnom, literally "valley of Hinnom." This word originated as the name for a place south of the old city of Jerusalem where the city's rubbish was burned. At one time, live babies were thrown crying into the fire under the arms of the idol, Moloch, to die there. This place was so despised by the people after the righteous King Josiah abolished this hideous practice that it was made into a garbage heap. Bodies of diseased animals and executed criminals were thrown there and burned.

gittith Gittith is a musical term possibly meaning "an instrument of Gath."

goad a sharp, pointed prodding device used to motivate reluctant animals (such as oxen and mules) to move in the right direction.

gospel Gospel means "good news" or "glad tidings," specifically the Good News of Jesus' life, death, and resurrection for our salvation, healing, and provision; and the hope of eternal life that Jesus made available to us by God's grace.

Hades Hades: The nether realm of the disembodied spirits. Also known as "hell."

Har-magedon Har-magedon, also called Armegeddon, is most likely a reference to hill ("har") of Megiddo, near the Carmel Range in Israel. This area has a large valley plain with plenty of room for armies to maneuver.

hin   *A hin was about 6.5 liters or 1.7 gallons.*

homer   *One homer is about 220 liters, 6.2 U. S. bushels, 6.1 imperial bushels, 58 U. S. gallons, or 48.4 imperial gallons.*

hypocrite   *a stage actor; someone who pretends to be someone other than who they really are; a pretender; a dissembler*

Ishmael   *Ishmael is the son of Abraham and Hagar. Ishmael literally means, "God hears."*

Jehovah   *See "Yahweh."*

Jesus   *"Jesus" is Greek for the Hebrew name "Yeshua," which is a short version of "Yehoshua," which comes from "Yoshia," which means "He will save."*

kodrantes   *A kodrantes is a small coin worth one half of an Attic chalcus or two lepta. It is worth less than 2% of a day's wages for an agricultural laborer.*

lepta   *Lepta are very small, brass, Jewish coins worth half a Roman quadrans each, which is worth a quarter of the copper assarion. Lepta are worth less than 1% of an agricultural worker's daily wages.*

leviathan   *Leviathan is a poetic name for a large aquatic creature, posssibly a crocodile or a dinosaur.*

mahalath   *Mahalath is the name of a tune or a musical term.*

manna   *Name for the food that God miraculously provided to the Israelites while they were wandering in the wilderness between Egypt and the promised land.*

From Hebrew man-hu (What is that?) or manan (to allot). See Exodus 16:14-35.

marriage   *the union of a husband and a wife for the purpose of cohabitation, procreation, and to enjoy each other's company. God's plan for marriage is between one man and one woman (Mark 10:6-9; 1 Corinthians 7). Although there are many cases of a man marrying more than one woman in the Old Testament, being married to one wife is a requirement to serve in certain church leadership positions (1 Timothy 3:2,12; Titus 1:5-6).*

maschil   *Maschil is a musical and literary term for "contemplation" or "meditative psalm."*

michtam   *A michtam is a poem.*

mina   *A mina is a Greek coin worth 100 Greek drachmas (or 100 Roman denarii), or about 100 day's wages for an agricultural laborer.*

myrrh   *Myrrh is the fragrant substance that oozes out of the stems and branches of the low, shrubby tree commiphora myrrha or comiphora kataf native to the Arabian deserts and parts of Africa. The fragrant gum drops to the ground and hardens into an oily yellowish-brown resin. Myrrh was highly valued as a perfume, and as an ingredient in medicinal and ceremonial ointments.*

Nicolaitans   *Nicolaitans were most likely Gnostics who taught the detestable lie that the physical and spiritual realms were entirely separate and that immorality in the physical realm wouldn't harm your spiritual health.*

omega   *Omega is the last letter of the Greek alphabet. It is sometimes used to mean the last or the end.*

Peniel *Peniel is Hebrew for "face of God."*

phylactery *a leather container for holding a small scroll containing important Scripture passages that is worn on the arm or forehead in prayer. These phylacteries (tefillin in Hebrew) are still used by orthodox Jewish men. See Deuteronomy 6:8.*

Praetorium *Praetorium: the Roman governor's residence and office building, and those who work there.*

quadrans *A quadrans is a Roman coin worth about 1/64 of a denarius. A denarius is about one day's wages for an agricultural laborer.*

rabbi *Rabbi is a transliteration of the Hebrew word for "my teacher," used as a title of respect for Jewish teachers.*

Rahab *Rahab is either (1) The prostitute who hid Joshua's 2 spies in Jericho (Joshua 2,6) and later became an ancestor of Jesus (Matthew 1:5) and an example of faith (Hebrews 11:31; James 2:25); or (2) Literally, "pride" or "arrogance" — possibly a reference to a large aquatic creature (Job 9:13; 26:12; Isaiah 51:9) or symbolically referring to Egypt (Psalm 87:4; 89:10; Isaiah 30:7).*

repent *to change one's mind; turn away from sin and turn towards God; to abhor one's past sins and determine to follow God.*

Rhabboni *Rhabboni: a transliteration of the Hebrew word for "great teacher."*

Sabbath *The seventh day of the week, set aside by God for man to rest.*

saints   *The Greek word for "saints" literally means "holy ones." Saints are people set apart for service to God as holy and separate, living in righteousness. Used in the Bible to refer to all Christians and to all of those who worship YHWH in Old Testament times.*

Samaritan   *A Samaritan is a resident of Samaria. The Samaritans and the Jews generally detested each other during the time that Jesus walked the Earth.*

sata   *a dry measure of capacity approximately equal to 13 liters or 1.5 pecks.*

Satan   *Satan means "accuser." This is one name for the devil, an enemy of God and God's people.*

scribe   *A scribe is one who copies God's law. They were often respected as teachers and authorities on God's law.*

selah   *Selah is a musical term indicating a pause or instrumental interlude for reflection.*

seraphim   *Seraphim are 6-winged angels. See Isaiah 6:2-6.*

sexual immorality   *The term "sexual immorality" in the New Testament comes from the Greek "porneia," which refers to any sexual activity besides that between a husband and his wife. In other words, prostitution (male or female), bestiality, homosexual activity, any sexual intercourse outside of marriage, and the production and consumption of pornography all are included in this term.*

shekel   *A measure of weight, and when referring to that weight in gold, silver, or brass, of money. A shekel is approximately 16 grams, about a half an ounce, or 20 gerahs (Ezekiel 45:12).*

Sheol   *Sheol is the place of the dead.*

Shibah   *Shibah is Hebrew for "oath" or "seven." See Beersheba.*

shigionoth   *Victorious music.*

soul   *"Soul" refers to the emotions and intellect of a living person, as well as that person's very life. It is distinguished in the Bible from a person's spirit and body. (1 Thessalonians 5:23, Hebrews 4:12)*

span   *A span is the length from the tip of a man's thumb to the tip of his little finger when his hand is stretched out (about half a cubit, or 9 inches, or 22.8 cm.)*

spirit   *Spirit, breath, and wind all derive from the same Hebrew and Greek words. A person's spirit is the very essence of that person's life, which comes from God, who is a Spirit being (John 4:24, Genesis 1:2; 2:7). The Bible distinguishes between a person's spirit, soul, and body (1 Thessalonians 5:23, Hebrews 4:12). Some beings may exist as spirits without necessarily having a visible body, such as angels and demons (Luke 9:39, 1 John 4:1-3).*

stadia   *stadia: plural for "stadion," a linear measure of about 184.9 meters or 606.6 feet (the length of the race course at Olympia).*

stater   *A stater is a Greek silver coin equivalent to four Attic or two Alexandrian drachmas, or a Jewish shekel: just exactly enough to cover the half-shekel Temple Tax for two people.*

tabernacle   *a dwelling place or place of worship, usually a tent.*

talent *A measure of weight or mass of 3000 shekels.*

Tartarus *Tartarus is the Greek name for an underworld for the wicked dead; another name for Gehenna or Hell.*

teraphim *Teraphim are household idols that may have been associated with inheritance rights to the household property.*

Yah *"Yah" is a shortened form of "YAHWEH," which is God's proper name. This form is used occasionally in the Old Testament, mostly in the Psalms. See "YAHWEH."*

YHWH (Yahweh) *"YAHWEH" is God's proper name. In Hebrew, the four consonants roughly equivalent to YHWH were considered too holy to pronounce, so the Hebrew word for "Lord" (Adonai) was substituted when reading it aloud. When vowel points were added to the Hebrew Old Testament, the vowel points for "Adonai" were mixed with the consonants for "YAH-WEH," which if you pronounced it literally as written, would be pronounced "Yehovah" or "Jehovah." When the Old Testament was translated to Greek, the tradition of substituting "Lord" for God's proper name continued in the translation of God's name to "Lord" (Kurios). Some English Bibles translate God's proper name to "LORD" or "GOD" (usually with small capital letters), based on that same tradition. This can get really confusing, since two other words ("Adonai" and "Elohim") translate to "Lord" and "God," and they are sometimes used together. The ASV of 1901 (and some other translations) render YHWH as "Jehovah." The most probable pronunciation of God's proper name is "YAHWEH." In Hebrew, the name "YAHWEH" is related to the active declaration "I AM." See Exodus 3:13-14. Since Hebrew has no tenses, the declaration "I AM" can also be interpreted as "I WAS" and "I WILL BE." Compare Revelation 1:8.*

VOLUMES IN THIS SERIES

Volume 1: The Pentateuch
- Genesis
- Exodus
- Leviticus
- Numbers
- Deuteronomy

Volume 2: History
- Joshua
- Judges
- Ruth
- 1 & 2 Samuel
- 1 & 2 Kings
- 1 & 2 Chronicles
- Ezra
- Nehemiah
- Esther

Volume 3: Poetry & Wisdom
- Job
- Psalms
- Proverbs
- Ecclesiastes
- Song of Songs

Volume 4: The Prophets
- Isaiah
- Jeremiah
- Lamentations
- Ezekiel
- Daniel

- Hosea
- Joel
- Amos
- Obadiah
- Jonah
- Micah
- Nahum
- Habakkuk
- Zephaniah
- Haggai
- Zechariah
- Malachi

Volume 5: New Testament

- Matthew
- Mark
- Luke
- John
- Acts
- Romans
- 1 & 2 Corinthians
- Galatians
- Ephesians
- Philippians
- Colossians
- 1 & 2 Thessalonians
- 1 & 2 Timothy
- Titus
- Philemon
- Hebrews
- James
- 1 & 2 Peter
- 1, 2, and 3 John
- Jude
- Revelation

Volume 6: Deuterocanon, Apocrypha, and Pseudepigrapha

- Tobit
- Judith
- Additions to Esther (additions found in the LXX namely Esther 10:4 – 16:24)
- Wisdom (also known as the Wisdom of Solomon)
- Ecclesiasticus (or Sirach)
- Baruch
- Epistle of Jeremy
- Prayer of Azarias (Daniel 3:24–97 in the LXX & Vulgate)
- Susanna (Daniel 13 in the LXX & Vulgate)
- Bel and the Dragon (Daniel 14 in the LXX & Vulgate)
- I Maccabees
- II Maccabees
- 1 Esdras
- Prayer of Manasses
- Psalm 151
- III Maccabees
- IV Maccabees
- 2 Esdras

FURTHER STUDY

Reader's Bibles are great, but if you want to learn more get a good study Bible. It will help you really dig into the text. Also, check out this stuff that I have found helpful:

 TheBibleProject.com

These guys are awesome. They make 5-10 minute explainer videos on every book of the Bible as well as common Biblical themes. Their "Read Scripture" series are little power lectures that get you into the main themes of each book and point you in some directions to explore in your own study.

 BillHull.net

This is my Dad. He's pretty rad. He writes books on discipleship and church leadership. This is where I would link you to Amazon if I could, but you will have to look them up yourself. If you are a pastor make sure to check out this thing he started at *TheBonhoefferProject.com*

 DownloadYouthMinistry.com

Are you a youth worker? God bless your over-worked and under-paid soul! DYM has a shocking array of resources to make your life easier and your ministry more effective. It was co-founded by Doug Fields. Doug also has some great books on marriage and parenting on his personal website *DougFields.com*

Printed in Great Britain
by Amazon